POETRY, KNOWLEDGE AND COMMUNITY IN LATE MEDIEVAL FRANCE

Edited by
Rebecca Dixon
Finn E. Sinclair
with
Adrian Armstrong
Sylvia Huot
Sarah Kay

D. S. BREWER

© Contributors 2008

All Rights Reserved. Except as permitted under current legislation
no part of this work may be photocopied, stored in a retrieval system,
published, performed in public, adapted, broadcast,
transmitted, recorded or reproduced in any form or by any means,
without the prior permission of the copyright owner

First published 2008
D. S. Brewer, Cambridge

ISBN 978–1–84384–177–7

D. S. Brewer is an imprint of Boydell & Brewer Ltd
PO Box 9, Woodbridge, Suffolk IP12 3DF, UK
and of Boydell & Brewer Inc.
668 Mt Hope Avenue, Rochester, NY 14620, USA
website: www.boydellandbrewer.com

A catalogue record for this title is available
from the British Library

The publisher has no responsibility for the continued existence or accuracy of
URLs for external or third-party internet websites referred to in this book,
and does not guarantee that any content on such websites is,
or will remain, accurate or appropriate

This publication is printed on acid-free paper

Printed in Great Britain by
CPI Antony Rowe, Chippenham, Wiltshire

Gallica
Volume 13

POETRY, KNOWLEDGE AND COMMUNITY IN LATE MEDIEVAL FRANCE

Covering the period from the late thirteenth to the early sixteenth century, this volume examines the role of poetry in French culture in transmitting and shaping knowledge, revealing the interplay between poet, text, and audience, and exploring the key dynamics of later medieval French poetry and of the communities in which it was produced.

REBECCA DIXON (University of Manchester) and FINN E. SINCLAIR (University of Cambridge) are research associates on the project 'Poetic Knowledge in Late Medieval France', funded by the Arts and Humanities Research Council (AHRC), UK.

Gallica

ISSN 1749–091X

General Editor: Sarah Kay

Gallica aims to provide a forum for the best current work in medieval French studies. Literary studies are particularly welcome and preference is given to works written in English, although publication in French is not excluded.

Proposals or queries should be sent in the first instance to the editor, or to the publisher, at the addresses given below; all submissions receive prompt and informed consideration.

Professor Sarah Kay, Department of French and Italian, Princeton University, 303 East Pyne, Princeton, NJ 08544, USA

The Managing Editor, Gallica, Boydell & Brewer Ltd., PO Box 9, Woodbridge, Suffolk IP12 3DF, UK

Previously published titles in this series are listed at the end of this volume.

CONTENTS

List of Illustrations   vii
List of Contributors   viii

Preface   xi
    FINN E. SINCLAIR

Introduction: L'Amour de Sophie. Poésie et savoir du *Roman de la*   1
Rose à Christine de Pizan
    JACQUELINE CERQUIGLINI-TOULET

PART I   LEARNED POETRY/POETRY AND LEARNING

1. Poetry and the Translation of Knowledge in Jean de Meun   19
    DAVID F. HULT
2. Apprendre à jouer? Fonctions de la partie d'échecs des *Eschés*   42
amoureux
    AMANDINE MUSSOU
3. Jean Gerson, Poet   56
    MISHTOONI BOSE
4. Gerson and Christine, Poets   69
    LORI J. WALTERS

PART II   POETRY OR PROSE?

5. Les *Razos* et l'idée de la poésie   85
    MICHEL ZINK
6. A Master, a *Vilain*, a Lady and a Scribe: Competing for Authority   98
in a Late Medieval Translation of the *Ars amatoria*
    DEBORAH MCGRADY
7. Deversifying Knowledge: The Poetic Alphabet of the Prose   111
Pèlerinage de la vie humaine
    STEPHANIE A. V. G. KAMATH
8. Prosifying Lyric Insertions in the Fifteenth-Century *Violette*   125
(*Gérard de Nevers*)
    DAVID J. WRISLEY

9. The Movement from Verse to Prose in the Allegories of Christine de Pizan SUZANNE CONKLIN AKBARI	136

PART III POETIC COMMUNITIES

10. The Songs of Jehannot de Lescurel in Paris, BnF, MS fr. 146: Love Lyrics, Moral Wisdom and the Material Book NANCY FREEMAN REGALADO	151
11. Refrains in the *Jeu de Robin et Marion*: History of a Citation JENNIFER SALTZSTEIN	173
12. Le Prince chez Meschinot, mise en forme d'un objet poétique/politique DENIS HÜE	187
13. Ways of Knowing in the *Songe veritable* and Christine de Pizan's *Livre de l'Advision Cristine* THELMA FENSTER	202
Conclusion: Knowing Poetry, Knowing Communities REBECCA DIXON	215
Bibliography	225
Index	243

LIST OF ILLUSTRATIONS

Plates

Les Eschés amoureux, manuscrit de Venise, Biblioteca Marciana, fr. app. 23, fol. 66r. Reproduced by kind permission of the Biblioteca Nazionale Marciana	54
Paris, BnF, MS fr. 146, fol. 57r: Initial page of the Lescurel lyrics Bibliothèque nationale de France	156
Paris, BnF, MS fr. 146, fol. 62r: Lescurel, #34, *Dit enté,* 'Gracïeus temps' Bibliothèque nationale de France	162
Paris, BnF, MS fr. 146, fol. 26v: *Fauvel, Motet enté* Bibliothèque nationale de France	163

Tables

Vernacular Love Lyrics in Paris, BnF, MS fr. 146	159
Refrain Concordances: *Le Roman de Fauvel* and Jehannot de Lescurel's Love Lyrics	160
Music of Refrain Concordances: *Le Roman de Fauvel,* ed. Rosenberg-Tischler; Lescurel, ed. Wilkins	170
Jeu Refrains with Concordances	175

Musical Examples

Refrain song, 'Robin m'aime'	173
Refrain 870 in *Le Jeu de Robin et Marion*	181
Refrain 870 in 'En mai / L'autre jour / Hé! Resveille toi'	181
Musical notation in 'Prenés l'abre'	185

LIST OF CONTRIBUTORS

Suzanne Conklin Akbari is Professor of English and Medieval Studies at the University of Toronto. Her books include *Seeing Through the Veil: Optical Theory and Medieval Allegory* (2004), *Marco Polo and the Encounter of East and West* (2008), and *Idols in the East: European Representations of Islam and the Orient* (2009).

Adrian Armstrong is Professor of French at Manchester University and a specialist on the *grands rhétoriqueurs*. He published *Technique and Technology. Script, Print and Poetics in France 1470–1550* in 2000 and has edited several late medieval texts including the *Œuvres complètes vol. I* of Jean Bouchet (2006).

Mishtooni Bose is Christopher Tower Student and Tutor in Medieval Poetry in English at Christ Church, Oxford. Her current research explores debates about clerical reform in the conciliar period and their impact on poetry and intellectual life in England and elsewhere. She discusses the confluence of charisma and vulnerability in Gerson's preaching in 'Advena, peregrinus: Jean Gerson's charisma', in *Charisma and Authority. Jewish, Christian and Muslim Preaching, 1200–1600*, ed. Katherine Ludwig Jansen and Miri Rubin, forthcoming.

Jacqueline Cerquiglini-Toulet is a professor at the Université de Paris-Sorbonne (Paris IV) and a member of the Institut universitaire de France. She specializes in medieval French literature, particularly poetry from Guillaume de Machaut to François Villon. Her most recent major work is the book-length 'Moyen Age' section of *La Littérature française: dynamique & histoire* (2007), a collectively authored volume co-ordinated by Jean-Yves Tadié.

Rebecca Dixon is Research Associate on the project 'Poetic Knowledge in Late Medieval France', funded by the AHRC (UK), and a member of the Department of French, University of Manchester. She completed her Ph.D., on fifteenth-century Burgundian prose literature, at Durham University, and is the author of several articles on later medieval literature, identity politics, and the relationship between text and image.

Thelma Fenster has published editions and translations of Christine de Pizan's narrative poetry, as well as articles on aspects of Christine's writing. In retirement from teaching at Fordham University, where she was professor of

French and Medieval Studies, she has been working on a substantial 'French of England' project with Jocelyn Wogan-Browne.

Denis Hüe is Professor of Medieval and Renaissance Language and Literature at the Université Rennes 2 Haute-Bretagne, and general editor of the *Medievalia* series. He is the author of *La Poésie palinodique à Rouen, 1486–1550* (2002), and has recently contributed a critical edition of Rimbaud's complete works (2007).

David F. Hult is Professor of Medieval French Literature at the University of California, Berkeley. His research interests focus on Chrétien de Troyes, Jean de Meun, allegory, literary theory and hermeneutics, text editing and related disciplines. His publications include *Self-Fulfilling Prophecies: Readership and Authority in the First Romance of the Rose* (1986).

Sylvia Huot is Professor of French at the University of Cambridge and a Fellow of Pembroke College, Cambridge. She has published widely on the *Romance of the Rose* and its medieval legacy. Her most recent book is *Postcolonial Fictions in the Roman de Perceforest. Cultural Identities and Hybridities* (2007).

Stephanie A. V. G. Kamath is an assistant professor at the University of Massachusetts, Boston. Her research interests include medieval allegory and vernacular translation, and she has co-authored a bilingual edition of René d'Anjou's *Livre du cuers d'amours espris* (2001).

Sarah Kay is Professor of French at Princeton University and a medievalist with wide-ranging interests. Her recent books include *A Short History of French Literature* (2003), co-written with Malcolm Bowie and Terence Cave, and *The Place of Thought. The Complexity of One in Late Medieval French Didactic Poetry* (2007).

Deborah McGrady currently teaches in the French Department at the University of Virginia. She has published several articles on reader response and reception in late medieval literature and is the author of *Controlling Readers: Guillaume de Machaut and His Late Medieval Audience* (2006).

Amandine Mussou is currently preparing a thesis on the *Eschés amoureux* under the direction of Professeur Jacqueline Cerquiglini-Toulet at the Université de Paris-Sorbonne (Paris IV).

Nancy Freeman Regalado is Professor of French at New York University. She has published *Poetic Patterns in Rutebeuf* (1970), *Le Roman de Fauvel in the Edition of Mesire Chaillou de Pesstain* (1990), with Edward Roesner and François Avril, and *Performing Medieval Narrative* (2005), with Evelyn Birge Vitz and Marilyn Lawrence.

Jennifer Saltzstein is Assistant Professor of Musicology at the University of Oklahoma. She completed her Ph.D. at the University of Pennsylvania in 2007. Her doctoral dissertation, entitled 'Wandering Voices: Refrain Citation in Thirteenth Century French Music and Poetry', is an interdisciplinary study of musical citation and its literary and cultural meanings, focusing on refrain use in romance, *trouvère* song, the motet, and in the works of Adam de la Halle.

Finn E. Sinclair is Research Associate on the project 'Poetic Knowledge in Late Medieval France', funded by the AHRC (UK). She is also Bye-Fellow in French at Girton College, University of Cambridge. Her publications include *Milk and Blood: Gender and Genealogy in the 'Chanson de Geste'* (2003) and articles on medieval French and Occitan literature, focusing in particular on gender, textuality, and authorship and authority.

Lori J. Walters is the Harry F. Williams Professor of French at Florida State University. She is the author of over 70 publications that fall into three main categories: Christine de Pizan, Medieval Romance, and the allegorical *Roman de la Rose*. Her current work explores the relationship between Christine de Pizan and Jean Gerson and presents evidence, gleaned from manuscripts and printed books, which sheds light on what she calls the 'spiritual partnership' of the two authors.

David Joseph Wrisley is Assistant Professor in Civilization Studies at the American University of Beirut. He is working on a book about the images of the Eastern Mediterranean in the literature of the medieval court of Burgundy.

Michel Zink is Professor of Medieval French Literature at the Collège de France. He has published widely on the literature, philology, historiography and history of France from the twelfth to the fifteenth century, including works on lyric poetry, Jean Renart, Chrétien de Troyes, Rutebeuf, and Froissart. In 2007 he was awarded the Balzan Prize for European Literature (1000–1500) for his contributions to the understanding of French and Occitan literature in the Middle Ages.

PREFACE

Finn E. Sinclair

This volume forms part of a collaborative research project 'Poetic Knowledge in Late Medieval France', which examines the role of poetry in French culture from the late thirteenth to the early sixteenth centuries in transmitting and shaping knowledge.[1] The project looks not only at the explicit content of the poetry but also, more importantly, at the kinds of knowledge that are implied by its form and context, at the types of expertise to which it gives rise, and at the nature of the communities it presupposes or creates.

The majority of the chapters presented here are drawn from the project's conference ('Poetry, Knowledge and Community in Late Medieval France', Princeton University, 1–4 November 2006) and the rest from papers given by invited speakers at its regular research seminars. These have all contributed substantially to the ongoing research of the 'Poetic Knowledge' project, exploring and developing key areas of thought and extending the horizons of what we mean by 'poetry', 'knowledge' and 'community', and the ways in which these concepts may be seen to interrelate. The chapters comprise studies of both canonical and less well-known French and Occitan verse literature, and cover a wide range of complementary subject areas including the status of poetry as an object of knowledge; poetry and philosophy; the relationship between verse and prose; citation; textual histories and textual communities; the transmission and revision of poetic texts; and the relationship between poetry, politics, and power. The wider implications of these individual studies will be drawn out in the volume's conclusion, which explores the significant role played by poetry (as opposed to prose) in the culture of knowledge of late medieval France.

The period covered by this volume extends from the late thirteenth to the late fifteenth century, encompassing the rich and influential developments in poetic form and content that flourished in the years between Jean de Meun's composition of his continuation of the *Roman de la Rose* and the poetic works of Meschinot. This may generally be thought of as the period during which prose writing came to the fore, transmitting a straightforward 'truth' that contrasted with the beguiling tortuousness of verse. Yet the rise of prose paradoxically freed up composition in verse, allowing for the exploration and development of

---

[1] This project is funded by the Arts and Humanities Research Council (AHRC), UK. The publication of this volume has been further supported by the Department of French at the University of Cambridge, the Bretey and Vinaver Funds of the University of Manchester, and the Department of French and Italian of Princeton University.

new generic and structural poetic forms, and for the expansion of the epistemic reach of poetry, as it encompassed philosophical, moral, didactic and political themes, among others. Knowledge and its transmission became an intrinsic aspect of many types of poetry, from verse encyclopaedias to poetic *dits*, aiding the development of these genres. Yet verse was not simply a means of disseminating various types of knowledge. The specific form of verse, with its formal intricacies and its particular literary context, created a space in which knowledge could be shaped and redefined. The community in which a verse text was produced and the community of readers for which it was destined also played a major role in shaping the kind of knowledge it contained, how this knowledge infused the poetic text, and how the text was received and interpreted. Poetry, knowledge and community were intimately interlinked during this period and it is their vibrant interaction and its literary and cultural implications that provide the focus of this volume.

The chapters are organised into three sections, 'Learned Poetry/Poetry and Learning', 'Poetry or Prose?' and 'Poetic Communities', reflecting the project's principal lines of investigation and providing a framework for their exploration. Jacqueline Cerquiglini-Toulet supplies an introductory essay for the volume, while each of its three sections opens with a longer chapter based on a paper given by one of the plenary speakers at the Princeton conference: David F. Hult, Michel Zink, and Nancy Freeman Regalado. Although the chapters fall into separate sections, they consistently dialogue between one another, as the epistemic, formal and social aspects of verse composition are seen to influence and respond to each other. This interaction enhances the scope and import of 'poetry', opening up the ways in which it may be seen to shape and transmit different forms of knowledge, and extending our notion of 'poetic community'.

Jacqueline Cerquiglini-Toulet's 'L'Amour de Sophie. Poésie et savoir du *Roman de la Rose* à Christine de Pizan' charts the way in which poetry developed from its earlier focus on love and the knowledge of love into a form that blended the philosophical with the love of knowledge. She focuses in particular on Christine de Pizan, for whom poetry embodied science and moral and theological knowledge, and studies the way in which Christine's redefinition of *poema* opened up its allegorical and epistemic dimensions.

The link between philosophy and poetry and the relation of *carmen* to *poetria* are expanded by Mishtooni Bose in Chapter 3, 'Jean Gerson, Poet'. Bose explores the relationship between poetry, song and mystical theology in Gerson's poems in Latin, considering how this reflects the interplay between the theologian-poet's ego and super-ego, between the charismatic individual and the authoritative exegetical poet. For Gerson, *carmen* is allied to the genre of the biblical psalm, and the song which the philosophical poet sings is the *canticordum*, the 'song of the heart'. Lori Walters's following chapter, 'Gerson and Christine, Poets', dialogues fruitfully with the above, turning to a consideration of Gerson's vernacular poetry and relating this to Christine de Pizan's desire to elevate poetry to a philosophical and theological level.

Amandine Mussou examines a different connection between poetry and learning in her essay 'Apprendre à jouer? Fonctions de la partie d'échecs des *Eschés amoureux*', although again the use of poetic allegory and its interpretation play a key role. Mussou highlights the way in which the poetic structure of the *Eschés amoureux* informs and enriches its didactic intent, that of transmitting an 'art d'aimer' as well as an 'art de jouer'. This concern with poetic form and learning is one of the key aspects of David Hult's wide-ranging study, 'Poetry and the Translation of Knowledge in Jean de Meun', which explores the role of translation and the relationship between textual form (verse or prose) and the transmission of meaning. His discussion, while prefacing the section on 'Learned Poetry', also points towards the following section, 'Poetry or Prose', where Michel Zink, in 'Les *Razos* et l'idée de la poésie', considers the nature of the knowledge transmitted by the prose *razos*, and the way in which these act as poetic supplement to the *cansos* of the troubadours. The dialogue between *razos* and *cansos* illuminates the fluidity of a poetics where 'knowledge' shifts in response to poetic form and interpretation.

Deborah McGrady, in Chapter 6, 'A Master, a *Vilain*, a Lady and a Scribe: Competing for Authority in a Late Medieval Translation of the *Ars amatoria*', also discusses the differing kinds of knowledge produced by gloss and supplement, here focusing on the thirteenth-century French prose translation of Ovid's *Ars amatoria* and its reassigning of knowledge and authority through the deployment of citation and commentary. For Suzanne Akbari the vernacular context of Christine de Pizan's writing provides an alternative focus for an examination of the implications of a shift from verse to prose. In Chapter 9, 'The Movement from Verse to Prose in the Allegories of Christine de Pizan', Akbari situates Christine's work in the context of late-fourteenth-century French translations of philosophical and scientific writings, arguing that the development of her work away from verse reflected an attempt to reconcile this translation project with the tradition of verse allegory. The interrelation of verse and prose, and the transition between the two, shapes Chapters 7 and 8 by Stephanie Kamath and David Wrisley. Kamath studies the signifying function of inserted lyrics in 'Deversifying Knowledge: The Poetic Alphabet of the Prose *Pèlerinage de la vie humaine*', where the fifteenth-century movement towards *dérimage* provides the context for the changing response of prose redactors to Guillaume de Deguileville's diverse lyrics, as new lyric insertions provided a grafting of knowledge to supplement the reinterpretation of existing modes of poetic discourse. A complementary study of lyric insertions is provided by Wrisley, whose 'Prosifying Lyric Insertions in the Fifteenth-Century *Violette (Gérard de Nevers)*' explores the importance of poetic performance, as the strategic preservation and reinterpretation of inserted lyrics is used to create a notion of identity, here at the Burgundian court. Through its preservation and memorialization of the lyric citations the prose text becomes an object of poetic and communal knowledge.

In the final section, 'Poetic Communities', Nancy Freeman Regalado's 'The

Songs of Jehannot de Lescural in Paris, BNF, MS fr. 146: Love Lyrics, Moral Wisdom and the Material Book' also studies the lyric and its reading community. Her essay examines the importance of compilation in the interpretation of the lyric in the later thirteenth and fourteenth centuries, arguing for a new appreciation of the form in terms of its moral and political significance as well as for its *technê*, its knowledge of art. The manuscript context of Jehannot de Lescurel's love lyrics encourages 'reciprocal reading' between texts, allowing a deeper moral and didactic reading to emerge. The notion of reading across texts is also significant for Jennifer Saltzstein, whose 'Refrains in the *Jeu de Robin et de Marion*: History of a Citation' engages with the reception history of Adam de la Halle's play, whose refrains connect it with a diverse body of musical and poetic works. Through his use of citation, Adam placed himself within a distinct regional and genealogical community of poets whose works resonate through his *Jeu*, to be recognized by its knowledgeable audience.

The political dimension of poetry and its relation to community concern both Denis Hüe and Thelma Fenster. In Chapter 12, 'Le Prince chez Meschinot, mise en forme d'un objet poétique/politique', Hüe explores the political and polemical aspects of Jean Meschinot's *Ballades des Princes*, situating it within the tradition of the 'conseils à l'aristocratie', yet illuminating Meschinot's use of an *amplificatio* that opens up the moral and universal dimension of the *ballades* and paves the way for the Humanistic writings of the Renaissance. Fenster's 'Ways of Knowing in the *Songe veritable* and Christine de Pizan's *Livre de l'Advision Cristine*', which follows, relates the importance of *fama* as pervasive, socially constructed knowledge to the political and literary context of early-fourteenth-century France. She reads both the *Songe* and the *Advision* as 'songes politiques' highlighting the subtle interplay between learning, knowledge and experience that appears in Christine's text and which encourages its interpretation as an epistemology.

The chapters outlined above provide a multiplicity of different perspectives on the relationship between poetry, knowledge and community in late medieval France. The definition and scope of each of these areas is brought into question, with the meaning of poetry itself, as verse, allegory, *carmen*, or *poetria*, consistently under examination. The nature of knowledge is equally scrutinized, as scholarly learning, experience, *fama*, or poetic tradition, and the idea of community is revealed as diverse and multi-faceted, encompassing intellectual affinities between individual authors, and audiences linked through geographical, traditional, and cultural networks of readership and transmission.[2]

---

[2] Conventions of quotation and transcription are as follows. All titles of Middle French texts appear in their most usual Middle French form within the chapters of this volume. Frequently quoted primary texts are initially fully referenced in a footnote; subsequent references are given within parentheses in the main text. The initial letter of each line in verse quotations is capitalized.

Introduction
L'Amour de Sophie
Poésie et savoir du *Roman de la Rose*
à Christine de Pizan

JACQUELINE CERQUIGLINI-TOULET

Aristote l'affirme au début de sa *Métaphysique*: 'Tout homme desire à savoir.' Depuis la redécouverte du philosophe au XIIIe siècle, la formule justifie et conditionne le travail encyclopédique en français. Ainsi s'ouvre *Placides et Timéo*:

> Aristotes dist en son livre de nature ou commenchement d'un livre, le quel livres est appelés le livre de metafisique, que tout homme couvoite et desire a savoir naturelment les secrés de nature.[1]

> [Aristote dit en son œuvre sur la nature au commencement d'un livre, qui est appelé livre de métaphysique, que tout homme convoite et désire savoir naturellement les secrets de nature.]

C'est le début du *Convivio* de Dante, des *Leys d'amors*, auparavant du *Bestiaire d'amours* de Richard de Fournival, pour prendre des exemples de rassemblement de savoirs de types différents. La formule revient fréquemment chez Christine de Pizan: énoncée de manière générale comme dans la ballade 98 des *Cent Balades*, 'Tous hommes ont le desir de savoir';[2] mise dans la bouche de Sénèque dans le *Chemin de longue estude* 'et par nature / Desire savoir creature';[3] ou commentée dans *Le Livre des Fais et bonnes meurs du sage roy Charles V*, 'Aristote dit "Tous hommes par nature savoir desirent", dient les dittioneurs', c'est-à-dire les commentateurs.[4] Mais très souvent, Christine

---

[1] *Placides et Timéo* ou *Li Secrés as philosophes*, éd. Claude Alexandre Thomasset (Genève, 1980), p. 1.
[2] Christine de Pizan, *Œuvres poétiques*, t. I, éd. Maurice Roy (Paris, 1886).
[3] Christine de Pizan, *Le Chemin de longue étude*, éd. et trad. Andrea Tarnowski (Paris, 2000), vv. 5179–80.
[4] Christine de Pizan, *Le Livre des fais et bonnes meurs du sage roy Charles V*, éd. Suzanne Solente, 2 vols (Paris, 1936 et 1940), II, p. 162.

rapporte la formule à elle-même, dans des variations multiples. C'est le cas en particulier dans *Le Livre du Chemin de longue estude*: 'Ainsi de grant desir ardant / Aloye par tout regardant (vv. 787–8) [Ainsi brûlant d'un grand désir j'allais par tout regardant]', 'Car moult desiray a savoir / De l'estre du lieu tout le voir (vv. 855–6) [car je désirais beaucoup savoir toute la vérité quant à la nature de ce lieu]', ou 'et moy comme celle qui vouloit / Tout enquerir (vv. 2066–7) [et moi qui voulais m'enquérir sur tout]'.

Ce désir de savoir caractérise un mouvement dans la littérature vernaculaire qui se met en place à la suite du *Roman de la Rose*. La lecture du livre, de Guillaume de Lorris à Jean de Meun, est conçue alors comme un parcours de l'amour à la connaissance, de l'amour mondain à la connaissance des secrets de nature. *Les Eschés amoureux* en vers sont un magnifique exemple de ce point de vue tout comme *Le Chevalier errant* de Thomas III de Saluces. Ce texte fait évoluer le héros du service du dieu d'Amour courtois au Dieu chrétien. Des vertus, comme Foi ou Espérance, connaissent des transformations significatives. Elles passent au cours du texte du domaine amoureux (la fidélité, l'espoir) à leur valeur théologale.

Choisissant d'étudier le phénomène chez Christine de Pizan, je me donne à la fois une facilité et une complexité qui tiennent à la même particularité: le genre féminin de Christine qui se veut *clergesse*. Je croise donc une tendance générale de la littérature des XIVe et XVe siècles à une idiosyncrasie. Comment décrire le mouvement qui mène d'un amour de l'amour à un amour de la connaissance quand le désir de savoir est celui d'une femme, éloignée du savoir par son sexe, exilée de l'amour par son statut de veuve?

Christine souligne dans l'*Advision Cristine* le caractère scandaleux du désir de savoir chez une femme:

> Si comme une fois respondis a ung homme qui reprouvoit mon desir de savoir, disant qu'il n'appertenoit point a femme avoir science, comme il en soit pou, lui dis que moins appartenoit a homme avoir ignorance, comme il en soit beaucoup.[5]
>
> [Ainsi qu'une fois je répondis à un homme qui critiquait mon désir de savoir disant qu'il ne convenait pas à une femme d'être savante – encore qu'il en soit peu –, je lui dis qu'il convenait moins à un homme d'être ignorant – encore qu'il en soit beaucoup.]

D'où vient ce désir? Du manque. Christine le dit de manière explicite dans *Le Livre de la Mutacion de Fortune*:

---

[5] Christine de Pizan, *Le Livre de l'Advision Cristine*, éd. Christine Reno et Liliane Dulac (Paris, 2001), 3.9, p. 109.

> Car je desir ce que n'ay pas,
> C'est le tresor que grant savoir
> Fait a ceulx qui l'aiment avoir.[6]

> [Car je désire ce que je n'ai pas, le trésor que le grand savoir donne à ceux qui l'aiment.]

Christine compare ce désir au désir amoureux:

> Si suis comme les amoureux
> Bien ardans et bien desireux,
> Qui ne pevent veoir, n'ouyr
> Ce dont desirent a jouir. (vv. 439–42)

> [Je suis comme les amoureux, bien épris et pleins de désir, qui ne peuvent ni voir ni entendre ce dont ils aimeraient jouir.]

Le désir amoureux est détourné, dérivé en désir de savoir qui par là même est érotisé.[7]

Guillaume de Machaut, dans la lignée des troubadours et des trouvères, concevait son écriture comme naissant dans l'amour, ayant l'amour comme moteur. Si cette dernière comportait des aspects didactiques, ils étaient subsumés sous le régime de l'amour, comme dans *Le Roman de la Rose*.[8] Christine, elle, envisage l'écriture lyrique, l'écriture d'amour non comme une matière totalisante, mais comme une étape dans son écriture, une propédeutique à ce à quoi elle aspire, l'écriture savante, c'est-à-dire une écriture qui ne trouve pas forcément son support d'exposition dans l'amour. Elle décrit cet apprentissage dans le *Livre de l'Advision Cristine*:

> Adonc me pris a forgier choses jolies, a mon commencement plus legieres, et tout ainsi comme l'ouvrier qui de plus en plus en son euvre se soubtille comme plus il la frequente, ainsi tousjours estudiant diverses matieres, mon sens de plus en plus s'imbuoit de choses estranges, amendant mon stille en plus grande soubtilleté et plus haulte matiere. (3.10, p. 111)

> [Je me pris alors à forger de jolies choses, plus légères au début, et comme l'ouvrier qui devient de plus en plus subtil dans ses œuvres à force de les pratiquer, en continuant à étudier des matières diverses, mon intelligence

---

[6] Christine de Pizan, *Le Livre de la Mutacion de Fortune*, 4 tomes, éd. Suzanne Solente (Paris, 1959 [pour les tomes I et II]/ 1964 [tome III]/ 1966 [tome IV], I, vv. 444–6.

[7] Sur la sublimation chez Christine, on se reportera à l'article de Sylvia Huot, 'Seduction and Sublimation: Christine de Pizan, Jean de Meun, and Dante', *Romance Notes*, 25 (1985), 361–73.

[8] Voir Sylvia Huot, *The 'Romance of the Rose' and its Medieval Readers: Interpretation, Reception, Manuscript Transmission* (Cambridge, 1993), chapitre 7 intitulé 'Poet of Love and Nature: Guillaume de Machaut and the *Rose*'.

s'imprégnait de plus en plus de choses étrangères, et mon style s'améliorait en subtilité et touchait de plus hautes matières.]

Le rythme même de la phrase, sinueuse, accumulant figures de parallélisme – 'ainsi comme … ainsi' et figures de relance (les participes présents: 'estudiant', 'amendant') – fait sentir ce parcours, ce 'chemin de longue étude'. 'Commenchier a choses legieres', c'est aussi la recommandation du dieu d'Amour à l'acteur dans les *Eschés amoureux*, s'il veut 'fort chose apprendre [apprendre des choses difficiles]'.[9] Pédagogie de l'apprentissage qui fait passer de l'amour à la connaissance. Une comparaison de Christine de Pizan à Guillaume de Machaut est intéressante pour mettre en lumière de tels transferts. On observe tout d'abord de l'un à l'autre l'infléchissement d'une formule qui caractérisait la poésie d'amour: le regret d'avoir commencé trop tard à aimer. Adam de la Halle, au XIIIe siècle, disait dans l'une de ses chansons: 'Je plaing souvent le tans que je perdoie / Anchois que je commenchasse a amer [Je regrette souvent le temps que j'ai perdu avant de commencer à aimer].'[10] La dame du *Voir Dit* énonce un constat identique. Parlant du commencement de ses amours avec le poète, elle lui écrit: 'Lequel fu trop tart a mon gré, car c'est le plus grant regret que j'aie que du bon temps que nous avons perdu (Lettre 26) [lequel vint trop tard à mon gré, car tel est le plus grand regret que j'aie que le bon temps que nous avons perdu].' Le poète répond: 'Et, mon tredoulz cuer, vous estes courecie de ce que nous avons si tart commencié: par Dieu, aussi sui je. Mais ves cy le remede: menons si bonne vie que nous porrons en lieu et en temps, que nous recompensons le temps que nous avons perdu et que on parle de nos amours jusques a cent ans cy aprés (Lettre 27) [Et, mon très doux cœur, vous êtes fâchée de ce que notre amour a commencé si tard: par Dieu, je le suis moi aussi. Mais voici le remède: menons une vie aussi agréable que nous le permettront les lieux et le temps, de telle sorte que nous compensions le temps que nous avons perdu. Et qu'on parle de nos amours dans cent ans encore].'[11]

Le regret, chez Christine, ne porte pas sur l'amour mais sur l'étude: avoir commencé trop tard à étudier. La Sibylle lui en fait la remarque dans le *Chemin de longue estude*: 'tart a m'escole / Es venue (vv. 1683–4) [tu es venue tard à mon école].' La façon, ensuite, dont Christine et Guillaume se représentent leurs dons d'écrivain va dans le sens de cette même évolution. Guillaume de Machaut voit deux sources à son écriture: Nature et Amour. Il

---

[9] *Die Liebesgarten-Allegorie der 'Echecs amoureux': Kritische Ausgabe und Kommentar*, éd. Christine Kraft (Frankfurt-am-Main, 1977), vv. 3611–18.

[10] Adam de la Halle, *Œuvres complètes*, éd. Pierre-Yves Badel (Paris, 1995), chanson XXX, vv. 12–13.

[11] Les deux citations renvoient à Guillaume de Machaut, *Le Livre du Voir Dit*, éd. Paul Imbs, révision: Jacqueline Cerquiglini-Toulet (Paris, 1999), pp. 432–4, p. 450.

s'en explique dans le prologue qu'il donne à ses œuvres complètes.[12] Nature gouverne la manière d'écrire à l'aide de trois 'enfants': Sens, Rhétorique et Musique. Amour propose la matière par l'entremise de trois autres 'enfants': Dous Penser, Plaisance et Esperance. Christine, quant à elle, dans la dédicace du manuscrit de ses œuvres qu'elle offre à Isabeau de Bavière, déclare qu'elle écrit: 'Du seul sentement que retiens / Des dons de Dieu et de Nature' (vv. 21–2).[13] On le constate: Amour a disparu. Ce n'est pas un fait de hasard. C'est ce même couple dont fait état la Dame Couronnee dans *L'Advision Cristine*: 'Amie, a qui Dieux et Nature ont concedé oultre le commun ordre des femmes le don d'amour d'estude' (1.6, p. 16). Nature et Amour, d'un côté, Dieu et Nature, de l'autre, les termes dans ces paires ne sont pas sur le même plan. Le rapport est horizontal dans le cas de Nature et Amour, vertical, hiérarchique dans celui de Dieu et Nature, ramenant en fait directement l'écriture à un seul principe: Dieu. C'est ce 'faux' couple qu'on retrouve chez Laurent de Premierfait lorsqu'il rend compte de l'écriture de Dante dans sa seconde traduction du *De casibus virorum illustrium* en 1409. Il s'agit d'un ajout au texte de Boccace: 'Dant donques, qui de Dieu et de Nature avoit receu l'esperit de poetrie, advisa que ou *Livre de la Rose* est descript le paradis des bons et l'enfer des mauvais en langage françois [Dante, donc qui avait reçu de Dieu et de Nature, l'esprit de poésie, se rendit compte que dans le *Livre de la Rose* est décrit en français le paradis des bons et l'enfer des mauvais].'[14] Christine, du point de vue de ses sources d'inspiration, est donc semblable à Dante et se distingue du *Roman de la Rose* et de Guillaume de Machaut. Elle-même d'ailleurs oppose Dante à Jean de Meun lors de la *Querelle du Roman de la Rose*.[15] Ultérieurement, on voit de nouveaux termes s'introduire dans le schéma. Une ballade anonyme du début du XVIe siècle[16] attribue à Art et Nature le talent d'Alain Chartier et le débat entre ces

---

[12] *Œuvres de Guillaume de Machaut*, éd. Ernest Hoepffner, 3 tomes (Paris, 1908/1911/1921), I, pp. 1–12.

[13] Il s'agit du British Library MS, Harley 4431. Maurice Roy édite la dédicace au tome I des *Œuvres complètes*, pp. xiv–xvii.

[14] Le texte est celui du BnF, MS fr. 226, fol. 268 cd, cité par Pierre-Yves Badel dans *Le Roman de la Rose au XIVe siècle. Etude de la réception de l'œuvre* (Genève, 1980), p. 486. Le passage se lit également dans *Debating the* Roman de la rose, *A Critical Anthology*, éd. Christine McWebb (New York, 2007), p. 422.

[15] Christine de Pizan, Epistre à Maistre Pierre Col dans *Le Débat sur le* Roman de la Rose, éd. Eric Hicks (Paris, 1977), pp. 141–2: 'Mais se mieulx vuelz oïr descripre paradis et enfer, et par plus subtilz termes plus haultement parlé de theologie […] lis le livre que on appelle le Dant […]: la oyras autre propos mieux fondé plus subtilment, ne te desplaise, et ou tu pourras plus prouffiter que en ton *Romant de la Rose*'.

[16] 'Que faiz-tu ore en cendre et sepulture / O maistre Alain qui par art et nature / As merité la palme de bien dire.' Cité par E. J. Hoffman, *Alain Chartier: His Work and Reputation* (New York, 1942), p. 234.

deux forces anime toute la poésie au tournant des XVe et XVIe siècle.[17] Dans la conception de la poésie comme amour de l'amour ou amour du savoir, l'examen de ces dyades est instructif.

Pourquoi le savoir est-il désirable pour Christine? Parce qu'elle en a été éloignée par l'*us*, la coutum, mais qu'elle sait qu'il existe car il s'est incarné pour elle dans deux figures aimées: son père Thomas, 'philosophe', dont elle se dit être le fils, et non la fille, et Charles V, son roi, 'philosophe', 'car ameur / De sapience en grant saveur / Yert (*Chemin de longue estude*, vv. 5013–15) [car il était amoureux de la sagesse et avait pour elle du goût]'. Comme il y a une exacerbation du désir amoureux par la distance, dans l'amour de loin, il y a pour Christine une exacerbation de son désir de savoir par l'éloignement qu'a induit son sexe. Qu'implique un tel transfert? Un double déplacement dans la pensée à la fois de l'amour, de l'écriture et de la société: le remplacement de Vénus par Diane, puissance tutélaire de Christine, la récriture implicite, continue, décalée du Jugement de Pâris. L'élue devrait être, pour la femme-poète, Pallas. Il est à noter que lorsque Christine pense l'union de la clergie et de la chevalerie chez le noble, elle met en parallèle Pallas et Espérance comme contrepoids dans leurs domaines respectifs, le savoir et l'amour, aux valeurs guerrières. Elle écrit dans l'*Epistre Othea*: 'Et sicomme Pallas, qui notte sagece, doit estre adjoustee avec chevalerie, doit estre la vertu d'esperance adjouxtee aux bonnes vertus de l'esprit chevalereux, sans la quelle il ne pourroit prouffiter [Et de même que Pallas qui désigne la sagesse doit être ajoutée à la chevalerie, de même la vertu d'espérance doit être ajoutée aux vertus de vaillance de l'esprit du chevalier, vertu sans laquelle il ne pourrait progresser].'[18] Par ces questionnements, Christine rencontre une interrogation de la fin du XIVe siècle: l'amour est-il toujours au centre d'une écriture pour les cours? Le savoir sur l'amour peut-il encore pour ce milieu faire office de savoir sur le monde? Joue-t-il toujours, aux deux sens du terme, son rôle de spéculation? L'implication biographique de Christine dans le traitement de ce problème donne à son écriture sa coloration particulière. Elle passe au crible de sa vie une question générale et la résout à sa manière propre.

Comment Christine se situe-t-elle par rapport aux arts d'aimer et ces derniers relèvent-ils pour elle du régime du savoir? De nombreux textes

---

[17] Voir en particulier le débat autour des *Douze Dames de Rhétorique* entre George Chastelain et Jean Robertet. On se reportera à l'édition de David Cowling, *Les Douze Dames de Rhétorique* / George Chastelain, Jean Robertet, Jean de Montferrant, (Genève, 2002), et à l'étude de Ludmilla Evdokimova, 'Des *Douze Dames de Rhétorique* à la *Complainte*: le prolongement du débat littéraire dans la réponse de Jean Robertet', dans *Poétiques en transition entre Moyen Age et Renaissance*, éd. Jean-Claude Mühlethaler et Jacqueline Cerquiglini-Toulet (Lansanne 2002), pp. 111–28.

[18] Christine de Pizan, *Epistre Othea*, éd. Gabriella Parussa (Genève, 1999), p. 223.

au Moyen Âge s'intitulent *Arts d'amour*[19] ou se donnent des titres qui, de manière imagée, soulignent les notions d'enseignement, de didactisme quant à l'amour: *La Clef d'amours*, par exemple, dont le dieu d'Amour exige de la part de son auteur qu'il le fasse en la manière d'un 'petit portehors', d'un livre que l'amant puisse toujours avoir avec lui. Livre à la visée pratique.[20] Peut-on séduire, en quelque sorte ou conduire une affaire amoureuse sans son art d'amour? La pose amusée est évidente mais dit l'importance accordée au livre, à l'enseignement en ces matières. À l'origine de ces textes, on trouve l'*Ars amatoria* d'Ovide et beaucoup de ce type d'œuvres en français se présentent comme des traductions glosées d'Ovide. Chrétien de Troyes rappelle dans les premiers mots de son *Cligès* qu'il a traduit l'*Ars amatoria*: 'Cil qui fist d'Erec et d'Enide, / Et les comandemenz d'Ovide / Et l'art d'amors en romanz mist [Celui qui composa *Erec et Enide* et mit en français les commandements d'Ovide et *L'Art d'amour*]'.[21] Pourquoi enseigner l'amour, et quel amour? Quel est le lien de l'amour et du savoir? Tous les mots employés, en effet, en dehors d'*art* sont ceux de *traité*, de *doctrine*, de *science*, d'*ensenhamen*.

Les grandes catégories d'amour envisagées se modèlent sur l'objet de l'amour: la femme, le prochain, Dieu. Pour ce qui est de l'amour de la femme, un autre livre, en dehors de l'*Ars amatoria*, a une influence: l'*Ars honneste amandi* d'André Le Chapelain, à la fin du XIIe siècle. On remarque la présence du modalisateur *honneste* qu'on a pris l'habitude de rendre en français moderne par *courtois*. L'ouvrage est traduit en 1290 par Drouart La Vache sous le titre *Li Livres d'Amours*.[22] L'amour de Dieu et du prochain est traité par Pierre de Blois dans son *De amicitia christiana* qui part de Cicéron. Pierre de Blois y indique: 'Aussi, Dieu ordonne-t-il aux êtres doués de raison la mémoire, la connaissance et l'amour: l'amour trouve un soutien dans la mémoire et dans la connaissance, et à leur tour ces deux facultés participent à la douceur de l'amour.'[23]

Quels types d'arts propose le Moyen Âge? Des arts d'aimer, des arts de mourir, des arts de rhétorique, des arts de chevalerie, des arts de la guerre. On peut noter que *Le Livre des Fais d'armes et de chevalerie* de Christine de Pizan est imprimé par Vérard en 1488 sous le titre *L'Art de Chevalerie selon Végèce*.[24] Ces arts, pratiques ou théoriques, relèvent de modes de comporte-

---

[19] Sur les Arts d'aimer au Moyen Âge, voir Michèle Gally, *L'intelligence de l'amour d'Ovide à Dante. Arts d'aimer et poésie au Moyen Âge* (Paris, 2005).

[20] *La Clef d'amors*, éd. Auguste Doutrepont (Halle, 1890), v. 102.

[21] Chrétien de Troyes, *Cligès*, éd. Charles Méla et Olivier Collet (Paris, 1994), vv. 1–3.

[22] *Li Livres d'Amours* de Drouart La Vache, éd. Robert Bossuat (Paris, 1926).

[23] Marie-Madeleine Davy, *Un traité de l'amour du XIIe siècle. Pierre de Blois* (Paris, 1932), p. 161.

[24] Sur cette transformation du titre et l'effacement de la personne de Christine par l'imprimeur on se reportera à Cynthia J. Brown, 'The Reconstruction of an Author in

ment ou de connaissance. Les arts d'aimer, précisément, entrent-ils dans les schémas de catégorisation du savoir? Il semble bien que oui. C'est en tout cas à un tel classement que procède l'auteur de l'*Art d'amours en prose*.[25] Ce dernier distingue les arts mécaniques de ce qu'il appelle les 'arts et sciences ensemble' (p. 65) qui comportent deux catégories: les arts libéraux et non libéraux. Les arts d'aimer font partie de cette dernière catégorie dans la sous-section 'arts ne defendus ne octroies' où ils se trouvent avec l'astronomie. Il est d'autres tentatives à la fin du XIIIe siècle et au début du XIVe siècle de classement de l'amour au sein de la connaissance ou de catégorisation de l'amour: *Arbre de Philosophie d'amour* de Raymond Lulle (la métaphore est empruntée à la nature), *Breviari d'amor* de Matfre Ermengaud (la métaphore est religieuse), *Leys d'amors* de Guilhem Molinier, ces lois étant celles de la poésie d'amour, à savoir des règles de versification et de rhétorique.

Comment se présentent les arts d'amour? Ceux qui suivent au plus près *l'Ars amatoria* s'offrent comme des livres de manières, des livres de comportement. Ils apprennent à l'amant à polir ses mœurs comme les arts de rhétorique apprennent à polir les mots. Ils donnent à ce dernier les moyens de prendre la dame au piège, et donnent à la femme des conseils pour tromper l'amant. C'est l'*ars* au sens de ruse et l'amour est bien homonyme dans ces cas là de l'hameçon, selon le jeu *aim*: *haim*. Les *Arts* qui subissent l'influence d'André Le Chapelain cherchent à caractériser l'amour, à en donner une définition, et proposent des modèles de conversation. Ils se préoccupent d'analyser la naissance de l'amour, son développement, souvent grâce à la métaphore de l'arbre. Nous sommes face à une phénoménologie de l'amour. Dans le *Commens d'Amour*, en prose, l'auteur souligne que l'amant ne doit pas être trop couard, c'est-à-dire timide, 'k'il ne laisse mie oubliier sa besoigne, et qu'il ne li face souvenir d'amer par amours par aucun biau mot, si comme d'amoureuses hystoires, ou de Troies ou d'autres et en contant biaus examples, si comme Paris ravi Helayne et Tristrans Yseut [de sorte qu'il ne laisse pas oublier son entreprise et qu'il lui fasse souvenir [à savoir: à sa dame] d'aimer par amour grâce à de belles paroles comme les histoires amoureuses de Troie au d'autres et en contant de beaux exemples comme le rapt d'Hélène par Pâris ou d'Yseut par Tristan].'[26] Le rôle d'incitation à l'amour de la littérature est très souvent souligné. C'est ce que fait l'*Art d'amours en prose* pour justifier son utilité: 'tel puet lire et oïr l'art d'amours qui, s'il ne l'eüst leü, ja n'eüst talent ne volanté d'amer (lignes 105–6) [tel

---

Print: Christine de Pizan in the Fifteenth and Sixteenth Centuries', dans *Christine de Pizan and the Categories of Difference*, éd. Marilynn Desmond (Minneapolis and London, 1998), pp. 215–35. Vérard ramène le livre de Christine à un manuel, un *art*.

[25] *L'Art d'Amours. Traduction et commentaire de l'*Ars amatoria *d'Ovide*, éd. Bruno Roy (Leyde, 1974).

[26] 'Li Commens d'Amours de Richard de Fournival (?)', éd. Antoinette Saly, *Travaux de Linguistique et de Littérature*, 10, 2 (1972), 21–55, p. 43.

peut lire et entendre l'art d'amour qui, s'il ne l'eût lu, n'aurait jamais eu désir ni volonté d'aimer].'[27] L'amour selon cet auteur n'est donc pas un sentiment naturel mais construit. Il y a à l'arrière-plan de cette question le problème de la *Nature* et de l'*Us* [l'usage] en amour que le XIIe siècle avait posé en termes sociaux. Dans l'*Altercatio Phillidis et Florae* [*Débat de Phillis et Flora*], *Usus* et *Natura* sont les noms des deux juges amenés à trancher la question de la précellence en amour du clerc ou du chevalier. Christine de Pizan pose le problème de manière plus générale en termes d'inné et d'acquis, de *Nature* et de *Nourreture*, la *nourreture* désignant l'éducation au Moyen Âge. Sa pensée en ce domaine est complexe. Elle la développe par la bouche de Raison dans *La Cité des dames*, raison qui oppose sens naturel et science acquise: 'Car l'un est don de Dieu par naturelle influence, et l'autre est acquis par lonc estude.' L'un, naturel, meurt avec celui qui le possède, l'autre acquise profite à tous et est transmise par les livres: 'Mais les sciences durent a perpetuité a ceulx qui les ont, c'est assavoir en loz, et prouffitent a maintes gens en tant que ilz les apprennent aux autres et en sont livres pour ceulx a venir [Mais les sciences durent toujours pour ceux qui les possèdent, à savoir par la louange qu'ils en retirent, et elles profitent à beaucoup, les uns les apprenant aux autres, et il en est fait livres pour ceux à venir].'[28] On comprend l'importance qu'a pour Christine le fait d'intervenir sur la question de l'enseignement de l'amour.

L'art d'amour en effet ne se présente pas uniquement sous la forme de traités didactiques. Il peut être développé en actes par le biais du roman ou du dit. C'est le cas du *Roman de la Rose* 'ou l'art d'Amours est tote enclose' (v. 38). Dans ce livre les maîtres qui incitent à l'amour érotique sont au nombre de deux: le dieu Amours lui-même qui énonce ses commandements à l'intention de l'amant, et la Vieille qui s'adresse à la dame représentée par Bel Accueil (vv. 12710–14516).[29] Ce dédoublement de la dame en un personnage féminin et masculin Bel Accueil, diversement analysé, est significatif. Celui à qui on apprend à tromper est grammaticalement de genre masculin. L'enseignement est théorique d'un côté, c'est celui du dieu Amour, l'enseignement est pratique de l'autre, la Vieille l'a appris par 'experimenz' (v. 12775) mais elle en possède maintenant 'la science' (v. 12786), elle peut enseigner en chaire: 'dont bien puis en chaiere lire' (v. 12787). Nombreuses sont les œuvres qui reprennent tel ou tel de ces enseignements ou qui remploient la formule même du *Roman de la Rose*: 'ou l'art d'amours est tote enclose'. C'est ce que fait Nicole de Margival dans son *Dit de la Panthère*: 'Qui veult d'amors

---

[27] *L'Art d'amours*, éd. Roy, p. 67.

[28] Christine de Pizan, *La Città delle dame/Le Livre de la Cité des dames*, éd. Earl Jeffrey Richards, trad. Patrizia Caraffi, 2ème édition (Milan, 1998), Livre I, chap. 43, pp. 196 et 198.

[29] Guillaume de Lorris et Jean de Meun, *Le Roman de la Rose*, éd. Félix Lecoy, 3 tomes (Paris, 1965/1966/1970), II.

a chief venir, / Dedens le *Rommant de la Rose* / Trouveras la semence enclose [celui qui veut venir à bout de la connaissance de l'amour en trouvera la semence enclose dans le *Roman de la Rose*].'[30] Jean Froissart dans son *Joli Buisson de Jonece* utilise ce moule formulaire, en changeant la rime, pour parler de son 'orloge amoureux': 'Ou grant part del art d'Amours loge [où loge une grande partie de l'art d'Amour]'.[31] Martin le Franc analysant l'œuvre de Froissart dans son *Champion des dames* la place par sa formulation dans l'orbite d'André Le Chapelain: 'L'orloge amoureux, ou l'art / De sage amour est bien traictié.'[32] L'adjectif *sage* fait écho en quelque sorte au *honneste* d'André Le Chapelain. On note qu'en 1389, l'*Horologium sapientiae* d'Henri Suso, écrite vers 1339, est traduite en français. Le parallélisme des titres: 'horloge amoureux', 'horloge de sapience', par leur recours à une image d'un même savoir technique dit la tension qui organise la pensée de toute l'époque entre amour et sagesse.

Quelle est la réaction de Christine face aux arts d'amour dans la lignée d'Ovide? Elle est violente. Cette œuvre d'Ovide pervertit les jeunes clercs qui, en étudiant le latin à travers elle, sucent avec le lait de la grammaire celui de l'antiféminisme. Il faudrait donc la rebaptiser, non par Art d'amour mais 'Art de grant decevance [Art de grande tromperie]' proclame Christine dans *L'Epistre au Dieu d'Amour* (v. 377), la déconstruire et la récrire.[33] Sa position est originale, de par son genre et son point de vue; même si elle fait parler le dieu d'Amour, elle est femme. Elle n'envisage pas en effet, des *Remedia amoris*, au sens ovidien du terme, à la différence de l'auteur des *Eschés amoureux*. Ce dernier, s'il fait bien prononcer les *Remedia* par Pallas, garde le point de vue d'Ovide. Pour Christine, en revanche, il ne s'agit pas de guérir les hommes de l'amour – entendons bien les mâles – pour qu'ils accèdent mieux au savoir. Elle n'adhère pas à la pensée qui veut voir dans la femme un obstacle aux livres pour le clerc. Il est question pour elle d'apprendre à ce dernier le respect de la femme et de permettre à celle-ci l'accès au savoir. Non pas apprendre les tours d'amour, sa pratique, ni même en connaître la théorique, si l'on reprend les termes employés par le *Roman de la Rose*[34] et

---

[30] Nicole de Margival, *Le Dit de la Panthère*, éd. Bernard Ribémont (Paris, 2000), vv. 1030–2.

[31] Jean Froissart, *Le Joli Buisson de Jonece*, éd. Anthime Fourrier (Genève, 1975), v. 446.

[32] Martin Le Franc, *Le Champion des dames*, éd. Robert Deschaux, 5 vols (Paris, 1999), III, vv. 12123–4.

[33] La réaction est la même dans sa lettre à Maistre Pierre Col, éd. Hicks, *Le Débat*, pp. 138–9: 'Ha! livre mal nommé *L'Art d'amours!* Car d'amours n'est il mie! mais art de faulse malicieuse industrie de decepvoir femmes puet il bien estre appellés.'

[34] La Vieille évoquant sa jeunesse: 'Bele iere, et jenne et nice et fole, / n'onc ne fui d'Amors a escole / ou l'en leüst la theorique, / mais je sai tout par la practique', vv. 12771–4.

Guillaume de Machaut,[35] mais accéder par la science, par la connaissance à la sagesse. Jacques Legrand, dans son *Archiloge Sophie*, donne avec le titre de sa première partie un tel programme: 'Le premier livre parle de l'amour de Sophie et des raisons qui doivent un chacun incliner a sapience amer.'[36]

Philosophie, au début du *De consolatione Philosphiae* de Boèce, chasse les muses des poètes, du chevet du malade, muses qu'elle traite de prostituées – 'scenicas meretriculas' et de sirènes. C'est à elle, Philosophie, que revient la consolation. Il y a une hiérarchie de la poésie à la philosophie. Christine de Pizan au moment de sa plus grande dérélicition, la mort de son mari, se montre elle aussi accompagnée des 'musetes des pouetes' (*Advision*, p. 107). Il s'agit des commencements de Christine dans l'écriture, 'si comme il appert au commencement des mes premiers dictiez ou principe de mes premieres *Cent Balades* [ainsi qu'il apparaît au commencement de mes premières compositions, au début de mes *Cent Balades*]'. Mais les muses ne sont pas chassées théâtralement et c'est par degrés que Christine va monter dans le domaine de la connaissance. Dans le *Chemin de longue estude*, elle pose bien les limites de son ascension et, topos de modestie, précise que son guide n'est pas Pallas elle-même mais la Sibylle, la Sibylle de Cumes, Almathée (vv. 507–11). Respectueuse de la pensée de Boèce, Christine place au sommet du Parnasse les philosophes, d'Aristote, 'le prince de grant scïence' (v. 1018) à son père Thomas. 'Petit plus bas' (v. 1051) elle situe les poètes et Virgile[37] est nommé en premier puis Homère, Ovide, Horace, Orphée.[38] Cette liste a souvent été commentée en lien avec celle qu'offre Dante au chant IV de l'*Inferno* (vv. 88–90).[39] Une formule mérite d'être relevée pour ma démonstration. Parlant de la fontaine des muses et des poètes, la Sibylle dit: 'Si tiennent la l'escole sainte / Qui de grant scïence est ençainte' (vv. 995–6). 'L'escole sainte' renvoie à l'expression de Dante 'la bella scola' (v. 94). Christine répond ainsi, par Dante interposé, au *Roman de la Rose*. La seule

---

[35] Le prince s'adresse ainsi au poète dans le *Livre de la Fontaine amoureuse*: 'Car je say bien que la pratique / Savez toute, et la theorique / D'amour loial et de ses tours' vv. 1505–7), éd. Jacqueline Cerquiglini-Toulet (Paris, 1993).

[36] Jacques Legrand, *Archiloge Sophie*, éd. Evencio Beltran (Genève, 1986), p. 28, lignes 15–16.

[37] Il est à remarquer que pour le Moyen Âge, Virgile est non seulement poète mais aussi 'philosophe', homme de savoir. C'est la vision et la légende du Virgile magicien qui se construit aux XIIe et XIIIe siècles.

[38] Tous ces noms commencent par O dans la graphie médiévale, c'est-à-dire un signe qui par sa rondeur indique la perfection (vv. 1065–6).

[39] Voir par exemple Kevin Brownlee, 'Le moi *lyrique* et la généalogie littéraire: Christine de Pizan et Dante dans le *Chemin de long estude*', dans *'Musique naturele': Interpretationen zur französischen Lyrik des Spätmittelalters*, éd. Wolf-Dieter Stempel (Munich, 1995), pp. 105–39.

école possible n'est pas celle des arts d'amour,[40] l'école régie par Vénus telle qu'elle a pu l'évoquer dans les *Cent Balades*[41] ou *L'Epistre Othea*.[42] L'école ici est sainte. Elle enclôt non l'amour mais la science et l'enclôt à la manière d'une matrice féminine. La rime *sainte-ençainte* polémique en quelque sorte avec la rime *close-enclose* du *Roman de la Rose*.

Boèce est présenté par Christine comme le fils de Philosophie, 'mon chier amé filz Bouece le tres souffisant philosophe [mon fils bien-aimé Boèce, le très grand philosophe]' dit Philosophie dans l'*Advision* (p. 94). Dans la question complexe des héritages que ce soit de son père charnel, Thomas, ou de sa mère rêvée – Nature dans *Le Livre de la Mutacion de Fortune*, Philosophie dans l'*Advision* –, Christine ne peut avoir que les restes. Ce sont les raclures, paillettes du trésor de son père dans la *Mutation de Fortune*, les miettes tombées de haute table dans l'*Epistre Othea* (vv. 41–2), ou s'adressant à Philosophie dans l'*Advision* les 'petites mietes de ton relief', les 'demourans des grosses viandes de tes tables' (p. 94). Mais Christine ne s'en tient pas à sa première liste, hiérarchique des poètes et des philosophes. Y revenant dans l'*Advision*, elle la présente cette fois de manière chronologique et les premiers qui arrivent dans l'énumération sont ceux qu'elle appelle à la suite de Boccace: les 'theologiens pouetes' (p. 61, ligne 65) à savoir les '.VII. Saiges' ou les 'poetes theologisans' (p. 63, ligne 36). Elle suit Boccace qui dans sa *Genealogie deorum* écrit:

> [poetae] a prisca gentilitate theologi nuncupati sunt; eosque primos fuisse theologizantes testatur Aristotiles; et, quanquam a non vero Deo seu a dictis de non vero Deo nomen tale sortiti sint, venientibus veris theologis, perdere nequivere.[43]
>
> [Depuis le temps des anciens païens, les poètes ont été appelés théologiens; et qu'ils ont été les premiers à pratiquer la théologie, Aristote en témoigne; sans doute, c'est à partir d'un Dieu qui n'était pas vrai ou de ce qu'on en disait qu'un tel nom leur est échu; mais lorsque sont venus les vrais théologiens, ils n'ont pas pu le perdre.]

Et Christine de commenter:

---

[40] Pour le traitement courtois du thème, voir *Li Dis de l'Escole d'amours* de Watriquet de Couvin, éd. Auguste Scheler, *Dits de Watriquet de Couvin* (Bruxelles, 1868), pièce XXVI, pp. 355–8.

[41] Ballade 52, v. 11: 'La grant Venus qui d'amours tient escole'.

[42] Histoire 73 sur le jugement de Pâris, glose: 'Aprés parla Venus par moult amoureuses paroles et dist: "Je suis celle qui tient escole d'amour et de joliveté et qui les folz fais estre sages et les sages fais foloier et les riches fais mendier et les exillez enrichir"' (Parussa, p. 303).

[43] Giovanni Boccaccio, *Genealogie deorum gentilium libri*, 2 vols, éd. V. Romano (Bari, 1951), XV, 8.

Si est cy assavoir que, comme les premiers en Grece renommez de science fussent appellez poetes theologisans – ainsi dis poetes, car de ce qu'ilz disoient ilz formoient dictiez et parloient saintement, theologisans aussi, qu'ilz parloient des dieux et des choses divines –, les premiers et les plus principaulx renommez d'iceulx furent trois, c'est assavoir Orpheus et son disciples Museus, et Linius de Thebes qui fut maistre d'Ercules. (p. 63)

[Il faut ici savoir que les premiers en Grèce à avoir été renommés pour leur science furent appelés 'poètes théologiens', ainsi nommés 'poètes' parce qu'ils donnaient à leurs propos la forme de compositions poétiques et qu'ils parlaient saintement, 'théologiens' également en ce qu'ils parlaient des dieux et des choses divines, et que les premiers et les plus renommés d'entre eux furent au nombre de trois: Orphée et son disciple Musée et Linos de Thèbes qui fut le maître d'Hercule.]

Christine cite également Hésiode – 'Exodus qui fut l'un des poetes theologisans' – et elle précise les 'theologisans pouetes qui precederent les naturielz philosophes' (p. 72, lignes 75–6 et 78).

La poésie, telle que l'entend alors le Moyen Âge, ne se limite ni à une question de versification,[44] ni au seul chant amoureux. Elle devient mythologique et philosophique. Pour Christine, la poésie n'est plus alors uniquement voix et charme mais écrit et science. Elle a partie liée avec le savoir et un savoir de type religieux, un savoir sur le monde et ses secrets. Les sirènes et leur chant sont conjurés. Convertissant la poésie païenne en savoir chrétien, l'allégorie permet la récupération de toute la science enfouie dans la fable. On sait le rôle essentiel, pour le français, joué par l'*Ovide moralisé* au début du XIVe siècle pour la 'conversion' d'Ovide. Des lecteurs de la fin du XVe siècle et du XVIe siècle, à leur tour, vont appliquer la même méthode au *Roman de la Rose*. Je lis les prémices de ce mouvement chez ceux qui, dès le XIVe siècle, citant la *Rose*, l'appellent non *Le Roman de la Rose* mais *Le Livre de la Rose*. On trouve parmi eux Philippe de Mézières dans son *Livre de la Vertu et du sacrement de mariage*,[45] Raoul de Presles dans le commentaire de sa traduction de la *Cité de Dieu* de saint Augustin,[46] et Laurent de Premierfait, nous l'avons vu, dans sa vie de Dante ajoutée à sa traduction du *De casibus* de Boccace.[47] La liste est significative. On quitte le domaine de l'amour pour celui de la morale et de la connaissance. La Rose devient l'allégorie du savoir. Le *Roman de la Rose moralisé* de Jean Molinet en témoigne. Telle est également la démarche de l'éditeur du *Roman de la Rose* de 1526 dans

---

[44] Sur cette question, voir notre article: 'Leçon. Sentier de rime et voie de prose au Moyen Âge', *Po&sie*, 119 (2007), 123–31.

[45] Philippe de Mézières, *Le Livre de la Vertu du sacrement de mariage*, éd. Joan B. Williamson (Washington, DC, 1993), p. 241: 'le Jalous ou Livre de la Rose'.

[46] On peut lire le passage dans McWebb (ed.), *Debating the Roman de la Rose*, p. 16.

[47] Voir note 14.

son préambule: 'Je dis doncques premierement que par la rose qui tant est appettée de l'amant est entendu l'estat de sapience.'[48] Cette tournure d'esprit globale, allégorique, est ce qui permet à Christine au dernier chapitre de son *Advision* de remercier Philosophie en la personne de Theologie:

> Et vraiement es tu toutes les sciences. Car tu es vraie phisique, c'est assavoir theologie, en tant que tu es de Dieu, car toutes les causes de toute nature sont en Dieu createur. Tu es ethique, car bonne vie et honnestes que tu sermonnes et aprens, c'est assavoir a amer ce qui est a amer, c'est Dieu et le prouchain; et cela, Theologie, monstres tu en la science de phisiques et de ethiques. Tu es logique, car la lumiere et la verité de l'ame raisonnable tu monstres. Tu es politique, car tu aprens a bien vivre, car nulle cité n'est mieulx gardee que par le fondement et lian de foy et de ferme concorde a amer le bien commun qui est tres vray et tres souverain.
> (p. 140, lignes 17–26 et 141, ligne 1)

> [Et vraiment, tu es toutes les sciences. Car tu es la vraie physique, c'est-à-dire la théologie, en tant que tu procèdes de Dieu car toutes les causes de toute la nature sont en Dieu créateur. Tu es éthique, car la bonne et honnête vie que tu enseignes et apprends, à savoir aimer ce qui est à aimer, c'est-à-dire Dieu et le prochain, c'est cela, Théologie, que tu montres dans la science de physique et d'éthique. Tu es logique, car tu montres la lumière et la vérité de l'âme raisonnable. Tu es politique, car tu apprends à bien vivre, car aucune cité n'est mieux gardée que si elle est fondée sur le lien de la foi et de la ferme concorde pour aimer le bien commun qui est très vrai et très souverain.]

Le désir de savoir, érotisé au départ chez Christine de Pizan car il fonctionnait comme substitut du désir amoureux, est devenu désir de Dieu. Toutes les branches de la connaissance, toutes ces sciences que Christine a illustrées, sont encloses dans la philosophie chrétienne qu'elle égale à Théologie. Dans le développement de son œuvre, elle passe d'une figure de poète de l'amour à la manière du Dante de la *Vita nova* ou de Guillaume de Machaut à une figure de poète 'theologisant', tel le Dante de la *Commedia*.

Christine de Pizan explore, intellectuellement ou par expérience, et expose les trois modes de vie – voluptueuse, active, contemplative – qui correspondent à trois âges de l'homme, selon la théorie des âges de la vie et aux trois déesses du jugement de Pâris: Vénus, Junon, Pallas. De la vie voluptueuse, Christine traite de manière critique dans sa poésie amoureuse. Elle parle de la vie active, du rapport à l'avoir, à l'argent que symbolise Junon, à l'héritage matériel, au moment de ses procès à la mort de son mari: 'Car

---

[48] Bernard Weinberg attribue cette édition à Guillaume Michel et édite le préambule. Voir 'Guillaume Michel, dit de Tours. The Editor of the 1526 *Roman de la Rose*', *Bibliothèque d'Humanisme et Renaissance*, 11 (1949), 72–85. Notre citation se trouve à la page 81 de l'article.

de Juno n'ay je nul reconfort' chante le refrain de la ballade VII des *Autres Balades*.[49] Elle choisit enfin la vie contemplative, la vie 'astracte et solitaire [retirée et solitaire]',[50] vie contemplative 'laquelle est vraie Sapience' ainsi qu'elle l'affirme dans l'*Advision* (p. 123) et vraie joie. Elle pourrait dire avec l'auteur d'un autre type d'art d'amour que les arts érotiques, l'auteur de *Li Ars d'amour, de vertu et de boneurté*: 'Vins et sons de musike esleechent le cuer, mais deseur psaltere et viele fait li désirs de sapience douce mélodie [Vin et musique réjouissent le cœur mais au-dessus du psalterion et de la vièle, le désir de sagesse fait une douce mélodie].'[51] Elle parle, elle, du 'doulx goust de science' (*Advision*, p. 123).

Christine a transformé le *carmen*, le chant, caractéristique de la poésie de ses prédécesseurs – Guillaume de Machaut en particulier –, en *poema*, poème philosophique.[52] Ce faisant, elle ouvre la voie à tout un courant de la poésie du XVIe siècle.

---

[49] Ed. Maurice Roy, tome I, pp. 214–15.
[50] Il s'agit du dernier vers de la *Mutacion de Fortune*, éd. Solente, t. IV, v. 23636.
[51] *Li Ars d'Amour, de Vertu et de Boneurté*, édité par Jules Petit sous le nom erroné de Jehan le Bel, 2 tomes (Bruxelles, 1867–69), II, p. 281. Le texte est attribué dans l'état actuel de nos connaissances à Jean d'Arkel.
[52] Sur la distinction entre *carmen* et *poema*, voir Fernand Hallyn, 'Poésie et savoir au Quattrocento et au XVIe siècle' dans *Poétiques de la Renaissance. Le modèle italien, le monde franco-bourguignon et leur héritage en France au XVIe siècle*, éd. Perrine Galand-Hallyn et Fernand Hallyn (Genève, 2001), pp. 167–217, p. 171. Fernand Hallyn s'appuie sur le *De laboribus Herculis* de Coluccio Salutati.

PART I
LEARNED POETRY/POETRY AND LEARNING

1

Poetry and the Translation of Knowledge in Jean de Meun

DAVID F. HULT

Although Jean de Meun is best known to us through his spectacularly successful, endlessly seductive *Roman de la Rose*, it would seem by all accounts that the bulk of his career as a writer was devoted to translation, if we judge by the well-known statement he makes in the dedication of his translation of Boethius's *Consolation of Philosophy* to the King of France, Philip the Fair:[1]

> Je Jehan de Meun qui jadis ou Rommant de la Rose, puis que Jalousie ot mis en prison Bel Acueil, enseignai la maniere du chastel prendre et de la rose cueillir et translatay de latin en françois le livre Vegece de Chevalerie et le livre des Merveilles de Hyrlande et la Vie et les Epistres Pierres Abaelart et Heloys sa fame et le livre Aered de Esperituelle Amitié.
>
> (Preface, lines 2–7; p. 168)
>
> [I, Jean de Meun, who previously in the *Romance of the Rose*, after Jealousy had imprisoned Bel Accueil, taught how to take the castle and pluck the rose, and translated from Latin into French the book of Vegetius on Chivalry and the book of the Marvels of Ireland (*Topographica hibernica* of Giraud de Barri) and the Life and Epistles of Peter Abelard and his wife Heloise and the book of Aelred on Spiritual Friendship (*De amicitia spirituali* of Aelred de Rievaulx).]

Now, as Rita Copeland has suggested, Jean's listing of his *curriculum vitae* in this spot has the effect of placing the Boethius translation in the context of Jean's vernacular production, thus making it function both in an interlingual manner (Latin to French) and an intralingual one, and thus stressing the

---

[1] Quotations from Jean de Meun's translation of Boethius' *Consolation* will be taken from V. L. Dedeck-Héry, ed., 'Boethius' *De Consolatione* by Jean de Meun', *Mediaeval Studies*, 14 (1952), 165–275. Unless otherwise noted, all translations from Old and Middle French are my own.

importance and the authority of vernacularity itself.[2] It also begs the question of the relative status of Jean's prose translations and that of the *Roman de la Rose* as a work of poetic translation. In what sense can we even consider the *Rose* a work of translation? How does Jean's use of poetry, that is rhymed verse, affect the nature of the translation, that is, the 'transfer' of knowledge from one linguistic context to another?

There is, of course, a special linkage between the *Roman de la Rose* and Jean's later translation of Boethius. Not only is the *Rose* sprinkled throughout with borrowings from Boethius, but at one point during the discussion between Reason and the Lover, the allegorical figure makes the following coy remark:[3]

> Mout est chetis et fols naïs
> Qui croit que ci soit ses païs:
> N'est pas vostre païs en terre,
> Ce peut l'en bien des clers enquerre,
> Qui Boece *de Confort* lisent
> Et les sentences qui la gisent,
> Donc granz biens aus gens lais feroit
> Qui bien le leur translateroit. (lines 5003–10)

> [He who believes that his country is here is very much a wretched captive and a naïve fool. Your country is not on earth. You can easily learn this from the clerks who explain Boethius's *Consolation* and the meanings which lie in it. He who would translate it for the laity would do them a great service, p. 105.]

I use the word 'coy' because, by making this reference to the important service someone might perform for a lay public by translating the *Consolation of Philosophy*, Jean seems to be hinting at, or perhaps even tacitly advertising, his own translation of Boethius. But of course Jean's translation of the Boethian text was, by all accounts, probably not completed before the last decade of the thirteenth century, some fifteen to twenty-five years after the putative date of the *Roman de la Rose*. The dedication to King Philip, whose reign began in 1285, would necessarily place it somewhat after that date. To be sure, groundwork on a future translation seems to have been accomplished in and through the *Rose*, with its rendering and, as Daniel Heller-Roazen has recently shown, his careful rereading of some of the most

---

[2] Rita Copeland, *Rhetoric, Hermeneutics and Translation in the Middle Ages: Academic Traditions and Vernacular Texts* (Cambridge, 1991), pp. 133–6.

[3] All quotations from the *Roman de la Rose* are taken from Guillaume de Lorris and Jean de Meun, *Le Roman de la Rose*, ed. Félix Lecoy (Paris, 1965–70). English translation is quoted from Charles Dahlberg, *The Romance of the Rose by Guillaume de Lorris and Jean de Meun* (Princeton, 1971), except where noted. Line numbers (Lecoy) and page numbers (Dahlberg) will be included in the text.

difficult philosophical passages in the Boethian dialogue.[4] But by putting Reason's remark in the conditional, is he suggesting that his project in the *Rose* does not partake of translation? Is he even more coyly referring to the snippets of Boethius we find in the *Rose* as themselves the *Boethius* he is referring to? Which, indeed, of the many possibilities for the term *translatio* (transfer, adaptation, paraphrase, explication, or what we commonly mean today by translation) should be understood here?[5]

As recent work on theories of medieval translation has shown – and here I am thinking most specifically of Rita Copeland's book devoted to the interrelation between translation and commentary in the medieval context – concepts and practices of translation in the twelfth to fourteenth centuries differed significantly from our common-sense understanding of that term. Whereas this lay conception of translation bespeaks a transfer from one language to another that remains subservient to an authoritative original, the copy as it were of a master model meant to offer the meaningful equivalent to another linguistic community, medieval traditions saw translation as a conflation of replication and explication, of transfer and interpretive commentary.[6] For Copeland, medieval translation is an act of empowerment and cultural appropriation.[7] A quite apposite statement to this effect is to be found in the following lines of the preface that Jean de Meun appended to his prose translation of the *Consolation*, from which I have already quoted. Jean speaks of the present undertaking: 'Boece de Consolacion que j'ai translaté de latin en françois (Preface, lines 7–8; p. 168) [Boethius's *Consolation*, which I have translated from Latin into French]'. He then proceeds to speak more specifically of his approach to translation, which was in some measure dictated by his patron's request:

---

[4] Daniel Heller-Roazen, *Fortune's Faces: The Roman de la Rose and the Poetics of Contingency* (Baltimore, 2003).

[5] See Copeland, *Rhetoric, Hermeneutics and Translation*, pp. 9–62, and the more recent remarks concerning twelfth-century translation by Peter Damian-Grint, 'Translation as *Enarratio* and Hermeneutic Theory in Twelfth-Century Vernacular Learned Literature', *Neophilologus*, 83 (1999), 349–67.

[6] In this respect, medieval translation provides an important historical illustration of what modern 'translation theory' sees as a dynamic relation between the original text and the act of translation as partaking in any of a number of transformational operations – hermeneutic, socio-cultural, economic and so on. As Lawrence Venuti has put it most succinctly, 'The history of translation theory can in fact be imagined as a set of changing relationships between the relative autonomy of the translated text, or the translator's actions, and two other categories: *equivalence* and *function*', by which terms he means the translation's correspondence and/or fidelity to the foreign text and its place in the new context of the receiving culture. See Lawrence Venuti, ed., *The Translation Studies Reader* (New York, 2004), pp. 5–6.

[7] Copeland, *Rhetoric, Hermeneutics and Translation*, p. 125.

> Et por ce que tu me deis – lequel dit je tieng pour commandement – que je preisse plainement la sentence de l'aucteur sens trop ensuivre les paroles du latin, je l'ai fait a mon petit pooir si comme ta debonnaireté le me commanda. Or pri touz ceulz qui cest livre verront, s'il leur semble en aucuns lieus que je me soie trop eslongniés des paroles de l'aucteur ou que je aie mis aucunes fois plus de paroles que li aucteur n'i met ou aucune fois mains, que il le me pardoingnent. Car se je eusse espons mot a mot le latin par le françois, li livres en fust trop occurs aus gens lais et li clers, neis moiennement letré, ne peussent pas legierement entendre le latin par le françois. (Preface, lines 9–18; p. 168)

> [Since you told me – and I take your words as a command – to take the meaning of the author in a straightforward fashion without following overly much the words of the Latin, I have done that with my modest skills just as your graciousness enjoined me to do it. Now I beg all those who will see this book to forgive me if it seems to them that in some places I have strayed too far from the author's words or that I have on some occasions put in more words than the author or on other occasions fewer. For if I had expounded the Latin by the French word for word, it would make the book too obscure for the laity and the clerics, even those who are moderately literate, could not easily understand the Latin from (or through) the French.]

Initially of interest in this preface is the audience Jean was aiming at for his translation. In fact he specifies three distinct audiences: first and foremost, the King, who is depicted as a reader of Latin, one experienced enough to specify how he wanted Jean to go about his translation but who would find the French easier to understand than the Latin. Then he mentions two other groups characterized as distinct in their abilities: the laity, who are presumably being depicted as illiterate (in either of the principal senses of the term, 'not being able to read' or 'ignorant of Latin') and who will understand the ideas of Boethius when reformulated in a clear, vernacular rendering, and a clerkly audience who will in some way, it is suggested, use the French translation in order to disentangle the difficulties of the Latin original. Is Jean referring to a manuscript format that would include both the original Latin text and his French prose translation, conceivably on facing pages, as we indeed find in some of the surviving manuscripts? This is not unlikely, given that the translator of a later, versified, version of the *Consolation* recommends precisely that in his epilogue: that his readers place a copy of the original Latin next to his translation, to provide extra pleasure in the reading:

> Mais chascun pri quë il assamble
> Mes dis avoec leur exemplaire
> Le latin; si li devra plaire.[8]

---

[8] Quoted from J. Keith Atkinson, 'A Fourteenth-Century Picard Translation-Commentary of the *Consolatio Philosophiae*', in *The Medieval Boethius: Studies in the*

[But I beg each [reader] to bring together my words with their model, the Latin; thus it ought to give him pleasure.]

As far as the question of technique is concerned, Jean here makes reference to what had been an ongoing debate among Classical and early Christian authors regarding theories of translation: whether translation should be based upon a transfer of meaning ('de sentence a sentence' as certain translators would put it) or whether it should be based upon close lexical transfer ('mot a mot'). While Copeland considers this to be a commonplace distinction in the classical tradition of translation theory, I am not aware of translations in the vernacular tradition prior to the last quarter of the thirteenth century specifying the mechanics of their work in this way.[9]

It is interesting to consider precisely what Jean has in mind here, especially when he makes word count (more or fewer than what is found in the original) a reason for which he might be reproached. A passage from Simon de Hesdin's translation of Valerius Maximus's *Memorabilia* echoes in many ways Jean's preface to the Boethius translation, especially in its stated purpose of transposing the text via the meaning and the glossing activity of the translator (*declarier*) which turns difficult Latin into clear and understandable French.[10] Simon's reference to the difficulty of Latin syntax, especially its compactness, corresponds to Jean de Meun's use of the word *plainement*, which recurs often in prose translators' prologues. As was convincingly argued by James Cline some time ago, the adverb *plainement* undoubtedly refers, in Jean's preface and elsewhere, to the 'opening up' of Latin syntax, its unpacking if you will, such as rendering an ablative absolute as a full clause with a conjugated verb.[11] However, it differs in one important way, it seems to me. Whereas Simon indicates the impossibility of doing a word-for-word translation, Jean does not. Or rather, his apology for the divergence from the Latin original in the number of words, along with his handing over of responsibility for his translating according to the text's meaning to his patron, might suggest that he had alternate possibilities in mind.

Whereas Simon's expressed difficulties in translating word for word seem due to syntactic issues, an anonymous translator who was his contemporary,

---

Vernacular Translations of 'De consolatione Philosophiae', ed. A. J. Minnis (Cambridge, 1987), pp. 32–62, p. 42.

[9] *Ibid.*, pp. 42–55. Although he does not touch upon French translations of Boethius, Jacques Monfrin's 'Humanisme et Traductions au Moyen âge', *Journal des Savants*, 148 (1963), 161–90, remains an important resource.

[10] Léopold Delisle, *Recherches sur la librairie de Charles V*, Part I (Paris, 1907), pp. 114–15.

[11] James M. Cline, 'Chaucer and Jean de Meun: *De consolatione Philosophiae*', *English Literary History*, 3 (1936), 170–81.

likewise working at the bidding of King Charles V, provides still another variation on this topos:[12]

> Aucunes foiz, où l'aucteur du livre et les docteurs et philosophes ont, pour le plus bel et rectorique latin querir, transporté les dictions, pourquoy le françois ainsi ordené seroit pesant et moins cler à entendre, j'ai la sentence mise rez à rez, si comme j'ay pensé que il l'eussent dit eulz meismes, se il parlassent françois.
>
> [Sometimes where the author of the book, as well as the scholars and philosophers, have transposed words, in order to seek out the most beautiful effect along with Latin eloquence, I myself – because French composed in this way would be ponderous and less easy to understand – I have rendered the meaning at the same level [as theirs], as I thought they themselves would have said it, were they to have spoken French.]

This translator seems to be speaking rather of the Frenchifying of difficult Latin words as an impediment to good translation, an approach that he prefers to avoid in favour of some sort of paraphrase.[13]

Critics who have compared passages in the *Roman de la Rose* inspired by Boethius's *Consolation* and corresponding passages in Jean de Meun's prose translation have typically found a close correspondence between the two, especially with regard to lexical choice.[14] But rarely is the most obvious difference between the two more than mentioned in passing: the fact that the *Rose* is in verse and that the Boethius translation is in prose. One might indeed ask why Jean chose to do his entire translation in prose, even when the form of the *prosimetrum*, Boethius's alternation of prose and versified sections, might have suggested likewise, in French, prose sections alternating with ones written in, say, rhymed octosyllabic couplets – the poetic form of the *Rose*, as well as the most common one used through this entire period for composing fictional as well as didactic works. From the numerous studies that have been devoted to the French translations of Boethius, which number about a dozen discreet ones from the thirteenth to the fifteenth century, we know that Jean de Meun's was not the first. This suggests either that he really was not familiar with those of his predecessors or that he was being even more coy than at first blush in his reference to a future translation of the *Conso-*

---

[12] Quoted from Léopold Delisle, *Mélanges de Paléographie et de Bibliographie* (Paris, 1880), p. 227.

[13] See also the comments made by Denis Foulechat, also a translator commissioned by Charles V, in the prologue to his translation of John of Salisbury's *Polycraticus*, where he speaks of the occasional lack of a term in French to properly render a Latin word, the polysemy of Latin vocabulary and the consequent need to depend upon context in order to determine the correct signification. Quoted in Delisle, *Recherches*, I, p. 88.

[14] See especially Ernest Langlois' important intervention, 'La Traduction de Boèce par Jean de Meun', *Romania*, 42 (1913), 331–69.

latio in Reason's speech.[15] But interestingly enough, placing aside Simun de Freine's late-twelfth-century verse adaptation of portions of the *Consolatio*, called the *Roman de Philosophie*, the three translations that almost certainly preceded Jean de Meun's, but that undoubtedly had little circulation, are likewise in prose. It is only in the first half of the fourteenth century (thus post-dating Jean de Meun) that two anonymous versions are produced that intermingle verse and prose, while, during the same period, two entirely versified translations, the one by the anonymous author we quoted above and the other by the Dominican Renaut de Louhan, were composed. It is the second of these two verse/prose translations, commonly titled *Le Livre de Boece de consolacion*, that was clearly the most widely circulated of all the French translations. Glynnis Cropp, whose edition of it appeared in 2006, lists some sixty-five surviving manuscripts that transmit all or part of this translation.[16] This version is not without its connections to Jean de Meun, moreover, for either the translator or one of the first copyists attached to it Jean de Meun's preface, including the dedication to Philip the Fair and Jean's list of his past literary accomplishments, and it is in this form that it is found in most of the surviving manuscripts.

In an important article that appeared some twenty years ago, Peter Dembowski suggests a sequence of steps in the history of rendering in the vernacular learned or didactic Latin works from the twelfth to the fourteenth century that helps to explain Jean's choice. 'The early French vernacularizations', Dembowski states, 'were, according to any modern criterion, not translations, but adaptations.'[17] It is only starting in the mid-thirteenth century, in a movement coinciding with the appearance and confirmation of prose as an important medium for the transmission of romance, historiography and hagiography alike, that prose will be used to produce what Dembowski terms 'service-translations'. These, like Jean de Meun's, served the Latin author and saw as their overt goal the transmission of that author's meaning and intention to contemporary audiences whose knowledge of Latin was limited or nil. If the *Rose* is not a 'service' translation in the way of Jean's later *De Confort*, it does partake in the exercise of interlingual transfer by the borrowing of snippets from a variety of Latin works with the intention of providing a new interpretive context for these passages. No less an authoritative reader than

---

[15] An excellent *mise-au-point* of this material, including an excellent bibliography, can be found in the article 'Boèce', signed by Pierre Courcelle and Sylvie Lefèvre, in the *Dictionnaire des Lettres françaises: Le Moyen Age*, updated by Geneviève Hasenohr and Michel Zink (Paris, 1992 [1964]), pp. 204–8; see also the recent overview by Glynnis M. Cropp, 'The Medieval French Tradition', in *Boethius in the Middle Ages: Latin and Vernacular Traditions of the 'Consolatio Philosophiae'*, ed. Maarten J. F. M. Hoenen and Lodi Nauta (Leiden, 1997), pp. 243–65.

[16] *Le Livre de Boece de Consolacion*, ed. Glynnis M. Cropp (Geneva, 2006).

[17] Peter Dembowski, 'Learned Latin Treatises in French: Inspiration, Plagiarism, and Translation', *Viator*, 17 (1986), 255–69, p. 257.

Jean Gerson declares in *Le Traictié d'une Vision faite contre Le Ronmant de la Rose*, through his spokesperson Eloquence Theologienne, that:

> *L'Art d'amour,* laquelle escript Ovide, n'est pas seulement toute enclose ou dit livre, mais sont translatés, assemblés et tirés come a violance et sans propos autres livres plusseurs, tant d'Ovide come des autres, qui ne sont point moins deshonnestes et perilleux.

> [Not only is the *Art of Love*, which Ovid wrote, entirely enclosed within the said book, but many other books, by Ovid as well as by others, are translated, assembled and, as it were, extracted violently and without apparent purpose – books that are no less immoral and perilous.]

Later he adds that 'tres grant partie de tout ce que fait nostre Fol Amoureulx n'est presques fors translacion des dis d'autruy [a very large part of all that our Foolish Lover says is practically nothing but a translation of others' writings]'.[18] In more recent discussions, both Douglas Kelly and Peter Dembowski have likened Jean's *Rose* to a nearly contemporary prose work, Brunetto Latini's *Tresor* – to quote Kelly, 'as a compilation drawn from heterogeneous sources'.[19] As Kelly summarizes this discussion of translation as adaptation and alteration of sources, 'Adaptation may even effect a total change in the source. [...] The final stage in such change is to pick and choose material in the source that may serve the purposes of the new author. Here we find Jean de Meun.'[20] Peter Dembowski makes a similar point: 'The difference between the *Tresor* and, to take another example, the second part of the *Roman de la Rose* is not in kind but in degree.'[21] Interestingly enough, then, the two works of Jean de Meun that I have been discussing can be seen to represent two extremes of the translational project in the late thirteenth century: the *Rose* could be characterized as adaptation gone berserk, while in the Boethius translation Jean is, in the words of Dembowski, a 'pioneer', 'one of the first, if not the first' of the so-called service translators.

At this juncture, and before proceeding to a discussion of Jean de Meun's 'poetic' translation project in the *Rose*, it is perhaps useful to linger a moment on one of the great formal innovations of the thirteenth century: the appearance of prose and its relation to the previously dominant mode of verse

---

[18] Christine de Pizan, Jean Gerson, Jean de Montreuil, Gontier et Pierre Col, *Le Débat sur le Roman de la Rose*, ed. Eric Hicks (Paris, 1977), pp. 76–7 and 80. It should be noted that the figure of the Foolish Lover is, in Gerson, a conflation of the Lover figure in the dream and the author of the poem, Jean de Meun (who is otherwise not named by Gerson).

[19] Douglas Kelly, '*Translatio Studii*: Translation, Adaptation, and Allegory in Medieval French Literature', *Philological Quarterly*, 57 (1978), 287–310, p. 292.

[20] *Ibid.*, p. 292.

[21] Dembowski, 'Learned Latin Treatises in French', p. 257.

composition.²² As is widely known, quite a polemic arose in the first quarter of the thirteenth century, according to which prose was allied with truth and historical writing, whereas verse was accused of being false, fictional, and excessive. In this regard, it is important to note that the word *prose* does not seem to appear in the French language prior to Brunetto Latini's use and discussion of the term in the early 1260s.²³ Before that time, prose could be called an oppositional mode, in that it is only designated as what it is not, that is, as a form that is not in verse or to be more specific, lacking rhyme: either using the expression 'sanz rime' or, less commonly, 'desrimé'. The terms of this polemic, as well as the growing importance of prose through this period, have led to a commonplace view of the contrasting profiles of prose and verse composition not too dissimilar to the following statement made by Robert Hanning some years ago: 'By the early thirteenth century, a French narrative claiming to be true, authoritative, and edifying or instructive would have its claims undermined by presentation in verse.'²⁴ But if this were the case, how could the *Romance of the Rose* go on to be received as an exemplary gold mine of learning and philosophy, as will be the case in the fourteenth and fifteenth centuries? Why is rhyme *necessarily* the result of hearsay? Why could not rhymed accounts have as their source written Latin prose?

One of the more interesting arguments for the inherent inauthenticity of verse is that of the need to add words to the text in order to fill out the rhyme. Johannes in his *Chronique de Turpin* states that his book is without rhyme in order that it may reflect the Latin of the history that Archbishop Turpin composed and wrote down just as he saw and heard it.²⁵ Somewhat surprisingly, similar claims regarding the need to distort or rework content (always seen as being inherently truthful) in order to fit the formal requirements of rhymed verse even find their way into verse compositions of the

---

²² The bibliography on the subject of prose composition has in recent years become quite abundant. Principal studies include Erich Köhler, 'Zur Entstehung des altfranzösischen Prosaromans', in *Trobadorlyrik und Höfischer Roman* (Berlin, 1962), pp. 213–23; Omer Jodogne, 'La Naissance de la prose française', in *Académie royale des sciences, des lettres et des beaux-arts, Bulletin de la classe des lettres et des sciences morales et politiques* (Brussels, 1963), pp. 296–308; Brian Woledge and H. P. Clive, *Répertoire des plus anciens textes en prose française depuis 842 jusqu'aux premières années du XIIIᵉ siècle* (Geneva, 1964); Wlad Godzich and Jeffrey Kittay, *The Emergence of Prose: An Essay in Prosaics* (Minneapolis, 1987); Gabrielle Spiegel, *Romancing the Past: The Rise of Vernacular Prose Historiography in Thirteenth-Century France* (Berkeley, 1993); and Claudio Galderisi, 'Vers et prose au Moyen Âge', in *Histoire de la France Littéraire: Naissances, Renaissances*, ed. Frank Lestringant and Michel Zink (Paris, 2006), pp. 745–66.
²³ See Mary B. Speer and Alfred Foulet, 'Is *Marques de Rome* a derhymed romance?', *Romania*, 101 (1980), 336–65, p. 361.
²⁴ Robert Hanning, 'Arthurian Evangelists: The Language of Truth in Thirteenth-Century French Prose Romances', *Philological Quarterly*, 64 (1985), 347–65, p. 355.
²⁵ Ronald N. Walpole, ed., *The Old French Johannes Translation of the Pseudo-Turpin Chronicle: A Critical Edition* (Berkeley, 1976), p. 130.

period. The scribal compiler of the *chanson de geste La Mort Aymeri de Narbonne* interpolates the following reflection, suggesting a tension between writer and singer:[26]

> Nus hom ne puet chançon de jeste dire
> Que il ne mente la ou li vers define,
> As mos drecier et a tailler la rime.
> Ce est bien voirs, gramaire le devise. (lines 3055–8)
>
> [No man can tell a *chanson de geste* without lying at the end of the line, in arranging the words and sculpting the rhyme. This is really true, grammar explains it.]

The narrator locates very precisely the space of lies, where he comes to the end of the verse. His use of the verb *taillier*, taken from the vocabulary of stone masonry, suggests not only the physical effort of the poet but also, for better or for worse, the nature of verbal artifice as one of the mechanical arts. The inherent adequation of verse and artifice suggests the very power (and truth value) of rhyme through an exercise of that power, while at the same time questioning its efficaciousness.

The author of a verse prologue to a now-lost prose work, a version of the *Prophetia Merlini*, even seems to admit to the difficulty of writing in verse as opposed to the relative lack of skill or authorial intervention required for prose composition.[27] The narrator again uses the idea of *taillier* in relation to poetic composition, contrasting the hands-on work of the rhyming poet with the relative passivity of the prose writer who, quite literally, does nothing himself.[28]

Although among such discussions the attacks against verse are preponderant, there is some evidence of verse writers' early frustration with minstrels (*not* clerkly writers) using the prose format of their stories as, shall we say,

---

[26] J. Couraye du Parc, ed., *La Mort Aymeri de Narbonne, chanson de geste* (Paris, 1884). While most scholars have attributed this rather self-contradictory comment to the *jongleur* that composed the poem, it should be noted that this passage appears in only two of the four MSS containing it, both late (fourteenth century). It is accompanied by an authorial designation and a reference to the written chronicle tradition of Saint Denis, all of which, taken together with the reference to 'gramaire', supports the editor's assertion (p. xxii) that the passage is a later interpolation undoubtedly attributable to a scribal compiler and not to the original *jongleur*/singer, who would have composed the *chanson de geste* in the late twelfth century. The scribe would thereby be registering disapproval of the text he was in the process of copying.

[27] John Koch, 'Anglonormannische Texte im Ms. Arundel 220 des Britischen Museums', *Zeitschrift für romanische Philologie*, 54 (1934), 20–56, p. 35.

[28] Gaston Paris, 'Par ci le me taille', *Romania*, 18 (1889), 288–9. A quotation provided by Paris indicates that this is an expression an architect or master in masonry would have used to tell his subordinates, the stonecutters, what to do (literally, 'cut it for me in this spot'), thus doing no work himself but taking credit for it.

an advertising ploy. Thus the putative author of the *Second Continuation* of the *Conte du Graal,* Wauchier de Denain, writing in the first decade or so of the thirteenth century, attributes the lies or omissions to those who tell stories 'without rhyming', and who mendaciously claim that their audience is hearing the entire story.[29] Aside from the inherent interest of such a 'counter-attack', the fact that Wauchier was also the author of a prose translation of the *Vies des pères* in which were inserted a series of six verse passages, provides one of many examples of the versatility of clerkly writers during this period, as well as their casual rapport (perhaps even identification) with the prosifiers who were beginning to make their appearance. In fact, whether or not we accept this authorial attribution, the narrator of the passage in the *Second Continuation* makes a concerted effort to align the clerkly with the poetic and the jongleuresque ('cil menestrel') with the prosaic, thus calling into question one of the most widespread commonplaces regarding the 'emergence of prose'.

The arbitrariness of the claim to veracity, echoed throughout prologues of the early thirteenth century, becomes particularly evident in a case such as that of the mid-thirteenth-century prosifier of Benoît's extremely popular *Roman de Troie.* As Benoît's editor, Léopold Constans, has claimed, the prosifier's principal source was the twelfth-century poem, which he followed closely, and yet he claims to be translating directly from a Latin original even as he pulls out the now-familiar criticisms of lying verse in order to justify his use of prose.[30] This devious prosifier's need to occult his true source resonates even more strongly when compared with the Benedictine monk Jean de Flixecourt's rather positive characterization of the 'rhymed' *Roman de Troie* in his prose translation of Dares' 'original' (1262):[31]

> Pour che que li roumans de Troies rimés contient molt de coses que on ne treuve mie ens u latin, car chis qui le fist ne peüst mie autrement belement avoir trouvee se rime, je, Jehans de Fliccicourt, translatai sans rime l'estoire des Troiens et du Troies de latin en roumans mot a mot ensi comme je le trouvai en un des livres du livraire Monseigneur Saint Pierre de Corbie ... si que chil qui veulent oïr lé batailles de Troies et ne pueent mie avoir le rommant qui est rimés, ou pour chou que il est trop grans ou pour chou que

---

[29] William Roach, ed., *The Continuations of the Old French Perceval of Chrétien de Troyes*, Vol. IV: *The Second Continuation* (Philadelphia, 1971), lines 26086–101.

[30] Léopold Constans, ed., *Le Roman de Troie*, Vol. 6 (Paris, 1912), p. 268.

[31] Quoted in Brian Woledge, 'La légende de Troie et les débuts de la prose française', in *Mélanges de linguistique et de littérature romanes offerts à Mario Roques*, 2 vols (Baden-Baden, 1953), II, pp. 313–24, p. 315. See also Françoise Vielliard, 'La traduction du *De excidio Troiae* de Darès le Phrygien par Jean de Flixecourt', in *Medieval Codicology, Iconography, Literature, and Translation: Studies for Keith Val Sinclair*, ed. P. R. Monks and D.D.R. Owen (Leiden, 1994), pp. 284–95. Jean de Flixecourt's translation is extant in only two MSS, MS 487 of the Royal Library of Copenhagen and Turin L. IV. 33 (Biblioteca Nazionale Universitaria), which was partially destroyed in the 1904 fire.

il ent est peu, si porroit avoir chestui legierement, car il est petis, et porroit bien savoir par chestui le verité de l'estoire.

[Since the *Roman de Troie* in rhyme contains many things that one doesn't find in the Latin, inasmuch as he who wrote it could not otherwise so beautifully have composed his poetry, I, Jean de Flixecourt, translated without rhyme the story of the Trojans and of Troy from Latin into French word for word just as I found it in one of the books in the library of My Lord Saint Peter of Corbie … so that those who wish to hear the battles of Troy and cannot possess the rhymed romance, either because it is too big or because there are few copies of it, could nevertheless obtain this one easily, for it is small, and could then find out from this one the true story.]

We note Jean's lack of embarrassment about the verse *Troie*, not only in terms of its aesthetic beauty, but also in terms of its renown and indispensability. His shorter prose version will fill a gap not because it is more truthful or even because it is more faithful to the original, but because it is more compact and therefore, presumably, either easier to transport or to have copied. Quite simply, and unlike the other prosifier, Jean refrains from attacking verse because he has nothing to hide: Benoît's poem is genuinely not his source.

Both the stereotyped nature of the claim to truthfulness throughout this period and the attempted hoaxes of prosifiers such as the *Troie* translator strongly suggest that we look more closely at some of the less obvious motivations behind those claims. The truth-telling topos is omnipresent in works of the twelfth and thirteenth centuries, both verse and prose, but to make it a characteristic inherent in one form and to use that argument in order to dismiss another form seems to be a novel formulation. Yet it could be claimed that the anti-verse side of the polemic is related to the prose writer's sense of rivalry, or even of technical inferiority, combined occasionally with a need to suppress the translator's true source. To suggest that writers or storytellers who use verse are necessarily illiterate (as is stated, for instance, in Nicolas de Senlis's prologue to his translation of the *Pseudo-Turpin*, where he says that rhyming storytellers only obtain their knowledge through hearsay) or mendacious is, after all, an astonishing claim to make in the period 1200–10, when almost all religious and historical narrative, not to mention didactic literature, was being written in verse. It is worth recalling that, while prose makes its grand appearance simultaneously in the work of a wide range of authors, the anti-verse polemics are found in only a very particular segment of them. As Omer Jodogne pointed out some years ago, these claims are uniformly found in works that are, or that pretend to be, translations from Latin, but not in any of the works composed directly in vernacular prose, such as the crusader chronicles of Villehardouin, or the prose romances, such as the *Perlesvaus*. Furthermore, in all cases there seems to be a real or imagined verse text, usually unspecified, standing in a position of rivalry with the prose account: the *Chanson de Roland* for the *Pseudo-Turpin*; the *Roman de Troie* for the prose *Troie*; a verse history, perhaps the now-lost version of Jehan de Prunai, for the Philip Augustus translation; verse bestiaries (of which there are several in the twelfth century) for Pierre de Beauvais' *Bestiaire*; a manuscript of Wace, or perhaps one of the several available verse translations of Geoffrey of Monmouth, for the *Merlin* prologue. Most interesting of all, the scribal editor of *La Mort Aymeri de Narbonne* seems to be disputing with, and thereby rivalling, the very text he is copying, along with the epic tradition it represents. It is sometimes forgotten that the rhetorical technique of disparaging one's adversary is a universal one and found in virtually every vernacular genre practiced in the twelfth and thirteenth centuries.[32] What is important is not so much the substance of the attack, which itself becomes somewhat arbitrary, but the valorisations revealed by these attacks.

When we turn to the translators of learned treatises later in the thirteenth century and into the fourteenth century, we find a rather different picture. The prologue of the tremendously popular verse/prose rendition of Boethius that I mentioned earlier says the following about the formal aspects of the work:[33]

> Et use de proses et de metres, c'est a dire qu'il parle d'une part plainement et sanz rymes et d'autre part par vers rymez, car es proses il use de raisons qui font a consolacion et es vers rymez entremesle aucunes delectables raisons qui font oublier la douleur.
>
> [And [the book] uses prose and meter, that is, it speaks on the one hand plainly and without rhyme, and on the other, through rhymed verse, for in the prose passages it makes use of arguments that lead to consolation while in the rhymed verses it combines pleasurable ways of speaking that make one forget one's sorrow.]

As mentioned previously, Brunetto Latini seems to have been the first writer to introduce the word *prose* into medieval French, in his *Tresor*, in a discussion of the relative qualities of verse and of prose. There he states that the teaching of rhetoric is likewise applicable to both manners of composition, except that (using the metaphor of the road or the path) 'la voie de prose est large et pleniere, si comme est ore la commune parleure des gens [the passageway of prose is wide and vast, just as is nowadays people's common speech]' while 'li sentiers de risme est plus estrois et plus fors, si comme celui ki est clos et fermés de murs et de palis [the path of rhyme is more

---

[32] See for instance the pseudo-Ciceronian *Rhetorica ad Herennium*, ed. and trans. Harry Caplan (Cambridge, MA, 1981), I. v. 8: 'Ab adversariorum persona benevolentia captabitur si eos in odium, in invidiam, in contemptionem adducemus [From the discussion of the person of our adversaries we shall secure goodwill by bringing them into hatred, unpopularity, or contempt]'.

[33] Glynnis Cropp, *Le Livre de Boece*, pp. 88–9.

narrow and more arduous, as one that is enclosed and fortified by walls and palisades].'[34]

With these issues in mind regarding the status of verse and prose at the time Jean de Meun was writing, as well as his serious goal in both the *Rose* and the translation of Boethius, I would like to turn to the question of poetry in the *Rose* and the role it plays in helping Jean carry out his stated intention. Indeed, in the many fine studies that have been published and that continue to appear dealing with the intricacies of Jean's learned sources and his manipulation of them, only rarely are questions of poetic effect brought into the discussion. And yet, judging by the documents in the early-fifteenth-century *Querelle de la Rose*, Jean's excellence as a writer and poet seems to be one of the few things that his detractors and supporters manage to agree upon. Eloquence Theologienne, the allegorical spokesperson for Jean Gerson in the latter's clever retort to Jean de Meun's supporters, refers to his 'beau parler en rimes et proses [his gift for speaking in verse and prose]'.[35] Christine de Pizan speaks of his 'moult beaulx termes et vers gracieux bien leonimes [very beautiful terms and elegant verses with really rich rhymes]', while Pierre Col considers him a 'tres divin orateur et poete, et tres parfait philosophe [very divine orator and poet and extremely accomplished philosopher]', later excusing his numerous quotations from Jean's text by saying, 'Je ne pouroye en prose aussi briefment reciter une chose comme maistre Jehan de Meung la dit en rime leonine [I could not express an idea in prose as concisely as Jean de Meun does it with his rich rhymes].'[36] In one of his epistles, Jean de Montreuil refers to him as a 'philosophum et poetam ingeniosissimum [a philosopher and poet of supreme genius]'.[37]

In previous work I have attempted to show how the discussion over language usage in Reason's speech is crucial for an understanding of Jean's own approach to language, inasmuch as it sets the stage for a view of language as free-flowing and open to metaphorical associations that lead to occasionally outrageous images popping up in unexpected contexts.[38] By establishing and then exploding the idea that words in a given language have a 'proper' meaning through the authoritative personification Reason, she who herself invented the words that denote things, Jean manages to lend his own words a slipperiness, if not an ambivalence, that invades the entire poem. Since the learned discussion between Reason and the Lover is a result of the latter's accusation of obscene or unseemly speech on the part of the goddess who

---

[34] Brunetto Latini, *Li Livres dou Tresor*, ed. Francis J. Carmody (Berkeley, 1948), p. 327.
[35] *Le Débat*, ed. Hicks, p. 66.
[36] *Ibid.*, pp. 13, 89, 108.
[37] *Ibid.*, p. 44.
[38] David Hult, 'Language and Dismemberment: Abelard, Origen, and the *Romance of the Rose*', in *Rethinking the* Romance of the Rose*: Text, Image, Reception*, ed. Kevin Brownlee and Sylvia Huot (Philadelphia, 1992), pp. 101–30.

invented language, it leads to questions of linguistic cover-ups that can go in two directions: either that of euphemism – glossing over an objectionable term with one that is acceptable among polite company, essentially an exercise in the creation of metaphor – or, quite the opposite, that of figurative language, the letter of which is simply a cover for a hidden meaning. This is the well-known hermeneutic that can be called integumental reading, as Jean, via Reason, sums up in the following way:[39]

> Si dit l'en bien en noz escoles
> Maintes choses par paraboles,
> Qui mout sunt beles a entendre;
> Si ne doit l'en mie tout prendre
> A la letre quan que l'en ot.
> [...]
> Et qui bien entendroit la letre,
> Le sen verroit en l'escriture,
> Qui esclarcist la fable occure.
> La verité dedenz reposte
> Seroit clere, s'el iert esposte;
> Bien l'entendras, se bien repetes
> Les integumanz aus poetes. (lines 7123–7, 7132–8)

> [In our schools indeed they say many things in parables that are very beautiful to hear; thus, one should not take everything one hears according to the letter. [...] He who truly understood the letter would see in the writing the sense which clarifies the obscure fable. The truth hidden within would be clear if it were expounded; you will understand it well if you call to mind the integuments of the poets, p. 136.]

While the use of the technical term 'integument' is a clear marker of the influence of the School of Chartres, used to refer to the interpretation of non-Biblical texts by use of the concept of hidden or veiled meanings, Armand Strubel, a recent editor of the *Rose*, has suggested that this method of reading can be likened to Hugh of Saint Victor's discussion of interpreting the Bible in the *Didascalicon*.[40] What is additionally intriguing is the prominence given to the word *letre* in this passage, which is crucial to both types of reading, reading *a la letre* and truly understanding *la letre* so as to perceive the true meaning (*sens* – equivalent to Hugh's *sententia*). But what differs

---

[39] On the term *integument*, see the classic article by Édouard Jeauneau, 'L'Usage de la notion d'*integumentum* à travers les gloses de Guillaume de Conches', *Archives d'histoire doctrinale et littéraire du moyen âge*, 24 (1957), 35–100.

[40] Guillaume de Lorris and Jean de Meun, *Le Roman de la Rose*, ed. and trans. by Armand Strubel (Paris, 1992), note to line 7166 (Lecoy's line 7134), p. 399. See Hugh of Saint Victor, *Didascalicon: De studio legendi*, ed. Brother Charles Henry Buttimer (Washington, DC, 1939), Book 6, Chapter 8 ('De ordine expositionis'), pp. 125–6.

from Hugh's discussion is that Reason provides no guidance for the Lover (or for us) regarding how to determine whether a given discourse should be read literally or integumentally. This uncertainty is encoded in her very discourse as she first says that her use of the dirty word for the male private parts was meant integumentally:

> En ma parole autre sen ot
> Au mains quant des coillons parloie,
> Don si briefment parler voloie,
> Que celui que tu i veuz metre. (lines 7128–31)

> [In my speech there was another sense, at least when I was speaking of balls, of which I wanted to speak but briefly, than the one that you wish to place there (my translation).]

But then, a few lines later, she adds:

> Mes puis t'ai tex .ii. moz renduz,
> Et tu les as bien entenduz,
> Qui pris doivent estre a la letre,
> Tout proprement, sanz glose metre. (lines 7151–4)

> [But afterward I offered to you two words – and you understood/ heard them well – which should be taken according to the letter, quite properly, without applying a gloss (my translation).]

Although Reason does not, in this passage, use the three terms of Hugh of Saint Victor – *littera*, *sensus*, *sententia* – to designate the three levels of reading activity (rather, seeming to use *letre* for the first two and *sens* for *sententia*), they do occur a few hundred lines earlier, when Reason reproaches the lover for having forgotten all of his studies:

> D'autre part je tien a grant honte,
> Puis que tu sez que lestre monte
> Et qu'a estudier covient,
> Quant il d'Omer ne te sovient,
> Puis que tu l'as estudié
> [...]
> Que vaut quan que tu estudies,
> Quant li sens au besoig te faut,
> Et seulement par ton defaut?
> Certes, tourjorz en remenbrance
> Deüsses avoir sa sentence. (lines 6747–51, 6756–60)

> [Besides, I consider it a great shame, since you know what is the importance of the letter and that one must study [it], when you don't remember Homer after you have studied him [...] What is the value of whatever you study when its sense fails you, through

your fault alone, at the very time that you need it? Certainly you should always have its significance in your memory, p. 131. (I have slightly emended the translation.)]

Now, one segment of *Rose* criticism has made the claim that Jean de Meun, in relegating the scheme of allegorical action set up by Guillaume de Lorris to a tertiary position and filling his poem with speeches that are essentially learned commentaries on a huge variety of issues, has demonstrated his disinterest in figurative speech and his attachment to the literal level of the text. Most recently, Alastair Minnis has suggested that Jean's preferred (though not exclusive) mode of discourse is that of satire which, in order to convey its message, resides on the literal level.[41] Jean does seem to be concerned with the letter of the text – you know what is the importance of the letter, Reason says – but I think in perhaps a slightly different way. Jean's commitment to the letter is related not simply to the relation between literal and figurative meaning production, but also to the materiality of language itself and, in particular, to the ways in which that materiality can manipulate meaning in the space of vernacular expression, namely French. Part of the translation project conceived by Jean in the *Rose*, I would suggest, is related to this attempt to construct a counter-discourse that runs alongside, and occasionally in disruption with, the denotative project of his very expression, as well as the acknowledged authority of Latin expression. Inasmuch as it is the topic of obscenity that generates the discussion of proper and improper language use, along with the question of euphemism, Jean manages to generate a sequence of images that by imaginative contagion all end up suggesting obscene possibilities: purses, harnesses, pilgrim's staff, relics, and so on. One would like to say that a purse is just a purse, but both Jean's theory and his practice will not allow us to do that. This verbal contagion is further amplified and rendered especially complex by the plays of voice, extending from the shared first-person pronoun to the sequence of authoritative personifications, voices embedded within voices, and the insistently unshakable presence of Jean de Meun's own voice. Or, as Gerson put it so neatly, 'Tout semble estre dit en sa persone [Everything seems to be said in his person].'[42]

But there is still another aspect of language usage that comes out in Jean's poetry, and specifically, through his use of rich rhyme: the ability for words to call upon, echo or enclose other words. In this regard, I think it is important to recall the discussions of prose and verse that I mentioned earlier. Not only does the defence of prose entail the attack of verse, but it also focuses in on several aspects of verse writing: its beauty, its excess, and the technical

---

[41] Alastair Minnis, *Magister Amoris: The 'Roman de la Rose' and Vernacular Hermeneutics* (Oxford, 2001) (see especially Chapter 2, 'Lifting the Veil: Sexual/Textual Nakedness in the *Roman de la Rose*').

[42] Hicks, ed., *Le Débat*, p. 74.

mastery required for it. Jean de Meun proved to be a brilliant poetic master in the *Rose*, which I believe accounts both for his success, for the poetic imitators he spawned, and for the praise lavished upon him by even his fifteenth-century detractors. And technical prowess is itself a topic metaphorized by Jean, most notably in the famous connection made by Genius between lovemaking and three mechanical arts: ploughing, forging and writing. Genius puts it most succinctly in his characterization of pederasts who do not use their instruments in the proper way, following in this Alain de Lille:

> Orpheüs veulent ansivre,
> Qui ne sot arer ne escrivre
> Ne forgier en la droite forge. (lines 19621–3)

> [They want to follow Orpheus, who did not know how to plough or write or forge in the true forge, p. 324. (I have slightly emended the translation.)]

This is the writer seen in his most literal guise, as a copyist transcribing the letter. As Genius had earlier specified:

> Il ne daignent la main metre
> En tables por escrivre letre
> Ne por fere anprainte qui pere. (lines 19533–5)

> [They do not deign to put their hands to the tablets to write a letter or to make a mark that shows, p. 322.]

Among other issues, this discussion highlights an aspect of Jean's *métier* that is quite distinct from the linguistic one generated through Reason's speech. Here, writing is seen not as a matter of producing signs within a semiotic system but as a mechanical science. The expression 'mechanical science' is not my own, but a borrowing from Hugh of Saint Victor's *Didascalicon*, which I cannot believe was not a hidden source for much of the material underlying, first, Nature's speech, and then Genius's interesting development. In the first book of the *Didascalicon*, Hugh discusses what he calls one of the two branches of wisdom, 'knowledge' (*scientia*), which pursues human works and 'is fitly called "mechanical", that is to say adulterate'.[43] There are for Hugh three works, 'The work of God, the work of nature, and the work of the artificer, who imitates nature. [...] The work of the artificer is to put together things disjoined or to disjoin those put together.'[44] Examples Hugh gives of

---

[43] *Didascalicon*, Book 1, Chapter 8, p. 16: 'scientia vero, quia opera humana prosequitur, congrue mechanica, id est, adulterina vocatur.' Translation from *The 'Didascalicon' of Hugh of St. Victor: A Medieval Guide to the Arts*, tr. Jerome Taylor (New York, 1961), p. 55.

[44] *Didascalicon*, Book 1, Chapter 9, p. 16: 'opus Dei, opus naturae, opus artificis

the artificer's work are the founder who casts a statue or who makes arms, the builder who constructs a house, and the weaver who creates fabric and clothing. One other branch is agriculture, which in part concerns itself with the sowing of arable land. While Hugh does not include the work of the scribe in his list, this is clearly Jean's intent. It is all the more interesting when we consider Hugh's qualification of the term mechanical as 'adulterate', calling upon, as its etymon, not *mechane* but *moixos/moechus*, meaning 'adulterer.' In a gloss attributed to Martin of Laon, the following explanation is given:

> 'Moechus' means adulterer, a man who secretly pollutes the marriage bed of another. From 'moechus' we call 'mechanical art' any object which is clever and most delicate (ingeniosa et subtilissima) and which, in its making or operation, is beyond detection (invisibilis), so that beholders find their power of vision stolen from them when they cannot penetrate the ingenuity (ingeniositas) of the thing.[45]

Following are a couple of examples of Jean's play with the mechanics of rhyme, the invisible means by which he supplements or, alternately, disrupts his text. A simple rich rhyme such as *amassent/amassent*: 'Car cil qui richeces amassent,/ S'en les amast et il amassent (lines 5107–8) [For those who amass wealth, if someone loved them and they themselves loved (my translation)]', suggestively ties together two concepts that are otherwise declared to be antithetical: acquisition, from the verb *amasser*, and loving, from the verb *amer* (here in the imperfect subjunctive). As far as true love is concerned, the two concepts are antithetical, but as the rhyme reveals, the cynical vision of a character such as La Vieille is perhaps closer to the truth.

Another example provides a more overt illustration of the poet's tricks, the dissection of words to create words. Toward the beginning of Ami's speech, the personified Friend will make a disparaging remark about the opponent of love, Male Bouche:

> Male Bouche si est bolierres,
> Ostez *bo*, si demorra *lierres*:
> Lierres est il, sachiez de voir,
> Bien le poez apercevoir
> Qu'il ne doit avoir autre non,
> Qu'il emble aus genz leur bon renon. (lines 7325–30)

---

imitantis naturam ... opus artificis est disgregata coniungere vel coniuncta segregare' (*The 'Didascalicon' of Hugh of St. Victor*, p. 55).

[45] M. L. W. Laistner, 'Notes on Greek from the Lectures of a Ninth-Century Monastery Teacher', *Bulletin of the John Rylands Library*, 7 (1923), 421–56, p. 439: 'Moechus est adulter alterius t[h]orum furtim polluens. Inde a m<o>echo dicitur mechanica ars, ingeniosa atque subilissima et paene quomodo facta vel administrata sit invisibilis in tantum, ut etiam visum conspicientium quodam modo furetur, dum non facile penetratur eius ingeniositas.' Translation in *The 'Didascalicon' of Hugh of St. Victor*, p. 191.

> [Male Bouche is a *bolierre* (trickster): take away the *bo* and what remains is *lierre* (thief): He is indeed a thief, you can be sure, and he deserves no other name, for he steals people's good reputation (my translation).]

Through a figure of etymology, Ami provides the true meaning of the trickster. But the play doesn't stop there for, thousands of lines later, in the Faus Semblant episode, the trickster par excellence reveals part of his strategy:

> Li plus fors le plus foible robe.
> Mes je, qui vest ma simple robe,
> Lobant lobez et lobeürs,
> Robe robez et robeeurs. (lines 11519–22)
>
> [The strongest one robs the weakest. But I, who wear my modest garment, tricking the tricked and the tricksters, rob robbers and those who have been robbed (my translation).]

Boler, bolierre, lierre, robe, rober, lober. Through this intricate poetic weave, Jean manages to intermingle some of his important themes: trickery, theft and, most important I think, costume – *robe* and *rober*, costume and, therefore, deceit as robbery. And it doesn't stop there. In the lines following those just quoted he says 'Par ma lobe entas et amasse / Grant tresor en tas et en masse (lines 11523–4) [Through my deceit I pile up and amass a huge treasure, in a pile and in a mass (my translation)].' While highlighting grammatical transformations, verbs becoming nouns and vice versa, which he does elsewhere, Jean here also, through previous associations, brings together Faus Semblant and love, through the key rhyming term 'amasse', which poetically contains the word, though it is far from his denotation here.

Another, more complex, example provides further evidence of Jean's poetic virtuosity. Immediately after his introduction of Nature, Jean launches into a discussion of the perpetuation of the species through a description of the pursuit of Death personified who runs after every single living specimen but who cannot, as he says, 'hold them all together [Mes nes peut ensamble tenir, line 15939]'. Even if a single one were to survive, the common form, and therefore the species, would continue to exist. This is of course antithetical to the later statement of Genius who, promoting sexual activity and procreation, states that if all men stopped using their instruments after sixty years no new men would be engendered; unless God was content with the world being void of humankind he would, as it were, have to go back to the drawing board. There is thus a tension created in the earlier argument between the species and the individual 'piece' as Jean calls it. The species lives through the individual, but the individual cannot produce by him- or herself. It takes two. But then, in the same passage, Jean adduces the example of the Phoenix who is single and the sole exemplar of its species, such that there could never be two at the same time: 'il n'an peut estre .ii. ansenble' (line 15946). The phoenix lives for five hundred years and then makes a huge fire and burns itself. But out of the ashes another phoenix is born, resuscitated by Nature. And even if Death devoured a thousand phoenixes, there still would remain one: Phoenix is the common form, which Nature re-forms in the guise of the individual ('C'est phenix la conmune fourme, que Nature es pieces refourme', lines 15965–6).

Now this paradox of the individual and the species, the individual that encloses the species and yet the individual that cannot through itself reproduce that species, is cunningly replicated in Jean's own linguistic twists. First, in introducing his topic, Jean places *pieces* and *espieces* at the rhyme:

> (Nature) toute s'antante metoit
> An forgier singulieres pieces
> Por continuer les espieces. (lines 15866–8)
>
> [Nature placed all her intent into forging single pieces in order to continue the species (my translation).]

The rhyme *pieces/espieces* necessarily contains the suggestion that we decompose the word *espieces* in Old French into *es pieces*, 'in the pieces', which by an effect of paronomasia dissolves the tension between species and specimen: the species is in the individual, thus mirroring the point being made and foreshadowing the status of the mythical Phoenix, which is individual and species simultaneously. But upon the introduction of the Phoenix, another important rhyme is introduced: 'Tourjorz est il uns seus phenix; et vit, ainceis qu'il soit feniz (lines 15947–8) [There is only ever one phoenix, and one only lives, before it is finished/dead].' The rich rhyme *phenix/feniz*, which unites the name of the seemingly eternal bird with an adumbration of death or destruction, *feniz*, hints at the grander paradox of this entire discussion. Single is double and double is single; the eternal figure is destroyed but arises from its destruction. But still another rhyme has its consequences not four lines after the *phenix/feniz* rhyme. Telling us about the Phoenix's auto-destruction, Jean says:

> Si fet un feu grant et plenier
> D'espices et s'i boute et s'art.
> Ainsi fet de son cors esart. (lines 15951–3)
>
> [[The phoenix] makes a big roaring fire out of aromatics and throws itself into it and burns itself, thus destroying its body (my translation).]

Not only does the carefully chosen word 'espices' echo the word 'espieces' which recurs throughout this passage, but at the rhyme, *s'art/essart* of course conjures up the word *art*. Not a simple coincidence, however, for only thirty lines later we find an important discussion of the competition between art and nature which will end up developing the paradoxical relation between Nature and Art's flawed attempt to imitate Nature. The development of the notion of Art here foreshadows not only Genius's connection of the mechanical arts and sexual behaviour – forging, ploughing, writing – but also Pygmalion's emblematic status as the artisan whose creation came to life. But, next to the immortality of art, next to the capacity of alchemy (a true art, 'art veritable,' Jean tells us) to alter pieces and species, with a repetition of the same rhyme, art is also, through the phoenix, associated with burning and destruction. The verbal echoes that extend from here and penetrate through various discourses in the *Rose* are too numerous to detail. Suffice it to say that through his rich rhymes and the verbal associations that permeate the poem, Jean's poetics is an incantatory one that provides a type of knowledge inducing us to make links well beyond simple straightforward arguments, links that, furthermore, constantly remind us that, however much we might want to believe that he is presenting a sequence of love 'authorities' representing different stances and opinions, there is one unifying authority behind them, or, to come back to our previous quotation from Gerson, 'tout semble estre dit en sa personne'.

In short, Jean de Meun gives a virtuoso performance, demonstrating what is possible in the French language and that could not be accomplished in Latin. If vernacularity was a key for Jean, it seems to me that this is his best demonstration of it. We do not know why Jean turned away from poetry after the *Rose* and devoted himself to service translations in prose. But we know even less why he would have chosen Guillaume de Lorris's love narrative as a vehicle for his philosophical and erotic ruminations. Having said that, when passing from the *Rose* to the prose translation, one is struck by the contrast between the exuberance of the former and the sobriety of the latter, which one commentator has referred to as 'lean'. Perhaps he felt he could not outdo his performance in the *Rose*; perhaps, as would be suggested by the *Testament* (if it is indeed by Jean), it represents a type of retraction. In this regard, the opening scene of the Boethius translation might present us with an intriguing self-portrait of the ageing poet himself, another indication of what it was that attracted Jean to this seminal text, a work, as translators after him would successfully highlight, that is Philosophy and Poetry at once:[46]

> Je, qui jadis parfis jolies chançonnetez en mon estude flurissant, sui maintenant contraint a commencier en plourant a faire vers de doloreuse matiere. Veéz ci que les desordenees Muses des poetes me ditent chosez a escrire et mi chetif ver arrousent mon viage des vrais pleurs. Toutevois ne pot nule pour icestes parvaincre que elles ne me fussent compaignes et poursuissent notre airre. Cestes qui jadis furent la gloire de ma jeunece beneuree et vert

---

[46] Dedeck-Héry, ed., 'Boethius' *De consolatione* by Jean de Meun', pp. 171, 173.

confortent maintenant les destinees de moy dolereus viellart, car viellece m'est venue plus tost que je ne cuidoie.

[I, who long ago confected pretty little songs in my burgeoning reflections, am now obliged, as I cry, to make poems of sorrowful content. Behold how the dishevelled Muses of the Poets dictate things for me to write down and my miserable verses bathe my face with heartfelt tears. Nonetheless, nothing could prevent them from being my companions and following along our path. These women who were formerly the glory of my green and fortunate youth now console my destinies – I, a sorrowful old man, for old age came to me sooner than I expected.]

But Lady Philosophy enters, and:

Quant elle vit les Muses des poetes estans entour notre lit et dictanz paroles a mes pleurs, elle en fu un petit esmeue et enfamblee de cruelz eulz et dist: 'Qui a lessié aprochier a ce malade ces communes putereles abandonnees au peuple qui tant seulement ne li assouageront pas ses douleurs par quelques remedez, mais enseurquetout les li norriront de doulz veninz? Car ce sont celles qui par painturez de entalentemenz qui ne sont profitables ne fructueuses ocient le blé planteureuz des fruiz de raison et tiennent les pensees des hommes en coustume et ne les delivrent pas de maladie … Mais alés vous en anceiz, vous qui estes Sereines douces jusque a destruction, et le me laisséz a curer et a guerir avec mes sciences'.

[When she saw the Muses of the Poets standing around our bed and dictating words adequate to my tears, she became a bit agitated and, flaming with fierce eyes, she said: 'Who allowed those common harlots to approach this invalid, they who prostitute themselves to the populace and who not only will not lighten his pains with some remedies, but worse, will nourish him with sweet poisons? For they are the ones who, through depictions of desirable things that are neither profitable nor fruitful, destroy the abundant kernel of the fruits of reason and keep men's thoughts in check, without delivering them from illness … You sirens, whose sweetness risks destruction, instead of doing this, go away and let me heal him with my wisdom'.]

2

Apprendre à jouer?
Fonctions de la partie d'échecs des *Eschés amoureux*

AMANDINE MUSSOU

En annonçant la partie d'échecs des *Eschés amoureux*, Déduit, dieu du jeu, insiste sur la valeur didactique de ce divertissement:

> Car li jone y aprenderont
> Et li aultre y reprenderont
> Aussy, matere et examplaire
> De miex jouer et de miex traire.[1]

> [Car les jeunes gens pourront apprendre à mieux jouer, tout comme les autres pourront se perfectionner, en prenant exemple sur cette partie.]

Pour les spectateurs intra-diégétiques regroupés autour du narrateur et de la jeune fille qu'il va affronter, il s'agit d'être éduqués.

Cet épisode ludique est une création originale de l'auteur des *Eschés amoureux*, rédigés vers 1370–80.[2] L'attribution de l'œuvre est une question actuellement discutée: selon Gianmario Raimondi et Françoise Guichard-Tesson notamment, Évrart de Conty, médecin de Charles V, auteur d'un vaste

---

[1] Gianmario Raimondi, '*Les Eschés amoureux*. Studio preparatorio ed edizione (II. vv. 3663–5538)', *Pluteus*, 10 (1999), à paraître; vv. 4607–10. Il n'existe que deux manuscrits des *Eschés amoureux*. Le manuscrit de Dresde, Sächsische Landesbibliothek, Oc. 66 est le plus complet, bien qu'il s'interrompe au bout d'environ 30,000 vers. Le manuscrit de Venise, Biblioteca Marciana, fr. app. 23 est fragmentaire. Aucune édition intégrale n'est à ce jour disponible. Cependant, outre cette édition partielle à paraître, Gianmario Raimondi a déjà édité une première partie du texte: '*Les Eschés amoureux*. Studio preparatorio ed edizione (I. vv. 1–3662)', *Pluteus*, 8–9 (1990–98).

[2] On situe la rédaction du poème entre 1370 et 1380 en raison d'une allusion à Du Guesclin dans le manuscrit de Dresde, fol. 100b. C'est en 1370 que Du Guesclin accède au rang de connétable; il meurt en 1380. Voir l'introduction de Christine Kraft à son édition de l'épisode du verger d'Amour, *Liebesgarten-Allegorie der Echecs amoureux, Kritische Ausgabe und Kommentar* (Frankfurt am Main, 1977), p. 31.

commentaire en prose du poème, *Le Livre des Eschez amoureux moralisés*,[3] et d'une traduction des *Problèmes* d'Aristote,[4] serait également l'auteur du poème initial, que la critique considérait jusque-là comme anonyme.[5]

Reprenant la trame du *Roman de la Rose*, le récit en vers retrace les pérégrinations du narrateur, au cours d'une *vision en veillant*, jusqu'à son arrivée au verger d'Amour.[6] Là, le jeune homme, également appelé 'l'acteur', se penche au-dessus de la fontaine de Narcisse et aperçoit un attroupement. Il s'en approche et assiste à une partie d'échecs opposant Déduit à une jeune fille. Le dieu d'Amour ordonne ensuite au narrateur de prendre la place du dieu du jeu. Les pièces de l'échiquier sont alors décrites minutieusement et le déroulement de la partie est rapporté en détail. Le narrateur est *maté en l'angle* par la jeune fille, fine connaisseuse des stratégies échiquéennes.

Le mat est à entendre en un sens allégorique: une fois défait, le narrateur s'éprend de sa redoutable adversaire. Survient alors Pallas, déesse de l'entendement, qui, dans un long discours couvrant plus des deux tiers des trente mille vers des *Eschés amoureux*, lui délivre une série d'enseignements très variés. Cette veine didactique était présente dès la partie proprement narrative du poème, puisque le parcours du narrateur était semé de rencontres diverses: Nature, Vénus, Diane et le dieu d'Amour avaient déjà prononcé des discours – bien moins longs que celui de Pallas, mais à la tonalité clairement didactique et souvent fondés sur un appel massif à un savoir mythologique.

La partie d'échecs est l'unique moment du poème où le discours est suspendu au profit du récit. Aucune figure n'intervient, ni pour donner des conseils au narrateur ni pour le mettre en garde. L'arrivée dans le verger d'Amour, si elle n'est pas non plus prétexte à l'insertion de discours édifiants, se fait néanmoins sur le mode descriptif. Le narrateur reconnaît les lieux et les acteurs évoqués par son illustre prédécesseur.[7] L'épisode de la partie d'échecs,

---

[3] Évrart de Conty, *Le Livre des Eschez amoureux moralisés*, éd. Françoise Guichard-Tesson et Bruno Roy (Montréal, 1993).

[4] Une édition des *Problèmes* d'Aristote traduits par Évrart de Conty a été entreprise sous la direction de Joëlle Ducos, Geneviève Dumas, Michèle Goyens et Françoise Guichard-Tesson, à paraître en dix volumes.

[5] Pour ces questions d'attribution, voir Françoise Guichard-Tesson, 'Évrart de Conty, poète, traducteur et commentateur', dans *Aristotle's Problemata in Different Times and Tongues*, ed. Michèle Goyens et Pieter de Leemans (Leuven, 2006), pp. 145–74 et, dans le même recueil, Caroline Boucher, 'Les *Eschés amoureux* d'Évrart de Conty', appendice à 'Des problèmes pour exercer l'entendement du lecteur: Évrart de Conty, Nicole Oresme et la recherche de la nouveauté', pp. 175–97.

[6] À la différence de l'amant du *Roman de la Rose*, le narrateur visite le verger d'Amour, non plus en songe, mais sur les conseils de Nature qui lui apparaît sous la forme d'une vision: 'Non pas en dormant ne en songe, / Mais tout en veillant sans menchonge (Raimondi ed., vv. 173–6) [Ni en dormant ni en songe, mais sans mentir, alors que j'étais éveillé].'

[7] Jouant de la référence au *Roman de la Rose*, le narrateur sollicite régulièrement la mémoire du lecteur et justifie ainsi certaines allusions rapides à tel ou tel élément du

qui marque la profonde bifurcation qu'impriment *Les Eschés amoureux* à leur texte-source, s'inscrit dans un premier temps dans cette veine descriptive. L'auteur s'empare de l'échiquier et des pièces du jeu comme d'objets poétiques à part entière. La partie en tant que telle est, en revanche, traitée sur le mode du pur récit, loin, semble-t-il *a priori*, de l'ambition didactique qui irrigue l'ensemble du poème. Le narrateur, pendant près de six cents vers, livre, sans les commenter, les échanges successifs.[8]

Malgré l'absence de discours, d'autant plus remarquable qu'elle est unique au cœur des trente mille vers du poème, l'épisode est riche d'enseignement. C'est cette tension, entre l'attrait poétique exercé par le motif de l'échiquier et la perspective didactique qui en régit l'inscription dans le récit, que nous souhaitons analyser. Il s'agira donc de voir dans quelle mesure, au plus fort du poétique, le savoir transmis n'en demeure pas moins central. Cette question est liée à celle du destinataire: qui doit être éduqué? S'agit-il des spectateurs qui assistent à la scène, comme en témoigne le vœu de Déduit? Le narrateur de ce récit d'apprentissage est-il également visé? Plus largement, le lecteur des *Eschés amoureux* pouvait-il apprendre à jouer aux échecs en lisant le poème? En suivant un parcours qui nous mènera de la diégèse à la réception du texte, nous nous proposons d'examiner les différentes fonctions de la partie d'échecs.

Gustave Flaubert propose une définition ironique des échecs dans le *Dictionnaire des idées reçues*: 'Trop sérieux pour un jeu, trop futile pour une science.'[9] Il souligne l'ambivalence foncière de ce jeu qui n'en est pas tout à fait un. Ce fonctionnement double est mis en récit dans *Les Eschés amoureux*. Jeu de la rationalité et du discours savant, les échecs s'inscrivent néanmoins dans l'univers du divertissement. Ils trouvent par ce biais une place de choix dans le verger d'Amour, où Oiseuse règne en maîtresse. Tendant à la fois vers l'acquisition d'un savoir et vers la futilité, les échecs mettent en jeu des attitudes contradictoires. Le poème loue la beauté de l'objet luxueux et l'attrait visuel qu'il exerce, tout en insistant sur la rationalité de la grille de l'échiquier, reproduisant par là même l'entre-deux qu'évoquera Flaubert cinq siècles plus tard.

Récit à la première personne, *Les Eschés amoureux* livrent les impressions du narrateur lorsqu'il aperçoit l'échiquier pour la première fois. La descrip-

---

décor planté au siècle précédent par Guillaume de Lorris, 'car la chose est aillours bien dite' (*ibid.*, v. 264).

[8] Nous avons conscience que la distinction entre 'description' de l'objet-échiquier et 'narration' de la partie d'échecs est difficile à maintenir, puisque tout acte de narration induit une part de description. Voir sur ce point Gérard Genette, 'Frontières du récit', *Figures II* (Paris, 1969), p. 56 *sqq*.

[9] Gustave Flaubert, *Dictionnaire des idées reçues*, texte établi et annoté par Albert Thibaudet et René Dumesnil (Paris, 1952), vol. II, p. 1007. La définition dans son intégralité est la suivante: 'Échecs (jeu des): Image de la tactique militaire. – Tous les grands capitaines y étaient forts. – Trop sérieux pour un jeu, trop futile pour une science.'

tion de l'objet est minutieuse et relève de l'*ekphrasis*.[10] L'objet en tant que tel est décrit en premier lieu, puis ce sont les pièces qui attirent le regard du narrateur. Un emblème est représenté sur l'écu de chacune d'entre elles.[11] Le déroulement de la partie est ensuite rapporté sur près de six cents vers.[12] En réalité, le narrateur retrace tout d'abord les neuf premiers échanges, puis les cinq derniers car, précise-t-il, 'J'aroie trop a escrire, / Se tout vous voloie descrire (Kraft ed., vv. 1591–2) [J'aurais trop à écrire, si je voulais tout vous décrire].' Le début de la partie se déroule selon une logique de parfaite symétrie. La jeune fille est sommée par le dieu d'Amour d'ouvrir le jeu; elle avance le second de ses pions.[13] Le narrateur lui répond en miroir, en avançant son pion équivalent.[14] À l'ordre tactique de l'avancée de la jeune fille répond tout d'abord l'absence de stratégie du narrateur, qui se contente d'imiter celle de son adversaire.[15] L'avancée raisonnée de la jeune fille culmine avec le *mat en l'angle* qu'elle inflige au jeune homme.[16] À l'inverse, l'avancée hasardeuse du narrateur ne semble obéir à aucun ordre préalablement construit. Il n'élabore ni stratégie de défense ni stratégie d'attaque. Si les débuts de la partie sont marqués par une reprise à l'identique, en miroir, des coups de son adversaire, la suite semble improvisée. Il avance un pion, fait reculer son roi

---

[10] Cette description s'étend sur plus de deux cent cinquante vers; voir Kraft ed., vv. 1033–1292.

[11] 'Mais encor plus m'esmerveilloient / De che que je vi, qu'il avoient, / Aussy pour descongnissanche / Ou pour autre seignifianche, / Trestuit fourmes et ymaigettes / Par dedens lors escus pourtrette (*ibid.*, vv. 1081–6). [Mais les pièces me fascinaient d'autant plus que je vis qu'elles avaient toutes, comme signe distinctif, ou pour une autre signification, des formes et des images peintes sur leurs écus].'

[12] *Ibid.*, vv. 1293–876.

[13] *Ibid.*, vv. 1311–18.

[14] *Ibid.*, vv. 1342–3.

[15] Au deuxième coup, la jeune fille avance son troisième pion et le narrateur fait de même. Pour une étude détaillée du déroulement de la partie, voir Wilfrid Fauquet, 'Le *giu parti* d'Évrart de Conty. Une version échiquéenne du *Roman de la Rose*', *Romania*, 123 (2005), 486–522. Fauquet propose dans cet article de lire la partie d'échecs des *Eschés amoureux* comme une récriture masquée du *Roman de la Rose*. Raimondi fait figurer, à la fin de l'édition à paraître, des schémas récapitulant les différents échanges, cf. 'Studio preparatorio' II.

[16] 'Quant la dame au gent cors paré / Ot bien tout son fait preparé, / Si qu'elle ne pooit falir, / Elle fit son päon salir / Et sa fierge tres avenant / Pour parfaire le remanant. / Quant ordené les ot a point, / Elle, dont je ne me plains point, / Du päonnet de bel arroy / Me vint dire eschec a mon roy (Kraft ed., vv. 1861–70) [Quand la jeune femme noblement vêtue eut parfaitement préparé sa victoire, de telle sorte qu'elle ne pouvait perdre, elle avança son pion et son aimable reine pour achever ce qu'il lui restait à faire. Quand elle eut ordonné ses pièces, la jeune fille, à qui je n'ai rien à reprocher, vint, de son joli pion, dire échec à mon roi].' La victoire est présentée comme l'aboutissement logique d'un raisonnement maîtrisé, comme en témoigne la prégnance du champ lexical de l'accomplissement dans ces quelques vers.

quand celui-ci est en danger et semble adapter à chaque coup sa conduite, sans tenter d'établir de plan d'ensemble.[17]

Tout au long de la partie, le narrateur est sujet à des moments d'absence. Ceux-ci le maintiennent dans un état second qui le conduit à la défaite. Dès le début de l'épisode, lorsqu'il aperçoit la jeune fille jouant aux échecs contre Déduit, il en oublie les préceptes de Junon et de Pallas, qu'il avait rencontrées auparavant.[18] C'est alors sous le signe de l'oubli que va se placer la partie pour le narrateur. Tandis que le temps continue de s'écouler pour la jeune fille, il semble s'arrêter pour le jeune homme. Dès le premier coup de son adversaire, il marque une pause, absorbé par la contemplation du pion qu'elle a avancé.[19] Au fil du texte, les adjectifs qui le qualifient évoquent cet état dans lequel il est plongé: il est tour à tour 'souspris', 'arresté', 'esbahis', 'estourdis' (Kraft, ed., vv. 1324, 1329, 1339, 1676) ['surpris', 'arrêté', 'étonné', 'étourdi']. Le narrateur est tout aux pièces de l'échiquier et oublie le véritable but du jeu. Ce choc esthétique suspend le déroulement de la partie.[20] Si la jeune fille évolue dans le temps de la stratégie, le narrateur évolue au contraire dans celui de la fascination.

Cette double appréhension du jeu est soulignée par le narrateur qui, alors qu'il se perd une nouvelle fois dans la contemplation d'une pièce, oppose son attitude à celle de son adversaire. Comparant son comportement à celui d'un papillon qui, voletant autour d'une chandelle, finit par s'y brûler, il précise:

> Tout en tel guyse m'alourdoie
> Au päon, que je regardoie;
> S'en oublïoie a moy desfendre.
> Mais celle n'avoit soign d'entendre
> Ne de penser aillours, ains tire
> A moy mater et desconfire. (Kraft ed., vv. 1495–1500)

[De la même façon je me laissais tromper par le pion que je regardais et j'oubliais de m'en défendre. En revanche, la demoi-

---

[17] Le narrateur se retrouve pris au piège: 'Je retraioie aussy sans faille / A men tour en mainte maniere, / Une heure avant et l'aultre arriere (*ibid.*, vv. 1666–8). [Je rejouais sans faute, à mon tour, de diverses façons, un coup en avant un coup en arrière].' Fauquet interprète les ultimes va-et-vient du roi du narrateur comme une métaphore érotique, 'Le *giu parti* d'Évrart de Conty', p. 513.

[18] 'Il ne me souvenoit lors gaires / De Juno ne de ses tresors, / Ne de Pallas aussy (Kraft ed., vv. 906–8) [Je ne me souvenais alors ni de Junon et de ses trésors ni de Pallas].'

[19] 'Quant je vi le trait gracïeus / Du doulz päonnet precïeus, / [...] Je fuy, se Diez pardon me faiche, / Tout souspris de premiere faiche, / Car je n'avoie pas apris / A veïr eschés de tel pris (*ibid.*, vv. 1319–26) [Quand je vis le coup gracieux de ce doux et précieux pion, je fus, que Dieu me pardonne, de prime abord extrêmement surpris, car je n'avais pas appris à observer des échecs d'une telle valeur].'

[20] Nous empruntons l'expression à Michèle Gally, *L'intelligence de l'amour d'Ovide à Dante. Arts d'aimer et poésie au Moyen Âge* (Paris, 2005), p. 164.

selle ne se laissait distraire ni par des paroles ni par des pensées, mais jouait pour me mater et provoquer ma défaite.]

L'oubli de soi revient à plusieurs reprises au cours de la partie et notamment au sujet du pion dit du *mirëoir concave*.[21] C'est sur le sixième pion du narrateur qu'un miroir est représenté. La pièce est l'objet d'un jeu de regards complexe. Lorsqu'il avance ce pion, le jeune homme s'aperçoit qu'il réfléchit tout l'échiquier.[22] Il observe alors l'objet et son image. L'état dans lequel il tombe, en s'oubliant dans cette dernière, est alors celui de la *melancolie*, propice à l'énamourement: 'Si m'y suis *melancoliiés*, / Tant que tous m'y suy *oubliiés* (Kraft ed., vv. 1711–12. C'est nous qui soulignons) [Et je me suis laissé aller à la mélancolie, si bien que je m'y suis tout oublié].'[23] Ces stases qui décrivent l'état du narrateur, tout à l'aspect de l'échiquier, ancrent l'épisode dans une temporalité poétique fondée sur le retour du même et non sur une chronologie linéaire orientée vers un but précis.

Les comportements diamétralement opposés des deux joueurs miment la double attirance que suscitent les échecs:

> Dans le jeu d'échecs, il y a d'une part le spectacle étonnamment séducteur et fascinant d'un personnel représenté et incarné. […] Mais dans ce même jeu, se trouvent aussi l'abstraction, l'épure d'une combinaison formelle, l'emblème de l'approche systémique, le graphique d'une structure, des forces dans des formes, réglées, ordrées et en nombre réduit; il s'agit apparemment du lieu où triomphe la pensée géométrique.[24]

---

[21] Voir au sujet de ce pion, Françoise Guichard-Tesson, 'Le pion Souvenir et les miroirs déformants dans l'allégorie d'amour', dans *Jeux de mémoire. Aspect de la mnémotechnie médiévale*, ed. Bruno Roy et Paul Zumthor (Montréal-Paris, 1985), pp. 99–108; et Michèle Gally, 'Le miroir mis en abyme: *Les Échecs Amoureux* et la réécriture du *Roman de la Rose*', dans *Miroirs et jeux de miroirs dans la littérature médiévale*, ed. Fabienne Pomel (Rennes, 2003), pp. 253–63.

[22] 'Car j'avoie bouté avant / Mon päonnet au mirëoir, / Qui me fit merveilles vëoir; / Car chilz mirëoirs me raporte/ Au devant, par sa vertu forte, / Tant de figure precïeuses, / Atraians et delicïeuses / Et tant de merv(i)eilleuses choses, / Qui sont sur l'eschequir encloses, / C'onques puis je n'os soingn d'entendre / A moy revengier ne desfendre (Kraft ed., vv. 1690–700) [Car j'avais avancé mon pion au miroir, qui me fit voir des choses étonnantes: car ce miroir, en raison de ses propriétés particulières, me présentait tant de précieuses images, séduisantes et délicieuses, et tant de merveilles qui se trouvaient sur l'échiquier, qu'à la suite de cela, je n'eus plus l'esprit à me venger ou à me défendre].'

[23] L'association de la mélancolie et de l'oubli est répétée à la rime quelques vers plus loin: 'Tout ainsy m'atrape et atrait / Chilz mirëoirs par son atrait, / Et sy m'y *melancolïoie*,/ Que tout mon gieu *entroublïoie* (*ibid.*, vv. 1727–30. C'est nous qui soulignons) [De la même façon, ce miroir m'attrape et m'attire et je devenais si mélancolique que j'en oubliais mon jeu]'.

[24] Jacques Berchtold (dir.), *Échiquiers d'encre. Le jeu d'échecs et les lettres (XIXème–XXème siècles)* (Genève, 1998), p. 17.

Cette double séduction s'incarne dans les deux joueurs des *Eschés amoureux*. Le jeune homme est absorbé par la plastique de l'objet et l'observe en poète. La jeune fille figure en revanche une approche méthodique du jeu; elle se comporte en technicienne. Dès son entrée dans le roman elle est d'ailleurs présentée comme une joueuse exceptionnelle, détentrice d'un savoir.[25] Le glissement de la dimension ludique évoquée par Flaubert à la fascination exercée sur le narrateur des *Eschés amoureux* se fonde sur l'idée d'une gratuité fondamentale de la partie.

Le narrateur n'apprend rien au cours de cet épisode: du moins, il n'apprend pas à jouer aux échecs, puisqu'il n'y joue pas réellement et demeure prisonnier d'une image. La partie d'échecs occupe un espace narratif défini au sein du poème. Or cette création originale joue un rôle structurel déterminant puisque la défaite du narrateur le conduit à vouloir mater en retour la jeune fille. Dès la fin de la partie, il souhaite apprendre à jouer aussi bien qu'elle afin de prendre sa revanche.[26] Ce désir est exprimé à plusieurs reprises dans la suite du texte. Non seulement le motif de la partie d'échecs réapparaît après l'épisode narratif qui lui est consacré, mais la récurrence de la métaphore des échecs au-delà du récit de la partie souligne cette idée fixe. C'est dans la bouche du dieu d'Amour que revient notamment cette métaphore filée. Lorsqu'il met en garde le narrateur contre l'usage de la sorcellerie en amour, il lui dit:

> Ch'est chose aussy contraire as mours
> Et trop perilleuse en amours,
> Et si n'est pas grant vaillandise
> D'entendre au mat par cheste guyse. (Kraft ed., vv. 4495–8)

> [Vouloir mater son adversaire de cette façon n'est pas raisonnable et très dangereux en amour, et ce n'est pas très valeureux.]

Il s'agit donc de continuer à jouer. Le motif du jeu irrigue tout le texte et contribue à la progression du récit. Le discours du dieu d'Amour ne perd pas de vue ce point de fuite: il faut éduquer le narrateur afin qu'il prenne sa revanche de la bonne manière. La partie d'échecs remplit donc une fonction dynamique. Si le narrateur n'a rien appris au cours de la partie, il faut qu'il s'exerce afin de mater en retour son adversaire. Un horizon textuel apparaît au-delà de la partie didactique du poème: il s'agit du retour du fil narratif, d'une nouvelle partie d'échecs. Toutefois, la revanche que prendrait le narrateur n'est décrite dans aucun des deux manuscrits, qui s'interrompent tous deux au cours de l'intervention de Pallas.

Le Livre des Eschez amoureux moralisés ne commente que le début du poème et s'interrompt après la partie d'échecs. Cependant Évrart de Conty

---

[25] Kraft ed., vv. 865–9.
[26] *Ibid.*, vv. 2760–6.

offre, à la fin, un résumé du texte qu'il glose. La revanche du narrateur n'y apparaît pas:

> Aprés le mat s'ensuit comment le dieu d'amours, qui du mat ot grant joye, se fist congnoistre a lui […]; et comment oultre aprés la deesse Pallas, c'est a dire sapience, ou prudence, ou raison, le vint enfin reprendre et blasmer sa folie […]. Et lui dist dame Pallas et moustra moult d'enseignemens beaulx et moult de belles choses prouffitables a meurs et a honneste vie et qui seroient belles a declairier, maiz pour certaine cause je m'en tairay atant quant a present.[27]

> [Après le mat, le récit raconte comment le dieu d'Amour, ravi par cette défaite, se fit connaître auprès du narrateur […]; puis comment ensuite, la déesse Pallas, c'est-à-dire sagesse, ou prudence, ou raison, vint le blâmer de sa folie […]. Dame Pallas lui délivra de nombreux enseignements et beaucoup de belles choses profitables pour qui veut mener une vie honnête, et qu'il faudrait éclaircir, mais pour une certaine raison, je ne vais pas en dire plus pour le moment.]

Évrart de Conty évoque uniquement les discours du dieu d'Amour et de Pallas. L'auteur présumé du poème ne fait pas référence à un texte qui intègrerait à la fin une seconde partie d'échecs. Comme le remarque Michèle Gally, 'une seconde partie d'échecs signifierait que le jeune homme a résisté jusqu'au bout aux arguments de Pallas et à la vie "sérieuse".'[28] Or nous n'avons aucune trace réelle de cette revanche qui joue pourtant un rôle moteur dans tout le poème. La répétition de ce motif au-delà de la partie d'échecs apparaît comme un procédé déceptif. Il remplit uniquement une fonction dynamique puisque le texte ne mentionne pas de retour final de la trame narrative et demeure inachevé.

Le narrateur ne cède pas à la tentation ludique, bien qu'il en exprime le souhait à plusieurs reprises. L'épisode de la partie d'échecs peut alors être entendu comme l'une des phases de son apprentissage. Avant de pénétrer dans le verger d'Amour, le jeune homme doit rejouer le jugement de Pâris et choisir entre Vénus, Junon et Pallas. Accordant son jugement à celui de son prédécesseur, il préfère la déesse de la beauté aux deux autres. Les mythographes ont proposé une lecture allégorique de cet épisode: chacune des déesses représente un type de vie.[29] Dans son discours Pallas évoque justement très longuement ces trois vies. Prenant place au cœur de la partie narrative des *Eschés amoureux*, soit au début de ce récit allégorique, la partie

---

[27] Évrart de Conty, *Le Livre des Eschez amoureux moralisés*, pp. 765–6.
[28] Gally, *L'intelligence de l'amour*, p. 121.
[29] Voir sur ce point Pierre-Yves Badel, *Le Roman de la Rose au XIVe siècle. Étude de la réception de l'œuvre* (Genève, 1980), p. 281 *sqq.*; et Jean Seznec, *La Survivance des dieux antiques: essai sur le rôle de la tradition mythologique dans l'humanisme et dans l'art de la Renaissance* (Paris, 1993), p. 127.

d'échecs figure la jeunesse du narrateur (le lieu commun de la *reverdie* développé au seuil du texte en témoigne).[30] Elle est associée à la vie voluptueuse incarnée par Vénus. L'âge adulte serait dans cette perspective associé à la vie active, que représente Junon et que Pallas décrit longuement dans son discours. La vieillesse correspondrait, quant à elle, à la vie contemplative incarnée par Pallas et qui, dans *Les Eschés amoureux*, se présente comme un horizon asymptotique puisque l'exposé de la déesse s'interrompt avant qu'elle n'ait pu évoquer cette vie.[31]

Si le narrateur n'apprend rien au cours de la partie d'échecs, l'ensemble du récit confère à cet épisode le statut d'étape au sein d'un processus d'apprentissage. Les errances amoureuses du narrateur dans sa jeunesse, dont la partie d'échecs est l'allégorie principale, servent de prétexte au déploiement du didactisme pur. Elles représentent une phase permettant ensuite l'accession à un savoir. Certes, le poème demeure inachevé et l'on ne peut pas assurer avec certitude que le narrateur se rangeait du côté de Pallas en renonçant à la tentation ludique, mais cette hypothèse demeure la plus probable.[32] L'épisode incite le narrateur à vouloir apprendre à jouer réellement, vraisemblablement pour renoncer en dernier lieu au piège de l'amour. Cette fonction d'appât est relevée par Alastair Minnis qui se place du point de vue de la réception du poème: 'It could be argued that the *frisson* of the *ars amatoria* is designed to entice the young aristocrat into the moral centre of the text, where unimpeachable doctrine holds sway.'[33]

L'analyse de la réception du texte permet de conférer à l'épisode une fonction didactique en lui-même. Le manuscrit de Venise contient dans ses marges des gloses latines qui explicitent le sens du poème, notamment au moment de la partie d'échecs.[34] Le poème se contente de décrire les pièces et leurs emblèmes, sans en donner la signification. C'est ainsi que nous apparaît le texte du manuscrit de Dresde. En revanche, dans le manuscrit de Venise, les gloses envahissent les marges et explicitent, en latin, le sens des symboles

[30] 'Estoye en asséz grant delit / une matinee en mon lit, / ou doulz printemps delicïeux;/ c'est le temps sur tous gracïeux / qui toute plaisance appareille, / ou la nuit au jour est pareille (Raimondi ed., vv. 73–8). [J'étais très heureux dans mon lit, un matin du doux et délicieux printemps; c'est la saison la plus aimable de toutes, qui prépare tous les délices et où le jour et la nuit sont égaux.]' La rubrique suivante annonce un développement sur le printemps: 'Cy parle l'acteur du printemps [...]' (*ibid.*, p. 108).

[31] Voir à ce sujet Badel, *Le Roman de la Rose au XIVe siècle*, p. 287 sqq.

[32] Alastair Minnis le souligne: 'The final part of the *Eschez amoureux* is lost – assuming, of course, that its author actually completed it. One can easily imagine it ending with florid affirmation of Christian salvation' (*Magister amoris. The 'Roman de la Rose' and Vernacular Hermeneutics* (Oxford, 2001), p. 261). Par ailleurs, mater la jeune fille remettrait en question le monde courtois dans lequel évolue le narrateur.

[33] *Ibid.*, p. 261.

[34] Ces gloses ont été identifiées comme étant de la main d'Évrart de Conty: il s'agit là de l'argument central pour prouver qu'Évrart est également l'auteur du poème. Voir Guichard-Tesson, 'Évrart de Conty, poète, traducteur et commentateur', p. 150.

en leur attribuant une signification allégorique. Le pion de la jeune fille orné d'un croissant de lune est alors assimilé à Jeunesse,[35] le fou du narrateur sur lequel figure un navire est, quant à lui, associé à Espérance *etc.* [36]

Dans *Le Livre des Eschez amoureux moralisés,* ces commentaires marginaux sont intégrés au corps du texte: la description de l'échiquier et des pièces est alors nettement étoffée. Françoise Guichard-Tesson et Bruno Roy ont mis en évidence ce processus unique d''occultation littéraire' dans la version en vers.[37] Le poème ne donne pas de clé et demeure obscur sans les commentaires marginaux. Le texte devait ainsi s'insérer dans une performance mettant en scène un élève et un précepteur. Les éditeurs de la version en prose parlent d'une 'personne-ressource indispensable à la compréhension du texte'.[38] Le récit en vers tenait alors lieu de support destiné à un apprentissage: les commentaires marginaux dressent un véritable art d'aimer devant accompagner l'éducation amoureuse du destinataire.

L'attribution d'une vertu à chacune des pièces correspond à la méthode des arts de la mémoire, tels que les décrit notamment Frances Yates.[39] Il s'agit d'associer à des contenus mentaux une image évoluant dans un espace. Le *locus* est ici l'espace défini par l'échiquier et les *imagines* sont les emblèmes figurant sur les pièces. Mary Carruthers, dans *Le Livre de la Mémoire*, souligne que le Moyen Âge, à la différence de l'Antiquité, conçoit la mémoire comme un espace plan, bidimensionnel, divisé en colonnes au sein d'une grille.[40] L'échiquier serait ainsi une figuration de l'espace mnésique, comme chez Jacques de Cessoles, qui, dans son *Liber de moribus hominum vel officiis nobilium sive super ludo scacchorum*, associe à chacune des pièces des attributs relevant de leur position sociale.[41] Cette fonction mnémotechnique joue tant pour celui qui compose le texte que pour celui à qui il l'adresse: une

---

[35] 'Primo ergo pedes in bello mulieris ponitur hic Jonesche, quia licet in facto amoris conveniat et viro et mulieri' (Kraft ed., lignes 58–9).

[36] 'Duo alphini sunt Espoir et Desir. Primus per navem significatur, que peregrinos portat ad portum salutis' (*ibid.*, lignes 298–9).

[37] Évrart de Conty, *Le Livre des Eschez amoureux moralisés*, Introduction, p. LXI.

[38] *Ibid.*, p. LXII.

[39] Frances A. Yates, *L'Art de la mémoire*, traduit par Daniel Arasse (Paris, 1975).

[40] Mary Carruthers, *Le Livre de la Mémoire. La Mémoire dans la culture médiévale*, traduit par Diane Meur (Paris, 2002). Voir notamment, dans le chapitre 'Les Arts de la mémoire', pp. 193 et 211.

[41] Voir l'édition de Ferdinand Vetter, *Das Schachzabelbuch Kunrats von Ammenhausen nebst den Schachbüchern des Jakob von Cessole und des Jakob Mennel*, dans *Bibliotehek älterer Schriftwerke der deutschen Schweiz* (Frauenfeld, 1892). Voir également la traduction de Jean Ferron: Jacques de Cessoles, *Le Jeu des eschaz moralisé*, éd. Alain Collet (Paris, 1999).

technique au départ destinée à aider la mémoire d'un locuteur, de l'orateur, est ici au service d'une communication, de la délivrance d'un message.[42]

Toutefois, quel est le véritable objectif didactique de cet art de la mémoire? Les *imagines* sur les pièces de l'échiquier représentent les vertus associées à un art d'aimer. Cette technique servirait à se rappeler les différentes allégories courtoises issues, pour une partie d'entre elles, du *Roman de la Rose*, ainsi que leur fonction. Le destinataire serait alors l'objet d'une initiation à l'art d'aimer: c'est ainsi que Beauté est le premier pion qu'avance la jeune fille, et que le jeune homme lui répond en choisissant d'avancer le pion représentant Regard. Cependant, l'inscription de ces allégories dans un cadre ludique permet d'envisager la chose autrement. Il faut se demander si l'allégorisation des pièces permet l'apprentissage des règles du jeu d'échecs. Or, sans l'aide d'un précepteur, la chose semble impossible. En effet, la description de la partie d'échecs continue d'occulter ce processus d'allégorisation: les pièces sont désignées par leur nom traditionnel ('la fierge' pour la reine) ou, quand il y en a plusieurs, par leur emblème ('un päonnet [...] / Qui la rose en l'escu portoit', Kraft ed., vv. 1314–18). L'équivalence allégorique n'est de nouveau posée que par les commentaires marginaux.

Non seulement les gloses, actualisées par un précepteur, devaient établir les équivalences, mais cette personne-ressource devait également illustrer les différents coups des joueurs. Un diagramme clôt l'épisode de la partie d'échecs dans le manuscrit de Venise.[43] Il représente la position des pièces, désignées par les allégories, sur l'échiquier au début de la partie. L'historien des échecs Harold James Murray explique la double occurrence de deux pièces sur une même case (en *do* et *dl*, les reines des deux adversaires figurent sur la même case qu'un pion) en affirmant que le diagramme représente un cas d''assise courte', technique inventée au Moyen Âge pour améliorer le jeu d'échecs.[44] En revanche, selon Wilfrid Fauquet, cette disposition est une composition échiquéenne représentant une position de milieu de partie destinée à illustrer l'intrigue du *Roman de la Rose*.[45] Les travaux de ces spécialistes mettent en évidence la complexité de la partie d'échecs retracée par le poème. Afin de comprendre exactement le déroulement de la partie, il est nécessaire de déplacer les pièces au fil du jeu. Certes, la partie n'est pas donnée dans son intégralité, mais elle pouvait, du moins pour l'ouverture et le finale, être reproduite sur un échiquier réel, dans le cadre d'un enseignement. Si les règles du jeu d'échecs ne sont pas détaillées dans *Les Eschés*

---

[42] Raymond D. di Lorenzo, 'The Collection Form and the Art of Memory in the *Libellus super ludo scacchorum* of Jacobus de Cessolis', *Mediaeval Studies*, 35 (1973), 205–21, p. 207.

[43] Biblioteca Marciana, MS fr. app. 23, fol. 66r.

[44] Harold J. Murray, *A History of Chess* (New York ; Oxford, 1913), p. 476 *sqq*.

[45] Fauquet, 'Le *giu parti* d'Évrart de Conty', p. 492 *sqq*. Voir également les annexes 'Suite de l'argumentaire en faveur de l'assise ordinaire' et 'Assise courte', p. 520 *sqq*.

amoureux, leur mise en récit et en pratique pouvait s'inscrire dans le cadre d'une performance didactique. Ayant ainsi pu s'initier aux échecs en lisant et commentant la partie fictive, on peut imaginer que l'élève pouvait ainsi prendre la revanche que le narrateur n'avait pas prise en jouant une partie réelle à l'issue de sa lecture.

Les Eschés amoureux ne sont, bien entendu, ni un manuel d'échecs, ni un recueil de problèmes d'échecs, mais le récit de la partie, bien que tronqué, est néanmoins vecteur de savoirs. Le destinataire était certainement un jeune noble puisque le jeu d'échecs était considéré comme devant faire partie de l'éducation de tout aristocrate. Jeu des rois et roi des jeux, les échecs étaient considérés alors comme la seule activité ludique facilitant l'acquisition d'un savoir.[46] La fonction de la partie est donc double dans *Les Eschés amoureux*: elle permet au destinataire d'apprendre à jouer avec l'aide d'un précepteur, mais aussi de transmettre des préceptes amoureux sur le mode d'un art d'aimer.

'Le jeu ne produit rien: ni biens ni œuvres. Il est essentiellement stérile. […] Cette gratuité fondamentale du jeu est bien ce qui le discrédite le plus.'[47] Le choix d'insérer un épisode ludique au cœur de la trame didactique des *Eschés amoureux* est problématique: si l'ambivalence de ce jeu de la raison ne le discrédite pas totalement, il n'en demeure pas moins que le narrateur ne *joue pas le jeu* et est pris dans les rets de la 'gratuité fondamentale' évoquée par Roger Caillois. Paradoxalement, l'objectif didactique du passage, tel qu'il était annoncé par Déduit au seuil de la partie, peut s'entendre quasiment au pied de la lettre. L'inscription de la partie d'échecs dans le cadre d'une performance permet de penser l'épisode comme le support d'un apprentissage. Il s'agirait d'apprendre à jouer au jeu de l'amour.

Cette veine didactique est informée poétiquement par la structure fascinante de l'échiquier. Dans la version en prose, l'allégorie de la partie d'échecs demeure, mais elle est explicitée, chaque coup étant commenté. Conformément à ce qu'indique Évrart de Conty au début de son ouvrage, l'obscurité du poème est dissipée au profit d'un enseignement clair.[48] Le passage à la

---

[46] Voir Jean-Michel Mehl, *Jeu d'échecs et éducation au XIIIe siècle: recherches sur le 'Liber de moribus' de Jacques de Cessoles*, Thèse de 3ème cycle (Strasbourg, 1975) et, du même auteur, *Les Jeux au royaume de France, du XIIIe au début du XVIe siècle* (Paris, 1990). Voir notamment 'Les Jeux et l'étude', pp. 335–8.

[47] Roger Caillois, *Les Jeux et les hommes. Le masque et le vertige* (Paris, 1967), pp. 9–10.

[48] 'Ce present livre fut fait et ordené principalment a l'instance d'un autre, fait en rimes nagueres et de nouvel venu a cognoissance, qui est intitulé *Des Eschez amoureux* ou *Des Eschez d'amours*, aussi come pour declairier aucunes choses que la rime contient qui semblent estre obscures et estranges de prime face. Et pour ce fut il fait et ordené en prose pour ce que prose est plus clere a entendre que n'est rime (Évrart de Conty, *Le Livre des eschez amoureux moralisés*, p. 2) [Ce livre fut écrit principalement à partir d'un autre, naguère écrit en vers, qu'on a récemment découvert et qui s'intitule *Des Échecs amoureux*

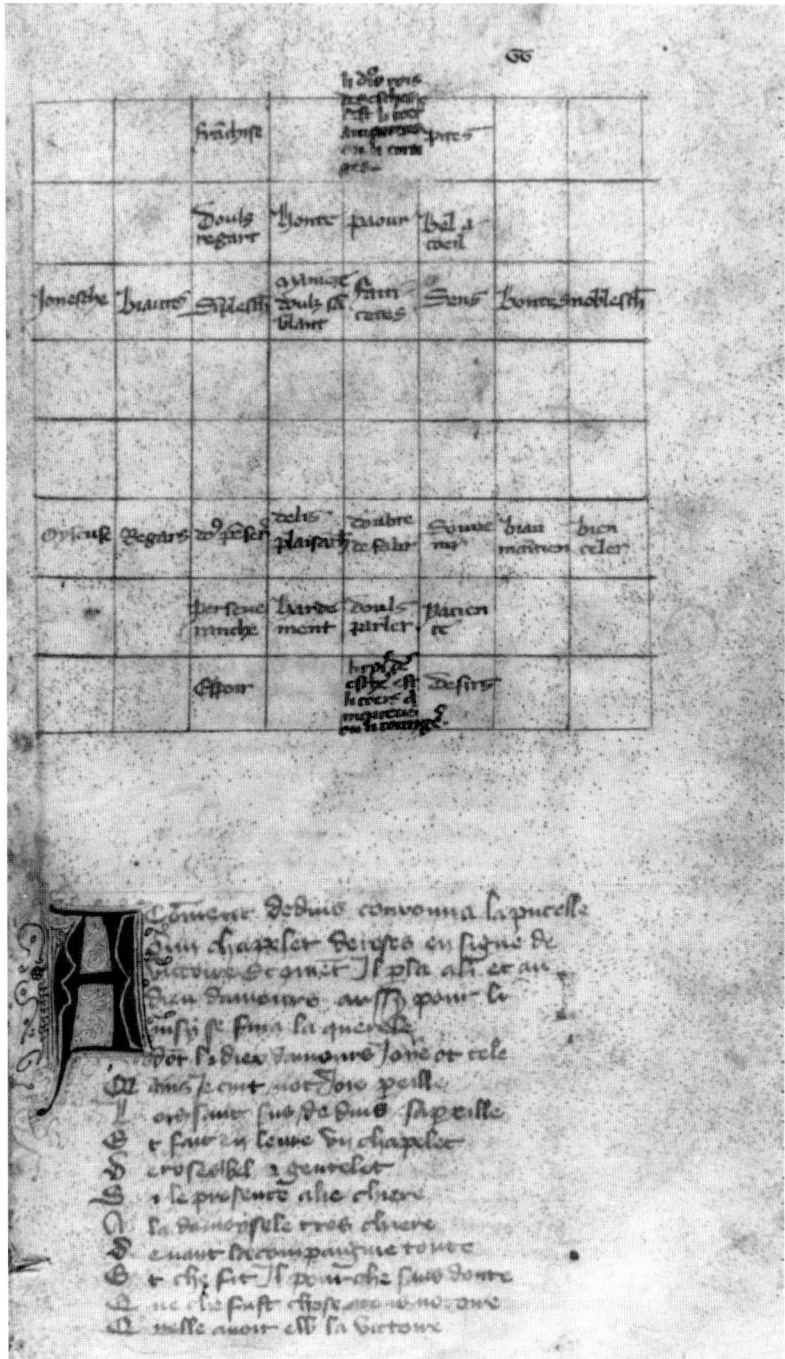

Les Eschés amoureux, manuscrit de Venise, Biblioteca Marciana, fr. app. 23, fol. 66r.

prose lève toutes les ambiguïtés qui pouvaient demeurer. Le caractère énigmatique du récit en vers encourage le lecteur à découvrir un sens caché, que la prose révèle immédiatement. Les perspectives ouvertes par les récents travaux au sujet de l'attribution du poème à l'auteur de son commentaire sont très riches: Évrart de Conty aurait ainsi choisi de gommer l'obscurité poétique de son propre texte, de lever le voile qu'il avait lui-même jeté sur le savoir qu'il souhaitait transmettre.

ou *Des Échecs d'amour*, pour éclairer certains points qui, en vers, semblent obscurs et étranges de prime abord. C'est pour cette raison que ce livre fut écrit en prose, car la prose est plus facile à comprendre que le vers].'

3

Jean Gerson, Poet

MISHTOONI BOSE

Pourquoi cette métamorphose? Pourquoi le théologien se transforme-t-il en poète?... Au XVe siècle, il est beaucoup trop tard pour inventer la poésie chrétienne: mais la poésie mystique d'expression latine?[1]

> Et quis in hoc evo scire poemata vult?
> Que meliora potest exclusus ab omnibus, exsul,
> Officiis? Sed nec carmina flere vetant.
>
> [And who in our time wants to learn poems? What better things has the man excluded, exiled, from every office, to do? But songs do not prevent one from weeping.][2]

In 1955, Max Lieberman observed that the poems of the prolific Jean Gerson had received far less attention from scholars than had his many other writings.[3] This remains the case. Gerson is still best known to Anglophone literary scholars as the avowedly anti-heretical critic of the *Roman de la Rose*.[4] But it

---

[1] André Combes, *La Théologie mystique de Gerson*, II (Paris, Rome and Tournai, 1964), pp. 313, 314.

[2] 'Carmen V: Legatur per modum dyalogi' ('Desipit an senium'), in *La Doctrine du chant du cœur de Jean Gerson. Edition critique, traduction et commentaire du 'Tractatus de canticis' et du 'Canticordum au pélérin'*, ed. Isabelle Fabre (Geneva, 2005), p. 456. This poem has a complex textual history and has been printed in different forms. I use Fabre's version rather than that appended to G. Matteo Roccati, 'A Gersonian text in defense of poetry: *De Laudibus Elegie Spiritualis* (ca. 1422–1425)', *Traditio*, 60 (2005), 369–85, and have translated from Fabre's version rather than using Roccati's translation. For a fuller understanding of what is at stake in the editing of Gerson's poems, see Roccati's discussion here and in 'À propos de la tradition manuscrite de l'œuvre poétique latine de Gerson: les manuscrits Paris, Bibl. Nat., Lat. 3624 et 3628', *Revue d'Histoire des Textes*, 10 (1980), 277–308. Unless otherwise credited, all translations from Middle French and Latin in this chapter are my own. I use the Douay-Rheims translation of the Vulgate.

[3] Max Lieberman, 'Chronologie Gersonienne IV: Gerson poète', *Romania*, 76 (1955), 289–333, p. 289.

[4] See most recently Renate Blumenfeld-Kosinski, 'Jean Gerson and the Debate on the *Romance of the Rose*', in *A Companion to Jean Gerson*, ed. Brian Patrick McGuire (Leiden, 2006), pp. 317–56.

has recently become possible to consider whether his poetry might fit with a number of new critical and historical narratives that seek to see Gerson whole and to consider him as an example of a new kind of public intellectual that emerged in late-medieval Europe and typically functioned as an intermediary between different social cadres, lay and clerical, scholastic and extramural.[5] One way of pursuing a similar line of enquiry is to consider how Gerson's poetic output interacted with, and sometimes may have substituted for, the kinds of diplomatic, pastoral and political action that had made him a prominent figure in French public life and further abroad. For example, the years 1417 and 1418 were years of personal and professional crisis for Gerson, as the Council of Constance drew to an end without his having achieved either of his personal aims (the establishment of a feast day for St Joseph and the posthumous censure of Jean Petit for heresy). He was forced into temporary exile, seeking shelter from supporters of the Burgundy faction of the French aristocracy, who might have been angered by his stance towards Petit.[6] But the period of professional frustration at Constance inaugurated a seminal moment in the development of his poetry. He wrote two major literary works during and after Constance: the Biblical epic *Josephina* and the *De consolatione theologiae*, in which he exploits and appropriates the stylistic resourcefulness of Boethius, alternating prose dialogues with poetry in a variety of metres. Far from remaining in Boethius's shadow, he confidently uses the *auctor* as a point of departure. It would be a worthwhile task simply to explore what poetry afforded Gerson at this particular period in his life: refuge, consolation, a new arena in which to consolidate his pastoral authority and to explore his identity as a Christian. But this was hardly the first occasion on which, to paraphrase André Combes, the theologian had transformed himself into a poet. Rather, Gerson had long been preparing himself for the virtuoso experimentation of this period by writing a large number of poems in a variety of metres and genres and in both Latin and French.

In this essay, I consider some of the continuities between Gerson's poetry and his other writings. It would be rash indeed to attempt to discern a single pattern, or common purpose, in such a large poetic output. It would be similarly unwise to interrogate his poetry for certain kinds and degrees of discursive complexity that are typically valued by modern critics, but for which he did not strive. His poems do not provide evidence of the particular creativity that springs from ambivalence towards bodies of knowledge. Rather, we are typically confronted with the desire to save theological appearances, to remain comfortably inside an unfolded doctrine rather than to relativize or

---

[5] For examples of these studies, see the following:McGuire, *A Companion to Jean Gerson*; Brian Patrick McGuire, *Jean Gerson and the Last Medieval Reformation* (Leiden, 2005), and particularly Daniel Hobbins, 'The schoolman as public intellectual: Jean Gerson and the Late Medieval Tract', *American Historical Review*, 108 (2003), 1308–37.

[6] McGuire, *Jean Gerson*, pp. 284–5.

even lampoon it (as Chaucer arguably had done with a variety of theological topics in *The House of Fame*, for example).[7] My aims in this essay, therefore, are twofold: firstly, to show that Gerson's writings invite close consideration of the kinds of knowledge that may be communicated in poetry; and secondly, to show how the roles of super-ego (that is to say, Gerson's clerical, authoritative, devotional *personae*) and ego (that is, the individual, avowedly sinful, often querulous versions of himself) interacted as provocatively in his poetry as they do in his other writings.[8]

It is the Latin poetry with which I will be concerned here, as space does not permit separate consideration of Gerson's vernacular poems. The most accessible modern edition of the Latin poems is the fourth volume of Glorieux's edition of the *Œuvres* (and in the tenth volume Glorieux added the innovative *Pastorium carmen*, Gerson's early imitation of Petrarch, after this had been separately edited by Ouy).[9] It should be noted, however, that this edition has been found unsatisfactory in certain important respects and should not be regarded as definitive.[10] The *Josephina* has been edited by Matteo Roccati on CD-ROM and in recent decades Roccati's welcome attention to Gerson's achievements in poetry, together with Gilbert Ouy's many penetrating analyses of his humanism and its multiple and complex manuscript contexts, have dominated critical discussion of this field.[11] Most recently, Isabelle Fabre

---

[7] For recent discussion of Chaucer in this respect, see Kathryn Kerby-Fulton, *Books Under Suspicion. Censorship and Tolerance of Revelatory Writing in Late Medieval England* (Notre Dame, IN, 2006), pp. 341–50.

[8] On this theme, see also my '*Advena, peregrinus*: Jean Gerson's charisma', in *Charisma and Authority. Jewish, Christian and Muslim Preaching, 1200–1600*, ed. Katherine Ludwig Jansen and Miri Rubin, forthcoming.

[9] Jean Gerson, *Œuvres complètes*, ed. Palémon Glorieux, 10 vols (Paris, 1960–73). All references to this edition will be given in the main body of the text and indicated by the letter G, followed by volume number in Roman and page number(s) in Arabic numerals. For general discussion of the routes through which some of Gerson's poems have made their way from manuscript to print, see Gilbert Ouy, 'Discovering Gerson the humanist: fifty years of serendipity', in *A Companion to Jean Gerson*, ed. McGuire, pp. 79–132.

[10] For constructive criticism of Glorieux's edition of the poems, see Matteo Roccati, 'Note a proposito delle poesie latine di Jean Gerson', *Studi Francesi*, 65–6 (1978), 341–9; 'Gerson e il problema dell'espressione poetica: note su alcuni temi e immagini ricorrenti nelle poesie latine', *Studi Francesi*, 77 (1982), 278–85 (especially fn. 3, p. 278 and fn. 12, p. 280). As Roccati's article alone shows, it is sometimes necessary to repunctuate the poetry in order to be able to make sense of it, and the reader cannot take for granted the reliability of Glorieux's nevertheless pioneering edition in this respect, as in certain others. Roccati himself frequently quotes directly from the manuscripts for this reason. Roccati has re-edited the poetry in an as-yet unpublished dissertation: 'Jean Gerson, Œuvre poètique latine', thèse de troisième cycle (Paris, E.H.E.S.S, 1980).

[11] Jean Gerson, *Josephina*, ed. G. Matteo Roccati (Paris, 2001). Gilbert Ouy, 'Gerson, émule de Pétrarque: le *Pastorium Carmen*, poème de jeunesse de Gerson, et la renaissance de l'églogue en France à la fin du XIVe siècle', *Romania*, 88 (1967), 175–231; Ouy, 'Discovering Gerson the Humanist' and the articles by him cited there.

has edited the *Tractatus de canticis*, making available this substantial prose text and its constituent poems in a reliable scholarly version and making possible new insights into Gerson's views of the relationship between poetry, song and mystical theology, some aspects of which will concern us here.[12] Nevertheless, this still leaves a large number of the poems largely or wholly unconsidered, and a route to some critical fresh ground may be forged via brief consideration of a far shorter but extremely significant poem, the *Epithalamium mysticum theologi et theologiae* (G. IV, 144–6), which survives in at least eight manuscripts (a fact that suggests a level of dissemination rivalling that of the *Josephina*).[13] Tracing the web of allegorical and theological materials and contexts focused in this poem sheds fresh light on some of the ways in which Gerson's poetic super-ego functioned. Here he speaks as the authoritative exegetical poet, his individual persona thoroughly concealed beneath the textual accretions of the Song of Songs, scriptural exegesis and the esoteric enigmas of mystical theology. But as has already briefly been suggested, many of Gerson's other writings are distinguished by the presence of an articulate and vulnerable ego. His various attempts to interpellate the ecclesiastical community simultaneously give expression to his private and public personae, his clerical authority and individual charisma, in distinctive and innovative ways. This essay will thus situate Gerson's poetry in the broader context of these two somewhat conflicting but utterly characteristic dimensions of his writings.

With the possible exception of the *Schola mystica* (G. IV, 105–6) or the *Carmen dicendum tempore tentationis* (G. IV, 11), Gerson's Latin poetry is technically, lexically and intellectually varied and ambitious. The alleged faultlines over which so many modern scholars hover anxiously – between, for example, scholasticism and humanism, or between humanism and mysticism – caused him few inhibitions. Gilbert Ouy has shown how Gerson as poet confidently absorbed and exploited the achievements of Petrarch and Sannazaro, and thus earned the status of innovator in the course of French literary history.[14] Gerson had also engaged purposefully with the long-established negotiations between the secular or profane arts of poetry and Christian subject-matter.[15] The negative connotations that had long called into question the suitability of poetry as a Christian discourse had notoriously been adumbrated in Boethius's articulation of analogous tensions between poetry and philosophy in *De consolatione Philosophiae*, and the famous opening

---

[12] Fabre, *La Doctrine du chant du cœur de Jean Gerson*.

[13] Roccati, 'À propos de la tradition manuscrite', p. 291 (fn. 3) points out that this text is placed at the beginning of a collection of Gersonian poems in MS Q (Paris, B.N. Lat. 3624), a sequence closed by the *Testamentum peregrini metricum*, composed when Gerson was in his mid-sixties.

[14] Ouy, 'Gerson, émule de Pétrarque'.

[15] On this topic in medieval French literature, see Michel Zink, *Poésie et conversion au Moyen Age* (Paris, 2003), especially pp. 99–121, and pp. 137–201.

scene of Boethius's dialogue is immanent in much of Gerson's thinking and writing about the relationship between poetry and knowledge. Detailed attention has already been paid to Gerson's handling of the suitability of poetry as a vehicle for Christian subject-matter in the prologue to the *Josephina*.[16] This tension also surfaces elsewhere in his writings, however. For example, in the fifth poem in the sequence *De canticis* III, Gerson broaches in dialogue form the question as to whether an old man, such as he had become by then, is merely revisiting the follies of his youth when choosing to write poetry. A poetic vocation is certainly affirmed here, but, in the restricted terms that we would expect from an attentive and absorbed reader of Boethius, Gerson insists that songs written with Christian piety may be fruitful ('cum pietate / Carminibus textis fructus inesse potest'), whereas 'scenica [trivial dramas]' are to be avoided.[17] This theme, clearly derived from the banishing by Boethius's Philosophy of 'scenicas meretriculas [thespian harlots]', is also affirmed in 'Vidit livor' (G. IV, 176–7). Allegedly written scarcely twelve days before his death, this poem stages an opposition between writings that have a 'painted face [facies picta coloribus]' and lack virtue (the term 'meretricula' in line 5 explicitly evoking Boethius) and the chaste, matronly verse that desires to please its spouse.[18]

Thus far, Gerson's writings might be judged little more than conventional in their rehearsal of a clichéd topos of Christian humanist poetics. But consideration of Gerson's particular resolution of the relationship between poetic discourse and divine pedagogy brings us much closer to the source of his distinctiveness. Throughout his writing, there is a perceptible, albeit not overemphasized, distinction between the respective connotations of the terms *carmina* (or *cantica*) and *poemata* or *poetria* (the latter being a term that he uses very rarely).[19] It is notable that among the titles given to the many poems in the Glorieux edition, most feature the term *canticum* or *carmen*. The range of *carmina* and their respective properties would be explored exhaustively and with great profundity towards the end of Gerson's life, in *De canticis*. The expressive resources and potential of the *poema*, on the other hand, are scarcely broached. Indeed, it is precisely when discussing the limitations of philosophy and other discourses to convey knowledge of God's judgments in the *De consolatione theologiae* that Gerson refers to *poemata* rather than

---

[16] Giovanni Matteo Roccati, 'La "Josephina" di Jean Gerson (1418): un poema virgiliano di contenuto biblico', *Studi Francesi*, 121 (1997), 4–15; Giovanni Matteo Roccati, 'Humanisme et préoccupations réligieuses au début du XVe siècle: Le Prologue de la *Josephina* de Jean Gerson', in *Preludes à la Renaissance. Aspects de la vie intellectuelle en France au XVe siècle*, ed. Carla Bozzolo and Ezio Ornato (Paris, 1992), pp. 107–22 (an article to which Roccati has appended his edition of the prologue).

[17] Roccati, 'Gerson e il problema dell'espressione poetica'.

[18] *Ibid.*, pp. 280–1.

[19] My observation here is briefly corroborated by Roccati, 'Gerson e il problema', p. 283 (fn. 27).

carmina, albeit in the immediate context of a work that uses poetic interludes as a means of defamiliarizing the teachings of theology, as Boethius had used poetry to enunciate philosophical problems and conclusions. In the second prose section of Book One, the messenger Volucer asserts to his monastic interlocutor Monicus (based on Gerson's brother, Jean the Celestine) that theology begins where Boethius's philosophy left off, and deals with matters that it exceeds the capacity of philosophical discourse either to explore or to express. Poetry is briefly but significantly associated with philosophy here, as Volucer seeks to establish that theology alone can broach the profound topic of God's judgments. Were philosophers or poets to attempt such a task, he asserts, they would get lost in the maze of their own thought, generate errors, and disagree among themselves ('[q]uod facere si vel philosophi vel poetae tentaverint, evanuerunt in cogitationibus suis, et vix aliud quam errores fabulosos, sibique dissidentes fingere potuerunt', G. IX, 189). The validation of Gerson's own poems under the rubric of *carmina* purports to solves this problem, as it aligns his literary productions with the scripturally-authenticated genre of the psalm; and it has been pointed out that Gerson invites his readers to elide his own poetry with that of the Biblical prophets, leaving ambiguous the point at which his writings are to be viewed as constituting a separate genre from theirs.[20]

Poetry as song can serve as an affective adjunct to ratiocinative discourses. The poetry of *De consolatione theologiae* is designed to reformulate what has already been discussed in such a way that the reader has access to a different mode of experience.[21] Towards the close of the work, Volucer breaks off his prose discourse and says that 'we are forced to grieve and lament in the following verses (G. IV, 237) [itaque lugere, plangereque compellimur]'. By suggesting that therapeutic grief-work can only be fully consummated in a poem, Gerson was validating the special work to be undertaken by this particular discourse. The heart was central to Gersonian theology, as Volucer also observes in a passage that makes unusually clear one of the ways in which Gerson's professional temperament might be said to anticipate that of Erasmus:

> [S]icut apud Ciceronem orator describitur, quod est vir bonus dicendi peritus, ita theologum nominamus bonum virum in sacris litteris eruditum; non quidem eruditione solius intellectus, sed multo magis affectus.
> (G. IX, 237)
>
> [Just as the orator is described by Cicero as one who is a good man expert at speaking, so we call a theologian a good man learned in the sacred

---

[20] *Ibid.*, p. 283.
[21] In *Jean Gerson and 'De consolatione theologiae' (1418). The Consolation of a Biblical and Reforming Theology for a Disordered Age* (Tübingen, 1991), Mark S. Burrows argues that the formal differences between poetry and prose are far less important here than their discursive continuity (p. 94).

writings, not in learning of the intellect merely, but much more of the heart.]²²

In the context of this holistic conception of the ideal theologian, the 'song of the heart' – the *canticordum* – could not but occupy a place of the greatest importance. For Gerson, the highest Christian poetry aspired to the condition of song, a form of utterance that derived authority from its continuity with one of the fundamental expressive modes of the Scriptures. But such discursive music forges a relationship with Christian doctrine that is not as analytical as it is experiential.

Gerson gave this topic his most considered and elaborate treatment in *De canticis*, a compendious, comprehensive and complex work. But it is solely to the relationship between *De canticis* and the *Epithalamium mysticum* to which I will now turn, to show precisely how Gerson transformed esoteric knowledge into lyric poetry. In Gerson's thought, the transference of knowledge or spiritual power is repeatedly imagined in terms of a marriage, and marriages require *epithalamia*. Thus, for example, in the opening lines of 'Felix theologus', the second poem in Book One of the *De consolatione theologiae*, Wisdom (clearly understood here as Theology) is described as having been the fortunate theologian's dedicated spouse from his childhood, and as binding him chaste with her love:

> Felix theologus, pulchra sophia
> Cui vult a puero se dare sponsam
> Quam castum tenero stringit amore. (G. IX, 28)

The theologian (in the first place Gerson, in his persona as *advena*), flees worldly things in favour of consolation through an allegorized marriage which makes him more powerful than Hercules or Orpheus. In the poem's closing lines, it is significantly asserted that no-one has sufficiently sung Theology's praises:

> Ergo nemo satis theologiae
> Laudes extulerit tanta patrantis. (G. IX, 29)

Gerson, who in his poetry went quite some way to remedying this alleged insufficiency, found the association between spiritualized marriage and intellectual enlightenment compelling and urgent. In *De canticis* I.iii, in which he explores the anagogical dimensions of song, his profound, elaborate and often original exploration of spiritual marriage required that he modulate briefly but significantly from an affirmation of poetry as spiritual song, in

---

²² Jean Gerson, *The Consolation of Theology. De consolatione theologiae*, trans. and intro. by Clyde Lee Miller (New York, 1998), p. 257.

an affective tradition clearly indebted to St Bernard of Clairvaux's readings of the Song of Songs, to a yet more esoteric, schematized and intellectual spirituality derived specifically from Richard of St Victor. His discussion of spiritual marriage focused on the scriptural marriages between Jacob, the Old Testament patriarch, and his four brides: Lia and Rachel, the daughters of Laban, and their respective maidservants, Zelpha and Bala.[23] The allegorical exegesis of this episode from Genesis came already freighted by association with patristic and scholastic readings of the patriarch Abraham's marriage with Sarah, and with Sarah's maidservant Hagar.[24] More specifically for Gerson's purposes, Jacob's marriages had featured in the spiritual pedagogy of Richard of St Victor's schematized treatise on mystical theology, *De duodecim patriarchis* (Benjamin Minor).[25]

Gerson refers briefly to this collection of allegorized marriages in *De consolatione theologiae* (G. IX, 239), but the theme is broached more thoughtfully in *De canticis*, where he describes the three modes of marriage ('unus viri cum libera, alius viri cum ancilla, tertius viri cum domina [one of a man with a free woman, another of a man with a maidservant, and the third of a man with his lady]').[26] Joseph's marriage with Mary is the only kind to come under the last category, but under the first two are comprised the marriages of Abraham and Jacob with their wives and the wives' respective maidservants. At this point he is obliged to undertake some nimble footwork in order to point *De canticis* in the direction of the particular set of interpretations that concerned him. After expounding St Paul's interpretation of the marriages of Adam, Abraham, Jacob and Joseph, Gerson turns to the Song of Songs, in order to see how it may illuminate each of them, taking into account what patristic and scholastic exegesis have already made of the various possible interpretations of this mysterious text. It is when exploring the symbolic marriage of the Holy Spirit with the soul that Gerson turns to Richard of St Victor, practically all of whose writings, he says, deal with the allegorized and mysterious marriage between the spirit and the soul, as expressed through a metaphor in which man is the superior, and woman the inferior, element.[27]

---

[23] Genesis 29:16–30:24. The birth of Benjamin, Rachel's younger son by Jacob, is related in Genesis 35:16–18 and all of Jacob's progeny by his four wives are listed in Genesis 35: 23–6.

[24] On interpretations of Hagar, see John L. Thompson, *Writing the Wrongs. Women of the Old Testament among Biblical Commentators from Philo Through the Reformation* (New York, 2001), pp. 17–99.

[25] Richard of St Victor's writings are in *PL* 196; Richard de Saint-Victor, *Les Douze Patriarches ou Beniamin Minor*, text and trans. by Jean Châtillon and Monique Duchet-Sucheaux, intro., notes and index by Jean Longère (Paris, 1997); *The Twelve Patriarchs; The Mystical Ark; Book Three of The Trinity*, trans. and intro. by Grover A. Zinn (London, 1979); Raymond D. Di Lorenzo, 'Imagination as the First Way to Contemplation in Richard of St Victor's *Benjamin Minor*', *Medievalia et Humanistica*, 11 (1982), 77–98.

[26] Fabre, *La Doctrine du chant du coeur*, p. 356.

[27] *Ibid.*, pp. 357–8.

In a further manoeuvre, Gerson authorises his own interpretation by bringing Richard's formulation of a marriage between spirit and soul together with the Song of Songs, and this launches him on a detailed and profound exposition of the Song's various properties and applications. The focus remains on the spiritual dimensions of such a marriage: for Gerson, the *epithalamium* is the 'canticum vie pro desponsatione divinali', that is, a song that begins in this life and ends with the hoped-for glory of a heavenly consummation.[28] In the ensuing discussion, he examines the structure of the *epithalamium*, the song of a bride and bridegroom united by faith, hope and charity; its status as a dramatic dialogue; and interpretations of the respective roles, feelings and words of the two interlocutors.[29] Subsequently Gerson argues that when regarded through the lens of symbolic and mystical theology (the former generating the moral and the latter the anagogical sense of the text), the *epithalamium* can be spiritually adapted to signify any kind of union between God and love, even between the spirit and the soul of Christ, Wisdom and the exultant spirit of Mary, or the spirit of Mary and her 'handmaid', the life of the senses (as represented by Hagar, Bala and Zelpha).[30]

The apparently inexhaustible and multivalent significance of the *epithalamium* as expounded in this lengthy prose text offers a suggestive point of comparison with the *Epithalamium mysticum theologi et theologiae*, a poem that focuses much of the argumentative essence of *De canticis* in only fifty-five lines (if one includes the rubrics indicating changes of speaker), and in the allusive and compressed form of the dramatic allegory. For all its lexical and structural simplicity, this is an extraordinarily concentrated work when one considers the sheer weight of theological knowledge which it synthesizes. Rachel sings the first and last strophes (Gerson points out in *De canticis* that 'sponsa preloquatur, sponsus respondeat') and Jacob sings the intervening sequence, dedicating himself to her in all-encompassing terms that sometimes make contact with the Old Testament narrative (Lia's fertile womb and the numerous progeny of the maidservants, together with Joseph and Benjamin, are briefly mentioned) and in a register frequently redolent of the *Canticum* itself (as when the theologian demands kisses and sacred embraces from his bride). The terms according to which he swears perpetual loyalty to her are ambitious: no matter in what walk of life God had placed him, he swears, he would love her; he would journey across the world for her and neither Scylla nor Charybdis would hold any terrors for him (G. IV, 145). The terms in which Rachel expresses herself likewise observe the moral and spiritual decorum with which Gerson associated this genre in *De canticis*, her opening words invoking 'sacred faith, glory and honour [per fidem sanctam, decus et honorem]' and her closing words approving the soaring rhetoric of

---

[28] *Ibid.*, pp. 358–9.
[29] *Ibid.*, pp. 359, 361–2.
[30] *Ibid.*, pp. 367–9.

Jacob's song of devotion, sealing the allegory with her declaration of love for him. The *Epithalamium* is, therefore, a poem in which allegory, epistemology, mystical theology and the *rites de passage* of institutional pedagogy are lightly but profoundly woven together, making clear how transparently Gerson believed poetry could handle esoteric learning and the chaste raptures of sublimated passion. But 'knowledge' here assumes the form, not of information, but of lyric meditation on particular kinds of religious and intellectual experience. Nothing is glossed, so that the particular mysteries with which the poem deals remain closed to the uninitiated, and the individuality of its author is displaced entirely by its esoteric freight.

Thus far, Gerson might be viewed as having taken refuge in Scriptural *imitatio* as a means of escaping or denying his own creative agency. In the *Epithalamium*, the clerical super-ego is serenely in charge. Nevertheless, in *De canticis*, when creatively fusing Richard of St Victor's mystical pedagogy with the exegetical resources of the Song of Songs, Gerson represents himself as having been inspired to do this while meditating in the privacy of his heart at night ('Visum est tamen michi nonnumquam meditanti in secreto cordis mei cubiculo per noctes').[31] Whether genuinely self-revelatory or not, this aside reveals much about Gerson's wish to depict himself in an archetypal pose that evokes poets, prophets and visionaries: all insightful but essentially isolated servants of God. 'Desipit an senium', one of the *carmina* included in *De canticis*, builds on this image of inspiration in isolation, associating the vatic and castigatory purposes of poetry approved by Gerson with the Book of Job:

> Nocte Deus dat, ait Job, carmina; rex tribulatus
> Misit, ait, Dominus carmen in ore novum.
>
> [Job says that God gives songs by night; the troubled king [David]
> Said that God had given him a new song in his mouth.][32]

Elihu's words in Job 33:14–16 serve as a suggestive gloss on this passage:

> Semel loquitur Deus et secundo id ipsum non repetit.
> Per somnium in visione nocturna quando inruit sopor super homines et dormiunt in lectulo.
> Tunc aperit aures virorum et erudiens eos instruit disciplinam.
>
> [God speaketh once, and repeateth not the selfsame thing the second time.
> By a dream in a vision by night, when deep sleep falleth upon men, and they are sleeping in their beds:

---

[31] *Ibid.*, p. 358.
[32] Job 35:10; Psalms 39:4.

> Then he openeth the ears of men, and teaching instructeth them in what they are to learn.]

The belief that God can sidestep the rational faculties and functions of man's waking life in order to grant special insight runs piquantly alongside Gerson's somewhat better-known role as the thoughtful critic and appraiser of latter-day visions and revelations. And herein lies the key to his complex subjectivity. For if Gerson speaks with several voices at different times in his life, and across different literary genres, two of the predominant modes are that of the professional, extraverted insider – politically engaged, writing for the moment, assiduously and fearlessly interpellating those around him – and that of the individual and introverted outsider – introspective, writing for family, intimates and ultimately himself. In aligning himself with those to whom God gives *carmina*, songs by night, he uncovers a complex articulation of self that his 'daytime' proclamations – whether sermons, or dissertations on revelations, institutional mores or modes of procedure against heretics, can only fitfully afford to acknowledge, even though, as might be expected, there is a strong subterranean link between Gerson the vulnerable prophet and castigator and Gerson the public preacher, diplomat and administrator.

The key to further exploration of this issue lies in the cluster of works by Gerson on St Joseph, a figure to whom he frequently recurred as a model.[33] The *Josephina* itself is an elaborate and layered life of the saint that for the most part follows the biblical account (albeit not in chronological order) and fills out the silences of scripture with a vivid exploration of the holy marriage and its impact on the infant Jesus. Part of Joseph's attraction as a role-model for Gerson is the fact that he is twice visited by a disambiguating angel. These revelations orientate him on the path of obedience through submission to divine will: once when he acknowledges the faithfulness of Mary and once when he is warned about the imminent danger to the Holy Family from Herod. Revelations and nocturnal visitations had their uses, therefore, for this critical analyst of visionaries.

Community took various forms, real and imagined, for Gerson. Sometimes, as at the Council of Constance, these different forms overlapped, as when the real congregations of his sermons were interpellated as the ideal representatives of a beleaguered Church in search of renewal. It is the Josephine strand in his writing that has been most substantially connected with his understanding of, and aspirations for, Christian community. As Pamela Sheingorn has argued, Gerson's strenuous and unsuccessful campaign to bring Joseph to the forefront of the Church's devotional life, and to lead a Christian renewal based explicitly on the inculcation of virtues that he associated with

---

[33] M. Lieberman, *Cahiers de Joséphologie*, 13 (1965), 227–72; 14 (1966), 271–314; 15 (1967), 6–113; 16 (1968), 293–316; Palémon Glorieux, 'Saint Joseph dans L'Œuvre de Gerson', *Cahiers de Joséphologie*, 19 (1971), 414–28.

this particular saint, reveal much about his sense of Christian community.[34] In a brief poem in elegaic couplets, *Ut festum Joseph celebratur*, Gerson interpellates the saint as 'peregrinis dux, via, vita, salus (G. IV, 15) [the leader, way, life, salvation to pilgrims]'. He is to play this cluster of roles alongside his more familiar roles as 'illustris virgo', 'justus propheta' (the prophetic link is interesting too vis-à-vis Gerson's own self-understanding) – husband of the Virgin and father of Christ. St Joseph is not only being placed at the head of the innumerable pilgrims who constitute the church militant; more personally yet for Gerson, he functions here as an adopted patron saint for one who long considered himself to be – and who, in the immediate aftermath of Constance, actually was – an *advena*, a *peregrinus*: a foreigner, a pilgrim, a stranger. The Josephine strand in Gerson's writing, which surfaces with prolonged eloquence in his poetry, thus taps into and articulates something acutely personal to Gerson: it lays bare, and enables him to explore, a painful but fruitful faultline in his life between the super-ego roles – inquisitorial, pastoral, diplomatic – with which he was, and is, so often and so completely associated, and his subjective, private, but no less authentic and clamorously articulated, sense of the difficulties of living life as a Christian like any other; which is to say, as a sinner. No less than the image of Joseph does the image of the pilgrim fill much of Gerson's poetry, as in *Descriptio peregrini*, when he asks who wrote the poem ('quis est qui carmina condidit ista?') and answers by obliquely naming himself, his first name meaning 'grace' ('Gratia nomen ei; cognomen et advena fecit / Esse peregrinus', G. IV, 15). He had proclaimed the felicitous significance of his surname 'Gerson' at Constance where, in a remarkable blending of private and public voices and subjectivities, he had preached the sermon *Obsecro vos* (1415) in which he pointed out the equivalence between the names 'Gersan' and 'Gerson' (used by Moses and Levi respectively for the first-born sons) and the Latin terms *advena* [*étranger*, stranger] and *peregrinus* [*pélerin*, pilgrim].[35] The *Descriptio peregrini*, written two years after this sermon, thus speaks to Gerson's sense of himself as being in a kind of exile which anticipates his actual period as a 'refugee' in the aftermath of the Council itself. This sense of distance from power is replicated through the structure of *De consolatione theologiae*, which ensured that the 'exile' Gerson was rendered more firmly present through his tantalizing absence from the immediate scene of the dialogue. In contrast with Boethius, who uses a first-person speaker in his dialogue with Philosophy, Gerson, always offstage but frequently invoked, remains an elusive object about whom Monicus seeks

---

[34] Pamela Sheingorn, '"Illustris patriarcha Joseph": Jean Gerson, Representations of Saint Joseph, and Imagining Community among Churchmen in the Fifteenth Century', in *Visions of Community in the Pre-Modern World*, ed. Nicholas Howe (Notre Dame, IN, 2002), pp. 75–108.

[35] McGuire, *Jean Gerson*, pp. 249, 284–5, Bose, '*Advena, peregrinus*'.

information from Volucer, and the indirectness with which the text communicates his mental and spiritual processing of the events at Constance confers greater authority on it precisely because it keeps the reader at a respectful distance from the text's object of desire. The apparently confident and hermeneutically inflexible gatekeeper of the *Querelle de la Rose* had a vulnerable and unusually articulate ego.[36]

Knowledge, therefore, assumes substantial but different forms in Gerson's poetry, occupying a number of points on a notional spectrum that ranges from catechetical pedagogy to mystical allegory. The particular knowledge with which Gerson's more ambitious poetry was engaged could often take the form of a mode of experience rather than of analysis, drawing even his hexametric poetry closer to the affective territory of the lyric. On the other hand, poetry could, for him as for others, serve as the means by which a self-conscious ego might articulate its needs and desires, private and public, interpellating and consoling by turns, and this dimension is shown by works as varied as the *Pastorium carmen*, the *Josephina* and the poetry of *De consolatione theologiae*. The poetry of *De canticis* has both of these dimensions, combining the rapturous and affective aspirations of the supra-historical Christian *carmen* with the autobiographical self-awareness of a melancholy and ageing man tethered to a particular moment in history. Sheingorn has argued persuasively that Gerson's campaign to interpellate the Church as a Josephine community failed in his own lifetime (whatever momentum it gained much later) because he could not control the range of unfavourable connotations that stubbornly clung to St Joseph.[37] But even the immediate failure of his campaign to have a feast-day devoted to St Joseph underlines how completely in Gerson's life authority and failure, vulnerability and charisma, were bound together, and this dual aspect, which regularly finds its way into his writing, is most appropriately symbolized by the ambiguous figure of St Joseph *peregrinus*.

Gerson's poems thus take their place alongside his many prose works as guides to a multivalent clerical subjectivity. This comprises tensions between the self inscribed, in its contingency and incompleteness, and the self effaced, taking refuge in authority and hierarchy, and it is to the tension between these two stances that Gerson's writings regularly draw our attention. Thus, while perhaps wishing that he had been a more nuanced reader of the *Rose*, modern scholars should not merely enumerate the categories, hierarchies and superegos amongst which his writings characteristically find their bearings, as if he were to be completely identified with them – for he showed himself more adept, nuanced and restless than that.

---

[36] Ouy points out that 'the ego […] is omnipresent in Gerson's works' ('Discovering Gerson the Humanist', p. 128).

[37] Sheingorn, '"Illustris patriarcha Joseph"', p. 77.

4

Gerson and Christine, Poets

LORI J. WALTERS

A Dieu s'en va et a mort amere
Jhesus veyant sa doulce mere.
Si devons bien par penitence
De ce deuil avoir remembrance. (St Jean 13:3)

[To God and to a bitter death goes Jesus, seeing his sweet mother. Thus we must through penitence have remembrance of this sorrow.]

My chapter takes up where Mishtooni Bose's leaves off, with a consideration of Jean Gerson's vernacular poetry.[1] You have an example inscribed above in a quatrain of Gerson's own invention, with which he opens his seven-hour-long 1403 Good Friday sermon. Although the bulk of Gerson's corpus is in Latin, he did write two volumes' worth of tracts, sermons, and poems in French, forming a hefty corpus had he written nothing else. The texts of Gerson's contemporary Christine de Pizan are exclusively in the vernacular. Although not as prolific a writer as Gerson, Christine's productions nonetheless constitute a weighty stack, numbering some forty texts in a variety of genres – lyric poetry, biography, mirrors for princes and princesses, and more topical political tracts. Although Gerson's Latin works far outnumber his French ones, the fact that he would use a quatrain he had composed himself to structure and animate arguably the most popular of his many sermons is a trustworthy indicator of his high regard for the potential uses of vernacular poetry.

In this chapter I develop further the notion, as explained by Bose, that Gerson distinguishes *carmen* from *poema*, suggesting that the former can be equated with the song of an elevated and culturally sanctioned kind (the Psalms being the model), whereas the latter is the more general term for

---

[1] The reader should refer to Chapter 3 for original references. In addition to the sources mentioned there, I have consulted a copy of Gilbert Ouy's unpublished translation of the *Josephina*, which has been very helpful in sorting out the text's rhetorical and theological complexities. I thank him for sharing his translation with me.

fictive discourse, and is less positively regarded. I argue that both Gerson and Christine attempt to raise their vernacular poetry to the level that Gerson prescribes for Latin *carmina*. Specifically, I relate Christine's poems which have the Psalms as model to those composed by Gerson. I claim as well that Gerson's French poetry played a central role in realizing two of his lifelong aims: healing divisions within France, and promoting the country, with himself as its chief mouthpiece, as the spokesperson for a united Christianity. I attempt to show that from her very earliest productions, her *Cent Balades* of 1399–1402, Christine helped Gerson to spread a feeling of community within the fractured nation-state. Responding to Gerson's own pronouncements on the matter, she concentrated upon members of the laity previously neglected by the monarchy: women, children, and other 'simple' people who were unable to obtain a Latin-based university education.

But first let me offer some reasons why it is not unusual to find the ideas of Christine and Gerson intersecting on poetry. The years 1400–2 found the two allied in their opposition to the *Roman de la Rose*. It has also recently been suggested that an unnamed *femelette* to whom Gerson gives spiritual counsel in his 1400 *Montaigne de contemplation* (G. VII, 16–55) was Christine.[2] The term was one that Christine identified with herself in the *Rose* quarrel, when she boasted what a mere *femelette* could accomplish when she armed herself with a proper understanding of Church doctrine.[3] The attitude that Gerson ascribes here to the *femelette* is one attributed to herself by Christine. In the *Montaigne* Gerson is engaged in instructing the *femelette* and other 'simple people' about the three steps of meditative contemplation: repentance, the discovery of a place suitable for solitary reflection, and perseverance.[4] When he describes the *femelette* absorbed in solitary contemplation in her chambers, he has her adopt the pose of the *seulette*, which Christine would later assume as her 'signature' persona.

It would appear, then, that Gerson gave Christine spiritual counsel sometime after the death of her husband in 1390, which was around the same time that he began to preach to the French court. Christine could have met him after hearing one of his many sermons.[5] Gilbert Ouy believes that Gerson and Christine would have been very well acquainted with each other, since they frequented the same circles and had many friends and benefactors in

---

[2] Earl Jeffrey Richards, 'Christine de Pizan and Jean Gerson: An Intellectual Friendship', in *Christine de Pizan 2000: Studies on Christine de Pizan in honour of Angus J. Kennedy,* ed. John Campbell and Nadia Margolis (Amsterdam, 2000), pp. 197–208. As in Bose, references to Jean Gerson, *Œuvres Complètes*, ed. Palémon Glorieux, 10 vols (Paris, 1960–73) are given in the main body of the text and indicated by the letter G, followed by volume number in Roman and page number(s) in Arabic numerals.

[3] Eric Hicks, ed., *Le Débat sur le Roman de la Rose* (Geneva, 1996), p. 132.

[4] The work begins with the line 'La cause d'escripre en francois et aux simples gens de la matiere de contemplation'.

[5] Ruth R. Rains, ed., *Les sept psaumes allégorisés* (Washington, DC, 1965), p. 31.

common.⁶ Given their network of associations, it is logical that Christine's poetry would be marked by Gerson's attitudes towards poetry. Even more significantly, Gerson actually refers to the concept of the meditative *seulette* in sermons, beginning with his 1397 sermon on the Annunciation, the 'Ave Maria' (G. VII, 546). He identifies the *seulette* closely with Mary at the Annunciation, mentioning it in his Good Friday sermon, quoted above. It in fact forms the conceptual basis of the quatrain and, as we will see below, it has connections to the Psalms.

To understand more fully how Gerson aligns his literary productions with the scripturally authenticated genre of the psalm, it is time to revisit the *Tractatus de canticis*. Song as *carmina* is for Gerson an expression of the living word of God, the very voice of the Holy Spirit or Sapientia, which according to Augustine resided in the heart. Gerson justifies his use of verse by reminding his readers that biblical prophets including Jeremiah, Job, David, and Moses all had recourse to poetry. According to Gerson, the wise Solomon composed 5,000 verses, and in every one of them 'Cantata est mulier fortis ab ore suo (4, 15) [The strong woman [i.e., Sapientia] sung through his mouth]'. Gerson then addresses his readers with the words, 'quisquis amas prosam metris ignoscito nostris (4, 1) [Whoever you are, lover of prose, be indulgent toward our verses].' He deserves their understanding, so he believes, because verse confers order on human passions, and metre guards against vice. Gerson situates the origins of all true poetry, and in effect of all good writing, in songs sung by a heart galvanized by Sapientia and the Holy Spirit.

For Gerson, singing the song of the heart starts the long and arduous transformation of the carnal self into something nobler. Gerson holds that the separation between human beings and God, albeit enormous, begins to be corrected when humans break out in song. Gerson relates poetry to song and to the desire for knowledge. All grow out of the imperfect nature of human understanding, the fact that we all see 'as in a glass darkly'. In despair because he could not bring his *City of God* to a conclusion, Augustine struggled to plumb the piece of wisdom Paul had expressed in II Corinthians, 13, returning to gloss it over and again. Augustine finally countered Paul's statement of human imperfection with another Pauline idea that gives him a way out of his predicament, 'It is sown an animal body, it will rise a spiritual body' (*Civitas* 22, 21; I Cor. 15:44).⁷ The Pauline paradigm in fact underlies the notion of the City of God as an upward ascent through material existence.⁸

This notion finds its origins in the Old Testament, most particularly in

---

⁶ Ouy expressed this opinion verbally in May 2004.
⁷ R. W. Dyson, ed. and trans., *The City of God* (Cambridge, 1998).
⁸ Northrup Frye, *The Great Code: The Bible and Literature* (New York, 1982), p. 76.

Psalm 87, the psalm about the City of God.[9] The Psalms' depiction of the transformation of David's cries of despair into a song of joy converge in the concept of the 'new man' who 'sings a new song'. The concept is implicit in Gerson's Latin poems, which have him imagining the soul ascending to heaven 'singing the psalms' ('cantantem in psalmis', 2, 98, which he repeats in 3, 38). The series of six *carmina* ends with Gerson uttering the reflection, 'Olim veniet spatiosor hora; Nunc satis a labiis te liberasse malis (6, 53–4) [An even more generous hour will come / It is enough that my impure lips have delivered this song].' Gerson thereby expresses his faith in human progress through song as *carmina*, which is equivalent to poetry shaped by biblical models.

Gerson's model of affective piety in the *De canticis* is the figure of 'pater Augustine (2, 87) [Father Augustine]'. He comments upon the future Church Father's change of heart being signalled by his copious shedding of tears, elicited 'vocibus Ecclesie (2, 87) [by means of the voices of the Church]'. Augustine's tears serve to substantiate the claim that for Gerson 'poetry' understood as song (i.e., *carmina*) is primarily affective in its impact. The story of Augustine's shedding of tears is well known through his *Confessions*, in which he continually relates his dialogues with God to the psalmist's. The universality of Augustine's Davidic voice is underscored by the fact that the French translation of the *Soliloquies*, referred to as the *Seul parlers* in the *Rose* Debate, recasts Augustine's original Latin text in light of his *Confessions*, which does not seem to exist as an independent translation in French.[10] The anonymous translator (who has been identified with Gerson, most believe erroneously) transforms the philosophical *Soliloquies* into a devotional dialogue between a human being and God, reminiscent of Augustine's original *Confessions* and its many even more passionately couched spin-offs, all of which exploit the Davidic subtext of lamentation and desire for consolation. In depicting Augustine's outpouring of tears, Gerson has this figure express a notion of spirituality grounded in the heart, which forms the basis of Gerson's obviously Augustinian and psalmist-inspired 'song of the heart'.

Gerson's *De canticis*, as well as many of his other works, develops the Latin *Soliloquies* and its French derivatives within the universal vision of the *City of God*, which, as we saw above, was derived from Ps. 87:3. In the Latin *Soliloquies*, a work whose importance for poetic composition has been

---

[9] Although I follow Bose in citing the Douay-Rheims translation of the Vulgate, in this case I base myself on the numbering of the Old Latin translation used by Augustine and by Christine in her *Epistre Othea*.

[10] Geneviève Hasenohr, 'Aperçu sur la diffusion et la reception de la littérature de spiritualité en langue française au dernier siècle du Moyen Age', in *Wissensorganisierende und wissensvermittelnde Literatur im Mittelalter, Perspektiven ihrer Erforschung, Kolloquium, 5–7, Dezember 1985*, ed. Norbert Richard Wolf (Wiesbaden, 1987), pp. 57–90, p. 74.

long overlooked, Augustine discusses the use of fables or lies to establish the truth. Grammar, he says, does not create falsehood, but from them it teaches and presents a true system. Fables use something patently false to teach something true. His commanding example is that 'there could be no true fable about the flight of Daedalus, unless it were false that Daedalus had flown!'[11] Although, as says Augustine, it is false that we are two persons, we can divide ourselves mentally, and in this way find truth.

Christine expresses ideas about poetry similar to Gerson's in her 1404 biography of Charles V, the king whom she would immortalize there as the 'Wise King Charles'.[12] If the book is full of explicit and implicit references to Augustine and Aristotle, it is because Christine has her own texts reflect the hierarchy she attributes to Charles, which represents these two authors as the chief monarchical authorities after Holy Scripture (*Charles V* 3, 12). Christine's discussion of knowledge and wisdom segues into a discussion of poetry in 3, 68 ('Cy dit de poesie'), where she establishes that poetry is one way that humans can perfect themselves through their reasoning powers. The passage bears close examination:

> Comme en general le nom de poesie soit pris pour fiction quelconques, c'est-à-dire pour toute narracion ou introduction apparaument signifiant un senz, et occultement en segnefie un aultre ou plusieurs, combien que plus proprement dire celle soit poesie, dont la fin est vérité.[13]
>
> [Since in general the name of poetry is taken for any type of fiction, that is, for all narrations or introductions apparently signifying one meaning and secretly signifying another or several, how much more properly can one speak of poetry as any fictive discourse whose end is truth.]

Poetry, she says, pertains to all narratives or presentations, having one apparent meaning and one or several figurative ones. The term 'poetry', however, more properly designates fictive discourses whose finality is truth. Truth, she continues, is found by clothing doctrine in pleasant discursive ornaments (she uses the term 'delectables') and dressing it with appropriate colours of rhetoric. We see that rather than restricting the sense of poetry to works in verse, Christine adopts a broader definition, making the term 'poetry' equivalent to 'allegorical fiction', whether that fiction is rendered in prose or in verse. Christine here ascribes to the term 'poesie' the highly specific sense acknowledged by various scholars since Marc-Réné Jung, who

---

[11] K. Paffenroth, trans., *Soliloquies: Augustine's Inner Dialogue* (New York, 2000), p. 77.

[12] Christine de Pizan, *Le Livre des fais et bonnes meurs du sage roy Charles V*, ed. Suzanne Solente, 2 vols (Paris, 1936, 1940). All references will be made to this edition.

[13] *Charles V*, II, pp. 176–7.

contends that the key concept in 'poetria' is not versification or rhyme, but rather this use of allegory or metaphor.[14]

Clearly applying exegetical methods to profane literature, Christine thereby claims that poetry, if it disguises truths under the cloth of properly conceived figures, can lead the reader to acquire poetic knowledge and to grow in wisdom. Otherwise said, when poetry is conveyed by the correct use of metaphor and rhetorical ornament, it can be on the same level as, and even be superior to, other forms of knowledge. Christine hereby supplies a reply to the oft-stated idea that verse falsifies the truth, by positing that poetic truth is not found on the level of literal meaning but rather must be inferred from the literal meaning of a text. However, if the literal meaning of a text is ignoble, or if its rhetorical ornaments are not 'delictables', it is unworthy of being the vehicle for conveying a higher meaning.[15]

A major responsibility of true poetic discourse is to hide divine secrets from the profane and to reveal them, at least partially, to only the most penetrating and worthy minds. Poetic discourse as Christine defines it is thus similar to the proleptic discourse of Scripture. It is of no surprise, then, that she places alongside secular poets such as Virgil, Ovid, Homer, Lucan, Orpheus, Plato, Boethius, and Martianus Capella Old Testament prophets like Daniel and Solomon, as well as the New Testament figure of Christ. As in the Old Testament generally, and particularly in sapiential books such as Wisdom and the Song of Songs, for Christine the figures of poetry prefigure or figure forth sacred truths.

We can see how close Christine's ideas on poetry are to Gerson's. To begin with, Boethius' consolatory prosimetrium, which figures in the above list, supplies the framework for Gerson's *De consolatione theologiae*, with Gerson implying that it is theology that provides the ultimate consolation. Christine makes the very same point when she has Lady Philosophy be transformed into Lady Theology at the end of her Boethian and otherwise Gersonian-inspired *Advision Cristine* of 1405. But it is even more important that Christine, like Gerson, views true poetry as conforming to scriptural models. If, as Bose affirms, 'Gerson invites his readers to elide his own poetry with that of the Biblical prophets', we will see below to what extent Christine does the same.

---

[14] Marc-René Jung, 'Poetria: Zur Dichtungstheorie des ausgehenden Mittelalters in Frankreich', *Vox Romanica*, 30 (1971), 44–64, pp. 58–9. I thank Finn Sinclair for supplying me with this reference.

[15] Here I believe that she is basing herself on Augustine's idea in the *Literal Interpretation of Genesis* that literal meaning cannot 'involve anything absurd or unworthy of God'. See R. J. Teske, '*Genesi ad litteram liber, De*', in *Augustine Through the Ages: An Encyclopedia*, ed. A. D. Fitzgerald (Grand Rapids, MI, 1999), pp. 376–7. I have made extensive use of other entries in this book, especially the following: E. L. Fortin, '*Civitate Dei, De*', pp. 196–202; J. McWilliam '*Soliloquia*', pp. 806–7; D. Kries, 'Political Augustinianism', pp. 657–8; J. V. Scott, 'Political Thought, Augustine's', pp. 658–61.

To begin with a more elementary comparison, we can observe that Christine and Gerson both object to the *Rose* on the grounds cited above, i.e., that its literal meaning is ignoble, its rhetorical ornaments unattractive and even repugnant. As a preacher, Gerson was justly concerned with providing instruction to everyone. Believing (probably rightly) that the majority of his parishioners would interpret the text on a literal level, he feared that a reading of the *Rose* could inspire them to commit licentious or otherwise immoral acts. From her perspective as a woman, Christine marks Jean de Meun for special censure because his rhetorical ornaments are not always 'delictables'. Some of those ornaments, like the comparison of holy relics to sexual organs, would cause a worthy lady to blush and hide her face in shame.[16]

These were more significant objections than they would at first appear to be. In the *Trois Vertus* (1, 12) Christine, repeating her oft-stated claim that noblewomen have the responsibility for setting a virtuous example at home and abroad, observes that such noblewomen routinely receive much of their instruction from uplifting texts in the vernacular. A book such as the *Rose*, read aloud to the Queen and her feminine court over their evening meals as was the common practice (1, 12), would embarrass its female audience.[17] Their embarrassment would not simply be a result of the licentious ending of the Rose quest. The noble ladies would also be offended by its suggestion that French women were daughters of Eve rather than near-clones of Mary.

The political stakes of representing 'French roses' in such a manner were high. Simply put, if French queens were akin to the easily seduced Rose, then France would lose its position of moral superiority within Christendom. (Phrased more bluntly, if the French queen was a whore, then France's hereditary monarchy was illegitimate.) This is no exaggeration; the legitimacy of the royal house was a burning issue during the reign of Isabeau de Bavière, queen of France from 1385 to 1422, thus during the lifetimes of Gerson (1363–1429) and Christine (c. 1364–1430). Queen Isabeau was rumoured to have had an adulterous relationship with her own brother-in-law, Louis d'Orléans. The question of legitimacy was also raised in regard to her son, the dauphin Charles VII. It is easy for us, judging the situation from the perspective of vastly different political systems and standards, to dismiss the objections of Christine and Gerson to the *Rose* as quaint or prudish. Their objections made a great deal of sense in early-fifteenth-century France. Christine and Gerson's campaign against the *Rose* takes its place among their broader efforts to defend France and indeed all Christendom against detrac-

---

[16] In the Debate Christine makes this point, which Gerson then comments upon in his letter to Pierre Col; see Hicks, *Le Débat sur le* Roman de la Rose, pp. 20, 56 and 168.

[17] In her dedication of the epistles in the Debate, Christine tells Queen Isabeau that she has heard that she 'se delicte a oïr lire dittiéz de choses vertueuses et bien dictes (Hicks, *Le Débat sur le* Roman de la Rose, p. 5) [takes pleasure in hearing read well composed poems about virtuous things]'.

tors as well as outright enemies, and this included composing vernacular poetry established upon sacred models.

Gerson conducted much of his defence of France from the pulpit. In his court sermons preached in French he did not hesitate to use poetic means to sway his listeners. And he was good at it. The comment made by his erstwhile opponent in the *Rose* Debate, Jean de Montreuil, reveals just how skilful Gerson was in captivating audiences using poetic techniques. Montreuil said he would go all the way to Rheims to hear Gerson preach a sermon on the Passion (quoted in G. VII.2, 449–519). In beginning his 1403 Good Friday sermon with a poem of his own invention, Gerson seeks to communicate to his listeners the impression that his lesson originates in a song overflowing from his own passionate heart, a song that they will also come to sing if only they take his lesson, as we now say, 'to heart'.

Gerson's song speaks of the union of the hearts of Christ and Mary at the moment when Christ experiences his Passion and sees Mary observing his suffering, both of them enduring their trials knowing they are preliminary to experiencing joy in heaven. Gerson's promotion of Mary here and elsewhere has intimate connections to the Psalms, since Mary was David's lineal descendant and it was her celebratory Magnificat that consoled David's despair. The quatrain's phonic and metrical patterning anchors the memory of their sorrows in the minds of Gerson's male and female listeners. Gerson exploits this technique to its full effect by repeating those verses, either in their complete form or as a couplet, numerous times throughout his seven-hour sermon. The result is that he creates a union, and one with a particularly bittersweet quality, of the hearts and minds of everyone present, as they come to know from the inside what it was like for Christ and Mary to observe each other in their sufferings and to look past them to their eventual consolation.

Gerson's poetic techniques overlap with those employed by Christine in her *Epistre Othea* of 1400.[18] Entries 6–100 of this text all begin with quatrains, many of which exhibit the same *aabb* rhyme scheme as Gerson's quatrain. Christine borrows her idea of poetic hermeneutics as a variant of biblical exegesis from Charles V's ideas about translation, which were organized according to three different methods: translation as simple text, translation as text and gloss, and translation as allegorized moralization (*Charles V* 3,12). Christine employs these same categories in several of her works: her *Livre de Prudence* is structured according to Text and Gloss, while her *Othea* combines the three, Text, Gloss, and Allegory, and her *Sept Psaumes allégorisés* relies upon the allegorized method.

Such governmentally sanctioned techniques of 'translation', based as they were upon techniques current in biblical exegesis, were adopted by both Christine and Gerson. In her *Othea* Christine connects these techniques to

---

[18] Christine de Pizan, *L'Epistre Othea*, ed. Gabriella Parussa (Geneva, 1999).

the Psalms. In the section marked 'Allegory' of *Othea* 87, Christine glosses the myth of Daphné with a statement that she ascribes to David in his Psalter, 'Glorisa dicta sunt de te, civitas Dei (Ps. 87:3) [Glorious things are said of you, O City of God].' This is the idea to which Augustine returns three times in his *Civitas*, where he points to its origins in the Psalms, a work upon which he expounds at great length, devoting his *Ennarationes in Psalmos* to their exposition. Christine, significantly, repeats the same quote from Ps. 87:3 at the conclusion of her *Cité des dames* of 1405, thereby connecting her text's echoes of Augustine to his source in David's Psalter.

Othea 87 additionally echoes *Othea* 67, where Christine quotes Psalm 101:8, the most famous of the penitential psalms, to say 'Vigilavi et factus sum sicut passer solitarius in tecto [I have watched and have become a lonely sparrow on the rooftops].' David is represented here as the solitary watchman for humanity, who has been transformed into its vigilant moral guide by virtue of having repented of his sins of adultery and murder. The subject of *Othea* 87 is Orpheus, whom Christine describes as a Christian poet like David, thus anticipating the list of poets she gives in *Charles V* 3, 12, where she specifically cites Orpheus as a divine poet. Gerson represents a similarly conceived Orpheus as a model poet in *Tractatus de canticis* 2, 41–4, where he explains that if the Ovidian account of Orpheus calming the Furies is made into a story designed to correct improper behaviour, his mythical song becomes consistent with Christian doctrine.

These references imply that both Christine and Gerson see themselves as Davidic-styled watchkeepers over public morality who compose 'poetry' possessing scriptural resonance. Christine for example creates a persona for herself as 'Dame Sibyll, dame de la Tour'. Consistent with her ideas about 'poetry', she inserts a letter from Lady Sibyll into both her prosimetrium *Duc des vrais amans* and her exclusively prose *Trois Vertus*. She also threads Davidic allusions into her earliest collection of lyric poetry, her *Cent Balades*. Subverting the desire of her patrons to hear joyous songs of romantic love, Christine creates a lyric collection characterized by reflection upon some of the moral issues currently facing the French court, mainly revolving around its corruption by deceit and treachery, themes being enunciated from the pulpit by Gerson around this very time.

It is significant in this regard that Gerson makes reference to the *seulette* at end of his 1403 Passion sermon, in referring to the contemplative rapture experienced between the Crucifixion and the Resurrection by the Virgin and St Jean, Christ's human surrogate. Through means particular to the biblical poetry inaugurated by David and Mary, Gerson tries to produce in his listeners a desire to imitate the type of higher love experienced by Mary, Christ, and St Jean. He accumulates repetitions in order to move hearts to devotion, which is his stated purpose in this sermon.

In a ballad marked by the quasi-obsessive repetition of the term '*seulette*', her *Cent Balades* 11, Christine creates a melopoetic image of herself as a widowed soul whose sufferings are unmatched by any other woman, an image corresponding to that of Mary in Gerson's 'Ad Deum vadit'. And Ballad 11 finds its echo in Ballad 14, lines 1–4 when Christine exclaims: 'Seulete m'a laissié en grant martyre / En ce desert monde plein de tristece [He has left me all alone in great martyrdom in this deserted world full of sadness].' These lines are a poignant restatement of Gerson's signature persona as *advena* or *peregrinus*, which he expressed in his motto 'Nostre conversatio est in coelis', which can mean 'Our true homeland is in heaven', or 'We were meant to speak with God in heaven'. Gerson's idea, tributary to Paul (Philippians 3: 20), is that in life we are in exile from our true home in heaven. Christine's refrain in Ballad 14 is: 'Qu'a tousjours mais je pleureray sa mort [I will never stop mourning his death].' Although the verse refers to Christine's loss of her husband, it also points beyond the personal to the universal by echoing Mary's lament at the foot of the cross, which was traditionally seen to be symbolic of the universal sorrow of the Church as it remembers Christ's sacrifice in its liturgy and many rituals.

Christine makes reference to her persona as a new Mary or a female Christ/David in the refrain of the last ballad of her *Cent Balades*: 'En escrit ai mis mon nom [In writing I have placed my name].' In employing the anagram '*escrit-cristine*', Christine affirms that her true identity resides in her textual persona as a female imitator of Christ rather than in her carnal self. Since '*escrit*' additionally contains the word '*cri*', she also connects her persona to David as well as to Christ and to Mary, since the word occurs in Psalm 101's opening line: 'Let my cry come unto thee'. Although the term given in the Vulgate is '*clamor*' ('Domine audi orationem meam et clamor meus ad te veniet'), Christine is surely translating '*clamor*' as '*cri*' here. We know that she does so in her *Sept Psaumes* of 1407, where she says 'Sire, exausse mon oroison, et mon cry viengne a toy'.[19]

Comparing *Cent Balades* 100 with Gerson's *Pratique du psalterium mystique* (G. VII, 421–3) brings out other connections between Christine's poetry and Gerson's.[20] The poem can be described as a verse drama staged by Gerson in the inner theatre of the reader's mind or heart. In this play the *cuer seulet* receives consolation from a figure called Comfort. Gerson depicts the despondent heart in his initial verse: 'Ung Cuer seulet mis en esmay crie souvent "Las, que feray?" [A solitary heart, finding itself in tribulation cries out often, "Alas, what will I do?"].' A personified Comfort answers by giving the heart, which is represented as a miniature human being having a face and an ear, a *psalterium* or *canticordum*, so that it can, in imitation of David, sing the canticles. Even more clearly than had Christine, Gerson, significantly in verse, associates the motif of the *cri de cœur* with the lamentations of David the psalmist.

---

[19] Rains, *Sept psaumes*, p. 22.
[20] Fabre, *La Doctrine*, p. 338, is unable to date Gerson's text with any precision.

As I have noted earlier, Christine identifies her role as keeper of public morality with her stance as the *seulette*. Christine places herself in the Davidic role of watchkeeper when she glosses 101.8, the line about the 'sparrow' David, with the prayer:

> Sire, ne prens pas garde a ma char, qui est pesant et endormie en pechié, mais avises mon esperit, qui est prompt et resveillés en solitude: reçois, se il te plaist, son oblacion.
>
> [Lord, disregard my flesh, which is heavy and asleep in sin, but counsel my spirit, which is quick and awakened in solitude; receive, if you please, its offering.]

She foregrounds the significance of her submission by employing the term 'oblacion', a liturgical term referring to a priest's act of offering the Eucharist up to God. Christine follows the quotation above with a reference to Jesus's baptism by St Jean, coupling it with a request to the Lord to protect her from giving 'faulx tesmoignage [false testimony]'. Is Christine here not insinuating ever so subtly that she is being baptized to do the Lord's work by means of her writing? This stance would be consonant with her self-depiction as the secretary of Divine Sapience in the gloss of her *Advision Cristine* (line 139).[21] Christine represents herself similarly when she has Christ baptize Saint Christine, his gesture endowing her patron saint with a tongue empowered to sing the Lord's praises even after her persecutors have savagely ripped it out by the root (*Cité des dames* 3, 10). In representing herself as a poet akin to the 'singer' David, Christine, like Gerson, equates writing grounded in sacred models as being equivalent to song.

Let me add to these speculations a final word on how Christine and Gerson conceived of 'poetry' as *carmina* or song. If Gerson's comparisons of himself to sacred figures seem to smack of hubris, this impression is counterbalanced by other factors. Take his quatrain, which is marked by the simplicity of the emotions expressed, along with the speaker's apparent vulnerability. The tensions in Gerson's *carmina* between 'the self inscribed, in its contingency and incompleteness, and the self effaced, taking refuge in authority and hierarchy', as noted above by Bose, can be discerned as well in a French poem such as this one. The quatrain produced by Gerson is, however, more telling than in its simple ability to reveal its creator's subjectivity. It stands as tangible proof of, and the speaker's truthful witness to, a song emanating from the heart of a latter-day Jean. Gerson tries 'with impure lips' to make the revelator's prophecies come true by singing his little ditty for others, aspiring in the process to have them to do the same. The song *is* his heart,

---

[21] Christine de Pizan, *Le Livre de l'Advision Cristine*, ed. Christine Reno and Liliane Dulac (Paris, 2000).

the gift he offers to others in the hope that it may redeem the egotism of the giver.

This study provides a fresh way of understanding early-fifteenth-century notions of community. The 'conjoined hearts' of Mary and Christ, united as Gerson presents them in his Good Friday sermon, was the primary image of the cooperation between men and women and of one heart with the next that the monarchy was promoting, through eloquent and passionately committed advocates such as Christine and Gerson, in order to create the feeling of nationhood in its citizens. This conjoining was reflected in the Church-state alliance and in the lineage system characteristic of all hereditary monarchies. In order for the concept of conjoining to form the basis of lasting community, it had to be communicated in a language understandable by the greatest number of people. Whereas works written in Latin would hardly penetrate beyond Gerson's clerical community, the communicative potential of French, at least in its spoken form, was virtually unlimited. This is the reasoning behind Charles V's translation campaign, which continued St Louis's *Grandes Chroniques de France*, the official history created by the translation of Latin chronicles preserved at the royal monastery of St Denis. Charles conceived of his translation programme, so reports Christine in *Charles V* 3, 12, in order to extend the wisdom and knowledge of the past to future generations, whom the King envisioned as being even more unschooled in Latin than the present ones. By 'translating' Scripture for the masses in their sermons, as Gerson did in his 'Ad Deum vadit', preachers made crucial contributions to this campaign.

Working thus in accordance with monarchical imperatives, Gerson and Christine strove to unify the divided nation and Church in their French productions. The *femelette/seulette* Christine directs the bulk of her efforts to women and other 'simple people' deemed by Gerson to be worthy of consideration. A survey of all the vernacular texts of the two extends well beyond the limits given for this essay. We can, however, observe Gerson affirming his belief in spiritual conjoining as the basis for social harmony when, in his 1397 French sermon on the Annunciation in which he alludes to the *seulette*, he reminds his listeners that he and they are all are bound to each other in the Lord, united as he says by a 'natural love that should exist between brothers and sisters all of one blood, of one flesh (G. VII, 549) [amour naturelle qui doit ester entre freres et seurs tout d'un sang, d'un char].' Gerson proposes a disinterested affection among people as the love that should bind everyone together. It is this type of spiritual kinship that I see as distinguishing Gerson's relationship with Christine. Echoing the use of the term '*nation*' in the *Grandes Chronique*s, Christine expresses her high hopes for the future of the 'noble nation françoise' despite momentary setbacks (*Charles V* 1, 5).[22]

---

[22] See Colette Beaune, *The Birth of an Ideology: Myths and Symbols of Nation in Late-Medieval France*, ed. F. L. Cheyette, trans. S. R. Huston, (Berkeley, 1991), and my

Through their words and deeds the *doctor christianissimus* Gerson and the 'holy widow' Christine become exemplary models for the entire community, a 'nation' held together, as proposed by St Louis's *Grandes Chroniques,* by its use of the vernacular.

What conclusions can finally be drawn from these preliminary studies of Gerson and Christine as poets? Like Bose discussing Gerson, I hesitate to overly generalize about these two figures, each of whose output was prodigious and whose *œuvre*, especially its complex manuscript transmission, calls for further study. But one caveat is indicated. When comparing Gerson's Latin and French poetry, it is easy to dismiss the latter. His Latin output is far greater, his innovations therein generously applauded. My study suggests, however, that just as has been the case for his sometime model Petrarch, Gerson's vernacular productions deserve to win him as lasting a place in history as do his Latin works. As for Christine, this chapter argues for discerning the presence of Gerson's moral concerns in her earliest lyrics. It also supplies a rationale for seeing the two of them as partners who consciously take up Augustine's imperative to defend Christianity by means of the pen, even while others were defending it by the sword. If France's future depended upon the active collaboration of women and men in all forms of Christian endeavour, that collaboration could have had no better incarnation than in the combined efforts of Christine and Gerson to have the country remain what the monks of St Denis had said it always was, the moral leader of the Christian world. For both Gerson and Christine, vernacular poetry was a potent arm to be wielded in defence of the Christian nation-state of France.

discussion in 'Christine de Pizan, Primat, and the *noble nation françoise*', *Cahiers de Recherches médiévales,* 9 (2002), 237–46.

PART II
POETRY OR PROSE?

5

Les *Razos* et l'idée de la poésie

MICHEL ZINK

Les *razos* illustrent à l'évidence la relation 'poetry, knowledge and community'. 'Poetry and community', puisqu'elles sont consacrées tout entières à la 'vie sociale en poésie'. 'Poetry and knowledge', puisqu'elles prétendent détenir un savoir sur les troubadours. Certes, ce savoir est au mieux incertain, au pire fantaisiste. C'est pourtant la somme de ce savoir qui donne le sentiment d'une communauté de poètes.

La relation entre 'poetry' et 'knowledge' peut s'entendre de plusieurs façons. De la façon la plus évidente: les *razos* prétendent apporter une information sur les poèmes des troubadours. De la façon la plus anachronique (et la plus plate): nous cherchons dans les *razos* des informations sur les troubadours. Mais nous savons bien, non seulement que les informations fournies par les *razos* sont la plupart du temps fantaisistes, mais encore qu'elles se fondent très souvent sur le poème qu'elles prétendent éclairer, autrement dit qu'elles sont une lecture des poèmes.

Quelle lecture? Pourquoi cette lecture? La question n'est pas nouvelle. Pourquoi une lecture aussi anecdotique de poèmes qui le sont si peu? Des réponses pertinentes peuvent être apportées dans des ordres différents. *Vidas* et *razos* ont certainement été utilisées comme prélude à l'interprétation des chansons, presque comme boniment, comme élément de *captatio benvolentiae*. La *vida* de Guilhem de la Tor dit qu'il accompagnait l'exécution de ses chansons d'un commentaire plus long que la chanson.[1] D'où leur ton volontiers détaché, humoristique, moqueur. *Vidas* et *razos* peuvent refléter la lecture de poèmes anciens en fonction d'une poétique nouvelle, en décalage par rapport à eux: c'est ce que j'ai moi-même soutenu,[2] et c'est ce qui pourrait me justifier de parler des *razos* dans un volume consacré à la poésie du Moyen Âge finissant. Les *razos* témoigneraient de l'émergence d'une idée

---

[1] 'Mas quant volia dire sas cansos, el fazia plus lonc sermon de la rason que non era la canso [Mais lorsqu'il voulait dire ses chansons, il consacrait au commentaire un discours plus long que la chanson même].' Jean Boutière et A.-H. Schutz, *Biographies des troubadours. Textes provençaux des XIIIe et XIVe siècles* (Paris, 1964), pp. 236–7.

[2] Michel Zink, *La Subjectivité littéraire autour du siècle de saint Louis* (Paris, 1985), pp. 49–53.

nouvelle de la poésie, qui sera celle de la fin du Moyen Âge, et avec d'autant plus d'évidence que ce sont des textes critiques.

Mais ces réponses sont-elles suffisantes? La mienne ne l'est pas, car elle suppose entre les poèmes d'une part, les *vidas* et les *razos* de l'autre, une rupture qui expliquerait l'incapacité des secondes à comprendre les premiers. Mais cette rupture existe-t-elle? Elle n'est pas réellement chronologique (Uc de Saint-Circ, auteur d'une grande partie des *vidas* et des *razos,* était lui-même un contemporain tardif des troubadours pour qui il les a composées).[3] Et il est de mauvaise méthode – à la fois trop facile et imprudent – de prétendre résoudre une difficulté en en rejetant la faute sur les textes, qui n'auraient rien compris. Mais si les *vidas* et les *razos* ont été conservées avec tant de soin, c'est qu'on leur a prêté une valeur et un intérêt qui dépassent celui du boniment qui précède la performance. Ce sont, en tout état de cause, des textes élaborés. Marie Louisa Meneghetti a admirablement montré ce qu'ils doivent au modèle des *accessus ad auctores*[4] et, en se référant à un article de Valeria Bertolucci Pizzorusso, à celui des vies de saints brèves.[5]

Ces textes élaborés sont conservés avec soin, et conservés d'une façon qui donne particulièrement à réfléchir dans les chansonniers qui ne les regroupent pas dans une section spéciale (au début du manuscrit, comme dans R, f. 1–3, ou à la fin, comme dans E, f. 189–210, ou dans P, f. 39–52), mais qui les intercale avec les poèmes de façon à en faire, selon leur vocation, des introductions aux poètes et aux poèmes, comme dans AIKH, produisant ainsi cette 'forme-chansonnier' gibeline et véneto-sicilienne, selon M. L. Meneghetti, qui se caractérise comme une anthologie par auteurs.[6]

Je disais en commençant que le savoir des *vidas* et des *razos* sur les troubadours est au mieux incertain, au pire fantaisiste. Comme je le rappelais aussi, j'ai cru pouvoir soutenir ailleurs que leur capacité herméneutique paraît modeste. On aurait tort cependant de négliger leur idée de la poésie – celle

---

[3] Maria Luisa Meneghetti, *Il pubblico dei trovatori. Ricezione e riuso dei testi lirici cortesi fino al XIV secolo* (Modène, 1984), p. 188.

[4] Meneghetti, *Il pubblico dei trovatori*, p. 303. Voir aussi Maria Louisa Meneghetti, 'La forma-canzoniere fra tradizione mediolatina e tradizioni volgari', dans *L'Antologia poetica, Critica del Testo* II/ 1 (1999), 119–40.

[5] Meneghetti, *Il pubblico dei trovatori*, pp. 285–6. Valeria Bertolucci Pizzorusso, 'Il grado zero della retorica nella "vida" di Jaufre Rudel', dans *Studi Mediolatini e Volgari*, 18 (1970), 7–26.

[6] Les *vidas* et *razos* sont conservées dans une vingtaine de manuscrits (Boutière, *Biographies des troubadours*, pp. xv–xx). Rappelons les cotes de ceux qui seront mentionnés ici: A = Rome, Vat. Lat., MS 5232; B = Paris, BnF, MS fr. 1592; E = Paris, BnF, MS fr. 1749; H = Rome, Vat. Lat., MS 3207; I = Paris, BnF, MS fr. 854; K = Paris, BnF, MS fr. 12473; P = Florence, Laurent., MS Plut. XLI; R = Paris, BnF, MS fr. 22543. M. L. Meneghetti remarque: 'Il salto di qualità ne modo di percepire la lirica volgare sarebbe insomma avvenuto tra Veneto e Sicilia, in una ambiente, in un ambiente ghibellino e imperiale' ('La forma-canzoniere fra tradizione mediolatina e tradizioni volgari', p. 137).

qu'elles appliquent aux chansons des troubadours et celle qu'elles incarnent en tant qu'œuvres poétiques.

Dira-t-on que ce ne sont pas des 'œuvres poétiques' parce qu'elles sont en prose? Mais le latin réservant généralement le mot poésie au seul mètre et plaçant souvent la poésie rythmique du côté de la prose, toute composition vernaculaire, à ce compte, est en prose. Aussi bien, les chansonniers qui les contiennent n'identifient pas graphiquement les vers et ne livrent pas tous, et de loin, les mélodies. Le style extraordinairement figé et formulaire des *vidas* et des *razos*, qui, disait Jean Boutière, permet si facilement d'en écrire des pastiches[7] (j'avoue m'y être risqué moi-même),[8] offre une poétique immédiatement repérable, aux rythmes très accusés, et qui, dans les chansonniers qui adoptent cette disposition, alterne avec celle des chansons de façon à créer l'effet d'un prosimètre, non seulement au sens que prend ce mot au XIIIe siècle (ouvrage où alternent la prose et le vers), mais au sens qui était le sien primitivement (ouvrage mêlant la prose au vers).[9]

Dira-t-on que ce ne sont pas des 'œuvres poétiques' parce qu'elles ne livrent pas le savoir et le sens de la fable antique, qui définissent longtemps le champ d'application des mots poète et poésie? Précisément; par le retour sur un passé récent, elles inaugurent la modernité en poésie, au moment même où les troubadours, qualifiés d'antiques, paraissent à Matfre Ermengaud des autorités suffisantes pour fonder un savoir poétique de l'amour.[10] Non seulement, comme l'a remarqué Maria Luisa Meneghetti se fondant sur un bel article de Martín de Riquer, elles se trouvent au regard des chansons dans la situation où les lais de Marie de France semblent se trouver au regard des lais bretons (développement narratif du récit implicite impliqué par une chanson ou un poème);[11] mais encore elles illustrent le programme annoncé par le prologue des lais: renoncer à une traduction du latin pour se consacrer à la préservation de la mémoire de poèmes appartenant à une autre tradition, préservation de la mémoire qui ne se confond pas avec la pure et simple reproduction ou conservation de ces poèmes, mais qui consiste, précisément, à en extraire et à en développer la narration implicite.

Je ne veux pas, cependant, m'appesantir trop longtemps sur la défense d'un paradoxe (les *vidas* et les *razos* comme œuvre poétique), mais plutôt essayer d'établir que la pénétration critique des *razos*, que leur capacité à aller droit au cœur de ce qui nourrit la poésie des troubadours et à le mettre en évidence, dépassent de beaucoup ce que l'on croit généralement. Mais

---

[7] Boutière, *Biographies des troubadours*, p. viii.

[8] Michel Zink, *Le Tiers d'amour. Un roman des troubadours* (Paris, 1998).

[9] Anne Turcan-Verkerk, 'Le *prosimetrum* des *Artes dictaminis* médiévales', dans *Archivum Latinitatis Medii Aevi* ou *ALMA* (2003), 111–74.

[10] *Le Breviari d'amor de Matfre Ermengaud*, ed. Peter T. Ricketts, 3 tomes (Leiden, 1976–).

[11] Meneghetti, *Il publicco dei trovatori*, p. 285. Martín de Riquer, 'La *avventura*, el *lai* y el *conte* en María de Francia', dans *Filologia Romanza*, 2 (1955), 1–19.

cette pénétration est souvent voilée à nos yeux par le fait qu'elle ne revêt pas la forme de l'analyse, mais celle de la mise en récit.

Ma démonstration prendra la forme d'une succession d'exemples. Et le premier d'entre eux sera le plus banal qui soit, la *razo* de la chanson de l'alouette (70, 43) de Bernard de Ventadour dans le chansonnier Sg, fondée, on le sait, sur la fiction que le troubadour était épris d'Aliénor d'Aquitaine, désignée comme la duchesse de Normandie:

> E apelava la B[ernart] 'Alauzeta', per amor d'un cavalier que l'amava, e ella apelet lui 'Rai'. E un jorn venc le cavaliers a la duguessa e entret en la cambra. La dona, que'l vi, leva adonc lo pan del mantel e mes sobra'l col, e laissa cazer e[l] lieg. E B[ernart] vi tot, car una donzela de la domna li ac mostrat cubertamen; e per aquesta razo fes adonc la canso que dis:
>
> 'Quan vei l'alauzeta mover...'. (Boutière, p. 29)
>
> [Et Bernart l'appelait 'Alouette', à cause d'un chevalier qui l'aimait et qu'elle appelait 'Rayon'. Et, un jour, le chevalier vint auprès de la duchesse et entra dans la chambre. La dame, qui le vit, leva alors le pan de son manteau et le lui mit sur le cou; et elle se laissa choir sur le lit. Et Bernart vit tout, car une suivante de la dame le lui montra en cachette; et sur ce sujet, il fit alors la chanson qui dit:
>
> 'Quand je vois l'alouette agiter...'.]

Cette *razo* est traditionnellement considérée avec le plus grand mépris, et cela pour deux raisons.[12] La première est que, non seulement elle tire sa matière de la chanson qu'elle commente (ce qui est en soi tout à fait habituel), mais encore elle le laisse voir maladroitement: 'Il l'appelait Alouette à cause d'un chevalier qui l'aimait et qu'elle appelait Rayon'. En voilà, une raison! En quoi le fait qu'Aliénor appelle le chevalier Rayon explique-t-il que Bernard l'appelle Alouette? Pourquoi l'un des mots appelle-t-il l'autre? Quel rapport y a-t-il entre un rayon et une alouette? Aucun, sinon que les deux mots sont associés dans les deux premiers vers de la chanson.

La seconde raison qui déconsidère cette *razo* est plus fondamentale. La gloire de la chanson de l'alouette n'est pas usurpée. Sa première strophe est admirable: l'accumulation des éléments habituels de l'incipit printanier y est remplacée par cette image épurée, unique, de l'alouette à contre-jour, dans un rayon de soleil. A peine une image (on voit mal à contre-jour, et l'alouette est si petite – un point face au soleil), mais plutôt une sorte de représentation presque abstraite du mouvement. Et quel mouvement! Ce geste suicidaire – se laisser tomber par 'oubli de soi-même' – qui évoque immédiatement

---

[12] 'Cette razo n'est qu'un essai d'interprétation, fort maladroit, des trois premiers vers de la pièce: "Can vei l'alauzeta mover / De joi sas alas contra'l rai, / Que s'oblid'e's laissa chazer..."' (Boutière, *Biographies des troubadours*, p. 29).

pour le poète la petite mort de la jouissance amoureuse, où la raison s'abolit (c'est ce que saint Thomas d'Aquin reprochera à l'orgasme, même atteint dans des circonstances légitimes), et fait naître en lui une sorte de 'jalousie sexuelle' de tous ceux qu'il voit jouissant de leur amour. Là-dessus, la *razo* ne trouve rien de mieux à faire que d'inventer une histoire grotesque de petit jeu érotique entre Aliénor d'Aquitaine et son amant, tandis que le poète les épie par le trou de la serrure avec la complicité de la bonne. C'est pitoyable.

Soit. Mais la *razo* n'en a pas moins saisi l'essentiel, et elle sait dire l'essentiel. L'essentiel, c'est, précisément, la jalousie sexuelle et le voyeurisme: 'quelle envie me prend de quiconque *je vois jouissant*' (et que l'on songe, s'agissant du voyeurisme, au souhait, formulé ailleurs par Bernard, de 'la suivre dans la chambre où elle se déshabille'). Le commentaire que je viens de faire de la strophe correspond exactement à ce que suggère la *razo*. Elle ne dit pas autre chose. Mais au lieu de le dire sous la forme du commentaire critique, elle le dit en racontant une histoire. Elle n'analyse pas la poétique de la chanson, mais elle lui substitue une autre poétique – celle du récit – dont l'effet et le sens sont les mêmes.

Or, ce type de jalousie, de frustration, d'irritation de la sexualité par le voyeurisme et par la comparaison avec le sort d'un amant plus fortuné, voilà ce que les *razos* développent avec prédilection, et à juste titre, car ce n'est pas seulement le thème privilégié des troubadours, c'est la racine même de leur perception poétique du monde et de la présence du monde dans leur poésie.

Les exemples se pressent, moins éculés peut-être que celui de la *razo* de la chanson de l'alouette, tous cependant bien connus, car tout ce qui touche aux *vidas* et aux *razos* est familier. Mais ne quittons pas la *razo* de la chanson de l'alouette avant de l'avoir rapprochée d'une autre, celle de la chanson de Raimbaut de Vaqueiras 'Ja non cuidei vezer' (392, 20), dans l'interpolation propre au manuscrit P.[13] Raimbaut de Vaqueiras, fils d'un pauvre chevalier et devenu jongleur, est le protégé du marquis Boniface de Montferrat, qui l'équipe et le restaure dans son état de chevalier:

> Don ell s'enamoret de la seror del marques, qe avia nom ma dompna Biatrix, qe fo molher d'Enric del Carret. Et troba de lei mantas bonas chansos. E appellava la 'Bel Cavalier'.
>
> Et per aiso l'apella[va] enaisi, qe a En Rambautz segi aital aventura, qe pozia vezer ma dompna Biatrix qant el volia, sol q'ella fos en sa chambra, per un espiraill; don neguns no'n s'apercebia.
>
> Et un jor venc lo marques da cassar; et entret en la chambra et mez la soa spaza a costa d'un leit, et tornet s'en foras. Et ma dompna Biatrix remas en [la] chambra; et despoillet se son sobrecot et remas en gonnella. Et tollc la spaza et se la ceinz a lie de cavalier. Et tra[i]s la for del fuor et geta la en alt, et pres la en sa ma et menet se l'al bratz d'una part e d'autra

---

[13] M. L. Meneghetti rapproche fugitivement les deux textes, mais dans une perspective sensiblement différente de celle qui est suggérée ici (*Il pubblico dei trovatori*, p. 297).

de la spala [correction Boutière, ms. 'spaza']; et tornet la em fuer, et se la desceinz et tornet la a costeil del leit.
Et En Rambau[t]z de Vaqera[s] vezia tot so qe vos ai dich per lo spiraill. Don per aso l'apellet pois totas vez 'Bel Cavalier' en sas chansos, si com el dis en la premiera cobla d'aqesta chanson qe comenza aisi:
'Ja non cuidei vezer ...'. (Boutière, pp. 451–4)

[Raimbaut devint donc amoureux de la sœur du marquis, laquelle avait nom madame Béatrice, et fut l'épouse d'Enrico del Carretto. Il composa sur elle maintes bonnes chansons, et l'appelait 'Beau Cavalier'. Et voici pourquoi il l'appelait ainsi: Raimbaut eut cette bonne fortune qu'il pouvait voir madame Béatrice quand il voulait, pourvu qu'elle se trouvât dans sa chambre, par un soupirail. Et personne ne s'en apercevait.

Un jour le marquis revint de la chasse; il entra dans la chambre, déposa son épée auprès d'un lit, et sortit. Or madame Béatrice était restée dans la chambre; elle ôta son surcot et demeura en robe de dessous. Elle saisit alors l'épée et la ceignit, à la façon d'un chevalier. Puis elle la tira hors du fourreau et la brandit; elle la prit ensuite en main et la ramena jusqu'à son bras, de part et d'autre des épaules. Après quoi, elle la remit au fourreau, la déceignit et la replaça auprès du lit.

Et Raimbaut de Vaqueiras voyait par le soupirail tout ce que je vous ai dit. Voilà pourquoi, dans ses chansons, il l'appela toujours par la suite 'Beau Chevalier', comme il le dit dans le premier couplet de cette chanson qui débute ainsi:
'Je ne crus jamais voir le jour ...'.]

Selon son habitude, P cite ici dans son intégralité la première strophe de la chanson avant de poursuivre la *vida* de Raimbaut. Le lecteur peut donc constater que, si la dame aimée du troubadour est en effet désignée dans cette strophe par le *senhal* 'Bel Cavalier', rien ne permet de déceler la moindre allusion à la scène décrite par la *razo*, même en supposant qu'elle soumet le texte à la même torture que celle de la chanson de l'alouette. Le poète dit seulement que, lui qui était rebelle à l'amour, il a été séduit par 'la beauté, la jeunesse, le noble corps gracieux et les gais propos charmants de son Beau Chevalier'.[14] De cet éloge si général, si banal, la *razo* tire une anecdote à la fois innocente – pour autant qu'il soit innocent d'épier continuellement une dame dans sa chambre par un soupirail – et très érotique (il est inutile de s'appesantir sur les traits qui la rendent telle). Une anecdote tout entière fondée sur le voyeurisme. Raimbaut n'a pas de rival et ne tire que du plaisir du spectacle qu'il contemple. Pourtant, de la *razo* de la chanson de l'alouette à celle-ci, l'imagination érotique est la même, révélant l'excitation que l'on attend de cette poésie.

---

[14] Mas beutat et jovenz, / E˙l gentilz cors plagenz / E˙ill gai ditz plasenti[er] / De mon Bel Cavalier / M'a[n] fait privat d'estraing' (vv. 7–12) (Boutière, *Biographies des troubadours*, p. 452).

Mais passons à des exemples où l'on voit, de façon explicite, les *razos* rapporter les poèmes qu'elles commentent à des situations de frustration, de jalousie, d'excitation sexuelle liée à la jouissance de l'autre et, comme si les auteurs des *razos* avaient lu René Girard, de rivalité mimétique.

On sait que René Girard a, dans ses premiers ouvrages, élaboré la théorie du désir mimétique et de la rivalité mimétique à partir d'exemples littéraires, dont le plus caractéristique est celui de *L'Éternel mari* de Dostoïevski.[15] Le mari ne peut désirer sa femme que s'il la voit désirée par d'autres et que si le désir des autres confirme que le sien est justifié. Il expose donc sa femme aux regards d'autres hommes et excite leur concupiscence jusqu'à ce que l'inévitable se produise et qu'il soit trompé.

Cette histoire a un équivalent célèbre dans les *razos* à propos de Raimon de Miraval. Sa *vida*, conservée dans tous les principaux manuscrits (ABEHIKPR), le présente comme un arbitre des élégances et de la vie courtoise, recherché à ce titre par toutes les dames, qui veulent toutes être courtisées par lui sans qu'aucune lui accorde jamais rien.[16] Il n'a donc lui-même de valeur que comme objet mimétique: ce qui est désirable en lui, c'est le fait que les autres le désirent; ce n'est pas lui en tant que tel. Mais de son côté, il ne désire que les femmes désirées par d'autres, telle la *Loba*, La Louve de Pennautier, aimée de tous les hommes. Il le paie quand elle accorde ses faveurs au comte de Foix. Puis il s'éprend d'Azalaïs de Boissezon, qui l'agrée comme soupirant, mais rien de plus; il n'a alors de cesse qu'il ne fasse connaître partout sa bonne fortune:

> E fes de leis maintas bonas chanson, lauzan son pretz e sa valor e sa cortezia; e mes la en si gran honor que tuit li valen baro d'aquela encontrada entendion en ela: lo vescoms de Bezers e˙l coms de Toloza e˙l reis Peire d'Arago, als cals Miraval l'avia tan lauzada que˙l reis, senes vezer, n'era fort enamoratz e l'avia mandat sos mesatges e sas letras e sas joias; el eis moria de volontat de leis vezer. Don Miravals se penet que˙l reis la vengues vezer, e˙n fes una cotbla, en la chanso que ditz 'Ar ab la forsa del freis':
>
> S'a Lunmbertz corteja˙l reis,
> Per tostems er jois ab lui;
> E si tot s'es sobradreis,

---

[15] René Girard, *Dostoïevski, du double à l'unité* (Paris, 1963) et *Critique dans un souterrain* (Lausanne, 1976). Pour une élaboration de la théorie du désir et de la rivalité mimétiques voir aussi Girard, *La Violence et le sacré* (Paris, 1972) et *Des choses cachées depuis la fondation du monde* (Paris, 1978).

[16] Boutière, *Biographies des troubadours*, pp. 374–5.

> Per un be l'en venran dui:
> Que la cortezi'e˙l jais
> De la bella N'Alazais
> E˙l fresca colors e˙ill pel blon
> Faun tot lo setgle jauzion.

Don lo reis s'en venc en Albuges e a Lombertz per ma dona N'Alazais; e˙N Miravals venc ab lo rei, preguan lo qu'el li degues valer et ajudar ab ma dona N'Alazais. Fort fo ereubutz et onratz lo reis e vegutz volentiers per ma dona N'Alazais. E˙l reis ades que fo asetatz apres d'ela, si la preguet d'amor; et ella li dis ades de far tot so qu'el volia. Si que la nueit ac lo reis tot so que˙ill plac de leis. E l'endema fo saubut per tota la gen del castel e per tota la cort del rei. E˙N Miraval, que atendia esser ricx de joi per los precx del rei, auzit aquesta novella. Fo˙n tritz e dolens.

(Boutière, pp. 392–400)

[Et il l'exalta dans ses chansons et dans ses dires, autant qu'il put et sut le faire; et fit sur elle maintes bonnes chansons, célébrant son mérite, sa valeur et sa courtoisie; et il la mit en si grand honneur que tous les valeureux barons de cette contrée étaient épris d'elle: le vicomte de Béziers, le comte de Toulouse et le roi Pierre d'Aragon, auprès desquels Miraval l'avait tant célébrée que le roi, sans l'avoir vue, était très amoureux d'elle et lui avait envoyé des messagers, des lettres et des présents; et il mourait du désir de la voir. Aussi Miraval fit-il son possible pour que le roi vînt la voir; et il composa à ce sujet un couplet, dans la chanson qui dit 'Ar ab la forsa del freis':

> Si le roi fait sa cour à Lombers,
> pour toujours la joie sera avec lui;
> et, bien qu'il soit très habile,
> pour un bien, il en recueillera deux,
> car la courtoisie et la joie
> de la belle Azalaïs,
> sa fraîche couleur et ses cheveux blonds
> rendent tout le siècle joyeux.

Le roi s'en vint donc en Albigeois, à Lombers, pour voir madame Azalaïs; et Miraval vint avec le roi, le priant de vouloir bien le soutenir et l'aider auprès de madame Azalaïs. Le roi fut très fêté, honoré et reçu volontiers par la dame; et, dès qu'il fut assis auprès d'elle, il la pria d'amour; et elle lui dit aussitôt de faire tout ce qu'il voulait. Aussi, cette même nuit, le roi eut d'elle tout ce qui lui plut. Le lendemain, cela fut connu de tous les gens du château et de la cour du roi. Et Miraval, qui s'attendait à être riche de joies grâce aux prières du roi, apprit aussi la nouvelle. Il en fut triste et dolent.]

Il y a dans ce récit une contradiction criante entre l'intention avouée du poète (ménager une entrevue entre le roi d'Aragon et Azalaïs pour que le roi puisse plaider sa cause à lui, Miraval, et obtenir qu'elle lui accorde des faveurs tangibles) et le résultat prévisible de la démarche. Une contradiction d'autant plus grande que Miraval s'efforce par ses chansons d'éveiller l'amour du roi et que la strophe qui fonde la *razo* en est un exemple: le roi est invité à venir faire la cour à Azalaïs; le poète l'assure qu'il sera payé au centuple (ou au moins au double); il célèbre la beauté de la dame. Et enfin, dans le dernier vers, il proclame que ses charmes 'faun tot le setgle jauzion [font jouir le monde entier]': on n'est pas plus clair. La contradiction est telle qu'on soupçonne que le poète, dans sa chanson, joue effectivement et délibérément le rôle d'entremetteur et que la *razo* enrichit le poème d'une possibilité de souffrance qui n'y est pas, mais qui est la vérité cachée de ce genre de situation. Le poème n'a d'intérêt, de profondeur, de résonances, que s'il dissimule la situation de 'l'éternel mari'.

Là encore, le récit qui tient lieu de commentaire du poème met le doigt sur l'essentiel. L'essentiel, qui nourrit l'ensemble de la *vida* et des *razos* de Raimon de Miraval, que cette *razo* particulière a su deviner dans le poème et qu'elle met en valeur par le décalage même entre le poème et l'argument qu'elle développe, est que chacun ne peut jouir qu'en imaginant ce que serait la jouissance d'un autre à sa place, et que, naturellement, cette imagination est une occasion de souffrance. La vérité poétique de la chanson, c'est le récit de la *razo*.

Le cas est loin d'être isolé; en témoigne la *razo* de la chanson 167, 52 de Gaucelm Faidit. D'après sa *vida*, ce bourgeois d'Uzerche s'est fait jongleur après s'être ruiné aux dés; porté sur la nourriture et la boisson, il devint obèse; il épousa une femme de mauvaise vie (*soldadera*), belle et instruite, mais qui devint encore plus grosse que lui.[17] La *razo* de la chanson 'Si anc nuls hom per aver fin coratge', contenue dans E et P, nous dit que Gaucelm s'était épris de la vicomtesse Marguerite d'Aubusson, qui lui faisait des promesses, mais ne lui accordait rien, si ce n'est qu'une fois, au moment de prendre congé, elle souffrit qu'il lui baisât le cou. En réalité, elle aimait Hugues de Lusignan, fils d'Hugues le Brun, comte de la Marche, qui était un grand ami de Gaucelm Faidit. Je cite la suite:

> La dona si estava el castel d'Albuso, on ella no podia vezer N'Ugo de Lasigna ni far plazer; per qu'ela se fes malauta de mort e vodet se az anar a ma dona Sancta Maria de Rocamador en orazo. E mandet dire a N'Ugo de Lasigna que vengues a Uzercha, az un borc on estava Gauselms Faiditz, e que vengues a furt e que desmontes en l'alberc d'En Gauselm e que ela desmontaria en aquel alberc e˙ill faria plazer en dreg d'amor, et ensenhet li lo jorn qu'el hi degues venir. Quan N'Ugo auzit aquesta cauza, fo alegres e joios, e venc en l'alberc d'En Gauselm Faidit. La moiller d'En Gauselm, quant ela˙l vit, l'acuillit molt fort, et ab gran alegreza e en gran crezensa, si com el comandet. E la dona venc e desmontet laintre e trobet N'Ugo de Lasigna en l'alberc, rescost en la cambra on ella devia jazer. Et ella, quan l'ac trobat, fo alegra e joioza, et estet dos jorns aqui; e pueis ela s'en anet a Rocamador et el l'atendet tor que venc. E pueis estet autres dos jorns

---

[17] Boutière, *Biographies des troubadours*, p. 166.

quan fo venguda, e cascuna nueit jazion ensems ab gran alegreza et en gran solatz. E no tarzet gaire, quan s'en foron tornat, qu'En Gauselms venc, e sa moiller li comtet tot lo fait. Gauselms, quant ho auzit, fo si dolens qu'el volc morir per so qu'el crezia qu'ela no volgues be si no a lui. E per so qu'ela al sieu leit l'avia colgat, en fo el mais dolens; don el fes per aquesta razo une mala chanso, la cals comensa:

'Si anc nuls hom per aver fin coratge…'

si com vos auziretz. Et aquesta fo la derreira chanso qu'el fes.

(Boutière, pp. 180–4)

[La dame demeurait au château d'Aubusson, où elle ne pouvait voir Hugues de Lusignan, ni lui faire aucun plaisir. Elle fit semblant d'être mortellement malade et fit vœu d'aller prier Madame Sainte Marie de Rocamadour. Et elle fit dire à Hugues de Lusignan de venir à Uzerche – un bourg où habitait Gaucelm Faidit –, d'y venir furtivement et de descendre chez Gaucelm; elle y descendrait aussi et lui ferait plaisir en droit d'amour; et elle lui indiqua le jour qu'il devait y venir. Lorsque Hugues entendit cette nouvelle, il fut gai et joyeux, et se rendit là bas au jour fixé; et il descendit dans la maison de Gaucelm Faidit. La femme de Gaucelm, quand elle le vit, l'accueillit très cordialement, avec grande joie et en grand secret, comme il le demanda. Et la dame arriva et descendit au même endroit; elle trouva Hugues de Lusignan au logis, caché dans la chambre où elle devait coucher. Et lorsqu'elle l'eut trouvé, elle fut gaie et joyeuse et resta là deux jours; ensuite, elle se rendit à Rocamadour et Hugues l'attendit jusqu'à son retour. Et quand elle fut revenue, elle resta deux jours encore, et chaque nuit ils couchaient ensemble, au comble de la joie et du plaisir. Lorsqu'ils s'en furent allés, Gaucelm ne tarda guère à venir et sa femme lui conta toute l'affaire. Il en fut si triste qu'il voulut mourir, car il s'imaginait que la dame ne voulait du bien qu'à lui seul. Et ce qui le chagrina le plus, c'est qu'ils avaient couché dans son propre lit. Aussi fit-il, sur ce sujet, une 'chanson méchante' qui débute ainsi:

'Si jamais homme, pour avoir cœur fidèle…'

ainsi que vous entendrez. Et cette chanson fut la dernière qu'il fit.]

Il n'y aurait guère là qu'un sujet de fabliau sans l'extraordinaire raffinement de sadisme de la *razo*. Sadisme des amants, mais aussi sadisme – excusable – de la femme de Gaucelm, que la *razo* a l'habileté de ne pas commenter. Boutière, dans une note, se demande pourquoi la *razo* dit que cette chanson est la dernière. On est tenté de dire que c'est parce que Gaucelm Faidit, qui a connu tant de péripéties et de déconvenues amoureuses, comme le content les autres *razos*, ne peut cette fois survivre poétiquement à cet excès du poison de l'humiliation sexuelle qui, à dose raisonnable, est au contraire l'aliment de la poésie.

Les deux derniers exemples que je voudrais présenter brièvement sont peut-être les plus parlants. C'est celui de Pons de Chapteuil et, plus encore, celui de Guilhem de Balaun.

Selon la *razo* des chansons 375, 20 et 18, dans les chansonniers E, P et Sg, Pons de Chapteuil aimait, comme l'a déjà dit sa *vida*, Azalaïs de Mercœur, femme du comte Odilon de Mercœur, auvergnat comme lui, et fille de Bernard d'Anduze, et il en était aimé. Voulant éprouver son amour, il feignit d'en aimer une autre, la femme du comte de Marseille.[18] Azalaïs de Mercœur, dépitée, ne voulut plus entendre son nom ni demander de ses nouvelles. Pons fit la cour à d'autres dames de Provence, puis, voyant qu'Azalaïs ne lui envoyait ni messager ni lettre, il se repentit de sa folle conduite. Il la supplia de lui pardonner, mais elle ne voulut rien entendre, malgré les chansons 'Si com celui qu'a pro de valedors (375, 20) [Comme celui qui ne manque pas de secours]' et 'Qui per nessi cuidar / Fai trop gran faillimen, / A dan li deu tornar (375, 18) [Celui qui, par une sotte opinion, / commet une très grande faute, / doit en subir un dommage].'

Bien que la seconde de ces chansons mentionne plus explicitement une faute du poète, la *razo* se fonde probablement sur la troisième strophe de la première: au cœur de cette chanson dédiée à Folquet de Marseille, désigné dans la tornada sous le *senhal* 'Plus Leial', qui se plaint de la façon la plus traditionnelle de la rigueur de la dame, cette strophe fait en effet allusion au fait que le poète aurait fait semblant de pratiquer le vagabondage sentimental. Mais, malgré une apparente analogie, il n'y a là rien de commun avec le calcul des plaisirs un peu sordide qui fonde la célèbre *razo* de Rigaut de Barbezieux[19] et celle de Gaucelm Faidit, Marie de Ventadour et Audiarde de Malemort.[20] Pons joue avec le feu jusqu'à ce qu'il s'inflige une inévitable souffrance. La cruauté de la dame, lieu commun des chansons, est donc vue fort lucidement par la *razo* comme le résultat recherché d'un jeu érotique et masochiste dont le poète est sans cesse tenté de repousser les limites.

Ce jeu morbide est poussé à l'extrême dans la *razo* de Guilhem de Balaun, et surtout il y est combiné avec cet élément plus fondamental encore que les *razos*, nous l'avons vu, sont si habiles à mettre en lumière: le désir et la jouissance, soit par procuration, soit par comparaison avec le désir et la jouissance de l'autre, accompagnés de toutes les souffrances, de toutes les excitations et de toutes les irritations perverses qui en découlent.

Cette longue *razo* de la chanson 208, 1, 'Lo vers mou mercejan vas vos [En criant merci, je vous envoie ce vers]', est conservée sous deux formes assez différentes, bien que l'histoire soit substantiellement la même, dans les manuscrits H et R.[21] Elle est donc assez difficile à citer, et je me contente de reproduire ici la traduction de Boutière, qui suit le texte de H en ajoutant les passages, parfois capitaux, propres à R.[22]

---

[18] Boutière, *Biographies des troubadours*, pp. 314–15.
[19] *Razo* (P) de 421, 2, 'Atresi com l'olifanz' (*ibid.*, pp. 153–5).
[20] *Razo* (E, N2, R, p) de 167, 59, 'Tant ai sofert lonjamen greu afan', et de 167, 43, 'No m'alegra chan ni critz / D'auzelh mon fel cor engres' (*ibid.*, pp. 170–3).
[21] *Ibid.*, pp. 321–8.
[22] *Ibid.*, pp. 328–31.

Ce qui frappe est moins l'idée baroque de Guilhem de Balaun (vérifier si l'amour est vraiment plus doux après une brouille et une réconciliation) que son entêtement suicidaire, que son acharnement à faire mal et à se faire mal, qui n'a rien à voir avec l'idée initiale puisqu'il en empêche la réalisation, et qui ne peut se résoudre qu'en se cristallisant, en *s'incarnant* dans la douleur physique, celle de l'ongle arraché:

> Elle [la dame] acceptait de tirer vengeance et de pardonner; mais elle exigeait que la vengeance fût telle: que Guillem s'arrachât l'ongle du doigt le plus long (*le plus court*) et vînt le lui apporter, *avec une chanson où il se blâmerait de la folie qu'il avait commise. [...] En entendant qu'il aurait son pardon, Guillem fut très joyeux [...] Il fit sur-le-champ mander un maître-chirurgien, se fit lier le doigt et arracher l'ongle, en souffrant une grande douleur. Il composa son 'vers',* monta à cheval et [...] se rendit à Jaujac, auprès de madame Gullelma. [...] *elle pardonna à Guillem, en le baisant et l'embrassant. Il lui dit sa chanson, et elle l'écouta joyeusement. Ils s'aimèrent ensuite beaucoup plus qu'auparavant.* (Boutière, p. 331)

Presque tous ces exemples peuvent être lus dans la perspective de E. Köhler: le troubadour de rang inférieur est cocufié par le grand seigneur. C'est la lecture de M. L. Meneghetti.[23] Mais les *razos* elles-mêmes ne tirent pas cette conclusion, qui pourtant saute aux yeux, et dont elles ne peuvent pas ignorer qu'elle saute aux yeux. Ce qu'elles disent est d'un autre ordre, et peut-être plus profond.

La poésie des troubadours, dit-on, est une poésie du désir. Soit. Mais toute poésie d'amour est une poésie du désir. La poésie des troubadours a ceci de particulier: qu'elle est une poésie du désir sous le regard de l'autre et une poésie du désir de la jouissance de l'autre. Une poésie du désir sous le regard de l'autre: c'est ce qui fonde cette poésie de la discrétion revendiquée, démentie par cette revendication même, qui ne peut être qu'un aveu affiché. C'est ce qui explique l'insistance sur les *lauzengiers*, c'est ce qui rend le mari nécessaire. Une poésie du désir de la jouissance de l'autre: c'est ce qui est au cœur de ce sommet de la littérature française du Moyen Âge qu'est, dans le poème de Thomas, le grand monologue de Tristan se demandant s'il doit épouser Iseut aux Blanches Mains (il y a une inégalité entre Iseut la Blonde et moi, puisqu'elle est obligée de coucher avec Marc et qu'elle ne peut s'empêcher de jouir avec lui, tandis que moi, je ne couche avec personne; je vais épouser Iseut aux Blanches Mains pour savoir l'effet que cela fait et pour éprouver la même chose qu'Iseut la Blonde, pour rétablir l'égalité entre nous).

Décrire une situation où le troubadour est cocufié par le grand seigneur, ce n'est pas faire de la sociologie, c'est utiliser une situation qui va de soi (le

---

[23] Meneghetti, *Il pubblico dei trovatori*, par exemple p. 196, p. 240 *sq. et passim*.

grand seigneur gagne toujours) pour faire sentir l'exacerbation d'une sexualité frustrée, humiliée, jalouse, taraudée par le voyeurisme. La vérité ultime de la poésie du désir, ce ne sont pas les conditions sociales; la vérité que l'on fait jaillir en s'aidant des conditions sociales, c'est celle de la poésie du désir. Que l'on songe à la *vida* de Peirol: Dauphin d'Auvergne favorise ses amours avec sa sœur, Sail de Claustra, puis en devient jaloux et use de son autorité sur le troubadour, son vassal, 'pauvre chevalier', pour les séparer: 'E l'amors de la dompna e de Peirol monta tan que'l Dalfins s'engellosi d'ella, car crezet qu'elle li fezes plus que convengues ad ella; e parti Peirol de si e'l loniet, e no'l vesti ni l'armet (Boutière, pp. 303 et 305) [Et l'amour de la dame et de Peirol atteignit un si haut degré que le Dauphin devint jaloux d'elle, estimant qu'elle lui accordait plus qu'il ne convenait. Il écarta Peirol de lui et l'éloigna, et cessa de le vêtir et de l'armer].'

Dauphin d'Auvergne trouve que sa sœur en fait trop pour le pauvre chevalier Peirol: réaction de classe. Mais 's'engellosi d'ella' est curieux: il n'éprouve pas d'amour incestueux pour sa sœur, bien sûr, mais il semble jaloux de la jouissance de Peirol, ou de la jouissance des amants, il 'envie celui qu'il voit jouissant', dirait Bernard de Ventadour.[24] Que l'on songe à l'aube de Guiraut de Bornelh, où l'ami veille sur les amours de son ami et l'avertit que l'aube approche et que les amants doivent se séparer: c'est une vision idéalisée, apaisée, qui nie cette jalousie, mais qui du coup la confirme – et l'ami intervient tout de même pour presser la séparation.[25]

Tout cela, les *razos* le disent, elles mettent les points sur les i, là où les poèmes sont évanescents et vagues. Et ainsi, elles jouent réellement leur rôle de commentaires critiques. En injectant l'anecdote dans la chanson, elles font apparaître que la chanson en elle-même est dénuée d'anecdote, qu'elle est lisse, qu'elle paraît s'inscrire perpétuellement dans le topos de la plainte amoureuse et qu'elle ne s'en évade ou n'y met du ragoût que sournoisement, mais d'une façon qui n'échappe pas à la *razo*, heureuse d'en rajouter. Elles font ainsi ressortir par contraste ce qu'est une poétique qui exclut le récit. En s'opposant aux chansons, en se posant en complément nécessaire aux chansons, elles développent sous forme narrative les implications d'une poétique, mais mettent aussi en valeur ce qu'est une poétique d'où le récit est absent.

C'est en ce sens qu'elles sont réellement porteuses d'un savoir sur la poésie des troubadours.

---

[24] Ou alors il faudrait aussi commenter le fait que c'est le frère de Béatrix de Montferrat, non son mari, qui entre dans sa chambre au retour de la chasse et y laisse son épée, dans la *razo* de Raimbaut de Vaqueiras!

[25] 'Reis glorios, verais lums e clartatz', 242, 64. Adolf Kolsen, *Sämtliche Lieder des Troubadours Giraut de Bornelh*, 2 tomes (Halle, 1910–35), I, p. 342. Ruth Verity Sharman, *The 'Cansos' and 'Sirventes' of the Trouvadour Giraut de Bornelh: A Critical Edition* (Cambridge, 1989).

6

A Master, a *Vilain*, a Lady and a Scribe: Competing for Authority in a Late Medieval Translation of the *Ars amatoria*

DEBORAH MCGRADY

Magister, auctor, prince des poètes: such are the illustrious titles accorded to Ovid during the Middle Ages. From the eleventh and twelfth centuries, recognized as the *ætas ovidiana*, to the sacred sixteenth-century renaming of his *Metamorphoses* as the *Bible des poètes*, the period testifies to Ovid's prominent role in both scholastic and vernacular realms. His early dominance was assured by the frequent usage of both the *Ars amatoria* and the *Remedia* to teach Latin and rhetoric. The addition to these works of glosses on topics ranging from grammar to ethics only enhanced Ovid's aura of authority. His status expanded to the vernacular realm, where so-called *fin'amors* depended on him for guidance in appropriate behaviors and practices. And yet, behind this grand narrative of Ovid's medieval dominance, so often reiterated by scholars, hides another account of the master's reception.

As Peter Allen argues, by the mid-thirteenth century, a growing ecclesiastic concern for Ovid's negative influence led to the reassessment of the master's role in society. Consequently the *Ars amatoria* eventually disappeared from classroom instruction and even from library shelves, as the 1338 Sorbonne catalogue indicates. So insidious was Ovid believed to be that by the fifteenth century he was purged from school handbooks, which now promoted the *auctores octo morales* from which Ovid was excluded.[1] Nevertheless, Ovid's rejection by the institution was countered by a fervent and sustained following in the vernacular. The best-known example of this appropriation concerns the *Ovide moralisé*, where an ethical rereading assured the master a renewed position of respect. Preceding this work, however, came a flurry of translations of the *Ars amatoria* that proposed a more aggressive engagement with the master. These mediated versions of Ovid often docu-

---

[1] Peter Allen, *The Art of Love: Amatory Fiction from Ovid to the* Romance of the Rose (Philadelphia, 1992), p. 56.

ment a critical gaze cast not only on the precepts expressed in the work but on the authority commonly afforded the master.

The impact of these translations on Ovid's later reception can be detected well into the fifteenth century, where simple reference to the *Ars amatoria* had the effect of placing Ovid in a particularly vulnerable situation. Take for instance Christine de Pizan's reflections on Ovid as recorded in the *Livre de la Cité des dames*, where the narrator expresses her astonishment that Ovid should be given the title of 'entre les poetes le plus souverain [the most sovereign of poets]' when his *Ars amatoria* as well as the *Remedia* did such a great disservice to women. Christine strips Ovid of his status as a master by recalling accusations of the debauchery that led to his castration and banishment in his own time as further justification for a new exile.[2] Where Christine sought to expel Ovid from the pantheon of writers, her contemporary Eustache Deschamps simply required that he share his fame with those who surpassed him in talent, such as the fourteenth-century poet and composer Guillaume de Machaut, of whom Deschamps writes: 'Machaut – noble poete et faiseur renommé, / Plus qu'Ovide vray remede d'amours [Machaut – noble poet and renowned writer, / More than Ovid a true remedy to love].'[3] Entertaining the question whether Ovid truly merited his formidable status, both Deschamps and Christine took advantage of a strong undercurrent of literary criticism that had, by this point, openly debated the master's authority as well as the love ethic long associated with him. It is telling that both writers are identified as having read the *Ars amatoria* in the same translation, a version singled out by scholars for its transgressive treatment of the original text.[4]

This version, the *Art d'amours en prose*, has only lately attracted serious scholarship that endeavors to rectify Gaston Paris's severe judgment of the work as presenting a 'singulier mélange de cynicisme et de gaucherie'.[5] Paris's remarks refer to the wordiness of the translation as well as to the integration of elaborate expository material in the form of an academically inspired prologue and abundant glossing. These glosses contain both expected commentary – paraphrase, clarification, and application of ideas – and unexpected, from digressions to refutations of Ovid. In each case, the commentary draws on supplementary material to reinforce its argument, but whereas convention dictates that supporting matter be drawn from the *auctores* to bolster the great *auctor*, the *Art d'amours en prose* freely intermingles the

---

[2] Maureen Cheney Curnow, 'The *Livre de la cité des dames* of Christine de Pisan: A Critical Edition', 2 vols, Ph.D. diss. (Vanderbilt University, 1975), I, ix.

[3] *Œuvres complètes d'Eustache Deschamps*, ed. Le Marquis de Queux de Saint-Hilaire, 11 vols (Paris, 1878), *ballade* ccccxlvii, vv. 3–4.

[4] Concerning Deschamps' familiarity with this translation, see Queux de Saint-Hilaire, vol. XI, 181; and on Christine, Marilynn Desmond, *Ovid's Art and the Wife of Bath: The Ethics of Erotic Violence* (New York, 2006).

[5] Gaston Paris, 'Chrétien Legouais et autres traducteurs et imitateurs d'Ovide au moyen âge,' *Histoire littéraire de la France*, 29 (1885), 489–97.

occasional maxim of Cato, Valerius Maximus and Solomon with aphorisms of the *vilain*, lyric complaints of ladies, and summaries of troubled romances. In all, the 112 glosses in Books I and II integrate 228 vernacular citations.

The work of its most recent editor, Bruno Roy, has revealed that the *Art d'amours en prose* was produced in two stages. The translation and commentary of Books I and II were first produced by an anonymous writer in the first half of the thirteenth century, while Book III was added later in the century by another anonymous translator.[6] Roy's edition sets the stage for new research that has focused especially on the relationship linking the learned text to the popular vernacular. These various studies allude to the threat that the glosses hold for the master text. For Ardis Butterfield, the increasing frequency with which lyric refrains appear in the glosses, eventually resulting in complete dialogues constructed of refrains, threatens to displace Ovid's voice as his words are overpowered by the masses singing in the margins.[7] Michèle Gally, on the other hand, offers a more positive reading, contending that these lyric citations as well as the proverbs enclosed in the glosses 'medievalize' Ovid, thereby assuring his continued vitality.[8] Gally's conclusions contrast sharply with those of the work's recent English translator, Lawrence Blonquist, who comments that, in comparison to the lively glosses, the now flattened prose of Ovid's work presents the master as pedantic, overly serious, and lacking the humor and cynicism that previously distinguished him.[9] In all cases, scholars speak of the challenges to Ovid's authority in the *Art d'amour en prose* as an unexpected and possibly unintended repercussion of aggressive mediating strategies. I contend, however, that the translator-commentator deliberately benefited from Ovid's problematic status in thirteenth-century France to address in his original rendition of the master text issues ranging from the ethical problems of *fin'amors* to evolving notions of vernacular authority, authorship, and reader responsibility. Using the *Ars amatoria* as a catalyst, the translator-commentator confronts established binaries that pitted the *auctor* against the *acteur*, Latin against vernacular, prose against poetry, learned against popular. Through its aggressive engagement with expectations, this complex work speaks to the Bourdesian notion that rigid social structures based on dichotomous distinctions can become the tools for constructing

---

[6] Bruno Roy, *L'Art d'amours. Traduction et commentaire de l'*Ars amatoria *d'Ovide* (Leiden, 1974). This study sets aside discussion of Book III by a second translator. For studies of that addition, see Roy, 13–16, and Michèle Gally, *L'intelligence de l'amour d'Ovide à Dante: Arts d'aimer et poésie au Moyen Âge* (Paris, 2005), esp. pp. 95–8.

[7] Ardis Butterfield, *Poetry and Music in Medieval France: From Jean Renart to Guillaume de Machaut* (Cambridge, 2002).

[8] See Gally, *L'intelligence de l'amour*, p. 62.

[9] *L'Art d'amours (The Art of Love)*, trans. Lawrence B. Blonquist (New York and London, 1987), xi–xii, xiv.

alternative social arrangements.[10] That these dichotomies are based on arbitrary contentions ultimately serves as an invitation to counterattacks, role reversals, and topsy-turvy viewpoints, just as we see in the *Art d'amours en prose*.

A brief comparison of the five extant thirteenth-century translations of the *Ars amatoria* reveals numerous shared traits among these otherwise distinct texts that document efforts to adapt Ovid to medieval social and literary expectations. Three of the five translations are identifiable by their authors' name: Maistre Elie, Jacques d'Amiens, and Guiart. The two remaining works, *La Clef d'amours* and the *Art d'amours en prose*, are anonymous.[11] The first collective characteristic concerns efforts to remain faithful to the source while facilitating medieval reception of Ovidian concepts through linguistic as well as contextualized adaptation. For this reason, Maistre Elie replaces the Roman theatre, previously designated as the ideal locale for meeting women, with the medieval church, now identified as the locus of seduction *par excellence*. Modernizing Ovid also entails adapting the master's message to contemporary concerns. For example, Jacques d'Amiens interrupts Ovid to record imaginary dialogues in which courtly conversation is modulated to the lover's prey, whether a simple bourgeoise or a noble lady. Both the *Art d'amours en prose* and the *Clef d'amours* turn to proverbs, and in the former case vernacular song, to give the work a contemporary voice counterbalancing Ovid's discourse. The textual cohabitation of the learned master and his modern counterparts affects both form and content in the *Art d'amours en prose*. Here Ovid's learned status is expressed through the use of prose, the oft-identified discourse of truth, to translate the master text, while framing glosses serve as repositories for contemporary voices recorded most often in poetic form. All of these translations emphasize the work's latent misogyny through first the exclusion of Book III, which addresses women, and then the vivid enhancement of Ovid's already unflattering portrait of women. Finally, an exaggerated binary system shapes each translation. The *auctor*, although now translated into the vernacular, retains an aura of authority contrasted with the coarse talk of the translators and other contemporary characters. In the case of the *Art d'amours en prose*, the use of prose and the incorporation of glosses enhance this distinction.

The survival of these works in fourteenth- and fifteenth-century copies attests to their long-term success. The *Clef d'amours*'s popularity continued well into the sixteenth century, with early printed versions of the work

---

[10] Bourdieu develops this idea in *La Distinction: critique sociale du jugement* (Paris, 1979). He discusses the specific instability of cultural capital and the ability to undermine it through criticism in *Choses dites* (Paris, 1987), p. 131.

[11] This list excludes lost translations, such as the missing version Chrétien de Troyes claims to have produced, and partial translations, as one could describe the *Roman de la Rose*.

produced in Paris, Geneva and Antwerp. But it is the *Art d'amours en prose* that appears to have enjoyed particular success in late medieval France. Fifteenth-century records testify to its dissemination at competing courts as well as among different social classes. Multiple copies are listed in the inventories of the king of France and the duke of Burgundy, in addition to copies linked with the duc de Berry, a member of the lesser nobility in Dauphiné, and a member of Parliament.[12]

That the *Art d'amours en prose* enjoyed such success surprises the modern reader, given that the other available translations were more lively, pithy, and engaging. In contrast the lengthy and frequent added glosses in this version demand careful reading and the often enigmatic nature of the commentaries requires thoughtful analysis. Even a scholastic reader would have likely been disappointed with the disposal of traditional learned topics to address instead the presumed needs and interests of a lay reader. To accommodate a lay audience, issues such as Ovid's rhetorical and poetic skills, as well as reflection on the ethical significance of his stories, give way to readings that address general comprehension. This added information ranges from fuller development of mythological references and allusions to ancient Roman customs, succinct summaries of Ovid's discourse, and/or contemporary exempla that enhance Ovid's message.[13] If in the first two instances the commentary defers to the master text, the last category of glosses does just the opposite. Rather than surround Ovid with learned writings to bolster his aura of authority, this commentary introduces examples from vernacular poetry, song, and proverbs – sources whose status as lesser works effectively dissipates Ovid's power. Moreover, far from deferring to the master text, these perceived inferior compositions introduce conflicting viewpoints expressed by wily *vilains*, dissatisfied and lascivious ladies, jaundiced *jongleurs*, and fast talkers or *bons barateurs*.

As already mentioned, thirteenth-century French vernacular translations of Ovid often turned to contemporary dialogue to enliven the master's text. But no version can compare to the *Art d'amours en prose*, where the now prosified or de-lyricized Ovidian text serves as a backdrop for lyric voices that are emphatically bawdy, populist and, frequently, conflicting. For example, when Ovid claims that women can easily be seduced with praise for their beauty and promises of beautiful things, the commentator interrupts in a very different key. For him, female beautification leads to unadulterated narcissism and ultimately discourages interest in men. The commentator confirms

---

[12] Only four copies are extant. They are Modena, Biblioteca Estense, MS y.G.3.20; Paris, Arsenal, MS 2741; Brussels, Bibliothèque Royale, MS 10988; Paris, BnF, MS fr. 881. For further manuscript details, see Roy, pp. 19–24.

[13] Compare with common topics covered in glossed Latin copies: Ralph J. Hexter, *Ovid and Medieval Schooling. Studies in Medieval School Commentaries on Ovid's Ars amatoria, Epistulae ex Ponto, and Epistulae Heroidum* (Munich, 1986).

this harsh reading by evoking the scene of women admiring themselves while intoning their refusal to accept just any lover: 'Ce ne sont pas bras a vilain dormir; Ja n'y dormira! [These are not arms where a peasant will sleep; never will he sleep here!].'[14] Later, when Ovid assures his male readers that they will triumph in seduction because women are easily deceived by false tears, the commentator counters that women typically mock their weepy-eyed suitors with their emasculating taunts: 'Vous ne me savés aimer, Vilain mal apris; Vous me le devés faire dix fois ou douze la nuit! (lines 1948–50) [You don't know how to love me, you uneducated peasant; you must be able to do it to me ten or twelve times a night!].' According to the commentator, rather than fall for smooth talkers, women attend to their own sexual gratification and consciously select their men based on these needs. Along with disputing Ovid's presentation of women as easily falling for men's seduction, the commentator expresses concern at Ovid's training men in deception. He laments that trickery is antithetical to man's character whereas it comes naturally to women. He further specifies that, once learned, this behavior should never be used against fellow man but reserved for trapping the greatest deceivers, women (lines 1443–56, 1883–94, 1896–1905, 2205–22, 2700–5, 2715–19). Suggesting that even Ovid cannot truly teach deception to the honest man, the commentator offers important additional assistance when he advises his male audience to pilfer courtly poetry and parrot the seductive discourse of the successful 'jouvencel amoureux' and the 'bons barateurs'. In these instances, the commentator fills his work with generic lines of courtly verse concerning women's beauty and men's claims of undying love for ready memorization and reuse (e.g., lines 1161–4, 2014–16, 2056–64, 2768–71, 2788–803, 2834–6, 2848–54, 2896–900). He accompanies these refrains with words of encouragement for his readers who are urged to pretend ('faire semblant') that they really will die if their love is unreciprocated (lines 1159–63).[15]

These representative examples vividly illustrate the commentator's usage of vernacular voices to challenge the master, his text, and eventually the courtly discourse he is said to have inspired. The commentator achieves this *tour de force* by countering Ovid's analysis of men's and women's behaviors with poetic evidence to the contrary. Where Ovid celebrates women's naivety, the commentator chooses lyric samples in which the truth of women's character rises as they sing together about their true feelings. Seemingly doubting Ovid's promise to teach men the art of seduction, the commentator advises them to consult more qualified lay masters. In his final analysis, the trans-

---

[14] Roy, *L'Art d'amours*, lines 1848–51. All references to this work will adopt the line numbering proposed by Roy. All English translations are my own.

[15] For further details on this topic, see Deborah McGrady, 'Maîtriser Ovide: Exemple d'une traduction de l'*Ars amatoria* à la fin du Moyen Âge', in *Ovide métamorphosé: les lecteurs médiévaux d'Ovide*, ed. Laurence Harf-Lancner, forthcoming.

lator-commentator dramatically reverses Ovid's assessment, redefining women as cunning and men as naïve. In a further exquisite turn of events, our commentator rejects contemporary binary views by identifying poetry as both the vehicle of hidden truths about deceptive women and a means for men to acquire the interpretative as well as linguistic skills needed to reassert control. Prose, on the other hand, becomes the conduit through which the faulty logic of a questionable master is exposed. Ovid's now prosified text proves obscure and false whereas poetry becomes transparent; the master emerges as naïve and his students – from the *jongleur* and the *barateur* to our translator – are revealed as perceptive. With these reversals, the *Art d'amours en prose* orchestrates a troubling clash of high and low culture and steers the audience to doubt the master text and favor instead its supposed subordinates, understood, in this case, as both the commentary that should exist to serve the master text and the enclosed lyric citations traditionally considered as offshoots of the same text.

As the commentary plays with established binaries pitting the learned against the popular and prose against lyric, it also invites reconsideration of the role of proverbs. Like lyric refrains, proverbs introduce a cast of characters that openly challenge the master text. Mixing the words of Cato and Solomon with those of the *vilain*, the commentary blurs the boundaries between learned and popular. At the same time it introduces a dramatic distinction between the lyric as a medium in which men and women reveal deception and the proverb where only men speak in frank terms. And yet, when our commentator pairs Ovid's advice not to dismiss too quickly old women as sexual conquests with the *vilain*'s truism that 'du poivre qui est noir fait on meilleur saveur que du pois qui est blanc et bel (lines 395–6) [one finds greater flavor in black pepper than in pepper that is white and pure]', it is Ovid who resorts to sparse language and the *vilain* who provides a poetic analogy to decipher. Here the common proverb, not the weighty text of a master, shocks the audience into a moment of poetic meditation. Such interpretative demands require readers not only to decipher the hidden significance of seemingly banal lyric and proverbial citations in the *Art d'amours*, but to re-evaluate a series of binaries structuring literary discourse, chief among them the privileged position accorded to Ovid over his vernacular counterparts.

Rather than exemplifying the aura commonly associated with annotation, the commentary in the *Art d'amours en prose* produces an alternative narrative that denies all but the most determined reader the chance to locate Ovid in this work. The commentary provides a space for different vernacular communities to counter the master. Ironically, the interlaced vernacular fragments generate a more cohesive commentary on sexual relations than the fragmented but complete vernacular translation of Books I and II of the *Ars amatoria*. Preparing his audience for the unconventional encounter with the so-called master, the translator announces in his prologue a radical reversal of expectations:

Je, qui la moralité et la sentence de ce livre translater vueil de latin en françois, fais assavoir a tous ceulx qui le liront que se ie vousisse, je l'eüsse plus ententivement exposé et attrait; mais science ne vault riens que chacun scet et puet sçavoir et regarder, car quant les mos sont obscurs, on s'arreste plus tost dessus pour savoir que c'est a dire; lors quant on y a pensé, si scet on que les mos et les paroles vallent et poisent. (lines 21–7)

[I who want to translate from Latin into French the morality and significance of this book want it known to all who will read it that, had I wanted, I could have more diligently exposed and developed it, but knowledge is worth nothing when everyone knows, can know, and can examine it. For when words are obscure, one lingers more readily over them to know what is said; for, when one has thought about it, one understands the value and weight of words and ideas.]

Openly rejecting the role of mediator and arguing instead for his responsibility to retain a level of obscurity and secrecy, our translator assigns to readers the obligation to decipher the work. To discover the truth hidden within, we must 'regarder' and 's'arrester' or linger over obscure, weighty words – 'les paroles ... poisent'. The translator-commentator's frequent revelation that the songs of women and the sayings of elderly men contain deeper meaning than initially expected primes the reader to recognize that vernacular insertions merit as much attention as the master text – if not more.

The physical fragmentation of the source text contributes to the instability of the translation and of Ovid in general. On numerous occasions, the commentator, whose conventional responsibility would be to break the master work into discrete parts that are then elucidated, chooses instead to interrupt Ovid in mid-sentence, thereby leaving ideas undeveloped and displaced, while the aside is privileged (e.g., lines 1112–18). This frequent disruption of Ovid's train of thought is exacerbated a third of the way through the translation when a dramatic role-reversal redefines the relationship between master text and commentary. As early as gloss xxxvii in Book I, the commentator abandons his expected subordinate position *after* Ovid, and instead preempts the discussion by announcing Ovid's point in advance of the master (lines 807–27). In some instances, without abandoning the *texte* (Ovid's space) for the *glose* (the acceptable outlet for his interventions), the commentator interjects in mid-sentence to point out that a topic has already been discussed in an earlier gloss: 'Il s'envola, lui et son fils, *si comme nous avons dit cy avant es gloses* (line 2308, emphasis added) [He flew away, he and his son, *just as we said before in the glosses*].' Eventually, the commentator goes so far as to take ownership of Ovid's text. Appropriation first appears when repetition in Ovid's discourse provokes the commentator to interrupt with reference to earlier passages that discussed the same issue. Thus when Ovid lingers once too often on the issue of jealousy, our commentator interrupts to point out 'c'est ailleurs prouvé la ou il dit ou je vous ay parlé de jalousie, car je di que ... (lines 1604–5) [This is proven elsewhere, there where he discusses and I spoke to you of jealousy, for I say that ...]'. By the second half of Book II, these efforts to negotiate ownership between Ovid and the commentator are fully abandoned. It becomes common to see glosses dramatically reduced to single, surprisingly authoritative, statements, such as 'De ceste mateier nous avons assés parlé cy avant (lines 2123–4) [On this matter we have sufficiently spoken above]' or even more authoritarian, 'je t'ay dit autresfoiz (line 2579) [I told you before]'. In other instances, as Butterfield observes, Ovid 'recedes into the distance' as the density and complexity of citations in the commentary create alternative narratives.[16]

Having already been prepared for a radical reversal of expectations in the prologue, readers discover over the course of the *Art d'amours en prose* that glosses obscure rather than reveal, poetry serves as gloss rather than the subject of glossing, translators provoke rather than mediate, and readers seek out hidden truths rather than passively learn from the *auctor* or the *magister*. In this respect, this work overturns the authority associated with the scholastic world, its privileged discourse and its glossing practices. This disruption is achieved first by dismantling the dominant structure through vernacularization. Even the decision to render Ovid in prose weakens the master, because it strips him of his rhetorical skills and dilutes his humor and cynicism. Then the work encloses the translation in glosses where the lively voices of a competing vernacular culture ultimately sap rather than enhance the work of authority. Finally the *Art d'amours en prose* constructs a new system in which the commentator, the *villain*, and the *jongleur* use this text alongside popularized platitudes regarding women to reveal truths not even known by the presumed master.

While other thirteenth-century translations of the *Ars amatoria* fell into disuse, the *Art d'amour en prose* enjoyed continued popularity. The reasons for its success can only be conjectured, but they surely include the fact that this version provides a relatively faithful translation of Ovid's work, that the glosses are rich in information shedding light on Ovid as well as on his extended influence, and, finally, that the complex architectonics complement the late medieval penchant for hybrid compositions while answering the expectations of the prosification and translation campaigns that occupied late medieval francophone culture.

For the book producers, this work required creative thinking on the level of the *mise en page* and the *mise en œuvre* to take full advantage of its richness. The four extant fifteenth-century versions testify to the book producers' active engagement as intermediary readers in the revival of the text for a

---

[16] Butterfield, *Poetry and Music*, p. 257.

new generation.[17] Not only do they take full advantage of advancements in layout but, in at least two of the four copies, there is evidence that the work served as a vehicle for promoting the vernacular in a period when the literary institution was just beginning to open up its pantheon to accommodate the vernacular writer.[18]

All four copies take advantage of the book medium to shape reception of this complex text. Three of the four copies call attention to the work's value by reproducing it as a single bound volume. All four codices introduce rubrics to distinguish between text and gloss, sometimes using red ink to set the extratextual material apart from the surrounding writing. The most innovative *mise en page* is in Bibliothèque de l'Arsenal, MS 2741. Here text and gloss are further distinguished through the use of different script, and marginal notation identifies each vernacular insertion by its generic form.[19] Nevertheless, by adopting a linear system in which gloss and source text share column space rather than framing Ovid with annotations, every copy accentuates an already difficult reading experience that demands shifting between the different narrative levels. Moreover, revealing the challenges of navigating the work in this intermediary stage of reception, each copy introduces errors, either by misidentifying different parts of the text, by leaving out passages, by fusing text and gloss in a single entry, or by failing to insert rubrics when necessary.

Although MS 2741 documents, in its physical form, special interest in the vernacular insertions, BnF, MS fr. 881 is unique in its insistence on placing the *Art d'amours en prose* within a vernacular poetic tradition. Constituting a self-consciously complex literary monument, MS 881 frames this text with a vernacular corpus that invites a contextualized reading of Ovid's mediated work. Reshaping the text and redefining its significance, this version of the *Art d'amours en prose* exposes the deeper issues addressed in this work: namely, Ovid's problematic status, the value of the vernacular, and the reader's obligation to participate in the making of meaning.

Both owner and producer of MS 881 are known. The original owner was a fifteenth-century parliamentary figure and book collector, Arnauld de Corbie, and the copyist responsible for this manuscript is Raoul Tainguy, a well-known scribe who dealt exclusively with two types of commission: French translations of classical authors, including Titus Livius, Ovid, Valerius Maximus, and Cato; and contemporary vernacular authors, such as Deshamps, Machaut

---

[17] On book producers as intermediary readers, see Deborah McGrady, *Controlling Readers: Guillaume de Machaut and His Late Medieval Audience* (Toronto, 2006).

[18] Jacqueline Cerquiglini-Toulet, 'A la recherche des pères: La liste des auteurs illustres à la fin du Moyen Âge', *Modern Language Notes*, 116 (2001), 630–43.

[19] See Butterfield for an enlightening study of the manuscript layout and a reproduction of a representative folio, pp. 257–8.

and Froissart.[20] MS 881 fuses these two traditions, for it opens with a translation of *De vetulla*, a pseudo-Ovidian text most likely composed in the thirteenth century by Richard de Fournival and then translated by the manuscript owner's colleague in Parliament, Jean Lefèvre. At the center of the 881 anthology is the *Art d'amours en prose*, followed by a collection of selected lyric works by Machaut.

Because the collection can be placed within the larger corpus of Tainguy's manuscripts, it is possible to detect Tainguy's unique reception of the work through a consideration both of practices that differ from his treatment of texts in other manuscripts and of signature practices that distinguish this copy from other extant versions. Alerting us to the importance of the combination of texts in MS 881 is the fact that this manuscript represents the sole known anthology in Tainguy's repertoire. By the same token, those practices now used to identify Tainguy, such as his frequent introduction of rubricated summaries of passages and his direct professional involvement in the promotion of the vernacular, play an important role in the reshaping of this work. For example, Tainguy offers an enhancement unique to this copy when he adds to the rubricated designations of *teuste* and *glose* lengthy rubrics summarizing the passage in question. In the process he insists on regularly inserting Ovid's name, even when speaking of the glosses. A representative example precedes the gloss, lines 1443–56 in the Roy edition, in which we find a strongly worded misogynous pronouncement on women's penchant for lies. In MS 881 this commentary is retroactively attributed to Ovid by an additional rubric reading, 'Comment Ovide a dit que tu doiz largement promettre a t'amie sanz rien lui donner [How Ovid said that you should make expansive promises to your ladylove while giving her nothing].' In such cases, the 881 rubrics effectively reattribute the *vilain*'s wisdom as well as the commentator's misogyny to the master himself. To read Tainguy's *Art d'amours en prose*, therefore, is to find a truly rehabilitated Ovid providing his medieval audience with strong counsel against love and proving his point by turning to the vernacular evidence. This reassertion of the master's authority in MS 881 has profound implications for the translator-commentator whose carefully cultivated authority is now weakened. Additional threats to the commentator emerge in the frequent abbreviation of passages. Unlike other extant versions, this copy trims down interventions or eliminates them altogether. In other cases, by accident or intention, text and commentary merge into a single segment now attributed to Ovid; or, worse, ownership is reversed, as when rubrics misidentify the lively and boisterous glosses as Ovid's text.[21] These

---

[20] For more on Tainguy's corpus, see Marie-Hélène Tesnière, 'Les manuscrits copiés par Raoul Tainguy: un aspect de la culture des grands officiers royaux au début du XVe siècle', *Romania*, 107 (1986), 282–368.

[21] The misattribution of glosses and text appears to have resulted from various moments of confusion, for text and gloss are confused at the outset until Gloss XXX; this

peculiarities of MS 881, combined with a failure to signal the presence of the inserted lyric material in this codex, appear to reaffirm the mastery of Ovid whereas the translator-commentator assumes a traditionally subordinate role.

Yet, if the *mise en page* appears to downplay the aggressive treatment of Ovid by the translator-commentator, the *mise en œuvre* reinforces the original distrust in a binary system that privileged Latin over the vernacular and poetry over prose. In the 881 codex valorization of the vernacular permeates the anthology, for the now vernacularized and prosified Ovid resides between two lay writers – Lefèvre the translator and Machaut the poet. This tri-partite arrangement invites a re-evaluation of the amorous dynamics associated with Ovid. By opening with *De la vieille*, the collection sets the stage for a rehabilitated Ovid. Here Ovid comes to abandon love for serious study when deceived. From this text the reader moves to the *Art d'amours en prose*, where not only do lyric and proverbial insertions communicate a harsh judgment, but the frequent conflation and confusion of *texte* and *glose* in MS 881 gives the impression that it is Ovid who speaks out on the dangers of love.

The reinvention of Ovid in the first two works of MS 881 prepares the linear reader to see Machaut and vernacular poetry in a new light. When we move to the final sampling of Machaut's poetic corpus, we are better equipped to recognize in these poems from the *Loange des dames* the overwhelmingly negative view of love expressed in Machaut's writings. Far from praising either women or amorous feelings, the MS 881 selection of 96 from the 256 poems from the *Loange* series underscores the dangers of such relations. An examination of the opening lines of *ballades* included in MS 881 makes this clear: we move from 'Gentil cuer souviengne vous / Des maulx que li mien sentit (*Lo* 236/fol. 102v) [Gentle heart, remember the pain that mine has felt]' to 'Helas amours que vous ay je meffait (*Lo* 84/fol. 108r) [Alas, Love, how have I wronged you?]' and finally, 'Helas dolent or vueil je bien mourir (*Lo* 237/fol. 110r) [Alas, miserable, I would prefer to die]'.[22] Having copied Deschamps's work, Tainguy may very well have been familiar with the designation of Machaut as 'Plus qu'Ovide, un vray remède d'amours.' Regardless, Tainguy supports these claims by following Ovid's translated and rehabilitated *Ars amatoria* with a vernacular *Remedia* – a 'vray remede d'amours'.

In the end MS 881 provides us with a new Ovid, one stripped of much of his past glory. Carrying further the lessons of the *Art d'amours en prose*, where we learn that proverbs and refrains disguise a truth missing in the

---

confusion reappears throughout the copy. Regardless of intentionality, the overall effect of reassigning to Ovid the lively sections of the work should not be ignored.

[22] All references are to, first, *Guillaume de Machaut. La Louange de dames,* ed. Jacqueline Cerquiglini-Toulet (Edinburgh, 1972; identified here as *Lo*), and second, MS fr. 881 foliation.

prose Ovid, MS 881 presents the audience with an immediate opportunity to apply this lesson beyond the work's textual boundaries. In the final folios vernacular poetry emerges as the exclusive medium allowed to pronounce on love. Moving from the translator-commentator's insertion of the poetic word to Tainguy's intimate affiliation of the vernacular poetry with the sanctioned voice of Ovid, we now encounter in the 881 codex the master of the vernacular poetic form, Machaut, who is accorded the final word. A sampling of Machaut's love poetry functions as a storehouse of warnings on the dangers of *fin'amors* and evidence of the wisdom of vernacular poetry. As such, Tainguy has prepared readers to view Machaut afresh as a didactic writer who criticized rather than promoted amorous discourse, a vernacular poet who contested the master, Ovid.

Tainguy's rendering of the *Art d'amour en prose* offers material evidence of late medieval investigations of sanctioned dichotomies as tools for establishing new literary aesthetics in which the wisdom expressed in the vernacular – whether by translators, *vilains*, or revered medieval poets – merited attention and celebration. It is of little surprise that, of the many translated classical works produced by Tainguy, this text figures at the center of such a complex orchestration. For the translator-commentator of the *Art d'amour en prose* had already begun the work of chipping away at literary expectations. MS 881 provides the careful reader seeking out the obscure and hidden truths celebrated by the translator-commentator the chance to discover a truth beyond the hidden perils of love. Tainguy brings to fruition the notion that vernacular poetry is the perfect medium of truth. What better way of proving his point than by choosing Machaut, not simply a descendant of Ovid, but a vernacular poet identified as offering the 'true' remedy to the master's failings?

Deversifying Knowledge:
The Poetic Alphabet of the Prose *Pèlerinage de la vie humaine*

STEPHANIE A. V. G. KAMATH

Nearly one hundred extant manuscripts, translations into English, German, Dutch, Spanish and Latin and an influence on the naming of New World islands attest to the widespread popularity of Guillaume de Deguileville's fourteenth-century pilgrimage allegories.[1] Deguileville's first allegory, the *Pèlerinage de la vie humaine*, circulated in two versions, the allegory composed c. 1331 and a longer version revised by the author c. 1355, distinguished hereafter as *Vie1* and *Vie2* respectively. In 1464, the shorter, more widely read *Vie1* inspired a *dérimage* dedicated to Jeanne de Lanval.[2] This prose version of the text was especially popular with late medieval and early modern readers, inspiring at least five print versions between 1485 and 1506, several being reissued multiple times.[3] Not all readers reacted favorably to the *dérimage*, however: two sixteenth-century editions containing a modernized form of Deguileville's *Vie2* begin with a verse prologue that derides the prose of the *dérimage*.[4] As this prologue indicates, these two adaptations of Deguileville's

---

[1] Both 'Deguileville' and 'Digulleville' are current spellings. On the relation to the New World, see Valerie Flint, 'Columbus, "El Romero" and the so-called Columbus Map', *Terræ Incognitæ*, 24 (1992), 19–30.

[2] On Jeanne de Laval's circle, see Anne-Marie Legaré, 'La réception du *Pèlerinage de Vie humaine* de Guillaume de Digulleville dans le milieu angevin', *Religion et mentalités au Moyen Âge: Mélanges en l'honneur d'Hervé Martin*, ed. Sophie Cassagnes-Brouquet et al. (Rennes, 2003), pp. 543–52 (esp. pp. 547–52).

[3] For a list of manuscripts and incunabla, see Eugene Clasby, trans. and intro., *The Pilgrimage of Human Life* (New York, 1992), pp. xxxv–xxxix.

[4] The prologue critical of the *dérimage* appears in two editions:
1. *Le Pelerinage de l'homme* (Paris: Anthoine Vérard, 1511); Cambridge, MA, Houghton Library, *FC.G9455D.511v
2. *Le premier pelerinaige* in *Le Romant des trois Pelerinaiges* (Paris: Barthole Rembolt and Jean Petit, n.d. [c. 1510–11 or 1514–18?]); Cambridge, MA, Houghton Library, *FC.G9455D.525v
Citations of *Vie2* refer by folio number to Vérard's edition unless otherwise noted. Vérard

first allegory – the *dérimage* and *Vie2* – assign contrasting values to verse. Yet each version uses distinct lyric passages to interrelate or to distinguish the voices of the allegory's intradiegetic narrator and characters and its extradiegetic author, sources and readers. I examine these distinct lyric passages in the *dérimage* and in Deguileville's *Vie2* to discover their functions and their relation to the allegory's acknowledged Latin and French sources.

The verse prologue critical of the *dérimage* overtly laments the replacement of poetry with prose:

> Pieca quelque ung ne scay pourquoy
> Le translata de rime en prose
> En quoy mal fist comme je croy
> Car mal a droit vient ceste chose
> Comme se le methamorphose
> L'en mettoit en langue rural...
> Touteffois ainsi qu'en latin
> Ovide plusieurs fables fainct
> Semblablement de pres actainct
> Poesie nostre guile ville
> Par quoi ne devoit estre enfrainct
> Aucunement son plaisant stile. (fol. 1r)

> [Recently someone, I don't know why, translated it from rhyme to prose. To my mind, he did wrong. For this is a clumsy thing, like putting the *Metamorphoses* into rustic language ... Just as Ovid made many fables in Latin, our Deguileville similarly comes close to allegory, so his pleasing style should not be disrupted at all.][5]

This complaint presents Deguileville's poetic style as authoritative and intrinsic to the allegory's meaning. The comparison between Ovid's Latin and Deguileville's pleasing style reflects a humanistic respect for Latin but also valorizes the vernacular author's authority, 'semblable [similar]' to that of Ovid. A subsequent complaint about the *dérimage*'s use of *Vie1*, rather than *Vie2*, as a base text, similarly identifies the author as an authority – the prologue insists that *Vie1* is imperfect because the author 'luy mesme l'atteste

---

published his edition of *Vie2* after having published multiple editions of the *dérimage*. One issue, *Le Pélerin de vie humaine* (Paris: Vérard, 1499), included a vellum copy for Henry VII. Unless otherwise noted, all citations from the *dérimage* refer by folio number to a facsimile of Henry's copy, *Le Pelerinaige de vie humaine: Reproduced in Facsimile from the Printed Book in the Library of the Earl of Ellesmere*. Intro. Alfred Pollard (Paris: Anthoine Vérard, 1499*)* (Manchester, 1912). Modern punctuation and i/j, u/v distinctions have been introduced where appropriate throughout the chapter. Françoise Bourgeois is preparing the first modern edition of the *dérimage* but I have not had access to her work.

[5] All Modern English translations are my own, with thanks to this volume's editorial team for their assistance.

(fol. 1r) [himself admits it]' in *Vie2*. The sixteenth-century critique thus associates verse with authorial voice, figurative language, Latin authority and *Vie2*. Verse is not entirely absent from the criticized medieval *dérimage*, but the function of verse within the prose narrative contrasts with the presentation of verse in *Vie2* and in its critical prologue. Instead of treating verse as a means of increasing the recognition of vernacular authors and their resemblance to classical authors, the *dérimage* employs verse to call attention to universal aspects of human identity through experimentation with allegorical voices. The differing functions of distinguishing verses are not exclusive of one another, however; as I will demonstrate, both respond to Deguileville's complex inheritance from an earlier French allegory.

Despite de-versifying the vast majority of Deguileville's first allegory, the *dérimage* retains in verse a lyric prayer, known as the *ABC* because it is composed as a stanzaic acrostic ordered by the letters of the alphabet. *Vie1* attributes its *ABC*, as well as other passages designated as inscriptions, charters, prayers or letters, not to Guillaume de Deguileville but to allegorical characters who appear within its narrative. The *dérimage* copies these aspects of *Vie1*, retaining the *ABC* in verse and also adding another rhyming passage in the voice of an allegorical character, a feature unnoticed until now in modern scholarship. Verse thus appears to have a different function within the *dérimage* from the one the sixteenth-century *Vie2* prologue envisions for verse – verse does not directly represent authorial style and intention. To understand the use of verse within the *dérimage*, as well as the claims made for verse in the *Vie2* prologue criticizing the *dérimage*, we must look to the allegorical techniques of the poem in which Deguileville found inspiration: the *Roman de la Rose* of Guillaume de Lorris and Jean de Meun, a text itself greatly indebted to Ovid. *Vie1* and its *dérimage* use distinct lyric passages in a way that differs from their employment in *Vie2*, yet the contrasting practices of both the prose adaptation and the verse recension represent developments in allegory inspired by the Ovidian *Rose*. In the *Rose*, an allegorical character presents the names of vernacular authors in a manner reminiscent of Ovid, yet defines the identity of the allegory's first-person voice as an open subject position – so open, in fact, that allegorical characters claim the authorship of particular verse passages for themselves. The allegorical practices of the *Rose* and the response to these practices in Deguileville's *Vie1* therefore offer an illuminating context for the uses of distinct lyrics in *Vie2* and the *dérimage*.

Medieval readers found the relation between Deguileville's allegory and the *Rose* notable and attractive. Deguileville's first allegory explicitly names the 'beau roumans de la Rose [fair romance of the Rose]' as its inspiration (line 11).[6] Medieval rubricators expanded on the connection, representing the two allegories as companions covering major bodies of knowledge: a manu-

---

[6] Quotations of *Vie1* cite by line number from Guillaume de Deguileville, *Le Pèlerinage de la vie humaine*, ed. J. Stürzinger (London, 1893).

script combining extracts from both texts declares Deguileville's allegory to be 'fais par poeterie, comme li Livres de le Roze, qui est en grant partie de philozofie, mes cilz pelerinages est de theologie [fashioned as an allegory, like the Book of the Rose, which is largely philosophical, but this pilgrimage is theological]'.[7] The poetic presentation of scientific and salvific arts in the form of allegorical dreams heralded a significant change in the theoretical structure of French narrative texts, a change illustrated in its visual representation. *Rose* manuscripts featured more complex rubrics of voice than any earlier French text had attracted, as scribes distinguish the speeches of the text's first-person voice as either those of 'l'acteur', the author of the poem, or of 'l'amant', the lover, the role assumed by the narrator-protagonist within the allegory.[8] The latter identity is clearly symbolic; the *Rose* addresses its readers as lovers and calls itself the 'Miroër aus Amoreus [Mirror of Lovers]'.[9] The first-person voice of the narrator-protagonist, who sometimes speaks as an author, thus also reflects the interpellated identity of the text's readers. Complicating the identity of this voice, the allegory of the *Rose* names both of its authors but identifies the first-person voice as one which neither of them quite controls. At the mid-point of the *Rose*, the god of Love represents himself as the work's author, naming the historical authors as his literary servants. Love first names Guillaume de Lorris by predicting his death in a lament modeled on Ovid's naming of great poets in *Amores* III.9; Love then names Jean de Meun by predicting his birth. This passage names the *Rose* authors and presents them as authorities through Ovidian allusion, but the allegorical voice relating these authors' names destabilizes the relationship of the external author to the shifting identity of the poem's first-person voice.[10]

The *Rose*'s interest in authorial naming and allegorical voice is especially pronounced in a passage that differentiates certain lines of verse as a charter written by the personification Genius. Genius's charter promises all lovers (including, presumably, 'the lover' identity of the *Rose*'s first-person voice) a new and better *locus amœnus* than that described in the *Rose*, citing the text by name. The allegory's creation of an internal character acting as an author crafts a hermeneutics of uncertainty in which only the reader, rather the disputed text or slippery authorial voices, can be the arbiter of

---

[7] Arras, B Mun., MS 845, fol. 103r. See Sylvia Huot, *The* Romance of the Rose *and its Medieval Readers: Interpretation, Reception, Manuscript Transmission* (Cambridge, 1993), pp. 231–8.

[8] See Sylvia Huot, '"Ci parle l'aucteur": The Rubrication of Voice and Authorship in the *Roman de la Rose* Manuscripts', *SubStance*, 56 (1988), 42–8.

[9] Guillaume de Lorris and Jean de Meun, *Le Roman de la rose*, ed. Félix Lecoy, 3 vols (Paris, 1965/1966/1970), line 10621.

[10] On the coercive effects of this unstable signature passage, see Noah Guynn, *Allegory and Sexual Ethics in the High Middle Ages* (New York, 2007), pp. 137–67.

knowledge.¹¹ The *Rose* thus demands that readers recognize the names of vernacular authors in relation to classical predecessors, while simultaneously expecting readers to interpret for themselves the knowledge conveyed by the competing compositions attributed to allegorical characters and to a first-person voice with multiple identities.

Manuscripts of Deguileville's *Vie1* imitate the innovations of the *Rose*. The manuscripts frequently feature rubrics that designate the text's first-person voice alternatively as 'l'acteur' or as 'le pelerin [the pilgrim]', the character assumed within the dream. Just as the *Rose* identified its readers as lovers listening to the story of the lover, the opening of Deguileville's allegory identifies its readers as spiritual pilgrims. Also like the *Rose*, *Vie1* features an allegorical character who both reveals the author's name and denies that the first-person voice of the text is entirely the author's own.¹² *Vie1* suggests its author's name when the personification Reason teaches the narrator his identity, saying 'Dieu est ton pere et tu son fil, / Ne cuides pas que soies fil / (A) Thomas de Deguileville (lines 5963–5) [God is your father and you his son; do not think that you are the son of Thomas de Deguileville]'. The passage insists on a universal spiritual identity for the allegory's first-person voice, but the specificity of the denied identity functions as a form of authorial signature, revealing the author to be Thomas de Deguileville's son. Reason's denial of the author's father resembles Love's prophetic denial of either of the *Rose* authors' living presence, identifying the author with a proper name but suggesting that the first-person voice of the narrator does not belong uniquely to the named individual. Even as the allegory draws readers' attention to the vernacular author's name, the antiphrastic presentation of this name by an allegorical voice teaches readers that they participate in the identity of the narrator's first-person voice – all children of god must heed Reason on their spiritual pilgrimage, just as all lovers serve the god of Love.

Along with the external feature of rubrication and internal play with authorial naming and identity, Deguileville's text expands upon the *Rose*'s experiment in presenting certain passages as verse composed by the allegory's characters. The author's role as the text's producer is rivaled by not one but many internal depictions of textual production. The *ABC* stands out among these distinguished passages as it has a prosodic form distinct from the surrounding verse. Although in the same meter as the narrative's octasyllabic couplets, the *ABC* has a stanzaic rhyme pattern (*aabaabbbabba*), in addition to its use of the first letter of each stanza to form an acrostic

---

¹¹ See Kevin Brownlee, 'Jean de Meun and the Limits of Romance', in *Romance: Generic Transformations from Chrétien de Troyes to Cervantes*, ed. Kevin Brownlee and Maria Scordilis Brownlee (London, 1985), pp. 114–34, p. 129.

¹² For discussion of naming strategies in Deguileville's allegory and the *Rose*, see my 'Unveiling the "I": Allegory and Authorship in the Franco-English Tradition, 1270–1450', Ph.D. diss. (University of Pennsylvania (2006)), pp. 25–74.

proceeding through the letters of the alphabet. The *ABC* is further distinguished by its introduction, which emphasizes the material form envisioned for this seemingly separate composition and invites readers to participate in voicing this passage. The prose version retains these features along with the *ABC*'s verse form.

The introduction to the *ABC* in both *Vie1* and the *dérimage* interrupts the narrative frame, forcing a shift between the voices of pilgrim and author, distinctions which rubrics imitating the manuscripts of the *Rose* sought to mark. Deguileville's *ABC* is presented as a gift to the narrator from the personification Grace of God. The lines introducing the *ABC* in *Vie1* and its *dérimage* remind the reader of this attribution but also, in each case, explicitly suggest an extratextual personal use of this document by readers. The first-person voice of the *ABC* is thus simultaneously the voice of the author, addressing readers, and the voice of Grace, the personification attributed authorship within the allegory. In addition, the *ABC* is spoken by the narrator's pilgrim character and also (the introduction suggests) the reader. I reproduce the lines introducing the *ABC* in the verse allegory and its fifteenth-century prose adaptation below, not to emphasize their minor differences but to demonstrate their shared shifts in perspective, layering the voices imagined as speaking this first-person prayer:

> Or vous di que l'escrit ouvri
> Et le desploiai et le vi.
> De touz poins fis ma priere
> En la forme et (en la) maniere
> Que contenoit le dit escrit
> Et si com Grace l'avoit dit.
> La forme de l'escrit orrez,
> Et si vostre a.b.c. (ne) scavez,
> Savoir le porrez de legier
> Pour dire le, s'il est mestier. (lines 10883–93)

> [Now I tell you that I opened and unfolded and read the script. On all points I made my prayer in the form and in the manner contained in the said script, just as Grace had spoken it. You will hear the form of the script, and if you don't know your a.b.c. you easily get to know it by reciting this poem, if need be.]

Or vous dis que je ouvriz l'escript et desploye et selon ce qu'il contenoit feis ma priere et comme grace de dieu le m'avoit dit. Et si bien vostre .A.B.C. scavez assez de legier scavoir le pourrez. (fol. V1r)

[Now I tell you that I opened and unfolded the script and made my prayer according to its contents and just as Grace of God had spoken it to me. And if you know your a.b.c. well, you can learn it easily enough.]

These passages introduce the *ABC* in terms that refer to the internal narrative frame of the allegorical action – the troubled narrator touches it as a material object and remembers its composition by Grace – yet both also incorporate the extradiegetic perspective of an authorial voice, in control of what is heard and seen in the text, who offers it to readers for use in their own lives. The *ABC* is the most literal passage within the allegory, in the sense of drawing attention to the letters composing language. Yet the invitation to learn to read the alphabet of Grace, to learn to pray as one learns to read, transfers the salvific message of the allegory to the most basic components of language.[13] Not only the acrostic but the meaning of the acrostic's voice depends upon metaleptic reading, since the text envisions a narrator who claims to write the allegory yet at the same time clearly acts as an allegorical figure for all humans, especially the text's readers. The *dérimage* maintains the attention of its source to the *ABC*'s multiplied voices, within and beyond the allegorical text, so that the *ABC* lyric retained within prose uses a shift in form to call attention to shifts in the identity of the allegory's voice.

Contrasting with the unstable identity thus created for the first-person voice of the *dérimage*'s *ABC*, Deguileville's *Vie2* contains passages distinguished as separate lyrics within the narrative that instead associate the voice of the allegory with named authorial identity. In *Vie2*, the *ABC* is moved to a later portion of the allegory and its acrostic form is no longer unique – a newly inserted acrostic, in stanzas of eight lines, each bound by a single end rhyme, spells out the author's name. In *Vie1*, only Reason's denial of Thomas de Deguileville reveals the author's name, but in *Vie2* attention is also drawn to the author's name by the use of verse, specifically by the use of an acrostic verse form, like that employed for the *ABC* in *Vie1*. Deguileville inserts the naming acrostic poem immediately after a new passage describing an encounter with a character who identifies himself as Ovid. Ovid curses the personifications attacking the narrator with an excerpt from the *Ibis*. Deguileville's subsequent naming acrostic employs macaronic verse, alternating lines of Latin and French, using the element of shared language to connect this acrostic with Ovid's preceding Latin verse. The writer of the sixteenth-century prologue critical of the *dérimage* and *Vie1* may well have had this passage in mind when comparing Deguileville and Ovid as stylistic masters. Whereas the *ABC* uses its first-person voice as an inhabitable identity teaching a lesson in salvific allegory, Deguileville's macaronic acrostic

---

[13] Such "allegory of letters" is not without echoes. Piers Plowman claims 'Abstynence the abbesse ... myn A.B.C. me taughte' in a later English allegory; see William Langland, *The Vision of Piers Plowman*, ed. A. V. C. Schmidt, 2nd ed. (London, 1995), *passus* VII line 133. Context heightens the resemblance: in Deguileville's *Vie1*, the *ABC* delivers the narrator from the onslaught of personified lust. For more on these poems' relation, see Guy Bourquin, *'Piers Plowman': Études sur la genèse littéraire des trois versions*, 2 vols (Paris, 1978), II, pp. 780–90.

poem uses both the narrator's and characters' voices to reveal the author's name and place in literary history.

The macaronic poem suggests through its form and placement a connection between the author and Ovid, but also indicates an alternative, allegorical authority for the author it names. The second stanza of the poem describes how the character Grace summons the first-person speaker by name from the margins of his scriptural reading:

> Vidi scriptum in margine
> Ou cestuy escript s'enracine
> Mirandam pulchritudine
> Grace dieu du ciel royne digne
> Me vocantam ex nomine. (fol. 96r)

> [I saw written in the margin, where this writing is rooted, Grace Dieu, worthy queen of heaven, marvelously beautiful, calling me by name.]

What the reader calls forth from the margins of manuscripts with marked initial letters for each stanza, edging beyond textual ruling, is the Latin form of the author's name, GVILLERMVS DE DEGVILVILLA (the V beginning the quoted stanza, for example, marks the second letter).[14] The reader's discovery of the author's name in the acrostic thus replicates the narrator's discovery of grace through scriptural reading. Grace, who offers the open-voiced alphabetic acrostic earlier in the allegory, now addresses by name the voice of an acrostic poem spelling the author's name. Like the *ABC*, this acrostic creates a situation in which the narrator's and readers' experiences mirror one another; both read textual margins just as earlier both read the alphabetical prayer for deliverance. But the content of the verse's acrostic shifts attention from a participatory identity for the first-person voice to the author's name.

Vie2 creates this focus on individual authorial identity not simply by incorporating the name in the acrostic but also by the acrostic's introduction, quite different from the introduction to the *ABC* in *Vie1* and the *dérimage*. Referring to Ovid, the narrator declares

> Que cil qui ne me congnoissoit
> De moy dueil et corroux avoit
> Pource le fiz et l'ay escript
> Et ne tiegne nul a despit

---

[14] See, for example, the colored capitals decorating the acrostic in the earliest illustrated copy, Paris, BnF, MS fr. 829, fols 127r–128v, and its marginal rubric 'cognomen peregrim', fol. 127v.

> S'en icelluy dueil j'ay assises
> Les lettres de mon nom. (fol. 96r)
>
> [Because this one who did not know me had grief and anger for my sake, I have made and written [the lament], and let no-one take it amiss if in this lament I have placed the letters of my name.]

This introduction invites readers to discover the author's name as intimately connected with the imagined sympathy of Ovid as well as the voice of the narrator. The narrator's account of his sufferings in the acrostic replicates the preceding allegorical narrative, suggesting the story in the acrostic is also universal and applicable to the readers, who are pilgrims like the narrator, according to the allegory. But this introduction insists on the individualized aspect of the acrostic's first-person voice and its Ovidian inspiration. Although the allegorical purpose of the narrative is not forgotten in differentiating this lyric, the emphasis falls upon a named authorial identity and a Latin literary inheritance rather than the universal nature of human spiritual identity.

Deguileville's *Vie2* does demonstrate an interest in using a change in form to draw attention to allegorical messages as well as authorial claims – but it assigns this function to Latin prose instead of acrostic verse. As noted above, the *ABC* appears at a different point within *Vie2*, much closer to the moment when the naming acrostic is inserted. In most *Vie2* manuscripts, the allegorical situation in which the *ABC* appeared in *Vie1* – a moment of great danger for the narrator – introduces instead a Latin prose treatise attributed to St Bernard (fols 63v–66v).[15] Like the *ABC*, this treatise saves the narrator from his attackers; however, unlike the *ABC*, it is the work of a named individual author recalled by the narrator rather than a material object which an allegorical character gives to the narrator. Like the additional acrostic of *Vie2*, the text now occupying the place of the *ABC* reflects a greater interest in named authors and Latin literary inheritance than *Vie1* demonstrates. Nonetheless, *Vie2* is using a passage written in a distinct textual form to invite readers' participation as it dramatizes its narrator's salvation by means of a text. Each version of Deguileville's allegory thus employs a unique change in textual form to underscore the significance of this rescue, be it the distinction between narrative verse and a unique verse form in *Vie1*, the distinction between narrative prose and a unique verse form in the *dérimage* or the distinction between narrative verse and Latin prose in *Vie2*. From this standpoint, the *dérimage* keeping the *ABC* in verse in the midst of prose narrative is not a change so much as a variation on earlier means of distinguishing by

---

[15] See, for example, Paris, BnF, MS fr. 825, fols 93v-98r. Certain versions of *Vie2* made other choices: Rembolt and Petit's edition reworks the Latin treatise in French verse (fol. 57r–57v). A medieval English verse translation of *Vie2* reworks the Latin treatise in English prose and verse; see John Lydgate, *The Pilgrimage of the Life of Man*, ed. F. Furnivall and Katharine Locock (London, 1899/1901/1904), lines 16275–17033.

form a passage that valorizes the role of textual creation in salvation as it invites participation, blending the voices of author, character and reader.

The distinct lyric passages of *Vie2* primarily advance authorial claims while those of the *dérimage* more strongly emphasize participatory allegorical voicing, but these functions are not mutually exclusive as textual interests in either version. Just as author-focused *Vie2* also invites participation in the first-person voice with a shift in form, certain *dérimage* manuscripts also demonstrate interest in authorial attribution. These manuscripts add a further name to the passage revealing the author's name, so that Reason describes the narrator's spiritual identity thus: 'Tu es filz et enfant de dieu ne cuides pas que tu soyes filz a thomas de deguilleuille ne a pierre gautier [You are the son and child of god; do not think that you are the son of Thomas de Deguileville or Pierre Gautier]'.[16] Whoever inserted Gautier's name – prose adaptor, scribe or patron – the alteration shows both recognition of this indirect form of authorial signature through allegory and an interest in its expansion. This interest resembles the *dérimage*'s use of lyrics. Keeping the *ABC* in verse calls attention to a passage multiplying rather than restricting the voices of the text, allowing the first-person voice to be not simply the author but also the universal pilgrim character, the reader, the Grace of God. Although the additional name in Reason's speech demonstrates an interest in individual attribution, it also further multiplies the identity of the text's voice.

On the whole, despite some interest in attribution, the *dérimage* uses verse primarily to place emphasis not on authorial identity but rather on the multiplied nature of the first-person voice of the text and its allegorical meaning. The *dérimage* not only retains the lyric *ABC* but also inserts a new series of couplets into Reason's speech shortly after she reveals the author's name through denial.[17] These verses further disrupt the narrator's identity by describing the antagonistic relationship of his body and soul. *Vie1* conveys carnal and spiritual opposition with a biblical analogy comparing body and soul to Delilah and Sampson, but the *dérimage* adds a rhymed series of contrasts describing the body, labeled as a 'proverbe' in the manuscript with the longest version:

---

[16] Rosamund Tuve noted this emendation in a 1504 Lyons edition and suggested it indicated the prose adaptor's name; see *Allegorical Imagery. Some Mediaeval Books and their Posterity* (Princeton, 1966), p. 216. I found the name in only two manuscripts: Geneva, B Publique et Universitaire, MS fr. 182, fol. 75v and Paris, BnF, MS fr. 1646, fol. 72r. The name also appears in two other print editions (Lyons: Huss, 1485, fol. H6v, and Paris: Vérard, 1499, fol. L5r).

[17] These rhymes, with variations, appear in the eight French *dérimage* manuscripts known to be extant: Paris, BnF, MSS fr. 1137, fr. 1646, fr. 12461; B de l'Arsenal, MS 2319; B de Ste Geneviève, MS 294; Geneva, B Publique et Universitaire, MSS fr. 181, fr. 182; Soissons, BM, MS 208. I appreciate the assistance of Justin Clegg, Leslie Morris, and Susan L'Engle in my attempts to locate two other manuscripts described in pre-WWII catalogues.

Plus est servy et plus se plainct;
Plus est nourry et plus se fainct;
Plus est paré et plus se demaine;
Plus est aymé et plus fait de peine;
Plus est creu et plus souvent ment;
Plus est peu, moins est content;
Plus est reprins et plus murmure;
Plus a hault pris, moins de Dieu cure;
Plus a d'avoir, moins luy souffit;
Plus a savoir, moins de bien dit;
Plus a mesprins, moins a cremeur;
Plus pres de Dieu, moins a saveur.[18]

[The more it's obeyed, the more it complains;
The more it's fed, the feebler it is;
The better it's defended, the more it laments;
The more it's loved, the more it sorrows;
The more it's believed, the more often it lies;
The more it's nourished, the less it's content;
The more it's replete, the more it rebels;
The more high praise it has, the less it fears God;
The more goods it has, the less it is satisfied;
The more knowledge it has, the less it speaks well;
The more wrong it has done, the less fear it has;
The closer to God, the less pleasure it has.]

The puzzle of the narrator's identity – located in the struggle between body and soul – is thus presented as a formally distinct riddle. The verses are distinguished from the surrounding prose not only by their rubric but by their couplet rhyme scheme, the parallel contradictions, and the feature of anaphora, calling attention to the opening of lines like the earlier acrostic *ABC*. The narrator must learn not only his alphabet but his dangerously doubled identity, 'plus [more]' than one. Although other manuscripts omit the 'proverbe' rubric that sets the verses apart in their longest form, the shorter verse sections are rendered distinct in other ways. For example, five manuscripts change their rubrication of the text's first-person voice after this passage.[19] Whereas most manuscripts of the allegory alternate employing the rubrics 'le pelerin [the pilgrim]' and 'l'acteur [the author]' for the first-person voice throughout the text, these five *dérimage* manuscripts use both rubrics only after the moment of dialogue between the body and soul which follows Reason's explanations of their relation. After the body's confrontation, these

---

[18] See Paris, BnF, MS fr. 1646, fol. 73r, and the print facsimile, fol. L.5v; both run the verse lines across the page like prose.
[19] Paris, BnF, MSS fr. 1377, fr. 12461 and B de l'Arsenal, MS 2319; Geneva, B Publique et Universitaire, MS 181; Soissons, BM, MS 208.

manuscripts employ 'le pelerin' rubric for the first time, emphasizing the function of this first-person voice as a character within the allegory rather than as its author. The new rhyming couplets differ from the retained *ABC* as they have a less consistent form and *mise en page* and are not presented as having a material form within the allegory. But these couplets resemble the *ABC* in function, as their distinction from surrounding prose draws attention to the complex identity of the allegory's first-person voice.

Reason's preaching of contradictions has a precedent in the *Rose*'s Reason character, and the insertion of proverbs echoes Jean de Meun's practice as a translator – Jean's otherwise rather exact rendering of the Abelard and Heloise letters adds proverbial expression.[20] The use of verse at this point in the *dérimage* to insert contradictory riddles forming part of a spoken or oral tradition is of particular interest, however, as the *dérimage* carefully elucidates other allegorical puzzles.[21] For example, the *dérimage* appends explicit interpretation to the nine-month dwelling from which the pilgrim emerges: 'cestadire du ventre de ma mere (fol. A6v, lines 221–3) [that is to say, the womb of my mother]'. The allegory's authorities for its figurations are also rendered more specific at times: 'saint Pol (line 3) [Saint Paul]' becomes, in the prose, 'monseigneur sainct pol lapostre (fol. A4r) [Sir Saint Paul the apostle]'. Yet even as the *dérimage* clarifies the verse allegory in this manner, it expands upon the puzzling divisions in the narrator's first-person voice. In the new verses, as in the retention of the *ABC* in verse, the *dérimage* shows greater interest in the use of formal difference to draw attention to the complications of human identity than in the use of verse to present authorial identity and an authoritative affiliation with Latin literature.

The fifteenth-century English prose translation of *Vie1* offers a rewarding comparison to the French *dérimage* since it also features added verse, although the addition appears only in one manuscript. In this manuscript, the new lyric is inserted at the narrative's close, another moment when the text discusses the division of the narrator's body and soul. As Reason's discourse on the enmity of soul and body forewarns, Sickness and Death arrive to divide the narrator's soul and body. Using the same techniques found in *Vie1*'s introduction to the *ABC*, the English prose presents the new lyric for use on this occasion. The narrator explains that 'Grace Dieu tuke to me a litill roule writyne on þis manere / with golde letters'; Grace offers this new verse document as useful not only for the narrator but the text's readers, describing the prayer as 'gude to ilk creature forto say'.[22] Just like the *ABC*'s introduction,

---

[20] Paul Chavy, 'Les Premiers Translateurs français', *French Review*, 47 (1974), 557–65, p. 561.

[21] On these versions' contrasting oral and written emphases, see Fabienne Pomel, 'Enjeux d'un travail de réécriture', *Le Moyen Age*, 109.3–4 (2003), 457–72.

[22] Melbourne, State Library of Victoria, MS 096 G.94, fol. 94r; see *The pilgrimage of the lyfe of the manhode*, ed. Avril Henry, 2 vols (London, 1988), II, Appendix.

the introduction to this new lyric asserts its value to every human, describes the material aspects of its written form within the allegory (the scroll, the gold letters), attributes it to Grace, and finally, sets it apart by putting it in verse. This version of the English prose translation reflects great interest in the use of the poetic alphabet found in the *Vie*, although, like the rhyming 'proverbe' added to the allegory's *dérimage*, the exact form of the added verse differs from that of the *ABC*.[23] In this English prose version, as in the 1464 *dérimage*, verse draws attention to the passage's inclusion of voices beyond the textual frame, envisioning the first-person voice as open to readers, at the very moment when the allegory itself is marking a division between the voice's components of body and soul.[24]

In conclusion, passages distinguished as separate lyrics and attributed to allegorical voices, including the first-person narrator's, serve universalizing and individual attributive functions in Deguileville's allegory, resembling the *Rose*'s complex use of voice and verse at its mid-point and in Genius's charter. Which of these functions receives emphasis differs significantly in the allegory's prose and verse adaptations. Although distinct passages of verse emphasized the first of these functions within fifteenth-century prose narratives, Deguileville's earlier authorial recension, *Vie2*, seems to anticipate in its use of such passages the attributive, author-promoting impulses of the *grands rhétoriqueurs*.[25] Whereas the 1464 *dérimage* draws upon common oral traditions of wisdom, inserting a new rhyming 'proverbe' within a character's speech, the early sixteenth-century edition of *Vie2* denounces the *dérimage*'s departure from the poetic form and authority of an 'acteur' comparable to Ovid, who writes allegorically 'pour aguiser lentendement / A tout chascun scientifique (fol. 1r) [in order to sharpen the understanding of each knowledgeable person]'.[26] Yet both the *dérimage* and *Vie2* teach readers to know Deguileville's name, and both use a difference in form to mark a special passage in which textual and extratextual voices intersect; the differing emphases of these two adaptations appear only through comparative examination. Lyrics within de-versified texts are easy to overlook and, when such lyrics are noted, the function of the difference in form is often discussed without attention to

---

[23] The form is non-acrostic *rime royal*, differing from Deguileville's stanza forms and the eight-line stanzaic form Geoffrey Chaucer used to translate the *ABC*. Chaucer's *ABC* translation frequently appears in English prose manuscripts; see John Thompson, 'Chaucer's *An ABC* in and out of Context', *Poetica*, 37 (1993), 38–48.

[24] English prose manuscripts generally employ fewer voice rubrics than the *dérimage* manuscripts; John Shirley's manuscript is an exception, referring to 'þauthor' as well as the pilgrim in its rubrics (London, Lambeth Palace, MS Arc.L40.2/E.44, fol. 20r, 40v).

[25] On form's importance to the self-promotional strategies of the *rhétoriqueurs*, see Adrian Armstrong, *Technique and Technology. Script, Print, and Poetics in France, 1470–1550* (Oxford, 2000).

[26] I cite from Rembolt and Petit's edition since Vérard's edition lacks the relevant stanza.

the range of choices in form found in the full textual tradition. To recognize the most meaningful aspects of form in the late middle ages, the roles of prose and prosody must be considered in relation to other textual effects, including the use of voice for authorial attribution and invitations of reader participation, the deployment of textual self-reference and intertextual allusion, and the significance of genre, as allegory's literary and hermeneutic inheritance differs from other romance-inflected forms like the chronicle. The case of the *Vie*'s poetic alphabet shows that the late thirteenth- and mid-fourteenth-century experiments in voice and verses, so striking within the allegory of the *Rose* and Deguileville, continued to be subjects of exploration and interest in the age of de-versification – and beyond.

8

Prosifying Lyric Insertions in the Fifteenth-Century *Violette* (*Gérard de Nevers*)

DAVID J. WRISLEY

One of the key features of the 'Burgundian century'[1] was the literary vogue for rewriting French verse romances of earlier centuries in fifteenth-century court prose. The *Roman de la Violette*, Gerbert de Montreuil's thirteenth-century romance famous for its poetic insertions, was itself recast in prose for Charles I de Nevers by 1467.[2] The prose *Roman de la Violette*, renamed the *Gérard de Nevers* by an anonymous fifteenth-century prosator, offers an important glimpse into the fate of the self-conscious artificiality of earlier French romances in the passage to prose. It provides a case study of how certain kinds of poetry in the fifteenth century were celebrated and perceived as vehicles of both knowledge and identity. In the revived chivalric mode of representation at the court of Valois Burgundy, identification with earlier poetic legends and communities, particularly those of the crusading movement and chivalric culture, gives rewarding insights into some of the forms that rewriting took in the Burgundian ducal milieu.

The fifteenth-century *mises en prose* are complex texts, and the passage from verse to prose text is rife with fascinating transformative processes: omission, compression, expansion, and gloss figure alongside other narratological shifts. The processes at issue are not easily summed up in the terms 'translation' or 'adaptation'. Christopher Callahan, in his study of the *Gérard* and the prose *Roman du Chastelain de Couci,* looks at the question of perfor-

---

[1] The 'Burgundian century' refers to the period stretching from 1363 to 1477, a period marked by the growth of the administration of the lands in the Low Countries belonging to the duchy of Burgundy. Of the four Valois dukes (Philip the Bold, John the Fearless, Philip the Good and Charles the Bold), Philip the Good is particularly known for his literary and artistic patronage. The prose version of the *Roman de la Violette* was composed at the end of his long reign (1419–67).

[2] The verse text is Gerbert de Montreuil, *Le Roman de la Violette ou de Gerart de Nevers*, ed. Douglas Labaree Buffum (Paris, 1928); the prose text is *Gérard de Nevers: Prose Version of the 'Roman de la Violette'*, ed. Lawrence F. H. Lowe (Princeton/Paris, 1928). All translations are mine.

mativity in fifteenth-century prose romance from a syntactical standpoint.³ He remarks that the prose romances, far from being 'flat' or performatively dull, are in fact lively and structured by complex hybrid figures of authority (including original narrator, prosator and patron) that require close critical attention. Finding an umbrella term to describe adequately the variety of transformations into prose is not easy. French-language criticism typically opts for the expression *mettre en prose* to describe the process itself, and for the resultant text, *mise en prose*. This is perhaps the most satisfactory term for the phenomenon. The expressions used by Callahan, 'dérimer [to de-rhyme]' as a description of the process, or 'roman dérimé [a de-rhymed romance]' for the end result, do not do justice to the reality of the *mises en prose*. The subtractive or negating prefix 'dé-' connotes for the modern critic the idea of restriction or a simplistic Monsieur Jourdain-style opposition of prose and verse. Rather than removing a formal characteristic of language, namely rhyme, 'putting into prose' is instead a fully-fledged literary transformation, the manifestation of another expressive medium altogether, or the translation of one formal idiom into another. The title of this chapter uses the verb 'to prosify' as the English equivalent describing that process. Connoting the shift from one kind of idiom into another, the verb 'to prosify' in English gives more critical space for describing the huge idiom of prose, an idiom which can and does contain fragments of poetic language. My argument about the *Gérard* begins therefore with an important distinction: the choice of the prose idiom does not exclude the strategic use of verse.

Those accustomed to reading fifteenth-century prose versions alongside the earlier verse texts are not surprised by the prose's radical departures from the poetics and significations of the verse text. Sometimes the prosator excises huge segments of the poem, summing them up in clever, or dismissive, turns of phrase. At other times the modifications are subtle, involving tiny omissions or additions, and only the attentive and patient reader will pick up patterns across the text. On the other hand, sometimes entirely new realms of meaning are introduced by prosification, releasing an unexploited potentiality in their verse narrative structure. Usually a number of these various transformations occur at the same time in Burgundian prose fiction, which can lead the reader to feel that the texts are inconsistent, naïve or even incoherent. The *mise en prose* can sometimes feel to the critic like a curious historical restoration – half refurbished, half distorted – or, in contemporary parlance, a new-old house.

It comes as no surprise that the Burgundian prosators tended to shy away from including narrative moments of poetic performativity in their prose texts, perhaps simply as a matter of taste. Removing sections of poetic density

---

³ Christopher Callahan, 'À l'ombre du jongleur disparu. La grammaire de la performance dans deux romans lyrico-narratifs dérimés', *Revue des Langues Romanes,* 101 (1997), 211–33.

from new versions of the romance could, in fact, be a convenient technique allowing the *mises en prose* to fulfill their prologues' often-stated intention of rejuvenating and updating old-fashioned styles of narration. Of the thirty-nine poetic insertions found in the *Violette*, only four are kept in their original form in the *Gérard*. Others are retained in part or in trace. That the *Gérard* removed poetic ornament from its narrative is quite typical of Burgundian prose narratives. The *Gérard* romance could easily have eliminated all traces of the lyric insertions of the *Violette*; importantly, though, it did not. It saves three couplets of conventional lyric, as well as a rich fragment of the *Chanson de Guillaume* found at the heart of the story in the *Violette*, thereby forming a prominent exception to the general excision of poetic language. This performative instance of epic song is maintained, and even showcased, by the prosator for his new readership. The figure of the jongleur is most certainly not gone; rather, in this section, he takes center stage.

Two apparently opposing tendencies can be seen in the *Gérard*. The prose text works to annihilate many of the poetic insertions for which the *Violette* has attracted so much critical attention while simultaneously retaining other fragments of poetry and setting them on a pedestal, allowing them a restrained performativity at key moments in the romance. This chapter examines some of the key transformations of the lyric insertions as they pass into prose, as well as the strategy of ducal identification created by the *Guillaume* fragment. Instead of asking the question what is left when a text is de-rhymed, I begin with a different question for the fifteenth-century *mises en prose*: in the passage to prose, what of poetry remains? Why is it that poetry is not fully expendable? In other words, just as critics have studied the poetics of insertion for the thirteenth and fourteenth centuries, we can examine the rhetoric of the poetic remainder for the fifteenth.

The *Violette* is said to belong to the 'cycle de la gageure [Wager Cycle]', a set of courtly narratives about falsely accused women who remain faithful to their men. It opens at the court of King Louis of France and recounts the story of a wager between an envious courtier, Lisiart, and the hero, the count of Nevers, to win the latter's beloved, Euriaut. Lisiart's villainous nature leads him to spy on the lady in her bath. Using the knowledge of the birthmark he sees on her breast (the 'violette' of the romance's title) he publicly (and deceptively) proves his conquest of her. The romance recounts Gerart and Euriaut's separation and Gerart's subsequent attempts to undo the treachery and to win back both lady and castle. Numerous wanderings are punctuated by battle scenes, the introduction of a magical potion and other typical romance subplots. The lyric insertions serve a variety of purposes in the original poetic narrative, namely to highlight characters' states of mind and to compare and link the two lovers together, acting as a sort of intratextual remedy for their separation in the plot.

The case of the *Gérard* merits special attention since it is not only an example of the prosification of a verse romance narrative, but of a particularly complex kind of verse narrative in which poetic insertions played an important role. In other words, the passage to prose is mediated from the outset by a number of complex factors inherent to the verse text itself. The phenomenon of fragments of lyric poetry, beginning with Jean Renart (*Roman de la Rose, ou de Guillaume de Dole*, c. 1228) and imitated quickly thereafter by Gerbert de Montreuil in the *Violette* (c. 1230), enjoyed a certain popularity in thirteenth- and fourteenth-century romance fiction, opening all kinds of possibilities for innovative literary subjectivity.[4] The lyric insertions are one of a number of means by which verse romance poetics creates social and literary associations, allowing the judgement and evaluation of characters' behavior. The question of the various literary functions of the poetic insertions inaugurated a whole set of modern critical debates concerning the economies of register, class and gender in these romances. It would be a mistake to assume that the poetics of insertion in these authors is identical, or even similar in all cases.[5] Each of the *Violette*'s almost forty lyric insertions, known for creating poetry inside of poetry, employs a different set of textual strategies, resulting in varied performative aspects.

The anonymous fifteenth-century prosator of the *Gérard* similarly treated different kinds of lyric insertions in different ways. The prosator had many examples of poetry to hand from which to pick and choose, and his manipulation of the source text's poetic insertions speaks to the kind of importance, and sense of distance from contemporary practice, that poetry maintained at the court of Burgundy. Poetry did not disappear from the prose version of the *Violette*; rather, the prosator made it into a literary monument. Poetry became a mark of identity and origin in an illustrious, albeit distant, past – the creative source for ducal self-fashioning in fiction. One might say very simply that identity and old poetry went hand in hand in fifteenth-century Burgundy.

A key feature which attracted the attention of the Burgundian prosators is how these earlier romances are repositories of stories of knightly deeds worthy of being preserved for human memory, and how they provide

---

[4] Maureen Barry McCann Boulton, *The Song in the Story: Lyric Insertions in French Narrative Fiction, 1200–1400* (Philadelphia, 1993); Sarah Kay, *Subjectivity in Troubadour Poetry* (Cambridge, 1990); Sylvia Huot, *From Song to Book: The Poetics of Writing in Old French Lyric and Lyrical Narrative Poetry* (New York, 1987); Emmanuèle Baumgartner, 'Les citations lyriques dans le *Roman de la Rose* de Jean Renart', *Romance Philology*, 35 (1981–82), 260–6; *eadem*, 'Sur les pièces lyriques du *Tristan en prose*', in *Etudes de langue et de littérature offerts à Félix Lecoy* (Paris, 1973), pp. 19–25; and Jacqueline Cerquiglini, 'Pour une typologie de l'insertion', *Perspectives médiévales*, 3 (1977), 9–14.

[5] Michel Zink, 'Suspension and Fall: The Fragmentation and Linkage of Lyric Insertions in *Le Roman de la rose (Guillaume de Dole)* and *Le Roman de la Violette*', *Jean Renart and the Art of Romance: Essays on* Guillaume de Dole, ed. Nancy Vine Durling (Gainesville, 1997), pp. 105–21.

powerful examples to princes aspiring to chivalric valor. In the attempt to recover and preserve this particular aspect of romance, fifteenth-century prosators often overlook other elements of the poetic narratives. The court writers in Burgundy, for example, interpret poetry through a very serious lens and rein in much of the self-conscious artificiality of romance, the *engin* which, as Sarah Kay has suggested, is such an important element in the use of lyric insertions.[6] Jane Taylor has argued that in the case of the Burgundian rewritings of Chrétien de Troyes's *Erec et Enide* and *Cligès* the 'ambiguity' or the 'mystery of Arthur's court' is domesticated, or re-acculturated: '[t]he prose text assimilates the mysterious or the ironic political system of Arthur's court to a model that would have been comfortably comprehensible to a Burgundian audience.'[7] The prosator in Burgundy willingly embraces and exaggerates romance verse narrative fiction when it features valiant deeds of great men and, where these deeds do not exist, the prosator sometimes even inserts them.[8] This is the double-faced mirror, reflecting and distorting, of prose romance from Burgundy.

The prologue of the *Gérard* text follows broader trends in the Burgundian *mises en prose* by expressing a prerogative of conserving and restoring the memory of chivalry. The narrative voice claims that the recountings of chivalric deeds in this text are consistently good examples which noble men can imitate: they 'ont esté et sont encores prise pour bonne exemple, miroir et fondation [were and still are good examples, mirrors and foundations]'. It underscores a revival of an ethos of chivalric culture rather than of language or a story *per se*. What is more, this emphasis on the deeds and the conquests of princes of the past who 'par leurs proeces et vaillances, au confort et a l'ayde de leur noble chevalerye ont fait leurs conquests [by their prowess and bravery made their conquests in the name of, and thanks to, their noble chivalry]' foregrounds a masculine world of deeds and the chivalric side of romance.[9] It is no wonder that for the title of the fifteenth-century version the prosator turns his back on the 'violette', the mark on the verse heroine's body, evoking her fidelity and serving as an emblem of what is playful and problematic about romance, and replaces it with the name and provenance of the male protagonist himself, Gerard de Nevers.

On the other hand, the prosator of the *Gérard* makes an important claim

---

[6] Kay, *Subjectivity*, pp. 171–214.

[7] Jane H. M. Taylor, 'The Significance of the Insignificant: Reading Reception in the Burgundian *Erec* and *Cligés*', *Fifteenth-Century Studies*, 24 (1998), 183–97, p. 190.

[8] A clear exception to this general trend is the scene of the Baghdadian sword, (called 'l'épée fine guerre') from the *Violette* (lines 1772–1829) which could perhaps also have served this purpose. Despite its epic allusions to Alexander and Charlemagne, the episode does not make it into the prose version.

[9] Both quotations from the prologue to the *Gérard* are from Lowe, ed., Gérard de Nevers*: Prose Version of the* Roman de la Violette, p. 2. References to this text will henceforth appear in the body of the chapter as *Gérard* followed by page number.

in the prologue about the origins of the *Violette*. In an interesting twist on the topos of the earlier romances' perceived linguistic difficulty, the prosator of the *Gérard* establishes a supposed Occitan origin for the *Violette*:

> [je] me suis ingeré et avachyé de moy traveillier a aplicquier mon petit sens et entendement a mettre et rediger par escript ce petit livret lequel *par avant estoit en langage prouvençal* et moult dificile a entendre.
>
> (*Gérard*, p. 2; emphasis added)
>
> [I have toiled and given all I can to apply my inferior sense and understanding in writing down this little book, which *originally was in Provençal* and was very difficult to understand.]

The *Violette* itself has, in reality, only two insertions originating in Occitan lyric and both these insertions have been linguistically rendered northern in the thirteenth-century text.[10] It therefore seems unlikely that in his attribution of provenance the prosator is making a specific reference to Provençal language found in the work; and it also seems unlikely that he is making a geographical attribution for the story, since the spatial frame of the *Violette*'s narrative is mostly the north and east of France. Such an explicative gloss to invent a source or to situate works in space and time is not uncommon to Burgundian fiction. The 'jadis [once upon a time]' of romance, as well as the pseudo-historical frame of 'realistic romances', are often replaced in the *mises en prose* with a specific historical time or place, and sometimes, specific mythico-historical actors make their way into the prose story.[11] It serves to pull prose romance away from a world where courtly exemplarities are the material for ludic fiction, and at the same time it creates a plausible (albeit sometimes falsified) tag for the origin of the work. The supposed southern origin of the work is more probably a distancing technique identifying a kind of poetic language and story in southern Europe. This lyrical south is an acquired taste in Burgundy, the prosator is arguing, but despite its exotic poetic quality, it deserves – at least to an extent – to be saved.

Only ten percent of the insertions remain in the prose text, so it is difficult to analyze comprehensively, as Maureen Boulton did for the *Violette*, how the prose text manages the expectations of lyric. Whereas in the verse romance, lyric insertions organized the textual space, stylized the emotional

---

[10] William Paden has also cautioned us to think twice about the Occitan insertions in the *Violette*, which are not only rendered exotic by a significantly different textual frame, but are also northern adaptations of southern language. See his 'Old Occitan as a Lyric Language: The Insertions from Occitan in Three Thirteenth-Century French Romances', *Speculum*, 68.1 (1993), 36–53.

[11] I make this point in more detail in my 'Burgundian Ideologies and Jean Wauquelin's Prose Translations', in *The Ideology of Burgundy: The Promotion of National Consciousness, 1364–1565*, ed. D'Arcy Jonathan Dacre Boulton and Jan R. Veenstra (Leiden, 2006), pp. 131–50, p. 138.

development of the plot, and even added a discursive gloss to the story, in the prose version the lyric chanson has sometimes been reduced to the status of a minor organizational technique. The weakest case of the prosified lyric insertion occurs when the text of the insertion has in fact totally disappeared. Nothing is left of the original insertion, except a mention in prose recalling the performative moment of lyric, here functioning as pure narrative transition: 'Puis aprés ce qu'il ot dit et fait sa complainte … (*Gérard*, p. 31) [And then when he finished uttering his complaint …]'. In other cases, the trace is nearly, or entirely, expunged.

In a few rare examples the text (or the content) of the lyric insertion is conserved in prose. In those cases, it is remarkable that the conservation of lyric actually seems to attenuate romance's insistence on the games of love. The initial lines of the *Violette* showcase the various ladies who have arrived at King Louis' court, each of whom acts as a mouthpiece, giving insights into different facets of the classic lyrical debates. The *Gérard* text eschews this lyrical spectrum of female perspectives on love, focusing instead on their gestural performance: the ladies, we learn, are simply dancing and singing. We read in direct discourse only two words from the duchess of Burgundy 'Amys, chantés (*Gérard*, p. 4) [Sing, friends]'; this one lady does, followed by the others in their turn. The insertion attributed to the sister of the count of Blois originally reads 'Ja ne mi marierai, / Mais par amors amerai [I will never marry, but in love I will love]'.[12] The prosator turns her couplet into a pithy paraphrase in indirect discourse: 'Quant la ducesse ot finee sa chanson, une moult belle pucelle, seur au conte de Blois, se prist a chanter, et dist que ja ne se maryeroit, mais toutte sa vye voldroit estre amoureuse (*Gérard*, p. 4) [When the duchess had finished her song, a very lovely lady, the sister of the Count of Blois, began to sing, saying that she would never marry, but she would like to be all her life in love].'

An analogous situation occurs just before the scene of renewed combat with the Saxons, where Florentine and Aiglente are jealously competing with each other. Florentine believes from listening to Gerard sing that she has won his heart, only to be quickly disabused of this notion (*Violette*, lines 3640ff). In the *Violette* he sings another couplet correcting her faulty interpretation, asking her to guess whom in fact he loves. The rather elegant tension created by her silence, and his opposing songs in the verse romance, is replaced in prose by a conversation (again in indirect discourse) in which she asks whom he loves, and he responds that he is suffering, begging her mercy and pity, repeating in a planar style more conventional concepts of lyric.[13] Poetic insertions as a means of creative characterization are minimized or reined in in the *Gérard*. In the *Violette* Gerard's vow to suffer until the woman who is

---

[12] *Le Roman de la Violette*, ed. Buffum, lines 119–20. References to this text will hereafter be given in the body of the chapter as *Violette* followed by line number.

[13] See Lowe, ed., *Gérard de Nevers*, p. 77.

the cause of his suffering is also touched by his love is followed by a poetic fragment 'Adeviner porés ciu j'aimme, / Par moi ne le sarés vous ja (*Violette*, lines 3365–6) [If you can, guess who I love, I will never tell you].' This couplet is both a gesture of challenge and a new vow to silence, immediately followed by Florentine's shock. The *Gérard* does away with such a gesture, breaking the scene with a rubric moving the narrative forward, directing us towards the coming siege: 'Comment Gerard se depparty de la court, et comment le lendemain ils alerent assegier ung chastel que le duc prist par les grans proeces de Gerart de Nevers (*Gérard*, p. 77) [How Gerard left the court and how the following day they went to besiege a castle which the duke acquired by the deeds of Gerart de Nevers].' The prose text expunges the couplet and puts Florentine's astonishment after the rubric's announcement of the siege, effecting a separation between action and emotion. The rubric places a different sort of exemplarity before the lyric game, the same one as is sketched in the *Gérard*'s prologue, namely the prowess of the ducal figure and the deeds of his vassals.

Sometimes the prosator keeps the reference to a lyric insertion because it contains an essential narrative clue. Such is the case of the *chanson de toile* fragment sung by the charming, attractive Marote. The lyric insertion is not included, but the prose text records the act of singing, creating a *mise en abyme* and subtly commemorating lost love. The prose, itself very poetic given its assonance and consonance, renders the situation as follows: 'Elle, quy estoit bien chantans, encommencha dire une chanson, et tant que en la chanson elle nomma Euriant (*Gérard*, p. 49) [She, who was delightful, began to sing a song, and in the middle of the song she named Euriaut].'[14] Singing is represented in the prose version as an activity befitting refined courtly figures, and its inclusion ostensibly indicates that it is worth noting for the prose reader that they are doing so. The contents of the song itself, however, are of secondary importance: prose adorned with a minimum of sonority, it seems, can achieve the same decorative and commemorative function.

The *Gérard* contains three other examples of verbatim, or near verbatim, citation of lyrics, all in the form of a single rhyming octosyllabic couplet.[15] In the *Violette*, the poetic narrative and the lyric insertion were linked in a game of intratextuality. The narrative inertia of the romance animated the asocial, highly private form of lyric, and the introspective lyric not only provided a

[14] For the text of the insertion in the verse, see *Le Roman de la Violette*, ed. Buffum, lines 2303–9.

[15] The editor Lowe has marked two of these in his edition as poetic citations, indented and therefore framed typographically as such on pp. 66 and 73. One of the others he put, I believe erroneously, into direct discourse, even though the language is almost a direct citation from the verse. On p. 70 of the *Gérard*, we read 'Je ne voy pas icy celle pour quy j'atens ma joye et mon bien [I cannot see here the woman in whom I find my joy and my happiness]', copying lines 3331–2 from the *Violette* 'Je ne le voi mie chi / Cheli dont j'atenc ma joie [I do not see here the one in whom I find my joy].'

perspective for social narratives to play with abstractions of love and desire, but also brought to a written text a constant reminder of the performative element of poetry. The *Gérard* conserves three cases of the lyric couplet, but no longer uses them particularly as a structuring technique. They are among the more generic of the lyric insertions, focusing on two themes: dying for a love to which the beloved is indifferent, and the inaccessibility of the beloved. In addition, the prosator has kept these three couplets originating from the same 300 lines of the verse romance which recount the scenes of the love philtre and Aiglente's attempted seduction. It seems that these couplets are a sign of lyric poetry. Being embedded in the prose narrative at this particular point of the tale does not add a significant interpretative element to the prose text's treatment of the threat of Aiglente's seduction. It is fair to say that the *Gérard* has a much tighter grip on these couplets than the *Violette*; instead of using them technically, it displays them as one would a rare ornament or jewel. The octosyllabic rhyming couplet, the basic signifying unit of high medieval lyrico-narrative poetry, has been left as a sign of fifteenth-century prose's distant source, thirteenth-century courtly fiction.

As the prose text proceeds, the number of totally effaced insertions rises. The simple reason for this phenomenon could be that the prosator lost interest in adapting these citations, and once he had marked his text's provenance with some decorative couplets, he abandoned the process. One could surmise also that as the prose text moves along a sufficient number of other textual transformations has occurred, meaning that the prosified lyric loses some of its power. The partial to complete excision of the lyric insertions from the prose versions allows other organizational schemes (for example, rubrics or miniatures) to control the narrative inertia. Such a technique might seem to reduce the instances of poetic performativity in the romances, but it also makes way for the textual performance of ducal identity based in deeds and valor to come into relief.

The liveliness of the romance texture created by the lyric insertions doubtless provided one of the elements attracting the prosator to choose this text. It is hard to mistake the *Violette* as anything but a romance. What is particularly special about the prose version of the romance however, is how, in the midst of the suppression of so much lyric and banalisation of the lyric that remains, the prosator leaves a trace of that original, distant dynamism in one particular epic fragment, a segment from the *Chanson de Guillaume*.[16] The ducal court of Burgundy often turned to the *chanson de geste* tradition as a 'sourcebook' to make claims about its illustrious dynastic origins and to fashion a revival of a crusading, chivalric tradition.[17] Girart de Roussillon was cast as an early Burgundian, as was Godefroy de Bouillon. One should not underestimate

---

[16] See Lowe, ed., *Gérard de Nevers*, p. 34.
[17] See the essays in Muriel Ott, ed., *L'Épopée médiévale et la Bourgogne* (Dijon, 2006).

how literature at the fifteenth-century court of Burgundy mined epic legends, such as those of Charles Martel, Charlemagne and Berthe, or imagined a renewed encounter with the Saracen. The *Violette* contained one such poetic fragment set in this kind of epico-chivalric context. Unlike the other poetic insertions in the original, it is not marked as specifically lyrical. It belongs to the category of narrative epic verse.

It is no wonder that the *Gérard* prosator conserved the fragment in its entirety. The scene is that of the court of Nevers. Gerard has dressed up as a jongleur; he has arrived soaking wet and exhausted, and has been waiting for some time at the door for someone to answer. With noble behavior, yet in ignoble garb, he asks to be excused to change his clothes and wash. The villainous Lisiart refuses his requests and insists that he stand up and perform immediately. Gerard does this reluctantly but, determined to impress, he sings a *laisse* from the *Chanson de Guillaume* and sings it well. The verse fragment covers a number of topics: chivalric manners, crusade against the Infidel, duels, justice debates and the proper behavior of those bound by ties of vassalage. From a purely topical perspective, it is easy to see how a Burgundian world of chivalric spectacle and dreams of renewed crusade would hold this poetic fragment up as the dearest jewel of all.

At the end of the insertion, the verse narrator insists that he 'lor dist vers dusch'a quatre (*Violette*, line 1430) [he recited up to four *laisses* of that song]', suggesting that these inserts are meant to give us just a taste of the lyrical performance at hand, and that in a live performance there would be much more. The *Gérard* includes the entire 21-line *laisse* labeled as 'Chanchon [Song]', but follows the song with a more restrained indication of how much more, if any, he actually sang: 'Gerars chanta de Guillaume au court nez moult grant espace (*Gérard*, p. 34) [Gerard sang about Guillaume au court nez for a long time].' The commentary in the prose text which follows also alters the verse version of the story. Whereas after the music Gerard sits down to table, but does not eat, imitating the discretion and manners of the knights in his song, the prose version insists that after the song Lisiart refuses to bring him anything to eat or drink, thereby intensifying the antagonism between the two characters.

That this poetic fragment, of all the other fragments, was kept entirely intact can be attributed to a few factors: firstly, its length and its epic narrative texture as opposed to others of a lyrical non-narrative quality; secondly, the overall tension at this part of the story requiring Gerard to defy Lisiart in a public context; and, lastly and most importantly, the mirror that it holds up for Burgundian identification with earlier poetic legends and communities. The Library of Burgundy is full of pseudo-historical literature related to the crusading movement and to the encounter with the Muslim southern and eastern Mediterranean. As such, to portray Gerard as a knight in disguise performing such a key moment as the decision to leave to provide reinforcements for Christians fighting against 'la geste Mahon (*Gérard*, p. 34) [the people of Muhammad]' would have immediate currency. This is, further, not the only recorded use of the epic legends at the banquets of the court of Burgundy. The court was quite famous for its elaborate tapestries woven on the occasion of spectacles, such as the tapestries of the life of Hercules, custom-made for the Feast of the Pheasant in Lille (1454). As Georges Doutrepont has noted, they also even had tapestries of the stories of Guillaume au court nez.[18] It comes as no surprise that this fragment caught the imagination of the prosator; indeed, it might well have been the impetus behind his choice of the *Violette* to be rendered in prose.

Prose versions from the fifteenth century are strangely discordant with the verse narrative written in earlier periods. They communicate in a more sober tone, and even with exaggerated seriousness, a recasting of aristocratic court scenes found in earlier verse romance. The *mises en prose* are rocky terrain, an uneven textual landscape in which remnants of a poetic past can often be felt just below the surface, as if masked or bound by new textual imperatives. For the ducal audience which consumed such modified poetic narratives, the prose texts act as spaces that display both local and distant culture, linking the two together and reaffirming local heritage in glorious pasts. The *mises en prose* collect, contain and showcase poetic knowledge, a knowledge linked intimately to notions of collective identity. In the reworking of the *Violette,* the possession and display of objects such as fragments of poetry, distant in both style and content, allows the prosator to anchor his text in a romance-styled court culture of the thirteenth century, all the while stressing the importance of that milieu's more chivalric elements. In the *Gérard* romance the *Chanson de Guillaume* epic fragment becomes an even rarer, more precious glimpse into the past, precisely because it uncannily locates in earlier poetry contemporary concerns in Philip the Good's court about chivalry, land and crusade. In the *Gérard* romance lyric fragments hang like tapestries, out of context perhaps, but admired as a sign of a past tradition. Romance narrative poetry in its most general sense is a body of shared stories, and the *mises en prose* at the court of Burgundy preserve this vernacular knowledge in poetry and present it for new aristocratic consumption. This knowledge, emanating from earlier *langue d'oïl* poetic fiction, has been handed over to a new regime of power. The passage to prose is neither neutral nor innocent. The prose versions of romances are invariably framed by radically different ideologies of power, gender and nation. A careful reading of the *Gérard* from other perspectives, such as gender or class, will no doubt reveal a plethora of other changes to the text, both macroscopic and microscopic, which gave shape to the Burgundianization of the *Violette*.

---

[18] Georges Doutrepont, *La Littérature française à la cour des ducs de Bourgogne* (Paris, 1909), p. 117.

9

The Movement from Verse to Prose in the Allegories of Christine de Pizan

SUZANNE CONKLIN AKBARI

Christine de Pizan is remarkable in many ways, not least as an author who produced an extraordinarily large volume of writing in a comparatively short period. Among these works are several allegories, some in verse and some in prose. Readers have tended to interpret Christine's movement from verse to prose allegory as simply a choice motivated by convenience or, somewhat more subtly, as an early manifestation of the complex and ornate prose style that would become ubiquitous in the later fifteenth century. This chapter argues that Christine's movement from verse to prose can fruitfully be understood in two complementary ways. First, it participates in an effort to integrate some of the rational and argumentative structures found in late-fourteenth-century French translations of philosophical and scientific writings within the originally poetic forms of medieval allegory; and, second, it is in step with Christine's definition of 'poesie' as a form of allegorical language that can be expressed through prose as readily as through verse. I have argued elsewhere that Christine's allegory exhibits features that depart from earlier allegorical models, especially with regard to the use of personification.[1] Her novel approach to allegory is perhaps nowhere so fully expressed, however, as with her redefinition of the mode as less a genre than a manner of expression. Christine innovatively constructs a notion of 'poesie' that establishes a range of texts – mythographic, historical, even scientific – as the object of allegorical exposition and as the source of hidden knowledge whose acquisition unites the interpretive community of perceptive readers.

Christine's first allegory, the *Epistre Othea*, combines verse and prose. This combination differs, however, from the prosimetrum form familiar from a number of allegories influential during the Middle Ages, including Boethius's *De consolatione Philosophiae* and Alain de Lille's *De planctu Naturae*: unlike these texts, in which the regular alternation of prose and

---

[1] Suzanne Conklin Akbari, *Seeing through the Veil: Optical Theory and Medieval Allegory* (Toronto, 2004), pp. 236–42.

verse reflects the dialogic interaction of narrator and personified interlocutor, the *Epistre Othea* features a four-part structure in which a short piece of verse is surrounded by an emblematic illustration and two distinct layers of prose commentary. This allegory differs substantially in form from Christine's subsequent works. The later works feature a linear narrative, in which Christine makes a journey or participates in the construction of a city, while the *Epistre Othea* is static and progress occurs only didactically, in the education of the reader. The work is organized according to formal and numerical principles, each chapter comprising three parts (or four, if we include the illustration),[2] and the work as a whole organized into one hundred chapters plus a prologue. Additional thematic groupings, including the seven virtues and vices, lists of deities, and so on, contribute to the rigidity of the numerical forms that organize the work.

It has been suggested that the page layout of the *Epistre Othea*, with the verse *texte* at the center and the glosses arranged about it, is meant to encourage a 'contemplative' reading of the work.[3] Without necessarily defining the *Epistre Othea* as a devotional work, we doubtless see here a reading practice encouraged by the manuscript layout, one that can be sharply distinguished from the very different organizing principles of Christine's later allegories. The *Epistre Othea* encourages the reader to consume it in two ways: linearly, through sequential reading that takes place over a span of time; and reflectively, as patterns within individual chapters and within the work as a whole emerge like visible forms in the mind of the thoughtful reader.

The 'contemplative' form of the *Epistre Othea*, with its designation of enigmatic verse as the oracular heart of the allegory, and expounded through prose commentary, gives way in Christine's later allegories to the more conventional allegorical form of the epic journey. In the *Chemin de longue estude* and the *Mutacion de Fortune*, the epic journey is recounted in poetic verse, whether expressed in terms of the narrator's climbing the ladder of intellectual ascent, in the *Chemin*, or in the form of the fateful voyage undertaken by the narrator in the first book of the *Mutacion de Fortune*. Subsequently, in the *Cité des dames* and the *Advision Cristine*, however, Christine moves from poetry to prose. This transition – sometimes dismissed merely as conformity to the fifteenth-century taste for prose, or simply as a time-saving measure – is worthy of closer attention, especially in the context of the *Epistre Othea*'s clear assignation of different functions to poetry on the one hand, and prose on the other. In the *Epistre Othea*, verse is appropriate

---

[2] Although the earliest manuscript of the *Epistre Othea* (Paris, BnF, MS fr. 848) has just four illustrations, see Sandra Hindman's study of the lavishly illustrated presentation manuscript in *Christine de Pizan's 'Epistre Othéa': Painting and Politics at the Court of Charles VI* (Toronto, 1986).

[3] Mary Ann Ignatius, 'Christine de Pizan's *Epistre Othea*: An Experiment in Literary Form', *Mediaevalia et Humanistica*, n.s. 9 (1979), 127–42.

to the oracular, enigmatic pronunciations of the goddess to the young knight Hector; conversely, the learned prose expositions of *glose* and *alegorie* provide much-needed commentary, designed to aid the youthful ruler in his effort to interpret rightly the directives of the goddess. *Glose* draws upon philosophical authorities for its interpretive force, while *alegorie* draws upon scripture and the Fathers of the Church. A strong sense of sequence is thus generated in the mind of the reader, where enigmatic verse comes first, followed by philosophical and, ultimately, theological exposition. Finally, the miniature conveys visually the meaning of the sibylline verse, dispensing entirely with the obscuring veil of language.

In a study of Christine's use of verse and prose, Earl Jeffrey Richards notes that '[t]he modern effort to see prose as the opposite of verse posits an antithesis that did not exist in medieval rhetoric.' He goes too far, however, in suggesting that the combination of prose and verse on the manuscript page of the *Epistre Othea* 'clearly shows […] that Christine viewed prose and verse as complementary in the most fundamental sense', even 'interchangeable'.[4] On the contrary, while the manuscript layout of the *Epistre Othea* demonstrates a 'complementary' relationship of verse and prose, it also clearly positions the verse as *prior*, that is, as oracular pronouncement in need of allegorical exposition, first through the philosophical interpretation of the *glose*, second through the theological interpretation of the *alegorie*.[5] Through figurative interpretation, the reader is led to a higher level of understanding. As Christine puts it, in the prologue to the first chapter of the *Epistre Othea* where she explains why the illustrations of the gods are obscured by clouds, 'deÿté est chose espirituelle et eslevee de terre [divinity is a spiritual thing, lifted above the earth]'.[6] To perceive clearly the meaning of the goddess's words, to look up at what is hidden within the clouds, requires the aid of the allegorical gloss.

Ascent is conveyed very differently in the *Chemin de longue estude*, where the narrator describes her figurative journey upward into the heavens under the tutelage of the Sibyl. In this work, the concatenation of the verse (emphasized, in certain passages, by the rhyme scheme) mimics the ascent enabled

---

[4] Earl Jeffrey Richards, 'Water without Salt and Ballades without Feeling, or Reintroducing History into the Text: Prose and Verse in the Works of Christine de Pizan', in *Christine de Pizan and Medieval French Lyric*, ed. Earl Jeffrey Richards (Gainesville, 1998), pp. 206–29, p. 210, p. 217.

[5] Compare the intelligent reading of Rosalind Brown-Grant, who points out that the *Epistre Othea* 'works precisely on the basis of a hierarchical progression from the pictorial to the spiritual, where the Latin 'autorité' quoted at the end of the chapter should be read as the ultimate point of reference to which the reader should aspire'. See 'Illumination as Reception: Jean Miélot's Reworking of the *Epistre Othea*', in *The City of Scholars: New Approaches to Christine de Pizan*, ed. Margarete Zimmermann and Dina De Rentiis (Berlin, 1994), pp. 260–72, p. 270.

[6] Christine de Pizan, *Epistre Othea*, ed. Gabriella Parussa (Geneva, 1999), p. 197.

by the ladder that Christine climbs through the spheres. Subsequently, in the *Mutacion de Fortune*, Christine continues to use verse, lapsing into prose only once, in her well-known account of Jewish history. In the *Cité des dames*, however, Christine moves into prose allegory for the first time, a form she maintains in her last allegory, the *Advision Cristine*. In both of these later works, architectural allegory provides a structuring principle that lends form to the allegorical narrative, governing the interpretive process in a way that is similar to – though not identical with – the four-fold structure of each chapter of the *Epistre Othea*, thereby enabling a form of 'contemplative' reading similar to the one suggested by the manuscript layout of her first allegory.

It is significant that it is only with the flowering of her prose allegories that Christine embarks upon an explicit definition of the nature of allegorical language. Peculiarly, Christine reserves the term 'alegorie' to refer specifically to allegorical exposition, what we would call 'allegoresis', and refers to allegorical language as 'poesie'. Significantly, the term 'poesie' designates a species of language, not a genre, and denotes a mode of expression found in a surprisingly wide range of works. 'Poesie', for Christine, does not correspond to our modern term 'poetry', for it can be as readily expounded through the medium of prose as of verse. Christine explicates the meaning of 'poesie' in several locations, including her biography of Charles V and the *Advision Cristine*. In the third and last part of her biography of the late king, Christine includes a digression 'de l'entendement et des sciences [concerning understanding and ways of knowing]'. The digression begins with an account of the senses and ends with a description of 'poesie', which, she says, uses figurative language to convey meanings that 'clerement ne se pevent enseigner [cannot be expressed clearly]'.[7]

Although Christine refers to this kind of language as 'poesie', her description of it closely resembles typical medieval characterizations of allegory. She writes that 'poesie' is generally taken to be any 'narracion ou introduction apparaument signifiant un senz, et occultement en segnefie un aultre ou plusieurs [narration or introduction openly signifying one sense, and covertly signifying another or many others]'. More properly, Christine continues, 'poesie' is a mode 'dont la fin est verité, et le proces doctrine revestue en paroles d'ornemens delictables et par propres couleurs, lesquelz revestemens soient d'estranges guises au propos dont on veult (3.68) [whose end is truth, and the process of which is teaching, clothed in words of delightful ornament and in the appropriate colors of rhetoric; with these clothes being of unusual styles in keeping with the purpose that one desires]'. In this definition, Christine uses several terms that are conventional to descriptions of allegory: the text signifies one thing openly, another covertly; it may have several levels of meaning; its purpose is to convey truth; and it clothes meaning

---

[7] *Le Livre des fais et bonnes meurs du sage roy Charles V*, ed. Suzanne Solente, 2 vols (Paris, 1936/1940), section 3.68. Translations of this work are mine.

with pleasant words, an allusion to the *integument* which is literally a veil or covering. Finally, among writers of 'poesie' Christine lists several allegorists, including Boethius, Martianus Capella, and Alain de Lille.

After offering this description of 'poesie', however, Christine abruptly withdraws from this mode of writing, stating 'pour cause que a maint pourroit le lengage sembler estrange, qui apris ne l'ont, et par consequent tourner a anui, retournerons a nostre premier objet (3.69) [because, to the many who have not learned it, this language may seem strange, and consequently bore them, let us return to our first objective]' – in other words, to the biography's narrative thread, currently at the account of Charles's death. Overtly, then, Christine indicates that a political biography is not the place for language that veils its meaning in order to restrict interpretation to a few. Covertly, however, she signals that, for those few who do understand such 'strange language', it may be possible to find a veiled significance in the biography of the former king. Put another way, the historical narrative of Charles's life is the ground for figurative explication, in the same way that sacred histories of the Bible are subject to exegesis, or the historical narratives evoked in Dante's *Commedia* are unfolded within the hermeneutics of the 'allegory of theologians'. The fact that Christine identifies this form of figurative language as 'poesie' suggests, moreover, that 'poesie' can refer to veiled language that does not necessarily have a fiction as its literal level. On the contrary, we can read historical narrative – such as the life of Charles V – as 'poesie' just as we can more conventionally read the *narratio fabulosa*, or 'fabulous narrative'.[8]

In her preface to Book One of the *Advision Cristine*, we find another exposition of the allegorical function of 'poesie'. Christine says that she, following the 'style of the poets', writes 'under the figure of metaphor or veiled speech':

> [S]ouventesfois soubz figure de methaphore, c'est a dire de parole couverte, sont muciees maintes secretes sciences et pures veritéz. Et en telle parolle dicte par poisie puet avoir mains entendemens, et lors est la poisie belle et subtille quant elle puet servir a plusieurs ententes et que on la puet prendre a divers propos.[9]

> [[O]ften, under the figure of metaphor or veiled speech, are hidden much secret knowledge and many pure truths. What is put in poetic language can have several meanings, and poetry becomes beautiful and subtle when it can be understood in different ways.]

---

[8] For a fuller exposition of the polysemous allegory of the 'end' of Charles V in Christine's biography of the French ruler, see Suzanne Conklin Akbari, 'Death as Metamorphosis in the Devotional Allegory of Christine de Pizan', forthcoming.

[9] Quotations are taken from the edition and translation of Christine Reno, 'The Preface to the *Advision Cristine* in ex-Phillipps 128', in *Reinterpreting Christine de Pizan*, ed. Earl Jeffrey Richards (Athens and London, 1992), pp. 207–27, pp. 208–9.

In this passage, 'poetic language' – 'parole dicte par poisie' – is polysemous, open to interpretation on a number of figurative levels, each of which is intellectually fertile and regenerative. 'Poesie' thus becomes, for Christine, a way to describe both allegory and myth, that is, all texts that can be subjected to allegorical interpretation. This conflation of allegory and myth as manifestations of 'poesie' is even more explicit in Christine's allusion to the 'poetic manner of speaking' in the *glose* to the first chapter of the *Epistre Othea*. There, she states that 'a ceste premiere [i.e., Prudence] avons donné nom et pris maniere de parler aucunement poetique et acordant a la vraye histoire [...] et a nostre propos prendrons aucunes auctoritez des ancians philosophes [to this first [virtue of Prudence] we have given a name and taken up a manner of speaking which is somewhat poetic and in keeping with the true history [...] and to aid this purpose we will take up some authorities among the ancient philosophers].'[10] Mythography, understood euhemeristically as being derived from actual historical events and personages, thus becomes material to be processed through the interpretive machine of allegory.[11] Moreover, as we saw in the account of 'poesie' in the biography of Charles V, historical narrative also can be allegorically expounded – that is, read as 'poesie'.

In view of the accommodation of allegory, myth and even history under the capacious definition of 'poesie' it comes as no surprise that, in the *Advision Cristine*, the term is further extended to comprise the *integumenta* of the philosophers. In book two of Christine's last allegory, in which the narrator interacts with the great shadow of the personification 'Opinion', the earliest poets' descriptions of natural phenomena are explicated in terms of allegory:

> Ces .III. pouetes dis [...] disoient que Occean, c'est a dire la mer ou l'abisme ou a tres grant inundacion d'yaues, et Thetis, qu'ilz disoient la deesse d'umeur, sont parens de generacion. Et par ce, dist il, comme par singuliere similitude ilz donnoient entendre que eaue fust le principe de la generacion des choses. Encore ceste sentence par autre fabuleuse narracion ilz covroient, disant que le sacrement et le serment des dieux estoit par l'eaue qu'ilz appellent Stix, laquelle est ung fleuve d'enfer.[12]
>
> [These three said poets [Orpheus, Musaeus, and Linus] [...] said that the Ocean [*sc.* Oceanus], or the sea or the abyss wherein exists a great flood

---

[10] *Epistre Othea*, ed. Parussa, p. 200.

[11] On mythography and allegory in Christine, see Renate Blumenfeld-Kosinski, *Reading Myth: Classical Mythology and its Interpretations in Medieval French Literature* (Stanford, 1997).

[12] *Le Livre de l'Advision Cristine*, 2.7. Quotations are taken from *Le Livre de l'Advision Cristine*, ed. Christine Reno and Liliane Dulac (Paris, 2001), and translations from *The Vision of Christine de Pizan*, trans. Glenda McLeod and Charity Cannon Willard (Cambridge, 2005), pp. 63–4 and p. 64 respectively. In this instance I have altered the translation slightly to render the text more literally.

of waters, and Thetis, whom they called the goddess of liquids, were the parents of generation. By this, he said, as by a particular metaphor, they made it understood that water was the principle for generation for things. Moreover, this meaning they hid by another fabulous story, saying that the gods' sacrament or oath was by the water that they called the Styx, which is the river of hell.]

In one respect, this passage is simply a manifestation of the 'manner of fictions' characteristic of 'poets', who conventionally deploy 'fabuleuse narracion' (the glossator's *narratio fabulosa*). The fact that their topic, however, is the 'things of nature' opens the way for a wider poetic understanding of natural philosophy. Further on in the same chapter, Christine describes how the philosophers of ancient times, like the poets, also expressed themselves through integumental language, that is, through the allegorical veil of 'poesie':

> Et puet estre ad ce ilz se mouvoient cuidans les vieux pouetes acorder avec eulx, ou puet estre pour les dis des philosophes nomans en plusieurs lieux les yaues sur le ciel. Toutesfois tant yceulx philosophes que aussi les pouetes, en tant comme a bon sens se puissent ramener au moins le plus des choses, en envelopement et soubz ombre parlerent: non les nouveaulx mais iceulx anciens, en tant que des sciences les portes vous ouvrirent, vous les devez excuser, amer et supporter. (*Advision* 2.7, p. 64)

> [And perhaps they were moved to this [i.e., to the belief that the first sphere is of water] believing that the ancient poets agreed with them or perhaps because the books of the philosophers mention in several places that the waters are above the heavens. Yet these philosophers as much as these poets, inasmuch as they might have been led by good sense to at least most of these things, spoke covertly and obscurely: not the new ones but these ancient ones, inasmuch as they opened the gates of knowledge for you, you must excuse, love and support. (*Vision*, p. 64)]

Here, Christine identifies philosophical discourse as being on a plane with poetic discourse, both of which communicate 'covertly and obscurely'. Such description of how philosophy should rightly be interpreted – that is, allegorically – is not common in early-fifteenth-century discourse. It is extremely common, however, in the twelfth-century discourse of neoplatonizing philosophers such as William of Conches, who in his glosses on Plato's *Timaeus* identifies the 'anima mundi', or world soul, as itself an *integument*, an allegorical veil deployed by the philosopher to refer to matters that are so high and lofty that – to use Christine's words in her biography of Charles V – they 'clerement ne se pevent enseigner (3.68) [cannot be expressed clearly]'.

Limitations of space prevent me from describing in detail how twelfth-century neoplatonizing philosophers deployed the notion of *integument* in order to describe how one might allegorically interpret not only the fables and myths of the ancient poets, but also the natural philosophy of Plato and his followers.[13] It is worth briefly pointing out, however, the extent to which many of the characteristic phrases that appear within Christine's definitions of 'poesie' – the 'fabuleuse narracion', the dichotomy of light and darkness, 'coverte' and 'ouverte' meaning – overlap significantly with definitions common in twelfth-century philosophical commentaries. There must certainly be intermediary sources for these discussions, which might profitably be sought in Nicholas Trevet's unpublished commentary on Boethius, which draws extensively on the twelfth-century commentary of William of Conches.[14] William's commentary includes several passages that correspond quite closely to certain sections of Christine's account in the second book of the *Advision Cristine* of how philosophy is coterminous with 'poesie', passages which are not drawn from the main source for this section, Aquinas's commentary on Aristotle's *Metaphysics*.

Based on this brief account, it is clear that Christine's broad definition of 'poesie' as a figurative mode of discourse that accommodates not just 'fabulous narration' and 'fiction' but also myth, history, and natural philosophy, corresponds significantly to the equally capacious definitions of *integument* produced in the late twelfth century. To note this correspondence is emphatically not to reduce Christine's use of allegory to twelfth-century forms of the mode. On the contrary, Christine's integration of 'poesie' with philosophical inquiry is very much in keeping with late medieval tendencies to bring together allegory and philosophical enquiry which we can see manifested, for example, in the work of Nicole Oresme.[15] As Claire Sherman has shown in her study of the manuscripts of Oresme's translations of, and commentaries on, Aristotle, Oresme lavishly deployed not just personification but also more substantial allegorical forms, such as what Sherman identifies as 'decision allegories', in order to facilitate his readers' efforts to understand and memorize salient details of the Aristotelian text.[16] Oresme's integration of allegorical modes into philosophical discourse might be seen

[13] On twelfth-century uses of *integumentum*, see Edouard Jeauneau, 'L'Usage de la notion d'*integumentum* à travers les gloses de Guillaume de Conches', *Archives d'histoire doctrinale et littéraire du moyen âge*, 24 (1957), 35–100. On its thirteenth-century vernacular uses, see Akbari, *Seeing through the Veil*, pp. 57–63.

[14] Trevet's commentary remains unedited, except for a typescript transcription by Edmund T. Silk. On Trevet's work, see Margaret T. Gibson, *Boethius, His Life, Thought and Influence* (Oxford, 1981) and Maarten J. F. M. Hoenen and Lodi Nauta, *Boethius in the Middle Ages: Latin and Vernacular Traditions of the* Consolatio Philosophiae (Leiden, 1997).

[15] On Christine's knowledge of Oresme's works, see Sylvie Lefèvre, 'Christine de Pizan et l'Aristote Oresmien', in *Au champ des escriptures: IIIe Colloque international sur Christine de Pizan*, ed. Eric Hicks (Paris, 2000), pp. 231–43.

[16] See 'Personifications and Allegories as Cognitive and Mnemonic Subject Guides' in Claire Richter Sherman, *Imaging Aristotle: Verbal and Visual Representation in Fourteenth-Century France* (Berkeley, 1995), pp. 35–174.

as a counterpart of Christine's own definition of 'poesie' as comprising not only fictional forms of language, but also scientific and philosophical ones.[17] More profoundly, we might wish to assess the extent to which Christine's exploration of Aristotelian metaphysics in the *Advision Cristine* informs the overall allegorical structure of the work. Christine's account of Aristotle's *Metaphysics*, adapted (with substantial additions) from Aquinas's commentary, appears in the second part of the *Advision*, and has been called the first rendition of the *Metaphysics* to appear in the vernacular.[18] Christine's presentation of the *Metaphysics* contributes to her assimilation of philosophical enquiry within the definition of 'poesie', leading to her use of the dichotomy of form and matter (highlighted in her précis of the *Metaphysics*) as the foundation of the philosophical allegory of the *Advision Cristine*.

Each of the three books of the *Advision* features a personification whose identity is constructed in terms of the dichotomy of form and matter. In book one, the opening scene features a great shadowy female, identifiable as Nature, who feeds a shadow in the form of a man, named Chaos. By replacing the standard feminine personification of matter, Silva, with an innovative masculine personification, Chaos, Christine implies that matter is (or can be) masculine. If matter can be either masculine (Chaos) or feminine (Silva), then form too presumably can be either masculine or feminine. This variability of gender assignation flies in the face of the conventional association of form and matter in popular assimilations of Aristotelian theory, epitomized in the philosopher's description of conception in terms of the stamp of the masculine form on the passive matter provided by the female. The popular spurious etymology of 'mater, id est, materia' only lent force to this gendered view of the relationship of form and matter.[19]

The second book of the *Advision*, comprising a discussion between the narrator and Opinion, also centers on the relationship of form and matter. This preoccupation appears throughout Opinion's learned discourse, most importantly perhaps in her account of Aristotle's view of the primacy of

---

[17] On scientific works using prose and verse, see Bernard Ribémont, 'Vers et prose dans l'écriture à caractère scientifique médiévale: L'exemple de l'encyclopédisme', in *Actes du XXe Congrès International de Linguistique et Philologie Romanes*, ed. G. Hilty (Tübingen, 1993), vol. 5, section 8 ('L'art narratif aux XIIe et XIIIe siècles'), pp. 341–52.

[18] On Christine's use of Aquinas, see Liliane Dulac and Christine Reno, 'L'humanisme vers 1400: essai d'exploration à partir d'un cas marginal: Christine de Pizan, traductrice de Thomas d'Aquin', in *Pratiques de la culture écrite en France au XVe siècle*, ed. Monique Ornato and Nicole Pons (Louvain-la-Neuve, 1995), pp. 161–78.

[19] On the feminine nature of matter, see Suzanne Conklin Akbari, 'Nature's Forge Recast in the *Roman de Silence*', in *Literary Aspects of Courtly Culture*, ed. Donald Maddox and Sara Sturm-Maddox (Cambridge, 1994), pp. 39–46, esp. pp. 39 and 43. On the feminine nature of personified matter ('Silva') in medieval neoplatonism, see Barbara Newman, *God and the Goddesses: Vision, Poetry, and Belief in the Middle Ages* (Philadelphia, 2003), pp. 55–64.

matter. Opinion cites Aristotle's statement that 'aurebours il appert que la terre soit tres proprement principe (2.12, p. 73) [however much it seems to go against the grain, the earth must be very appropriately the principle (p. 72)].' By making Aristotle the authority for Opinion's subsequent assertion that the earth is the origin of all things, characterized by 'souveraine simplicite [et] souveraine perfection (2.12, p. 74) [absolute simplicity [and] absolute perfection (p. 73)]', Christine continues to call into question the negative effect of the conventional association of woman with matter. The relationship of form and matter is central to book two of the *Advision* on the level not just of the philosophical discourse but also in the poetic form of personification, as Opinion is characterized as being made up of pure form, yet form that can be broken down into constituent parts. Opinion is 'une grant ombre femmenine sans corps [a great feminine shadow without body]' (2.1), who soon reveals herself to be made up of innumerable smaller shadows, each of a different color and form: 'une grant tourbe en y avoit de toutes blanches, une autre de toutes vermeilles, les autres yndes, autres de couleur de feu, autres d'eaue, et ainsi de toutes les couleurs (2.1, pp. 51–2) [There was one mass of all the white, others of all the reds, others blue, others the color of fire, others of water, and so on with all the colors (p. 53)].' By describing the colors that constitute Opinion as being like fire or like water, Christine suggests that, in Opinion, compounded matter is broken down into its elements. The imposition of form upon matter highlighted in the opening passage of the *Advision* is reversed in the opening of the second book, as synthesis is countered by dissolution.

In the third book, the varied colors of Opinion are replaced by the brilliant white light of Philosophy, who appears as 'une telle tres luisant espere qui toute la chambre emplissoit de tres grant resplandeur (3.1, p. 93) [a sphere shining so brightly that filled the whole room with great light (p. 89)]'.[20] This represents a third stage in a progression of synthesis and dissolution that structures the allegory: the elements compounded within the body of Chaos are dissociated in the fragmented body of Opinion, whose multi-hued parts are subsequently reintegrated in the pure light of Philosophy. This progression also moves from matter (the body of Chaos) to form (the body of Philosophy), and has at its center a sophisticated commentary on Aristotle's *Metaphysics* focusing precisely on the relationship of matter and form. I would therefore argue that, in the *Advision Cristine*, we find a novel mode of structuring allegorical interpretation, one which represents a new twist on earlier efforts to perform the same task, such as the distinctive page layout of the *Epistre Othea* and the architectural allegory of the *Mutacion de Fortune* and the

---

[20] On the relationship of Opinion and Philosophy in *Advision*, see Benjamin Semple, 'The Critique of Knowledge as Power: The Limits of Philosophy and Theology in Christine de Pizan', in *Christine de Pizan and the Categories of Difference*, ed. Marilynn Desmond (Minneapolis and London, 1998), pp. 108–27.

Cité des dames. While the *Advision Cristine* also includes architectural allegory, in the form of the linked university and cloister of the third book, it is unique in drawing upon philosophy (specifically, Aristotelian metaphysics) to provide a structuring principle that guides the act of allegorical reading. Sarah Kay has recently argued, in her brilliant analysis of the *Chemin de longue estude*, that several of Christine's works exhibit a concern with the nature of form as defined in the Aristotelian tradition and question the extent to which general knowledge can be abstracted from the particular.[21] In the *Advision Cristine*, however, the dichotomy of form and matter is not merely the object of philosophical inquiry, but the narrative structuring principle itself. This dichotomy provides a continuum along which metaphorical tropes and figures are arranged to facilitate the reader's linear progression and intellectual ascent: here, poetic knowledge *is* philosophical knowledge.

In the last lines of the *Advision*, Christine retrospectively provides emblems to facilitate the reader's understanding and memory of the allegory: 'Ainsi me depars de mon advision, laquelle je ay partie si comme en trois differences de trois pierres precieuses en leurs proprietez (3.27, p. 142) [Thus I take leave of my vision, which I have divided as if by the three different properties of three precious stones (p. 134)].' Each book, she writes, can be represented by a precious stone: diamond, cameo, and ruby. The diamond is 'dur et poignant [hard and sharp]', like the swords used by the knights in the current civil strife reviled in the first book by the crowned lady who personifies France. 'Ha!', she exclaims, 'La generacione perverse qui en lieu de dens usent de glaives, non mie pour mordre mais pour tout trenchier (1.21, p. 38) [Oh! Perverse generation that uses swords in the place of teeth, not to bite but to cut in pieces (p. 42)].' Just as the knight in the service of justice epitomizes virtue, so the diamond emits shining light whose 'virtu … est moult grande [virtue … is very great]'. When his strength is placed in the service of Avarice, however, who continually hoards wealth, like the diamond set in gold he becomes 'obscur et brun [obscure and brown]', propagating the figurative darkness of an unjust state. Like the diamond, the cameo is characterized by both light and darkness. Unlike the diamond, however, it displays both light and darkness simultaneously, just as human learning – opinion – generates both wisdom and deception. Unlike other stones, the cameo bears an 'emprainte [imprint]', reinforcing the importance of the discussion of form and matter in the second book as well as the importance of this dichotomy as the foundation of all intellectual inquiry. Finally, the ruby emblematizes Philosophy, which refines the understanding the more one contemplates it: 'cler et resplendissant et sans nue obscure, qui a proprieté de tant plus plaire comme plus on le regarde (3.27, p. 142) [clear and shining and without any

---

[21] See *The Place of Thought: The Complexity of One in Late Medieval French Didactic Poetry* (Philadelphia, 2007), pp. 150–76.

obscuring cloud, [and] which has the property of being more pleasing the more one gazes upon it (p. 134)]'.

In the *Cité des dames*, Christine describes the sibyls as 'pierres precieuses' because of their gift of prophecy. Similarly, in the *Advision Cristine*, the precious stones emblematizing the three books highlight the gift of foresight offered in them through the medium of prophecy. The prophecies of the first book concern the future of France, as the crowned lady declares 'O amie chiere, note la prophecie du temps de ma gloire! (1.20, p. 37) [Oh dear friend, take note of the prophecy of the time of my glory! (p. 40)].' Those of the second book concern Christine's own intellectual efforts, as Opinion tells Christine that

> ceste lecture sera de plusieurs tesmoignee diversement [...] Maiz, aprés ta mort, venra le prince plain de valeur et sagesce qui par la relacion de tes volumes desirera tes jours avoir esté de son temps et par grant desir souhaidera t'avoir veue. (2.22, pp. 89–90)
>
> [several people will bear witness to this commentary in different ways [...] But after your death, there will come a prince, full of valor and wisdom, who – because of the content of your books – will wish you had lived in his time and will greatly long to have known you. (p. 86)]

The prophecies of the third book concern the fate of the soul, as Philosophy tells what steps one must take in order finally to see God face to face. Philosophy's final command to 'veoir la benoite Trinité ainsi que elle est (3.26, p. 140) [see the blessed Trinity just as it is (p. 131)]'[22] is echoed in Christine's final display to the reader, the trinity of precious stones that represent the three books of the *Advision Cristine*, and which she invites the reader to gaze upon. Contemplation of that lesser trinity implicitly leads to the contemplation of the greater.

The metaphor of 'pierres precieuses' used in the *Cité des dames* to describe the sibylline stones upon which the City is founded is reworked in the closing lines of the *Advision*, in the hierarchy of three stones that emblematizes the three books of the allegory. An earlier description of knowledge in the form of precious stones, however, specifically reinforces the conflation of poetic and philosophical knowledge: Opinion pauses in her philosophical discourse, and refers the interested reader to the fuller account to be found in Aristotle's *Metaphysics*. While most readers will be satisfied with what Opinion has offered thus far, others will need to search more widely in the bountiful treasury of knowledge:

---

[22] I have revised McLeod and Willard's translation, reading 'veoir' here as a verb ('to see').

> Et ainsi comme en une riche marcerie ou tresor sont avec perles diverses pierres precieuses de plusieurs vertus, couleurs, et pris, lesquelles au goust et plaisirs de divers bargigneurs sont requises, soient ycestes choses ou tresor de ton volume reservees aux hommes scienceux de soubtil entendement, et passent oultre les moins expers aux choses plus legieres et communes. (2.13, pp. 74–5)

> [Just as in a rich shop or treasure chest there are with the pearls precious stones of particular virtues, colors, and prices, which at the pleasure and taste of sundry bargaining clients are sought, so these things in the treasure trove of your volume must be reserved for learned men of subtle understanding, and let the less expert proceed to lighter and more commonplace matters. (pp. 71–2)]

These figurative gems are at once the creation of the poetic sensibility of the author and a timeless, unaltered repository of ancient 'vertu', available to the reader who is 'de soubtil entendement'. Through the preservation and production of these 'pierres precieuses', Christine positions herself together with the ancient philosophers and her present (and future) readers as members of a single interpretive community, united by their common recognition of 'vertu' and their ability to see past the veil of 'poesie'.

PART III
POETIC COMMUNITIES

10

The Songs of Jehannot de Lescurel in Paris, BnF, MS fr. 146:[1]
Love Lyrics, Moral Wisdom and the Material Book

NANCY FREEMAN REGALADO

Among the questions raised by the title, *Poetry, Knowledge and Community in Late Medieval France*, I have chosen one: how could the formal features of medieval French love lyrics and their contextualization in a material book be used to shape knowledge for a particular community of readers?

One of the primary functions of verse in the vernacular works of the French Middle Ages (beyond the representation of the speaking voice) is to present knowledge, information and learning as moral wisdom. Paradoxically, medieval French love lyrics are not governed by the signifying practices of verse. Although they express moral judgments about their particular subject – opposing *bone amor* to *felonie* – medieval French love lyrics are courtly performance pieces most deeply expressive of *technê*, of knowledge as art rather than as learning, political wisdom, or spiritual truth. There are, of course, citations in vernacular motets which dig deep into written learning, yielding 'seemingly endless layers of meaning'.[2] But the impact of monophonic French love lyrics depends principally on their intense effect of psychological sincerity and their flaunting of poetic form rather than on allusions to learned, religious or classical traditions of knowledge.

As the courtly lyric enters into writing in the later thirteenth and the fourteenth century, however, the material book serves as a powerful technology

---

[1] I am deeply indebted to Elizabeth A. R Brown for her work on the historical and manuscript context of BnF, MS fr. 146, including our 1992 Oxford seminar on Lescurel (organized by Margaret Bent and Andrew Wathey), and to Edward H. Roesner who, for decades, has led my way into BnF, MS fr. 146. I am also warmly grateful to members of the 2001 and 2007 New York University seminars on BnF, MS fr. 146, co-taught with Brown and Roesner.

[2] S. Clark and E. E. Leach, ed., *Citation and Authority in Medieval and Renaissance Music Culture: Learning from the Learned* (Woodbridge, 2005), p. xxiii. See Sylvia Huot, *Allegorical Play in the Old French Motet: The Sacred and the Profane in Thirteenth-Century Polyphony* (Stanford, 1997).

for remotivating the vernacular lyric in new contexts through patterns of compilation that open the way for the love lyric to express high visions of knowledge as moral wisdom. Book compilation provides a change of footing for vernacular song, a shift of frame that could alter its significance. This is a period of extraordinary experimentation in ways poets and compilers could arrange lyrics in books in order to express moral knowledge. Notable examples include Dante's *Convivio* (c.1307) where the poet's love lyrics are embedded in philosophical commentary in Italian prose. Teodolinda Barolini shows how in Petrarch's *Rime sparse* (1327) the spiritual themes in the lyrics themselves are sustained by the compilational order of the *canzioniere* so that the material sequence of love lyrics marks out a moral progression towards conversion.[3] Anne Walters Robertson uncovers the 'schemes and patterns' of Machaut's cycle of motets 1–19 (composed in the 1320s), where the interplay of citation and sequential order leads to a mystical *scens*.[4] The compilations of the later fourteenth and fifteenth centuries that combine verse and prose or that set out sizeable arrangements of *forme-fixe* pieces are unthinkable without the support of the material book.[5] The moral and spiritual meanings of love lyrics set within large-scale compositions in the fourteenth century depend thus upon contextualization in books – through commentary in Dante, or in arrangements such as those of Petrarch and Machaut which are shaped by writing, book compilation, and page layout.

My question is the following: in what ways can knowledge as wisdom emerge not just from commentary and sequence, but also from the ways authors and compilers lead readers to consider different kinds of texts together as they manipulate the pages of a book, a practice I call reciprocal reading?[6] To demonstrate how reciprocal reading can lead readers to moral and political wisdom, I have chosen a set of love lyrics that have seemed particularly resistant to such a reading: the thirty-four *ballades*, *rondeaux*, and *diz entez* attributed to Jehannot de Lescurel and copied into the famous

---

[3] Teodolinda Barolini, 'The Making of a Lyric Sequence: Time and Narrative in Petrarch's *Rerum Vulgarium Fragmenta*', *Modern Language Notes*, 104 (1989), 1–38.

[4] Anne Walters Robertson, *Guillaume de Machaut and Reims: Context and Meaning in his Musical Works* (Cambridge, 2002), p. 8.

[5] See the chapters by Suzanne Akbari, Denis Hüe, and David Wrisley in this volume.

[6] Nancy Freeman Regalado, 'The *Chronique métrique* and the Moral Design of BN fr. 146: Feasts of Good and Evil', in *Fauvel Studies: Allegory, Chronicle, Music, and Image in Paris, BnF MS fr. 146*, ed. Margaret Bent and Andrew Wathey (Oxford, 1998), pp. 467–94 [hereafter *FS*]. Elizabeth Wright is completing a study of reciprocal reading in BnF, MS fr. 146 in the light of the non-linear reading style required of *Fauvel* readers who must ponder its complex page layout, bilingual texts, interpolated music, illustrations, and intertextual allusions ('Late Medieval Reading Practices Revealed in BnF fr. 146 and its Texts'). On reading BnF, MS fr. 146, see also Michelle Bolduc, 'The Dissociation of Contrast; The Authorial Sanctity of Chaillou de Pesstain in the *Roman de Fauvel*, BnF fr. 146', in *The Medieval Poetics of Contraries* (Gainesville, 2006).

Fauvel manuscript, BnF, MS fr. 146 (hereafter fr. 146), composed about 1316–17 when Philip V, the second son of Philip the Fair, ascended the throne of France.[7] Fr. 146 begins with an anonymous non-lyric *complainte*, 'Helas com j'ai le cuer plain d'ire' (fol. Ar–v).[8] It is followed by an index of all the musical pieces and *dits* compiled in fr. 146 (fol. Br–v), divided into three groups: 169 musical insertions in *Le Roman de Fauvel* amplified by Chaillou de Pesstain (fols 1r–45r), 106 in Latin, 60 in French, 3 bilingual, arranged in the index by musical genre and number of voices;[9] 8 *dits* (verse compositions represented as spoken) by Geffroi de Paris, 2 in Latin, 6 in French, (fols 46r–55v);[10] 34 '*balades Rondeaux et diz entez sus refroiz de Rondeaux*' (stanzas of spoken verse 'grafted' onto musical refrains) by Jehannot de Lescurel (fols 57r–62v), arranged in alphabetical order A–G (E missing).[11] Fr. 146 ends with an anonymous *Chronique métrique* of the kingdom of France for the years 1300–16 (fols 63r–88r).[12]

Fr. 146 is dominated by the *Roman de Fauvel,* which contains two books.[13] In Book I (dated 1310) all estates of man show their greed and corruption by currying Fauvel, the horse of hypocrisy. In Book II (dated 1314) attributed to Gervès du Bus, a royal notary, the horse Fauvel seeks to wed Fortune, who marries him off to Vainglory. Chaillou's expanded *Fauvel* (dated 1316–17) includes nearly 3,000 lines of *addicions* describing Fauvel's wedding, 169 musical interpolations, and 78 miniatures. The interpolated *Fauvel* and the other works compiled with it in fr. 146 play an intricate game that takes many paths to a single, overarching lesson in kingship. Its moral purpose is a lesson in right rule for the new king Philip V who ascends the throne in January 1317. If the virtue of Virginity is praised and the vices of Carnality and Adultery are condemned with special severity in fr. 146, it is because this moral

---

[7] *Le Roman de Fauvel in the Edition of Mesire Chaillou de Pesstain (facsimile of BnF MS fr. 146)*, ed. Edward Roesner. Introduction by François Avril, Nancy Freeman Regalado and Edward Roesner (New York, 1990) [hereafter *Facsimile*].

[8] J. C. Morin, ed. and trans., 'The Genesis of Manuscript Paris, Bibliothèque Nationale, Fonds Français 146, with Particular Emphasis on the *Roman de Fauvel*', diss. (New York University, 1992), Appendix A.

[9] Index, text of musical insertions, and verse *addicions* edited by E. Dahnk, *L'Hérésie de Fauvel* (Leipzig, 1935) [hereafter Danke]. Text and music of monophonic songs in Samuel N. Rosenberg and Hans Tischler, ed. and trans., *The Monophonic Songs in the 'Roman de Fauvel'* (Lincoln, 1991) [hereafter Rosenberg-Tischler].

[10] W. Storer and C. Rochedieu, ed. and trans., *Six Historical Poems of Geffroi de Paris, Written in 1314–1318* (Chapel Hill, 1950); Lesfranc Holford-Strevens, 'The Latin *Dits* of Geffroy de Paris', in *FS*, pp. 247–75.

[11] *The Works of Jehan de Lescurel,* ed. N. Wilkins. (Rome, 1966) [hereafter Wilkins].

[12] *La Chronique métrique attribuée à Geffroy de Paris*, ed. A. Diverrès (Paris, 1956).

[13] *Le Roman de Fauvel par Gervais du Bus*, ed. Alfred Långfors (Paris, 1914–19) [hereafter Långfors]; *Le premier et le secont livre de Fauvel in the version preserved in B.N. f. fr. 146*, ed. P. Helmer (Ottawa, 1997).

theme alludes to the political scandal (recounted in the *Chronique métrique*) that finally brought Philip V to the throne.[14] Accusations of adultery were brought against the three daughters-in-law of Philip the Fair in 1314. The lovers of two were horribly executed, one wife died in prison in 1315, but one was exonerated: Jeanne de Bourgogne, wife of the new king Philip V, who, in a struggle for the succession, succeeded his older brother in place of Louis X's daughter (whose bloodline was perhaps contaminated by adultery).

Elizabeth A. R. Brown has shown how false love is condemned and loyal love praised at key points throughout the manuscript.[15] Moreover, the *Roman de Fauvel*, the poems of advice by Geffroi de Paris, and the *Chronique métrique* – all composed in the verse appropriate to moral reflection – contribute directly to the lesson in kingship that emerges out of this period of turmoil. The puzzler, in fr. 146, is how the thirty-four Lescurel love lyrics might serve this high moral purpose. They have an exceptional status as a single-author collection of three-stanza love lyrics known only in this manuscript.[16] The sole theme of the Lescurel lyrics is love, expressed through the stereotypical motifs of the courtly song, as in the initial *rondeau* refrain (fol. 57ra; Wilkins #1) repeated in 'A vous, douce debonnaire' (fol. 57rb; Wilkins #3) (Plate 1).

> **A vous, <u>douce</u> debonnaire**
> **Ai mon cuer donné;**
> **Ja n'en partiré**.
> Vo vair euil mi font atraire
> **A vous, <u>dame</u> debonnaire**:
> Ne ja ne m'en quier retraire,
> Ains vous serviré
> Tant [comme] vivré.
> **A vous, <u>douce</u> debonnaire**
> **Ai mon cuer donné;**
> **Ja n'en partiré**.[17]

---

[14] See A.V. Clark, 'The Flowering of Charnalité and the Marriage of Fauvel', in *FS*, pp. 175–86, and Nancy Freeman Regalado, 'Allegories of Power: The Tournament of Vices and Virtues in the *Roman de Fauvel* (BN MS fr. 146)', *Gesta*, 32 (1993), 135–46.

[15] Elizabeth A. R. Brown, '*Rex ioians, ionnes, iolis*: Louis X, Philip V, and the *Livres de Fauvel*', in *FS*, pp. 53–72.

[16] These defining elements of the Lescurel repertory stand out when compared to other structural types of song collections comprehensively described by Eglal Doss-Quinby, 'The Douce 308 *chansonnier* within the Corpus of Trouvère Songbooks', in *Lettres et musique en Lorraine du XIIIe au XVe siecle*, ed. M. Chazan and N. F. Regalado, in preparation.

[17] Translations mine unless otherwise indicated; the polyphonic *rondeau* is recorded on CD *Fontaine de grace: Jehan de Lescurel: ballades, virelais et rondeaux*. Ensemble Gilles Binchois, dir. Dominique Vellard. Virgin Veritas: 7243 5 45066 2 8, No. 1.

[**To you, sweet lovely, I've given my heart; I'll never be parted from it.** Your fair eyes draw me **to you, lovely lady**: I never wish to turn away, Instead I will serve you as long as I live. **To you, sweet lovely, I've given my heart; I'll never be parted from it.**]

The subject and language of this love lyric – its expression of intense feelings of love, its absolute sincerity – are as utterly familiar as the *rondeau* form with its repeating refrain, one of the 3-stanza *formes fixes* that dominate the late medieval French courtly lyric. The apparent simplicity of the text is belied by its elegantly heterometric lines, its *mise en page*, and its musical development. Everything on the manuscript page makes this piece a high art form. The lyrics are repeated twice: first, its music fills most of column a, where the refrain appears in a showy polyphonic setting for three voices, written out in score form over the refrain, the only polyphonic piece in the Lescurel repertory; second, the full text of the *rondeau* is centred in column b in a monophonic setting. The initial decorated capital A is immense, twenty-five lines high, almost twice as tall as the fifteen-line capital F which opens the *Roman de Fauvel* (fol. 1), and this letter A is repeated six times in large, four-line, pen-flourished capitals on fol. 57r, four times reiterating the key word *Amours*.

In a personal communication (2 February 2007), musicologist Edward Roesner has generously contributed a musical analysis which describes the striking art of Lescurel's initial *rondeau*, 'A vous, douce debonaire'. 'There are very few polyphonic settings of *rondeaux* and like pieces before the second third of the fourteenth century, apart from motets that incorporate *rondeau* elements. It is the only polyphonic *rondeau* in fr. 146, and indeed the only polyphonic vernacular song apart from the motets. The only significant corpus of such works before Machaut is by Adam de la Halle.[18] This work may be a homage to Adam: like his polyphonic *rondeaux*, it is for three voices and it is set homorhythmically (all three voices move at essentially the same pace and declaim the text simultaneously). It places the 'main' voice in the middle of the texture, not in the bottom voice. In this, it stand apart from nearly all other examples of polyphonic writing from France in the thirteenth and early fourteenth century, which usually build up from the bottom. Instead, it resembles some compositional practices cultivated in medieval Britain in its striking emphasis on tertian sonorities, on the use of 3rds and 6ths in prominent positions, rather than the more 'open' consonant intervals of the 5th and 4th favoured in France. The tertian quality is also observable in Adam's *rondeaux*.' Speaking of its structural function in the compilation, Roesner adds, 'The complete *rondeau* appears monophonically

---

[18] *Adam de la Halle Œuvres complètes*, ed. and trans. Pierre-Yves Badel (Paris, 1995), pp. 453–62.

Plate 1. Paris, BnF, MS fr. 146, fol. 57r: Initial page of the Lescurel lyrics.
col. a, top: A vous douce debonaire [*sic*] (*rondeau polyphonique*)
col b, centre: A vous douce debonaire (*rondeau monophonique*)

in column b, but in a somewhat different rhythmic grid, suggesting that this is, in fact, a separate entry in the Lescurel collection, independent of the opening polyphony. The polyphonic setting would have had special importance; it may have been intended as a sort of dedicatory entry, like a large historiated initial, to launch the collection.'

Musicologist Wulf Arlt confirms the remarkable art of Lescurel's lyrics: there is nothing hesitant about the poet-musician's exhibition of lyric forms in this collection and his 'extreme individualization', that is, his expressive matching of musical cadences and ornaments with emotions in the texts.[19] Arlt notes that all thirty-four pieces are of exceptionally high quality, although there is an agreeable variety of tone and register. A half-dozen adopt a woman's voice, and there are shifts between pieces of high seriousness and others where girls' names and diminutives recall dance songs. Overall, the Lescurel lyrics constitute a display of masterful variations on the *forme-fixe* genres: there are 9 distinct types of *ballade* in 15 examples, 9 types in the 12 *rondeaux*, and each of the 5 *virelais* is different.[20] They reflect 'the creative upheaval in contemporary Paris', for they are 'the first monophonic songs in which the new mensural procedures of polyphony […] are adopted and exploited in the melodic conception'.[21] Musically, they are 'the work of an exceptionally fine craftsman' (Wilkins, p. v.). They show thereby a high degree of knowledge as *technê*. But nothing in the Lescurel lyrics themselves suggests any moral, political or spiritual meaning.

What can be the relation of the *rondeau* 'A vous, douce debonnaire' and the love lyrics that follow to the moral knowledge – the lesson in kingship – that is the purpose of fr. 146? In *Manuscripts and their Makers*, the Rouses declare that Lescurel's songs 'remain the anomalous element in the manuscript, whose relationship to the content and tone of the rest is yet to be convincingly explained'.[22] In our 1990 *Facsimile*, we suggested that they were 'incongruous' embellishments, perhaps 'raw material' copied 'wholesale' without selection and adaptation (pp. 30, 52–3). That answer – our best guess at that time – is no longer good enough! Every part of fr. 146 appears exquisitely fitted to its moral purpose, and I believe this is true of the Lescurel repertory as well.

The moral and political wisdom to be gathered from reading the Lescurel lyrics is not explicitly inscribed in their texts, however, nor does it derive from commentary, sequence, or learned citations. Instead, these lyrics are made

---

[19] Wulf Arlt, 'Jehannot de Lescurel and the Function of Musical Language in the *Roman de Fauvel*', in *FS*, pp. 25–34, p. 27; see id, 'Jehannot de L'Escurel', in *Grove Music Online,* ed. L. Macy (15 Oct 2006), <http:www.grovemusic.com>.

[20] Arlt notes that the *virelai* is not distinguished from the *ballade* in the index or in the *Fauvel* ('Jehannot de Lescurel', p. 26).

[21] *Ibid*, pp. 29 and 26.

[22] Mary Rouse and Richard Rouse, *Manuscripts and their Makers: Commercial Book Producers in Medieval Paris, 1200–1500*, 2 vols (Turnhout, 2000), I, p. 230.

to feed into a programme of moral and political wisdom through contextualization in the material manuscript. The process of reciprocal reading of the Lescurel lyrics with the whole – the interpolated *Fauvel*, the *dits* of Geffroi, and even the *Chronique métrique* – appears deliberately cued first by form and theme, and then by a system of recurring refrains or lyric concordances which are reinforced by symmetries in page layout and accented by key words, repetition and visual highlighting.

To begin with: form. The fr. 146 manuscript contains not one but two massive ensembles of courtly love lyrics: thirty-four in the Lescurel repertory and thirty-nine in the *Fauvel*, which showcases the most forward-looking vernacular genres: *rondeaux* and *ballades*, as in Lescurel, but also *lais* and motets, all mensurally notated and all (except for some refrains) unique to this manuscript.[23] (See Table 1: Vernacular Love Lyrics in fr. 146.) These two ensembles of love lyrics are strongly linked in fr. 146: indexed together at beginning of the manuscript, they are associated by language, style, musical form, and their common theme of love. Moreover, Joseph Morin found codicological evidence that the Lescurel lyrics were originally intended to follow *Fauvel* in the manuscript, so 'the compilers' interest in music would appear all the more striking.'[24]

In addition to the thematic and formal parallels, several textual cues in the form of recurring refrains or lyric concordances associate the two sets of love lyrics, inviting readers to consider the relationship between them. (See Table 2, Refrain Concordances.) Refrain concordances are tags of identical text that recur, sometimes with similar music, in different works.[25] In the courtly lyric, refrain concordances are drawn from a fund of common motifs.[26] Their occurrence signals a poetic register, but does not point to a single source, freighted with authority, as do the citations in the Latin lyrics in the fr. 146, although they can serve as 'proof texts' in a lover's plea.[27] Moral knowledge, in the Latin lyrics, is amplified by looking vertically down through citations on the textual surface to probe the depths of significant allusion to the centuries of texts which they recall. Roesner recently devoted seventy-seven pages to an account of the resonant depths of citations in just

---

[23] Ardis Butterfield, 'Writing Music, Writing Poetry: *Le Roman de Fauvel* in Paris BN fr. 146', in *Poetry and Music in Medieval France from Jean Renart to Guillaume de Machaut* (Cambridge, 2002), pp. 200–14, p. 203.

[24] 'Jehannot de Lescurel's Chansons, Geffroy de Paris' *Dits*, and the Process of Design in BN fr. 146', in *FS*, pp. 321–36, p. 333, to which Emma Dillon adds palaeographic evidence from the index for 'the ordering of the *dits* and Lescurel songs' (*Medieval Musicmaking and the 'Roman de Fauvel'* (Cambridge, 2002), pp. 151, 166–8).

[25] See the chapter by Jennifer Saltzstein in this volume.

[26] See Ardis Butterfield, 'The Refrain and the Transformation of Genre in the *Roman de Fauvel*', in *FS*, pp. 105–59, and eadem, *Poetry and Music in Medieval France*, pp. 243–5.

[27] Butterfield, *Poetry and Music*, p. 247.

Table 1. Vernacular Love Lyrics in fr. 146

Roman de Fauvel: interpolated love lyrics sung by Fauvel

fols 16v–29v: 3 *rondeaux*, 9 *ballades*, 2 *lais*, 14 refrains, 1 *motet enté* (including 11 refrains).
Note: fols 23v–27v constitute a continuous lyric and semi-lyric composition including: 2 *ballades*; 1 semi-lyric piece (545 lines in rhymed couplets in which are inserted 13 refrains); 1 *ballade*; 17 non-musical sextets; the *motet enté* (with 11 refrains); 32 non-musical sextets; 4 *ballades*; 1 *rondeau*.

Jehannot de Lescurel – 34 love lyrics

fols 57r–59v, #1–32 12 *rondeaux* (1 polyphonic) intermingled with 15 *ballades* and 5 *virelais*.
fols 60r–62v, #33–34. 2 *diz entés sus refroiz de rondeaux* (respectively 24 and 28 9-line stanzas, each ending in a musical refrain).

the first three Latin motets on fol. 1r of fr. 146,[28] and Leofranc Holford-Strevens has discovered similar riches in the *Fauvel* motets attributed to Philippe de Vitry. The Lescurel lyrics offer no such wealth of learned citations. Instead a thin web of four textual and musical concordances, supported by formal and codicological arrangements and by common motifs of courtly love, spreads horizontally over the surface of the pages of fr. 146, weaving the Lescurel lyrics into the manuscript programme of moral wisdom and inviting readers to construct the signifying relationships that link the Lescurel repertory to the other works in fr. 146.

The first of the Lescurel lyrics, the refrain of the *rondeau* 'A vous, douce debonnaire', offers a delicately modulated verbal reprise of the opening line of Fauvel's first love song, 'Douce dame debonaire (fol. 16vb, p. mus. 42 [19]) [Sweet, gracious lady]',[29] highlighted by the first of the miniatures showing Fauvel as a false lover with a human face. Roesner notes that the typically florid music of the first Lescurel refrain probably derived from the simpler *Fauvel* incipit.[30] Is it a scribal error – as Wilkins suggests (p. 37) – that substitutes *dame* for *douce* in the second repetition of the refrain in the Lescurel *rondeau* copied in the centre of fol. 57r, or is this variant a deliberate

---

[28] Edward Roesner, 'Labouring in the Midst of Wolves: Reading a Group of *Fauvel* Motets', *Early Music History*, 22 (2003), 169–245.

[29] Numbering of *Fauvel* lyrics is that of Dahnk (followed by Rosenberg-Tischler); translations from the *Fauvel* monophony are by Rosenberg-Tischler.

[30] Butterfield notes Lescurel's characteristic 'use of melismas, whereby he instantly gives greater linear space to the text' (*Poetry and Music*, p. 285).

Table 2. Refrain Concordances

Fauvel's love lyrics

1. p. mus. 42 (19)
Ballade, 'Douce dame debonaire'

fol. 57ra and rb
lines 1–2
'Douce dame debonaire!'
'Fauvel, que te faut?'

2. p. mus. 43 (20)
Ballade, 'Ay amours tant me dure'
fols 16vb17ra
'Pour quoi m'estes vous si dure'
'Pour quoi [m'estes vous si dure]'
'Pour quoi m'estes vous si dure'

p. mus. 64 (48)
Lai, 'Pour recouvrer alegiance'
fol. 28terva, St. 21.3.2 (different music)
'Et pour quoi m'estes vous si dure'

3. Motet enté (42), 'Han, diex! ou pourrai ie trouver'
fol. 26vb, §9
'Elle me dit crueusement: **fui de ci!
de toi n'ai que fere.'**

4. p. mus. 60 (45),
Ballade, 'Jolis sans raison clamer'
fol. 27vb
'Diex! vo cuer comment l'endure?'
'Diex! vo cuer comment l'endure?'
'Diex! vo cuer comment l'endure?'

Jehannot de Lescurel's love lyrics

#1, 3, *Rondeau*, 'A vous, douce debonnaire'

'A vous, douce debonnaire
'A vous, <u>dame</u> debonaire'
'A vous, douce debonaire'

#33, *Dit enté*, 'Gracieuse faitisse'
fol. 60vc
Ref. 21 **'Diex vo cuer comment l'endure?'**

#34, *Dit enté*, 'Gracieus temps'
fol. 62rb
Ref. 22 **'Fui de ci; de toi n'ai que faire!'**
Ref. 23 **'Pour coi m'estes vous si dure?'**

nudge to make the two pieces coincide by bringing both *douce* and *dame* into prominence? The placement of the concordance 'douce (dame) debonnaire' demonstrates also the significance of positioning. The four textual concordances between the *Fauvel* love songs and the Lescurel lyrics are strategically placed at the beginning and end of the courtship scene in *Fauvel* Book II, and at the beginning and end of the Lescurel repertory.

Repetition and location enhance textual and musical links between the two ensembles, heightening their visibility for the reader's eye. Thus the refrain 'Pour quoi m'estes vous si dure [Why are you so cruel to me]' of Fauvel's second *ballade*, 'Ay Amours tant me dure (fols 16vb–17ra; p. mus.43 [20]) [Alas, Love, the pain I have]', emphasized because it is repeated three times at the top of fol. 17ra,[31] recurs as a lyric refrain at the bottom of the centre column on fol. 62rb, in St. 23 of the last Lescurel piece, *Dit enté* #34, 'Gracïeus temps est, quant rosier [Fair is the season, when the rose]' (Plate 2). The third concordance is the refrain 'Diex! vo cuer comment l'endure? [God! how can I endure your attitude (lit. 'heart')]' of Fauvel's *ballade* 'Joli sans raison clamer (fol. 27vb, p. mus. 60 [45]) [Groundlessly I call myself cheerful]', which stands out in the centre of the group of lyrics that ends Fauvel's wooing and under the last line of music in column b. The same refrain recurs in St. 21 of Lescurel's penultimate piece, *Dit enté* #33, fol. 60v 'Gracïieuse, faitisse et sage [Fair, elegant and wise]' at the bottom of column c. A fourth concordance, the refrain 'Fui de ci; de toi n'ai que faire [Begone; I want nothing to do with you]' appears both in the centre of the *motet enté* in the *Fauvel* (fol. 26vb; § 9 [42])[32] (Plate 3) and, prominently, in St. 22 of Lescurel's final *Dit enté* #34, in the middle of the centre column (fol. 62rb) (Plate 2).

I am grateful to musicologist Alan Richtmyer for a personal communication offering musical analysis of three refrain concordances in *Fauvel* and Lescurel. He concludes that the beginnings and endings of the tunes of refrain concordances 'Pour coi m'estes vous si dure' and 'Fui de ci; de toi n'ai que faire' are 'very closely related' in pitch and duration, as is the musical outline of the fourth, 'Diex, comment vo cuer l'endure'. Their placement on the gamut, however, renders them 'modally quite different'. Musical setting thus provides additional cues to concordances among the two groups of love lyrics in fr. 146.

Moreover, the formal similarity of Fauvel's *motet enté* and Lescurel's two *diz entez* is striking. They are examples of an unusual type of semi-lyric

---

[31] This refrain also recurs in the last *Fauvel* love lyric, the *lai* 'Pour recouvrer alegiance (fol.28tera, p. mus 64 [48]) [To obtain relief, XIb [2.3.3]]', but with different music.

[32] On the 'spiralling process of citation' in this piece, which is 'put into a key structural position in the manuscript', see Butterfield, 'Refrain', pp. 111–12.

Plate 2. Paris, BnF, MS fr. 146, fol. 62r: Lescurel, #34, *Dit enté*, 'Gracïeus temps'.
col. b, below centre: Ref. 22 Fui de ci de toi n ai que faire.
col. b, bottom: Ref. 23 Pour coi m estes vous si dure
col. c, bottom: Ref. 26 Fausse amour ie vous doins congié i ai plus loial trouvée

Plate 3. Paris, BnF, MS fr. 146, fol. 26v: *Fauvel, Motet enté.*

composition in which stanzas of spoken verse are built on musical refrains.[33] The opposition between song and spoken verse in the love lyrics of Fauvel's courtship carries a deeply symbolic value, as does that between human and animal and between Latin and French in fr. 146: all express the great struggle between good and evil. In Fauvel's *motet enté,* as in the long semi-lyric composition that surrounds it, Fauvel's inability to sustain song, to stay in tune, is a sign of his moral worthlessness, which reduces him to speech.[34]

The page layout of the Lescurel repertory further amplifies the opposition between song and speech. The thirty-two musical lyrics exactly fill up the first three folios 57r–59v while the semi-lyric *diz entés* are laid out on the last three folios 60r–62v. The *mise en page* of the first thirty-two lyrics is dense: their text and music fill out the entire width of every line, for they are written out in musical style, like prose, with a punctum after each verse (Plate 1). They form a striking contrast with the more ragged effect of the *diz entez,* where each verse begins on a new line with a small capital and where the variable length of the refrains gives an impression of irregularity similar to that of Fauvel's *motet enté* on fol. 26v.[35] The conspicuous symmetry of the Lescurel repertory – three folios of music, three folios of spoken verse – takes on significance in the context of fr. 146. It resonates with the larger moral pattern carried by the contrast of song and spoken verse, which begins with the non-lyric *complainte* on folio Ar–v and which is such a feature of the interpolated *Fauvel* in fr. 146, starting with folio 1.

There is one additional resonance between Lescurel's *diz entez* and the overall setting of the *Fauvel* love lyrics: both are dialogues. Lescurel #33, 'Graciëuse, faitisse' gives twelve stanzas to a lover's *congé*, his farewell to his lady, and twelve to her lament; in #34, 'Gracïeus temps', the lady dismisses her would-be lover. The *Fauvel* love lyrics too are not a monologue but part of a dialogue in which Fortune, singing mostly in Latin (the language of high seriousness), dismisses her importunate lover. Refrain concordances, the opposition between song and speech emphasized by *mise en page*, and dialogic exchange – these elements weave a surface web of correspondences that link the Lescurel lyrics to the *Fauvel*, thus drawing them into its programme of moral and political wisdom.

One feature, however, distinguishes the *Fauvel* love lyrics: all are sung by Fauvel, the evil horse of hypocrisy. This is a unique phenomenon: to my knowledge, there are no other depictions in French medieval lyric of a lover

---

[33] See Maureen B. McC. Boulton, 'The Song as Refrain: Lyrics as Elements of Form', in *The Song in the Story: Lyric Insertions in French Narrative Fiction, 1200–1400* (Philadelphia, 1993), pp. 152–4.

[34] See the analytic description of the mingling of lyric and speech on fols. 23v–27v in Butterfield, *Poetry and Music*, pp. 205–12.

[35] Each verse of the *diz entez* ends with a punctum, as do the lines of the index (Br–v); Geffroi's *dits*, the *Fauvel,* and the *Chronique métrique* do not have line-end punctuation.

singing as a hypocrite, although many love songs condemn false singers, the detestable *losangiers*. Characterization of the singer in the fr. 146 *Fauvel* is almost entirely an effect of contextualization, depending on two features. The first is the transitional lines written into Chaillou's *addicions*, such as the rubric introducing the *virelai* 'Providence la senée [Providence, the wise]': 'Lors a Fauvel ceste balade/ Mise avant de cueur moult malade (fol. 23v; Dahnk, lines (51–2) + p. mus. 55 [26]) [Then Fauvel, sick at heart, came forth with the following ballad]'. Only two love lyrics in the *Roman* make internal reference to Fauvel. Fortune calls Fauvel by name in the *ballade* 'Douce dame debonaire!/Fauvel, que te faut?' (Dahnk, p. mus. 42, fol. 16v [19]), the first of the horse's love songs, and the story of Fauvel's wooing is summarized in 'Providence la senée'.

The second element characterizing Fauvel as a false singer is the series of nineteen miniatures illustrating the story and songs of Fauvel's wooing, which offer insistent reminders that the singer is a foul beast. In fr. 146 Fauvel is represented with a horse's face and body when he is curried by all the estates of man and when he rises to rule over the world.[36] In sixteen of the miniatures set among his love lyrics, where Fauvel sings as a false lover, his horse's face is concealed by a human semblance while his horse's hindquarters reveal his bestial nature. However, in three of the miniatures painted among the love songs, his horse's face is exposed, forcibly reminding readers of Fauvel's true nature, as on fol. 26v, where Fauvel appears first in Min. 42, column a, alone with his horse's face, seated smiling under a tree filled with birds (Plate 3). Then he kneels before Fortune on his horse's hocks in Min. 43, in the centre of column c, where his hypocritical human face sings his 'faux soupir (Långfors, line 2110) [false sigh]', the stanzas where he reiterates his passion, as in the lines below the miniature: 'Or est en vous du tout ma dame / de ma vie et ma mort, par m'ame! (Danke, lines 772–3) [Now, by my soul, my life and death depend entirely on you, my lady].' Such illustrations warn readers, as they turn the manuscript pages, to remember they are reading 'fausses musiques (Långfors, line 1353) [false music]': the *Fauvel* satire puns on the medieval term for accidentals in music. Readers of the material book will neither be ensnared by the beauty of Fauvel's lyrics nor forget the vile nature of the singer.

My colleague E. B. (Timmie) Vitz has proposed the term 'contamination' to describe one possible effect of how contextualization may extend symbolic meanings from one locus to another.[37] The notion of contamination is central to the *Fauvel* of fr. 146, for it describes the inescapable effect of the reader seeing the Fauvel songs on the manuscript page, reading them with the satire,

---

[36] See *Facsimile*, pp. 44–5; Mühlethaler, *Fauvel au pouvoir*, pp. 119–42, and, for numbering of miniatures, *ibid*, pp. 414–33.

[37] Evelyn Birge Vitz, *The Crossroad of Intentions; A Study of Symbolic Expression in the Poetry of François Villon* (The Hague, 1974), pp. 29–63.

and looking at them next to the miniatures that reveal the hindquarters of the beast below the blandishments of the lover's smooth face.

What might readers think when they come upon the Lescurel lyrics, reading them against the backdrop of false Fauvel's songs, his image, and the satire which describes his hypocrisy? Does the contamination evident in the setting of the *Fauvel* love lyrics infect those of the Lescurel repertory? Compilation in fr. 146 opens the way to a possible effect of guilt by association. Or do the Lescurel lyrics offer an effect of contrast, a moral counterbalance, as does the description of the great and good Parisian feast of 1313 in the *Chronique métrique*, which offsets the feast of evil Fauvel in the satire?[38] The final Lescurel lyric, *Dit enté* #34, 'Gracïeus temps', offers an answer by pointing to the world of history and the adultery scandal to warn readers against false love; it thus rejects contamination and shifts the Lescurel lyrics explicitly towards one major theme of the *Fauvel* satire: its condemnation of carnality and false love.

One proper name links 'Gracïeus temps' to the adultery scandal that gave rise to the lesson in kingship in fr. 146. In contrast with the other Lescurel lyrics, this final *dit enté* tells a story. The poet falls asleep in a garden and dreams of a fair company of lovers (St. 1–6). The dream vision is, of course, the royal road to moral truth in medieval literature, as in Geffroi's *dit*, 'Un songe [A Dream]', which immediately followed 'Gracïeus temps' at an early stage of copying.[39] The poet awakens to find the gay crowd has returned to the city (St. 9–16). As he returns, he meets a woman of queenly beauty – 'Dame tres digne d'estre amée; / Car de biauté / Je li donnai la royauté (St. 9) [A lady worthy of love, for I judged her to be the queen of beauty]' – and he declares his love. They meet again (St. 20–1), and the poet addresses her as 'Jenette'.

There are a couple of prettily diminutive female names in the Lescurel lyrics – Biétris (#9, line 1); Gillette (#32, line 2) – but Brown has demonstrated that 'Jenette' would have opened the poem towards history for contemporary readers, for it is a diminutive of the name of Queen Jeanne de Bourgogne, the rehabilitated wife of Philip V.[40] This signal pointing to the adultery scandal and to the exoneration of Queen Jeanne is strongly confirmed in *Dit enté*, #34, St. 22–8 (fol. 62r) (Plate 2), where the lady rebuffs the poet sharply in an exchange that includes two of the now-familiar refrain concordances (in bold):

> 'Més honte te pourchacerai,
> Se plus m'en parlés, et serai

---

[38] Regalado, 'Chronique métrique'.
[39] Morin, 'Lescurel's Chansons,' in *FS*, pp. 326–7.
[40] Brown, 'Rex ioians', p. 63.

> A mon povoir en ton contraire.
> **Fui de ci; de toi n'ai que faire!'**. (St. 22)

> ['I'll try to shame you; If you continue to speak to me of love; I'll do all I can to discourage you. **Begone! I want nothing to do with you**'].

The poet protests in St. 23, singing, '**Pourquoi m'estes vous si dure?'**, to which the lady gives an astoundingly uncourtly answer (St. 24): 'I won't love you because I'm married!'

> Car mariée
> Sui a celi qui bien m'agrée,
> Ne d'autre amer n'arai pensée
> Jour de ma vie.
> Miex me p*lai*roit ester ravie
> Morte de Paris en Pavie,
> Ne je ne changerai ma vie
> **Ja pour homme dont je soie requise.**

> [For I'm married to one who pleases me well any day of my life. I'd rather be carried off dead from Paris to Pavia, I'll never change my life. **Never, for any man who woos me**.]

In St. 27, the lady repeats her firm stance, adding a cascade of adjectives praising her husband and affirming her loyalty:

> Trouvée l'ai par marriage
> En bel et gracieux et sage
> Et raisonnable,
> P*lai*sant, jolis et aimable
> Et a touz gens e[s]t agréable
> Qui m'atalente.
> N'est droiz qu'a autre amer m'assente,
> Puisque j'aim personne si gente.

> [I found him in marriage so fair and gracious and wise and reasonable, pleasant, jolly and loving and so agreeable to all that I desire him. It's not right that I consent to love another since I love such a noble person.]

The *bien mariée* is a rare figure indeed in the courtly lyric of the thirteenth and early fourteenth century, which prefers *mal mariées* who are only too happy to be rid of their husbands. Lescurel's exceptional theme of loyal love in marriage feeds the political wisdom of fr. 146, which proclaims that the well-being of the nation depends on the moral health of the king and the faithful constancy of his wife. Readers of fr. 146 might find additional allusions to the careless lovers of the daughters-in-law of Philip the Fair in St. 26, which denounces all lying seducers of young women:

> E! plus estes plains de mensonges,
> Vous homes, que ne soit uns songes,
> Et vous plaigniez
> Et si bien mal avoir faignez.
> Face Dex tiex gens mahagniez;
> Car il deceuvent
> Les jeunes fames, et deceuvent
> Leurs vouloirs, quant il s'aparçoivent
> Que nice sunt pour tel pensée
> **Fausse Amour, je vous doins congié;**
> **J'ai plus loial trouvée.**

> [You men are all as full of lies as any dream. You complain and pretend to suffer. May God curse such evildoers. For they seek to deceive young women, and deceive their desires, when they sense their foolish gullibility. **False love, adieu! I've found a more loyal love.**]

The final St. 28, moreover, condemns those who have falsely accused this 'Queen'.

> Jolie dame bien doit plaire,
> Més Dex doint anui et contraire
> A la persone
> Qui souvent s'amour tost et donne,
> Mal ait qui a li s'abandonne!
> Tout ensement
> Courtois sunt au commencement,
> Puis plains de faus apensement.
> Pour telle gent qui fauce [et] ment
> **L'en dit que j'aim faucement.**[41]

> [A pretty lady should please, but may God punish anyone who gives and takes back love often. Unlucky is she who gives herself to him. Such ones are courtly at first, but then full of devious intentions. It is because of such liars **it is said that I love illicitly**.]

The message of loyal love is confirmed elsewhere in fr. 146 by praise of Dame Constance, who offers hospitality to the Virtues in the *Roman de Fauvel* (Långfors, MS E, lines 278–83) and of Queen Jeanne in Geffroi de Paris' 'Un songe' (lines 295–306), and by the account of her rehabilitation in the *Chronique métrique* (lines 6011–56).[42]

---

[41] Although Wilkins believes #34 is incomplete (p. vi), the sense of the final stanza is completed by the refrain, bringing this *Dit enté* to a satisfactory grammatical and moral closure.

[42] Chaillou de Pesstain's *addicions* to the *Roman de Fauvel* include borrowings from the *Roman du comte d'Anjou* (1316), a romance about a falsely-accused queen by Jehan

Three additional cues point the Lescurel love lyrics out into the world of history where the lesson in kingship must guide the prince: handwriting, an author's name, and the alphabet. In a personal communication (14 June 2007), Brown generously summarizes her conclusions about the hands in fr. 146: the *Roman de Fauvel* and the poems of Geffroi de Paris are copied in a chancery hand 'that links the whole fr. 146 production to the royal writing office and to those who worked within it (including Gervès du Bus)'. In contrast, the index and the Lescurel lyrics 'are copied in a liturgical hand found not so often in the chancery (except for very formal work)' while the *Chronique métrique* is written in a book hand 'also used in the chancery (for tax rolls)'. Yet similarities between the hand of the Lescurel songs and that of the *Chronique métrique* (particularly in contrast with pieces copied in a chancery hand) may invite the reader to associate Lescurel with the chronicle and history.

The author's name deepens the moral potential of these love lyrics, connecting them up with recent events and with condemnation of carnality. The name 'Jehannot de Lescurel', inscribed in the index (fol. Bv), was also detected by Wilkins (p. 1) in an immense acrostic perceptible only to a reader of the manuscript page – 'Dame, Jehan de Lescurel vous salue [Lady, Jehan de Lescurel greets you]' – in the *virelai* 'Dis temps plus qu'il ne faudrait flours (fol. 59va–b, #29) [Ten times more than the flowers needed]'. Was this a tainted name in Paris in 1316–17, the years of the making of fr. 146? Two contemporary chronicles record that a young, land-owning bourgeois of Paris named Jehan de Lescurel, a *clerc* of Notre-Dame, was hanged in 1304 for crimes including rape of nuns and murder. The Rouses have put paid to the romantic legend that this hoodlum was the composer of the avant-garde lyrics in fr. 146,[43] which Roesner affirms could not possibly have been written as early as 1304. Brown insists that the names of authors in fr. 146 are not necessarily transparent references to real persons but rather signs pointing to a time, a milieu, and to a moral judgment.[44] Was the name Jehannot de Lescurel taken perhaps from the gallows and applied ironically to the love lyrics as a cautionary warning against the perils of carnal love?

One last clue to historical circumstances lies in the alphabetical order of the Lescurel collection that runs from A-G, omitting E.[45] We are forever in the debt of Jeffrey Dean and Leofranc Holford-Strevens, who, in the course of our 1992 presentation at Oxford, explained the order of Lescurel's lyrics

---

Maillart, the king's notary, perhaps alluding to Queen Jeanne (Regalado, '*Chronique métrique*', p. 491 and N. B. Black, *Medieval Narratives of Accused Queens* (Gainesville, 2003), pp. 66–83).

[43] Rouse and Rouse, *Manuscripts and their Makers*, I, pp. 228–30.

[44] Brown, 'Rex ioians', p. 55.

[45] Margaret Bent notes that 'alphabetical order up to G is given particular prominence in fr. 146' ('Fauvel and Marigny: Which Came First?', in *FS*, pp. 35–52, p. 47, fn 26).

Table 3. Music of Refrain Concordances
Fauvel, ed. Rosenberg-Tischler; Lescurel, ed. Wilkins

1. 'Douce dame debonaire' - 'A vous, douce (dame) debonaire'
Fauvel, p. mus. 42 (19), fol. 16vb

Lescurel, #3, fol. 57rb

2. 'Pour quoi m'estes vous si dure'
Fauvel, p. mus. 43 (20), fol.. 16vc-17ra

Lescurel, *Dit enté* #34, St. 23, fol. 62rb

3. 'Fui de ci de toi n'ai que faire'
Fauvel, Motet enté §9 (42), fol. 26vb

Lescurel, *Dit enté* #34, St. 22, fol. 62rb

4. "Diex! vo cuer comment l'endure?
Fauvel, p. mus. 60 (45), fol. 27vb

Lescurel, *Dit enté* #33, St. 21, fol. 60vc

and the sense of the missing 'E'. A–G is not a sign that the Lescurel repertory is incomplete, as some have thought.[46] It can be taken as a complete set of Dominical letters, a calendar device identifying Sundays in a given year. The missing 'E' points the reader to 1315, 'l'année malle [the bad year]' bemoaned by Geffroi de Paris in his poem 'De la comète et de l'eclipse (fols 54r–55r) [On the comet and the eclipse, line 192]' and deplored in the *Chronique métrique*; the bad year when the papal seat remained vacant after the death of Clement V in 1314; when the first wife of Louis X, Marguerite of Burgundy, died or was murdered so the king could remarry; when Enguerran de Marigny, the powerful minister of Philip IV, was hanged on 30 April 1315; and when unseasonable cold and torrential rains led to crop failures and widespread famine (lines 6835–7618). For readers of Lescurel in fr. 146, the alphabet could thus lock the lyrics into the misfortunes and triumphs of the world of history.

But can we ever know what medieval readers thought as they read Lescurel and turned the pages of fr. 146? One such reader was moved to leave a written record of his poetic associations to the Lescurel lyrics. In the empty space left on fol. 62v next to the final lines of Lescurel's *Dit enté* #34 this reader wrote down (using French rather than Picard spelling) the first two angry stanzas of Adam de la Halle's *Congé*, which end:

> Adiu de foiz plus de .c. mile!
> Ailleurs vois oïr l'Evangile,
> Quar ci fors mentir on ne fait.[47]

> [Farewell, a hundred thousand farewells! I'm going to listen to the Gospels somewhere else, for here everyone is a liar.]

That reader was surely responding to the poetry on the pages he had just read: the lover's *congé* in *Dit enté* #33 and the denunciation of liars in the adjoining final stanza of *Dit enté* #34, 'Pour telle gent qui fauce [et] ment [For those people who speak falsely and lie]'. But it is worth noting that he recalled Adam's moral and satirical verse rather than any love lyrics by the great poet-musician; this reader's mind was turned to moral judgment of his world, and not to love.

By now, concordances, cues, and echoes are positively bristling around the Lescurel lyrics, linking them to the *Roman de Fauvel,* to Geffroi's poems of advice, to the events recorded in the *Chronique métrique,* and to the moral purpose of the makers of fr. 146. It is the readers' task, however, to perceive and recollect the horizontal patterns of arrangement and association that draw the Lescurel lyrics towards moral wisdom, just as they must recognize the

---

[46] Wilkins, p. i; Ch-V. Langlois, 'Jean de Lescurel, poète français', in *Histoire Littéraire de la France,* 36 (Paris, 1927), pp. 114–15.

[47] Ed. Badel, p. 404, lines 23–5.

learned citations that give such vertical depth to the Latin lyrics in fr. 146. The manuscript is not just a repository for preserving texts and circulating accumulated knowledge. It is a dynamic form which engages readers in drawing moral lessons, in producing and not just receiving moral wisdom. In fr. 146, knowledge is a construction of the book – which brings works together – and of the reader, whose thoughts and understanding fulfil its purpose.

All the material cues to reciprocal reading – concordances, elements of page layout, proper names, and letters – do not impinge on the formal beauty of the Lescurel lyrics, which remain intact on the pages of the manuscript. We must ask again why this unique group of superb love songs was compiled with the other works in fr. 146? The concluding theme of *Dit enté #34*, 'Gracïeus temps', which opposes false love to loyal love, suggests that the Lescurel lyric – untainted, uncontaminated – may have been included and perhaps even composed for fr. 146 to provide a positive counterbalance to the negative weight of Fauvel's 'fausse musique'.

We can, I believe, go even further. The very art, the aesthetic superfluity, of the Lescurel lyrics points to their essential role in this compilation. They draw our attention to the significance of the aesthetic in the medieval construction of authority and knowledge. Poetry is not merely an ornamental container for knowledge; it is, rather, one of its constitutive elements, an instrument of *savoir-faire*, *savoir*, and *sagesse*. Indeed, some formal sign of aesthetic weight is essential to the material expression of knowledge. Poetry is a particularly visible and audible marker of the aesthetic in the expression of knowledge, for it keeps the reader's mind and sense perception fully engaged. Moreover, the poetry in fr. 146 defines the community of its makers and readers: their trilingual knowledge of Latin, French and music in writing and in performance; their pleasure in the artistry of the page and in representations of their world; their deep concern for kingship. Poetry in fr. 146 provides the element of artistic splendour, the weight of beauty necessary for moral wisdom directed to the king and his counsellors.[48] Lavish and monumental, the Lescurel lyrics convey materially the prestige of the court and the readers to whom the moral teaching of fr. 146 is directed and for whom and by whom this manuscript was produced. The mirror for the prince requires gleams of glory and this the Lescurel lyrics give in full measure.

---

[48] Similarly, the impressive *lai*, 'En ce dous temps d'esté', which interrupts the charivari of the *Roman de Fauvel* in BnF, MS fr. 146, converts the representation of the raucous ritual into a festive royal spectacle (Nancy Freeman Regalado, 'Masques réels dans le monde de l'imaginaire: le rite et l'écrit dans le charivari du *Roman de Fauvel*, MS B.N. fr. 146', in M. L. Ollier, ed., *Masques et déguisements dans la littérature médiévale* (Montreal, 1998), pp. 112–26, and *Facsimile*, p. 15).

11

Refrains in the *Jeu de Robin et Marion*: History of a Citation

JENNIFER SALTZSTEIN

On a stage, possibly at the Angevin court in Naples in 1283, a young woman walked forward and began to sing:

Robin m'achata corroie
Et aumizoniere de soie:
Pour quoi donc ne l'ameroie?
Aleuriva!
Robin m'aime…

[**Robin loves me, Robin has me, Robin has asked for me and will have me**. Robin bought me a belt and a silken alms-purse, why then would I not love him? Aleuriva! **Robin loves me**…][1]

This little piece is a refrain song built around the line 'Robin m'aime'. Hearing the name 'Robin', a medieval French audience would have immediately identified our songstress as a shepherdess named Marion. The two were stock characters from the *pastourelle*, a popular thirteenth-century poetic genre centred on an encounter between Marion and a *chevalier*. As many critics have shown, the encounter, told from the narrative perspective of the *chevalier*, could end in the shepherdess' refusal of him, her assent to a sexual escapade, and sometimes even her rape.[2]

---

[1] Translation from Eglal Doss-Quinby, Joan Tasker Grimbert, Wendy Pfeffer and Elizabeth Aubrey, ed., *Songs of the Women Trouvères* (New Haven, 2001), p. 213.

[2] On the *pastourelle* and its sub-genres, see Pierre Bec, *La Lyrique française au moyen âge: contribution à une typologie des genres poétiques médiévaux* (Paris, 1977),

Though the young woman singing certainly belongs to the *pastourelle*, this is not the genre here. The song, of course, opens Adam de la Halle's *Jeu de Robin et Marion*, a late-thirteenth-century theatrical adaptation of the *pastourelle* that converts the poetic genre into a dramatic performance.[3] Kevin Brownlee's key analysis of Adam's play explores the implications of this generic transformation. Importantly, Adam's theatrical version erases the controlling narrative perspective of the *chevalier*, relegating him to the role of one of many characters in the play.[4] When Marion enters this play singing, then, she is singing in her own voice for the first time in the history of the *pastourelle* genre. No longer a quotation relayed by the poet-narrator, Marion's song reaches the audience directly, without mediation.

But in this moment, as she sings the refrain song 'Robin m'aime', Marion's voice also seems curiously fragmented. She functions simultaneously as a performer, a stock character from a popular genre, and a character in Adam's new work. Is the song she sings her own, conveying her devotion to Robin and her joy at the gifts he has given her? Or is she just singing one of her favourite popular songs? This question lies at the crux of our understanding of how such a song citation would have been heard. In fact, Marion's refrain may have been well known to thirteenth-century French audiences. It survives in two *pastourelle* songs that predate Adam's play, one of which was widely transmitted.[5] We cannot be sure, then, whether the assembled understood this as Marion's song, as a well-known song cited from elsewhere, or both.

What function might such a citation have had in Adam's play? The opening burst of female vocality surely served as a generic marker, reminding audiences of the conventions upon which the *Jeu* rests through its citation of the *pastourelle* songs.[6] This act of citation is not unique. The play cites twelve

---

pp. 119–35; William D. Paden, trans. and ed., *The Medieval Pastourelle* (New York, 1987), pp. ix–xiii; and Michel Zink, *La Pastourelle: poésie et folklore au Moyen Age* (Paris, 1972). On rape in the *pastourelle*, see Kathryn Gravdal, 'Camouflaging Rape: The Rhetoric of Sexual Violence in the Medieval Pastourelle', *Romanic Review*, 76 (1985), 361–73; Kathryn Gravdal, *Ravishing Maidens: Writing Rape in Medieval French Literature* (Philadelphia, 1991); and William D. Paden, 'Rape in the Pastourelle', *Romanic Review*, 80 (1989), 331–49.

[3] Line numbers refer to Adam de la Halle, *Le Jeu de Robin et Marion*, ed. Jean Dufournet (Paris, 1989).

[4] Kevin Brownlee, 'Transformations of the Couple: Genre and Language in the *Jeu de Robin et Marion*', *French Forum*, 14 (1989), 419–33.

[5] Refrain 1633, 'Robin m'aime', appears in R573.III, 'Au tens nouvel', by Perrin d'Angecourt, transmitted in four *chansonniers*, and in R85, 'A l'entrant de mai'. All refrain numbers refer to Nico H. J. van den Boogaard, *Rondeaux et refrains du XIIe siècle au début du XIVe* (Paris, 1969). Numbering for monophonic songs and motets follows Hans G. Spanke, *Raynaud's Bibliographie des altfranzösischen Liedes* (Leiden, 1955) and Friedrich Gennrich, *Bibliographie der ältesten französischen und lateinischen Motetten* (Darmstadt, 1957–58).

[6] See Joseph Dane, *Res/verba: A Study in Medieval French Drama* (Leiden, 1985), p. 104.

other refrains, four of which have extant concordances in a variety of musical and poetic sources, as seen in Table 1.[7] These sources may shed light on our understanding of not just the *Jeu*, but of the functions of refrain citation in Adam's output as a whole. I will examine the history of several of Adam's refrains and their subsequent circulation in later musical works. Re-situating Adam's refrain citations within a transmission history suggests new modes of reading and interpretation. This context also suggests important connections between refrain citation and the creation of authority and authorial identity, questions central to Adam's writerly persona.

Table 1. *Jeu* Refrains with Concordances[8]

1. '**Robins m'aime, Robins m'a / Robins m'a demandee, si m'aura**' (refrain 1633) appears in:
    1.1 *Jeu de Robin et Marion* by Adam de la Halle, lines 1–2
    1.2 'Au tens nouvel' by Perrin d'Angecourt (*chanson avec refrains*), KNXV (R573.III)
    1.3 'A l'entrant de mai' (*chanson avec refrains*), K (R85.III)
    1.4 'Mout me fu grief' (M297) / 'Robin m'aime' (M298)/ 'Portare' (motet), Mo 292v, Ba 52v

2. '**Bergeronnete, douche baisselete / donnéz le moi vostre chapelet**' (refrain 252) appears in:
    2.1 *Jeu de Robin et Marion* by Adam de la Halle, lines 172–4
    2.2 'L'autre jour je chevachoie' (*ballete*), *I* (R974)

3. '**Hé! Resveille toi Robin! Car on en maine Marot**' (refrain 870) appears in:
    3.1 *Jeu de Robin et Marion* by Adam de la Halle, lines 342–3
    3.2 'Hier main quant je chevauchoie' by Huitace de Fontaines (*chanson avec refrains*), P (R1700.IV)
    3.3 'En mai' (M870) / 'L'autre jour' (M871) / 'Hé! Resveille toi' (motet), Mo 297r, Reg. nr.4

---

[7] On the refrain, see Van den Boogaard, *Rondeaux et refrains*; Eglal Doss-Quinby, *Les Refrains chez les trouvères du XIIe siècle au début du XIVe* (New York, 1984), and Jennifer Saltzstein, *Wandering Voices: Refrain Citation in Thirteenth-Century French Music and Poetry*, Ph.D. diss. (University of Pennsylvania, 2007).

[8] The following manuscript abbreviations are used in footnotes and tables: Ba = Bamberg, Staatsbibliothek, MS Lit. 115; Ha = Paris, BnF, MS fr. 25566; I = Oxford, Bodleian Library, Douce 308; Iv = Ivrea, Biblioteca Capitolare 115; K = Paris, Bibliothèque de l'Arsenal, 5198; k = Paris, BnF, MS fr. 12786; Mo = Montpellier, Bibliothèque interuniversitaire, Section médicine, MS H196; N = Paris, BnF, MS fr. 845; O = Paris, BnF, MS fr. 846; P = Paris, BnF, MS fr. 847; R = Paris, BnF, MS fr. 844: Reg = Rome, Biblioteca Vaticana, Reg. Christ. 1543; X = Paris, BnF, nouv. acq. fr. 1050; V = Paris, BnF, MS fr. 24406.

    3.4 'Prenés l'abre / Hé! Resveille toi' (polyphonic *virelai*), Iv 28r
    5.5 'Salut d'amours' II, verse 8

4. **'Aveuc tele compaignie / doit on bien joie mener'** (refrain 200) appears in:
    4.1 *Jeu de Robin et Marion* by Adam de la Halle, lines 421–2
    4.2 *Renart le Nouvel* by Jacquemart Gielee, line 6632
    4.3 *Le Tournoi de Chauvency* by Jacques Bretel, line 3118
    4.4 'Salut d'amours' I, verse 8

The refrain 'Hé! Resveille toi Robin, car on en maine Marot', Table 1.3, is one of the most widely transmitted of the refrains cited in Adam's play, appearing in works from a wide variety of genres. The text of the refrain itself has a latent narrativity, expressing an event central to the conventions of the *pastourelle* genre: the abduction of Marion. The *pastourelle* and its narrative conventions will thus be key to any interpretation of this refrain network.

The works that cite 'Hé! Resveille toi' respond to its implied narrative in different ways, showcasing an array of narrative possibilities in the *pastourelle* genre. I will begin by considering the refrain's effect in Adam's *Jeu*, where ideas of the *pastourelle* genre abound. The structure of the play itself relies on a fusion of the *pastourelle classique* and a *pastourelle* sub-genre often called the *bergerie*.[9] In the *bergerie*, the *chevalier* still functions as the poet-narrator, but the encounter is absent. The *chevalier* passively observes the shepherdess with her lover and friends. Adam's play opens as a *pastourelle classique*, with the encounter between the *chevalier* and Marion. But the second half of the play more closely resembles a *bergerie*, focusing on the pastoral couple, Robin and Marion, and de-emphasizing the *chevalier*. In the *Jeu*, the refrain appears just after the *chevalier*'s second attempt to abduct Marion. Gautier, a friend of the couple, sings the refrain to Robin to warn him that the *chevalier* is about to take Marion away.[10]

To better understand what the refrain brings to the play and its generic innovations, I would like to spend some time considering its earliest extant source, the song, 'Hier main quant je chevauchoie', written by Huitace de Fontaines. The song's five verses tell a *pastourelle* story, each verse ending in a different refrain. This song has frequently been classified as a rape scenario.[11] Though the idea of abduction is clearly central to the refrain, the song as a whole is more ambiguous than previous examinations suggest. In the first verse, the *chevalier* goes out riding and comes upon Robin sleeping.

---

    [9] For a description of *pastourelle* sub-genres including the *pastourelle classique* and *bergerie*, see Paden, *The Medieval Pastourelle*, pp. ix-xiii.
    [10] Lines 358–60.
    [11] Gravdal, for instance, lists the poem as a rape example in *Ravishing Maidens*, p. 166, n. 4.

Soon after, he hears Marion, who sees Robin sleeping and sings an appropriate refrain to end the second verse: 'Dormez qui n'amez mie / J'aim si ne puis dormir [Sleep, you who do not love me; I'm so in love that I can't sleep].'[12] The *chevalier* greets Marion in the third verse, telling her he loves her. It seems as though she has accepted his advances in the fourth verse: the poet-narrator begins with the lines 'Quant la tose entalentee / Vi de fere mon voloir [When I saw that the desiring girl was willing to do my bidding].' The *chevalier* then lifts Marion onto his horse and holds her tightly. At the end of verse four, however, Marion cries out unexpectedly, singing the refrain 'Hé! Resveille toi'.

> Quant la tose entalentee
> Vi de fere mon voloir,
> Maintenant l'en ai levee
> Sus le col du palefroi
> Si l'enportai en l'aunoi
> Estroitement acolee
> Et ele s'est escrïee
> Au plus haut qu'el onques pot:
> '**Hé! Resveille toi, Robin**
> **car on en maine Marot**'.
> Quant oi fet de la bergiere
> Ce que j'aloie querant
> Ma coroie et m'aumosniere
> Li ai tendu maintenant.
> Puis si m'en tornai; atant
> Robin vint aval la pree
> Et a Dieu l'ai conmandee
> Regrettant et dolent m'en part.
> **A Dieu conmant je mes amors**
> **Qu'il les me gart.** [13]

[When I saw that the girl was inclined to do my bidding, I lifted her onto my horse's neck. I carried her to the sheepfold, holding onto her tightly then she cried as loudly as she could '**Hey! Wake up Robin! For someone is taking Marion.**' When I had done with the shepherdess that which I had wanted, I then handed her my belt and purse, then I turned away from her as Robin came across the field. And I commended her to God, regretful and sad to take leave. **I commend my loves to God that he may keep them for me.**]

---

[12] Refrain 598. I thank Kevin Brownlee and Amy Heneveld for their assistance with this translation.

[13] Hans Tischler, *Trouvère Lyrics with Melodies: Complete Comparative Edition* (Neuhausen, 1997).

This is the anticipated narrative event of the genre, and the refrain is used exactly as one would expect. But why is Marion crying for Robin's help after she has agreed to go off with the *chevalier*? It is clear that he has his way with her in the opening of the fifth verse, then hands her his belt and purse in time to see Robin come across the field toward her. Ardis Butterfield reads this stanza as containing a rape and a cynical taunt by the *chevalier*, seeing it as an important subtext for Adam's *Jeu*, since the placement of the refrain after the kidnapping scene enacts Gautier's mockery of Robin for missing his chance to rescue Marion despite his proximity to the scene. She explains that Robin 'does not awake even when Marion screams as loudly as she can: "Hé! Resveille toi, Robin / Car on en maine Marot". He only appears in the final strophe after the *chevalier* has raped Marion, in time to be taunted with the *chevalier*'s insulting final refrain: "A dieu conmant je mes amors qu'il les me gart"'.[14]

Though others have also viewed this song as a rape scenario, I would like to offer a reading that may differently inflect our interpretation of the refrain 'Hé! Resveille toi' in the *Jeu*. It is also possible that the *chevalier*'s belt and purse might have been what the couple was after all along. William Paden has described examples within the *pastourelle* genre where sexual favours are exchanged for these charged objects. He has also noted instances where the shepherdess pretends to accept the *chevalier*'s offer in order to escape.[15] It seems at least possible, then, that Marion's assent and mercurial change of heart were part of a ruse she and Robin devised in order to get hold of the *chevalier*'s money and luxurious effects. Indeed there are aspects of the song that strongly imply such a ruse. In verse three, for example, it seems as though Marion has accepted the *chevalier*'s advances. It is only at the end of the verse that she sings the refrain in protest. Further, both Marion and the *chevalier* knew exactly where Robin was the entire time: the *chevalier* watches as she finds him sleeping in verse two and hears Marion sing her reproachful refrain. This refrain could be interpreted as bait for the *chevalier*. Marion sings 'Dormez qui n'amez mie / J'aim si ne puis dormir', complaining that Robin does not measure up to a courtly cliché. It is possible to read the refrain as an invitation directed at the *chevalier* and his courtly advances. Under this interpretation, 'Hé! Resveille toi' could function as a signal already worked out between the two lovers, to ensure that the exchange takes place quickly.

We might, then, view this song as a humiliation of the *chevalier*. Here, he leaves Marion 'Regrettant et dolent' after recognizing her insincerity. It is certainly not unprecedented for Robin and Marion to humiliate the *chevalier*. In fact, the presence of so many humiliating representations of the *chevalier*

---

[14] See Ardis Butterfield, *Poetry and Music in Medieval France: From Jean Renart to Guillaume de Machaut* (Cambridge, 2002), p. 159.

[15] Paden, 'Rape in the Pastourelle', pp. 335–6.

led Michel Zink to argue strongly against the idea that the *pastourelle* was simply an élitist genre designed to deride the lower classes.[16]

We must be cautious about assuming that Adam was citing this song directly, but it resonates strongly with a number of aspects of the *Jeu*. Butterfield notes that the refrains often connect the play to *pastourelle* songs that provide narrative models for the *Jeu*.[17] In the case of 'Hier main quant je chevauchoie', the song I have just discussed, a number of interpretations are possible. Since she reads the song as a rape scenario, Butterfield argues that the placing of the refrain not during but after the kidnapping scene in both the song and the *Jeu* underscores Robin's ineffectiveness in both cases. In the alternative reading suggested above, the song could act as a narrative model for the cunning that Marion will exhibit in Adam's play in resisting the *chevalier*.[18] In either interpretation, the cited song creates an important narrative subtext designed, it seems, for a perceptive audience.

Other refrains from the play may have had a similar impact on audiences knowledgeable of their other poetic and musical contexts. The opening song, 'Robin m'aime', appears in two *pastourelles avec refrains*, as seen in Table 1.1. Together, these songs showcase opposite ends of the *pastourelle* narrative spectrum. The song 'Au tens nouvel' by Perrin d'Angecourt contains one of the more graphic rape scenarios found in the *pastourelle* corpus. In the song 'A l'entrant de mai' on the other hand, Marion not only refuses the *chevalier*, but sees through his seduction attempt, berating him for his falseness and hypocrisy. An audience familiar with these songs would be reminded of the narrative spectrum of the *pastourelle* from the outset of Adam's play.

Another example, the refrain 'Bergeronnete, douce baisselete' from the song 'L'autre jour je chevachoie' bears an intertextual narrative connection to the play, one so strong that it may have been an intentional reference. In 'L'autre jour je chevachoie', a *chevalier* sings the refrain 'Bereronette, trés douce compaignete' to Marion, asking for her *chapelet* as part of his attempt to woo her. Marion refuses, citing her devotion to Robin. When the refrain appears in the *Jeu*, it is Robin, not the *chevalier*, who sings the refrain to Marion after they have finished eating together. Assuring Robin of her devotion, Marion agrees to place her *chapelet*, the testimony of her love, on his head.[19] Adam's play rewrites the song's short narrative, emphasizing the mutual affection between Robin and Marion.

---

[16] Michel Zink, *La Pastourelle* (Paris, 1972), pp. 60–1.

[17] Butterfield, *Poetry and Music*, p. 152.

[18] Marion's cunning in the play, however, relates to her verbal prowess. See Brownlee, 'Transformations', pp. 421–5.

[19] Robert Mullally argues that this sequence refers to the *tour de chapelet*, a dance that also appears in the *Tournoi de Chauvency*. See 'Balerie and Ballade', *Romanica*, 104 (1983), 533–8. Françoise Ferrand sees this scene as a parody of the chivalric world. See 'Le *Jeu de Robin et Marion*: Robin danse devant Marion, sens du passage et sens de l'œuvre', *Revue des Langues Romanes*, 90 (1986), 87–97.

These examples show that the refrains in the *Jeu* can reference alternative narrative scenarios possible in the *pastourelle* genre and create intertextual readings. The refrains in the play have other functions, however. When read against their other surviving versions, some of the refrains in the *Jeu* can also be seen to foreshadow Adam's generic transformations, particularly the important combination of *pastourelle classique* and *bergerie*. Two of the other extant versions of the refrain 'Hé! Resveille toi', both of which predate Adam's play, mix these elements. The opening of 'Hier main quant je chevauchoie', the song I have just discussed at length, feels more like a *bergerie* than a *pastourelle*: the *chevalier* observes Robin and Marion for nearly three full verses, waiting to speak until the middle of the third verse. It is only then that the song resembles a *pastourelle classique*.

The mixture *pastourelle* and *bergerie* is perhaps even more striking in another work that includes this refrain, the motet 'En mai (M870) / L'autre jour (M871) / Hé! Resveille toi', transmitted in the Montpellier motet codex. This motet shares the melody and rhythm given for the refrain in Adam's play note for note, as seen in Example 1, below. We cannot know whether the notation for Adam's version of the refrain was copied from this motet or from some other common exemplar. The refrain is positioned in the tenor voice, the normal locus for the cited chant fragment in the motet form. Rhythmically, the repeated mode 1 patterns do not differentiate the citation from a conventional chant tenor. But musically, the melody of the refrain citation is repeated such that it resembles a *rondeau*. Example 1 shows the two primary phrases of the refrain, labelled as A and B. The tenor repeats the refrain's two phrases in the *rondeau* form ABAABAB.[20] There is an artful self-consciousness in this manipulation that marks the tenor as a cited song.

The upper voices of 'En mai / L'autre jour / Hé! Resveille toi' express the anxiety of separation. In the triplum, the poet-narrator observes as Marion worries that Robin has left her for another woman. In the motetus, the narrator sees Robin searching for Marion. Both anxieties are allayed at the end of the short texts.[21] Generically, the upper texts are representative of the *bergerie* type while the tenor refrain, 'Hé! Resveille toi, Robin, car on enmaine Marot', articulates the defining narrative event of the *pastourelle classique*, the possible abduction of Marion. Once again, the motet combines two *bergerie* texts in the upper voices with the tenor refrain 'Hé! Resveille toi', a generic marker indicating the *pastourelle classique*. It is possible that Adam cited the music and text of 'Hé! Resveille toi' from this motet, which would serve as another model for the play's hybrid construction.

---

[20] Though *rondeau* structure varies in the late thirteenth century, the tenor resembles the form Adam used in 'A Dieu conmant amouretes', a polyphonic *rondeau*.

[21] See Sylvia Huot, 'Intergeneric Play: The Pastourelle in Thirteenth-Century French Motets', in *Medieval Lyric: Genres in Historical Context*, ed. William D. Paden (Urbana, 2000), pp. 297–316.

Example 1: Melodic Comparison of 'Hé! Resveille toi'

Refrain 870 in the *Jeu de Robin et Marion*

Refrain 870 in 'En mai / L'autre jour / Hé! Resveille toi'

In addition to recalling narrative and generic models for a new work, I now wish to posit that refrains also express the circumstances of the poets who cite them, particularly their place in a larger community of writers. In thirteenth-century Arras, it seems that poets drew on a common stock of refrains. Tracing the distribution of refrains cited in the four *Renart le nouvel* manuscripts, Van den Boogaard discovered that the majority of their other surviving contexts were works contemporary to Jacquemart Giélée's romance, especially *Meliacin*, *Le Tournoi de Chauvency*, and the *Cour d'Amour*. Further, the refrains in *Renart le nouvel* that were also found in the chanson repertory were strongly connected to Oxford, Bodleian, MS Douce 308, which also transmits the *Tournoi de Chauvency*. The transmission of refrains in the *Renart le nouvel* manuscripts thus reflects an insular, local pattern of citation.²² Building on Van den Boogaard's findings, Butterfield has argued that the refrain citations and their function within these works correspond to a particularly *arrageoise* sensibility, inspired by the *puy* and its tradition of poetic performance and competition.²³ These studies encourage us to think about refrain citation as regional, and as a means for creating or articulating identity, here, the civic identity of Arras and its poetic rituals.

If refrain citation could express civic identity, it may have expressed other types of identities as well, for example, authorial identity. Indeed, in addition to the stock of common refrains Van den Boogaard found in poetic sources connected to Arras, there are indications that *arrageois trouvères* may have cited refrains from the songs of their contemporaries and predecessors. For example, 'Ma loial pensée tient mon cuer joli' (refrain 1287), appears in songs by Perrin d'Angecourt and Gillebert de Berneville. We also find shared refrains in songs by Colart le Boutelier and Adam de Givenci as well as between Colart and Pierre de Corbie.²⁴ It would be difficult to view these connections as coincidental; either the refrains were drawn from a stock of popular material known in Arras or they represent direct citations from one song to the other. Such engagement surely enabled these poets to define their own poetic identity by inviting comparison between their songs and those of other local *trouvères*, articulating their place within a regional poetic tradition.

Refrain citation may also have been central to the ways that Adam de la Halle constructed his authorial persona. We have already seen that refrains that Adam cited in his *Jeu de Robin et Marion* often referred to literary and musical models that would aid his audience in interpreting the *Jeu de Robin et Marion*. It is also significant that several of the models Adam invoked through his refrain citations came specifically from Arras. Of all of the refrains in Adam's poetic corpus, only three are found in the songs of *trouvères* from generations before Adam's period of activity: 'Robin m'aime', 'Hé! Resveille toi', and 'Bonne amourete'.²⁵ The refrain 'Hé! Resveille toi'

---

²² Nico H. J. van den Boogaard, 'Jacquemart Gielee et la lyrique de son temps', in *Alain de Lille, Gautier de Châtillon, Jacquemart Giélée et leur temps*, ed. Henri Roussel et François Suard (Lille, 1980), 333–53, p. 351.

²³ Butterfield, *Poetry and Music*, pp. 138–42. Though very little historical evidence supports the existence of the *puy*, a number of literary texts describe it as an organization of *trouvères* that held poetic contests in Arras. On the lack of historical evidence documenting the *puy*, see Carol Lynne Symes, 'The Makings of a Medieval Stage: Theatre and the Culture of Performance in Thirteenth-Century Arras', Ph.D. diss. (Harvard University, 1999), p. 254. For literary references to the *puy*, see Rosanna Brusegan, 'Culte de la Vierge et origine des puys et confréries en France au Moyen Age', *Revue des langues romanes*, 95 (1991), 31–58.

²⁴ Refrains 1585 and 1375.

²⁵ The transmission of 'Hé! Resveille toi' appears in Table 1.3. 'Bonne amourette' is used in the following sources: Adam de la Halle's *rondeau* of the same name in Ha 34v and k 77v; Perrin d'Angecourt's 'Quant voi l'erbe amatir' (R1390.IV) in KNXVO; the monophonic motet 'Bone amourete m'a souspris' (M1073) in R 3v; and *Renart le*

appears in Huitace de Fontaines' *pastourelle avec refrains*, 'Hier main quant je chevauchoie' (R1700). Little is known about Huitace, but Gillebert de Berneville dedicated a song to him in the mid-thirteenth century. Since all of Gillebert's other dedications honour prominent figures in the Arras poetic circle, it is reasonable to assume that Huitace was also connected to Arras, and that he was a contemporary of Gillebert, who flourished in the mid-thirteenth century. The two remaining refrains, 'Robin m'aime' (refrain 1633) and 'Bonne amourete' (refrain 289), appear in songs by Perrin d'Angecourt.[26] In the case of 'Robin m'aime', discussed above, the earliest extant source of the refrain is 'Au tens nouvel' (R573), a *pastourelle avec refrains* attributed to Perrin. The refrain 'Bonne amourete' (refrain 289), featured in Adam's *rondeau*, also appears in Perrin's song 'Quant voi l'erbe amatir' (R1390), the oldest extant source of this refrain. Both of these songs, particularly the latter, are widely attested in the surviving *chansonniers*.

This evidence does not indicate with certainty that Adam was intentionally citing the songs of the earlier *trouvères*. Anonymous songs and motets also transmit the refrains in question, and these could have been Adam's sources. It is also possible that Adam was unaware of all these songs and motets and was citing other sources that have not survived. But assuming, for the moment, that the songs I have just discussed *were* Adam's sources for the refrains in question, it seems significant that the songs are all by *trouvères* who are slightly Adam's senior, with strong connections to Arras. By citing refrains from songs by prominent *arrageois trouvères* active in the generation before him, Adam places himself within a specifically *arrageois* poetic tradition. We can view these citations as a sounding genealogy: a lineage that reverberates through the refrains, conjuring the memory of their earlier versions, and placing Adam within a well-defined poetic circle.

Though we have very little biographical information about Adam, his works themselves construct a rather elaborate authorial persona. In the *Jeu de la feuillée*, this persona is tied both to his home city of Arras and to Paris, the city of his scholastic ambitions.[27] The competing urban centres articulate his dual identity as *trouvère* and scholar. In the *Jeu de Robin et Marion*, I have suggested that Adam is using song citation to place himself, *qua* author of the play, within an *arrageoise* authorial genealogy. If this is the function of the cited songs, the technique seems to fuse the two identities maintained by the protagonist of Adam's *Jeu de la feuillée*. Citation, of course, is central to

---

nouvel, line 2552. There are connections between Adam's refrains and songs by Guillaume d'Amiens, but since Guillaume was active in the early fourteenth century, Adam's works themselves may have been his source for the refrains.

[26] The transmission of 'Robin m'aime' appears in Table 1.1.

[27] See, for example, Jean Dufournet, *Sur la Jeu de la feuillée: études complémentaires* (Paris, 1977), p. 11.

Latinate strategies of authorization.[28] Using this Latinate technique to create a vernacular authorial genealogy centred on his bourgeois home in Arras unites the two sides to Adam's authorial persona that appear in his earlier works. In this way, Adam is aligned with broader strategies through which vernacular authors authorized their works.[29]

Up until this point, I have focused on Adam's *engin*: his skilful poetic use of refrain citations for generic, narrative, and authorial purposes. I now wish to consider how Adam's refrains might have been heard by later generations. Though not listed in Boogaard's catalogue of refrains, there is an additional source for 'Hé! Resveille toi' that survives in the fourteenth-century Ivrea motet codex, the highly unusual polyphonic *virelai*, 'Prenés l'abre'.[30] No text appears in the manuscript, it is simply marked 'tenor,' but the melody of 'Hé! Resveille toi' is unmistakable. The piece, which appears in example 2, seems acutely aware of the refrain's history in the pieces already discussed.

> [Take then the bough, sweet Peronel, betwixt you and Sir Simon; dance we as the drums beat on, for love of Marion, our belle. For here I see Walter Trenel, who brings with him a platter to this dell, it will be his gift to Marion.][31]

As we can see by comparing the other notated versions of 'Hé! Resveille toi' in example 1, the *virelai* refrain appears at the same pitch level as the thirteenth-century versions, with the same rhythmic values, paying homage to the notational history of the refrain in the motet and Adam's play. The second half of the tenor is then given a fresh musical setting, which opens with a juxtaposition of triple and duple rhythmic groupings characteristic of the new notational technologies of the *ars nova*. These artful rhythmic manipulations are also present in the upper voice of the piece. The modal rhythms of the tenor's first half sound distinctly old-fashioned against the precious syncopations of the upper voce and the tenor's second half. The old and the new are juxtaposed in 'Prenés l'abre', demonstrating a musical history of notational innovation.[32]

---

[28] See, for example, Mary Carruthers, *The Book of Memory: A Study of Memory in Medieval Culture* (Cambridge, 1990), pp. 102–3, and Alistair J. Minnis, *Medieval Theory of Authorship: Scholastic Literary Attitudes in the Later Middle Ages* (Philadelphia, 1984), p. 10.

[29] On the use of Latinate techniques to authorize vernacular works, see Nancy Freeman Regalado, 'Des contraires choses: la fonction poétique de la citation et des exempla dans le *Roman de la Rose* de Jean de Meun', *Littérature*, 41 (1981), 62–81; Minnis, *Medieval Theory of Authorship*, pp. 160–210; and id, *Magister Amoris: The Roman de la Rose and Vernacular Hermeutics* (Oxford, 2001), pp. v-vii and pp. 63–80.

[30] Ivrea, Biblioteca Capitolare 115. See Wyndham Thomas, ed., *Robin and Marion Motets* 3 (Newton Abbot, 1985), p. ii.

[31] *Ibid.*, p. 26.

[32] On these notational languages, see Dorit Tanay, *Noting Music, Marking Culture: The Intellectual Context of Rhythmic Notation, 1250–1400* (Holzgerlingen, 1999).

Example 2: 'Prenés l'abre'

The *pastourelle* genre all but disappeared in the fourteenth century. Paden hypothesizes that that Jean de Meun's continuation of the *Roman de la Rose* established an 'authoritative secular erotic' that made the *pastourelle* and its expression of sexual desire redundant.[33] When *pastourelle* texts appear in fourteenth-century manuscripts such as the Pennsylvania *chansonnier*, they still refer to the shepherds and shepherdesses characteristic of the earlier versions. But the abduction narrative is absent in these later works; their subjects tend to be much more polite and courtly, focusing on weddings and celebrations. The most significant difference is the lack of the participant narrator, which aligns fourteenth-century *pastourelles* with the *bergerie* rather than the *pastourelle classique*, since their narrators observe the actions of the pastoral characters without being involved in the plot.[34] Frequently, the narrator is not introduced at all.

---

[33] William D. Paden, 'Flight from Authority in the Pastourelle', in *The Medieval Opus: Imitation, Rewriting, and Transmission in the French Tradition*, ed. Douglas Kelly (Amsterdam, 1996), pp. 299–325.

[34] See William Kibler, 'The Development of the Pastourelle in the Fourteenth Century: An Edition of Fifteen Poems with an Analysis', *Mediaeval Studies*, 45 (1983), pp. 22–78.

'Prenés l'abre' exhibits all of these characteristics of the fourteenth-century *pastourelle*. The *virelai* form opens with the refrain, pre-empting the male narrative perspective of the *pastourelle* and *bergerie*. The text describes dancing, singing, playing musical instruments and other bucolic amusements. There is no *chevalier* narrator, nor any mention of the sexual exploits that are so common in the thirteenth-century texts. Just as it does in the motet, 'En mai / L'autrier / He resvelle toi', the cited tenor refrain here in the *virelai* suggests the abduction narrative that is missing from the bucolic text. The charge of the citation is rather different in this later work, however. Citing 'Hé! Resveille toi' below this idyllic pastoral scene is a reminder of the earlier, ribald tradition, recalling the encounter and the possible abduction. The composer of this *virelai* seems acutely aware that the cited refrain carries the heritage of the *pastourelle* into this new context, where it serves as a marker of the genre's history. The citation prompts a musical memory of a time when the genre had darker implications, a memory made possible by the refrain's indirect allusion to the threat of rape. This somewhat obscure *virelai* not only encourages narrative rereading and reinterpretation in light of the refrain's history, it also provides an important commentary on the *pastourelle* genre and its history.

Though centred on a single work, Adam's *Jeu de Robin et Marion*, the examples explored here suggest that refrain citation was a rich practice with wide-ranging implications. We have seen that refrain citations can have multiple poetic functions within a single work, alternately highlighting narrative, genre, community, or history. Together, these examples also imply understanding of and familiarity with the network of pieces connected through refrain citation on the part of poets, composers and their audiences. This understanding suggests that refrains prompted diverse modes of reading and listening; that they both required and fostered poetic knowledge.

What might medieval audiences have heard when refrains were sung? I have suggested that they listened through these refrains, hearing other songs behind them. These songs, then, served as sounding memories of alternative narratives and regional authorial lineages, and could even chart the history and dissolution of a genre. Returning to 'Robin m'aime', the refrain with which I began, we might wonder whether, paradoxically, audiences of the *Jeu de Robin et Marion* strained to hear a female singing subject through these layers of citation. Though loosed from the poetic constraints of a male narrative *je* and the secondary status of reported speech, the promise of direct female expression is here layered with textures of history, memory, and genre. Marion's voice, though resonating through a female performing body, is bounded by citation. The other songs that echo through her voice complicate our sense of her presence. Refrain citation creates community, but also distance. It is perhaps this distance that most fascinates about refrains, which so often speak from beyond the text, from a place just out of reach.

12

Le Prince chez Meschinot, mise en forme d'un objet poétique/politique

DENIS HÜE

Les *Ballades des Princes* de Jean Meschinot ne font pas partie, aux yeux de la critique moderne, des œuvres politiques majeures du XVe siècle. Il y a probablement deux raisons à cela, la première étant que ces textes n'ont plus été édités depuis le début du XVIe siècle, peu accessibles et partant, peu lus. La seconde est l'étonnante faveur qu'ont rencontrée les *Lunettes des princes*. Œuvre plus célèbre, probablement à cause de son nom suscitant la curiosité, et qui a connu le privilège exceptionnel d'être publiée au XXe siècle deux fois en douze mois,[1] elle a comme éclipsé ce cycle de ballades – ainsi que, avouons-le, l'ensemble de l'œuvre lyrique du poète, sur lequel il faudra bien se pencher un jour.

Pourtant, ce cycle de vingt-cinq ballades en douzains de décasyllabes se signale à l'attention des chercheurs par sa richesse aussi bien formelle que thématique; si elles s'inscrivent dans une série, commencée avant le poète, de conseils à l'aristocratie (*Bréviaire des Nobles* de Chartier, ou plus tard le *Doctrinal des Princesses* de Jean Marot), elles s'en distinguent par une ampleur et un projet plus proprement politique, alors même qu'elles s'astreignent à de très exigeantes contraintes formelles.

Le titre complet, tel que le porte l'édition *princeps*, est:

> S'ensuyvent xxv balades composees par ung gentilhomme nommé Jehan Meschinot. Sur xxv princes de balades [a] luy envoyees de missire Georges Ladventurier serviteur de monseigneur de bourgongne Et trouverez au commencement de chascune desdites balades le refrain: et a la fin le prince fait par ledit Georges.[2]

---

[1] *Les Lunettes des princes de Jean Meschinot*, éd. Christine Martineau-Genieys (Genève, 1972); *Les lunettes des princes*, éd. Bernard Toscani (Paris, 1971).
[2] Édition Larcher, Nantes, 1493. f Ai (non signé). George Chastelain a en effet ce surnom de l'Adventurier. Dans toutes les citations de manuscrits et d'éditions anciennes, la ponctuation et l'orthographe ont été modernisées, et les vers numérotisés là où il le faut.

[Suivent vingt-cinq ballades composées par un gentilhomme nommé Jean Meschinot, sur vingt-cinq Princes de ballades que lui avait envoyées messire Georges l'Adventurier, serviteur de monseigneur [le duc] de Bourgogne. Et vous trouverez au commencement de chacune de ces ballades le refrain, et à la fin le prince fait par George [Chastelain].]

En fait, le texte est rapidement classé dans le genre méprisé des paraphrases, et la teneur, qui est de philosophie politique, n'est pas de celles qui attirent le lecteur. C'est en quelque sorte la hauteur de vue de ce cycle de ballades qui a rendu sa lecture problématique. Divers auteurs ont travaillé au siècle dernier sur ce cycle, à commencer par Arthur de la Borderie, qui voit en elles un brûlot polémique des poètes breton et bourguignon attaquant Louis XI; Arthur Piaget, l'accablant de sarcasmes, montre qu'il n'en est rien et associe ces textes à l'année 1453–54, autour du Banquet du Faisan. Plus récemment, Christine Martineau revient à l'hypothèse Louis XI, et fonde l'essentiel de son analyse sur ce point. À mon sens la discussion est assez vaine, dans la mesure où il nous manque un certain nombre des éléments historiques qui pourraient aider à dater précisément le texte et à mesurer ses enjeux; il ne s'ensuit pas qu'il faille renoncer à les étudier.

Je voudrais montrer, dans les pages qui suivent, qu'une telle approche positiviste, strictement historicisante, ne suffit pas à rendre pleinement compte d'une œuvre complexe et vraiment intéressante, qu'il importe d'auner non pas à la mesure de nos attentes critiques ou de celles plus historicistes des générations passées, mais à celle d'un public du XVe siècle – avec la facilité pour nous de percevoir une attente et une esthétique bien plus stables que les turbulences du siècle.

Pour cela, il n'est sans doute pas inutile de situer en quelques lignes l'auteur, son œuvre et les enjeux politiques et poétiques qui influent sur sa composition. Meschinot, poète breton de petite noblesse, est né vers 1420 dans la région de Nantes, meurt en 1492 selon certains, plus tard selon d'autres;[3] il sera toute sa vie un fidèle serviteur des ducs de Bretagne. On le voit, au cours des années, figurer dans les comptes de Jean V (1389–1399–1442),[4] François Ier (1414–1442–1450), Pierre II (1418–1450–1457), Arthur III (1393–1457–58), François II (1435–1455–1488) et enfin Anne de Bretagne (1477–1488–1514). Ses fonctions sont multiples: il semble avoir servi dans la maison ducale, mais aussi en armes lorsque l'on craint des attaques contre le duché. Dès 1440, on voit figurer dans les comptes de la maison du duc des dons 'pour un rondeau': le serviteur est très exactement un poète de cour, mais il abandonnera bien vite la veine courtoise non seule-

---

[3] Mireille Dhombres, qui a consacré une étude non publiée à Meschinot, m'a dit avoir retrouvé des traces du poète dans les comptes du château de Nantes bien au-delà de 1492.

[4] La deuxième date correspond à l'année d'accès au duché.

ment pour des pièces de circonstance qui jalonneront son œuvre, mais surtout pour une poésie plus austère. Il faudrait peut-être chercher dans sa biographie l'épisode douloureux qui lui fait considérer le monde avec un pessimisme amer, et Ch. Martineau s'efforce d'en retrouver les traces; nous n'en saurons rien de certain, mais pouvons constater que les vers d'ouverture des *Lunettes des princes* résument son approche du monde:

> Aprés beau temps vient la pluye et tempeste,
> Plaings, pleurs, souspirs viennent aprés grant feste.[5]

> [Après le beau temps viennent la pluie et la tempête,
> Plaintes, pleurs, soupirs viennent après les grandes fêtes.]

Cette œuvre, composée entre 1461 et 1465 d'après Ch. Martineau, connaîtra un grand succès: plusieurs manuscrits la conservent et plus d'une trentaine d'éditions la reprennent jusqu'après 1530, suivie des autres œuvres du poète: ce sont les *Lunettes des princes* qui font vendre. Ce prosimètre mêle l'autofiction (Désespoir vient loger chez le poète), l'allégorie (Raison donne au poète des Lunettes chargées de lui faire mieux voir le monde) et le discours moral (chacune des vertus cardinales développe ses préceptes). Dès lors, la notoriété de Meschinot est établie, ainsi que l'élévation morale de son œuvre. C'est ce qui lui permettra à diverses reprises de se constituer comme la voix de la Bretagne[6] et de se lamenter sur la maladie du prince, ou pour l'interdiction qui frappe la ville de Nantes; il tient toujours le discours de la sagesse et de la hauteur de vue:

> Frere qui parlez de L et C,
> Les autres lettres confundant,
> Dictes : quant viendroit a l'essay,
> Seriez vous tant effundant
> De ce sang humain com fundant
> Vont voz motz de menaces plains?
> Aprés jeux viennent pleurs et plaings.[7]

> [Frères qui parlez de L et de C, confondant les autres lettres, dites: quand vous en viendriez aux actes, verseriez-vous autant de sang humain que le font vos paroles pleines de menaces? Après les jeux viennent les pleurs et les plaintes.]

---

[5] Éd. Martineau-Genieys, p. 1, vv. 1–2.

[6] J'ai développé ce point dans 'Du Je courtois à la Prosopopée, Jean Meschinot', dans Danielle Buschinger, éd, *Figures de l'Ecrivain au Moyen Âge* (Göppingen, 1991), pp. 151–65.

[7] Tours, Bibliothèque municipale, MS 905, f 79v. Les lettres semblent renvoyer à Louis XI et à Charles le Téméraire.

On le voit, ces vers partent de l'allusion politique pour arriver à une vérité plus générale et plus élevée, l'importance de la vie humaine; l'aboutissement proverbial de la strophe renforce cette indiscutable sagesse. Mais son œuvre n'est pas seulement de circonstance: le talent de Meschinot est de savoir reprendre les préoccupations morales de l'homme, et de les approcher dans des démarches à la fois austères et d'une humanité qui fait mouche, comme lorsqu'il présente l'homme redoutant le châtiment 'Criant mercy com l'enfant a sa mere / Qui deservy auroit estre batu [demandant pardon comme l'enfant à sa mère, quand il aurait mérité d'être battu]'.[8] Le ton austère et la capacité à répéter obstinément les mêmes préceptes moraux sont largement compensés par une richesse de langue, une sensibilité et une justesse qui touchent. L'abondance des éditions prouve la grande popularité de ce poète, estimé par un public sensible à sa stature humaine et à un ton très personnel; mais cette estime est aussi partagée par les poètes qui mettent très souvent Meschinot au nombre des grands maîtres, aux côtés de Chartier, Jean de Meun ou des frères Greban.

La tradition critique pense que le poète a fait parvenir à Chastelain un exemplaire des *Lunettes des princes*, et que celui-ci lui a envoyé en retour une série de sixains intitulée *Les Princes*.[9] L'hypothèse est satisfaisante, ne serait-ce que par le parallélisme des titres, et correspond à ce que l'on sait des échanges poético-épistolaires du temps: rien d'étonnant à ce que les vers de Chastelain suscitent en retour les *Ballades des Princes*. Mais cette filiation pose cependant de nombreuses questions qu'il importe d'élucider.

Les *Princes* de Chastelain figurent dans quelques manuscrits comme une œuvre indépendante. Il s'agit alors d'une suite de vingt-cinq sixains de décasyllabes *aabccb*, commençant tous par l'ouverture anaphorique *Prince*. Pour Kervyn de Lettenhove, leur premier éditeur, ces vers attaquent Louis XI. Près d'un siècle après leur publication, A. Piaget a montré que ces textes participaient d'une tradition générique établie, attestée dans un manuscrit:[10]

> Le poème qu'il faut intituler *Les Princes* n'est pas isolé. Il fait partie d'un petit cycle qui, outre les *Princes*, comprend *les Dames*, *les Gouges*, *les Coquards* et *les Serviteurs*. Ces cinq poèmes sont composés de mêmes sixains rimant *aabccb* en vers de dix syllabes.[11]

---

[8] *Paraphrase biblique* IV: *Celum et terra transibunt*, etc., vv. 7–8. Ce texte est édité en appendice à mon article 'Psaumes, prières, paraphrases et récritures', *Le Moyen Français*, 51–52-53 (2003), 349–73, p. 365.

[9] Ceux-ci figurent dans l'édition Kervyn de Lettenhove des œuvres du chroniqueur, t. VII (Bruxelles, 1863), p. 457–63.

[10] Bruxelles, KBR, MS 11020–33. Il contient *les Princes* de Chastelain, *les Serviteurs* anonyme, *les Dames* d'Olivier de la Marche; la table annonçait également *les Gouges* de Bouton.

[11] Arthur Piaget, '*Les Princes* de Georges Chastelain', *Romania*, 47 (1921), 161–206, p. 167.

Les auteurs de ces textes sont Olivier de La Marche, pour *les Dames*: il s'agit d'une suite de neuf strophes présentant des dames se refusant au jeu d'amour, infidèles ou méprisantes, et à qui l'auteur annonce un châtiment. Claude Bouton et le Bâtard de Bourgogne, semble-t-il, sont les auteurs des *Gouges* qui s'organisent en dialogue: ce texte, conservé dans deux manuscrits, peut être la trace d'un concours de poésie à rire comme il s'en est fait en tout temps, d'une tonalité plus leste et moins convenue que le texte d'Olivier de La Marche, puisqu'il est question d'y énumérer les types de *gouges*, femmes lascives et immorales:

> Gouge qui veult les coquars et novices
> Et qui s'en fait servir du plat des cuisses
> Pour estre mieulx a son gré tricotee
> Et pour sçavoir si les sotz le font bien[12]

> [Gouge qui recherche les niais et les novices, pour s'en faire servir du plat des cuisses et être 'tricotée' à sa convenance et pour savoir si les idiots le font bien]

Chacune d'elles, 'Gouge qui …', donne lieu à des descriptions sarcastiques et inventives, qui constituent plus une sorte de définition générale de ce qu'est une gouge qu'une vraie typologie.

La dernière série est constituée de 44 sixains dévolus aux *Coquards*, nom générique des sots vains, présomptueux et coquins. Ici, il s'agit encore d'annoncer une typologie qui montrera les divers types d'hommes; mais le type même de l'énumération montre combien l'on est dans une sorte de galerie de portraits qui ne répondent pas à une classification précise. Il existe enfin un poème, *les Serviteurs*, dont le projet est, de même, de faire une sorte de portrait des divers mauvais serviteurs, le déloyal, le flatteur, le négligent, l'infidèle, le bavard, le traître, le dépensier …

La suite anaphorique de sixains de décasyllabes a donc pu constituer un genre en soi, au moins dans le milieu bourguignon et pendant une certaine période, autour des années 1460 – c'est en tout cas de cette époque que datent la plupart des textes que l'on vient de mentionner. Elle se caractérise, outre sa forme, par un ton satirique ou polémique, qui revient à décrire une catégorie de personnes au comportement inacceptable et dont les conséquences seront fâcheuses. C'est également ce ton qu'adoptent les *Princes* de Chastelain, comme un simple exemple le montrera:

> Prince flateur, menteur en ses parolles,
> Qui blandist gens et endort en frivolles
> Et riens qu'en doeul et fraude n'estudie,
> Ses jours seront de petite duree,

---

[12] Piaget, '*Les Princes*', p. 170.

> Son regne obscur, sa mort tost desiree,
> Et fera fin confuse et enlaydie.
>
> [Prince flatteur, aux paroles mensongères, qui enjôle les gens et les endort en discours vains et ne s'applique qu'en tromperies et préjudices, ses jours seront de petite durée, son règne obscur, on souhaitera vite sa mort et il fera une fin honteuse et laide.]

Il s'agit bien pour Chastelain de s'inscrire dans une tradition textuelle établie, et d'envoyer à l'auteur des *Lunettes des princes*, très probablement à la suite d'une correspondance, un texte peut-être déjà écrit, et dont le titre, comme la haute teneur, pouvait correspondre au ton du poète breton. Nous en avons sans doute la trace dans le manuscrit conservé à Nantes[13] et composé pour Bouton, qui contient les *Lunettes des princes* et les *Ballades,* et ne contient qu'elles: seul manuscrit de ce type, il provient d'un milieu bourguignon et propose non seulement un bon texte pour les *Lunettes*, mais probablement le meilleur pour les *Ballades des Princes*. Il s'appuie probablement sur les sources mêmes de l'échange épistolaire dont il conforte l'existence.[14]

Reste cependant à s'interroger sur la double visée de ce texte, dans la mesure où c'est à la fois l'ensemble des intentions de Chastelain et la réception qu'en a Meschinot qui sont à préciser. On considère aisément que l'invective contre le mauvais prince, lorsqu'elle est composée par un poète bourguignon du milieu du XVe siècle, vise Louis XI. En fait, la suite des textes anaphoriques le montre, il s'agit pour le plus souvent d'une description générique, dans laquelle il est difficile de rechercher des indications précises. La fragilité des hypothèses de Piaget le montre aisément:

> Olivier se donne pour 'le serf et le serviteur d'une' et, après avoir fait l'éloge de la dame idéale, il termine par ce vers 'Si prie a Dieu que telle soit ma dame.' Ce vers, peut-on imaginer, décèle un Olivier jeune et amoureux. Avons-nous là une discrète allusion à sa première femme, Odette de Janley? Le poème daterait ainsi de 1454 environ.[15]

Faut-il, alors, mettre en cause le commentaire que faisait Kervyn de Lettenhove sur ce texte – '[i]l est à peu près inutile d'apprendre au lecteur que ce prince est Louis XI'?[16] Probablement; ou plus exactement, même si le modèle est pareil, l'objet est différent. Il semble que le projet de Chastelain, dans ce texte, n'est pas tant de décrire une personne que d'inventorier les

---

[13] Nantes, B.M., MS 651. Toutes les citations des *Ballades des Princes* renverront à ce manuscrit, et apparaîtront désormais dans le corps du texte.

[14] On connaît d'autres exemples de ce type de correspondance regroupé dans un manuscrit de peu ultérieur cf. le BnF, MS fr. 2202, qui reprend les échanges de Perréal et de Jacques le Lieur.

[15] Piaget, '*Les Princes*', p. 169.

[16] Éd. Kervyn, p. 457, note 2.

aspects d'un mauvais prince; aspects d'autant plus faciles à saisir certes qu'un modèle se trouve à portée; mais dont l'importance particulière – fût-il le roi de France – s'efface devant le général.

Pour Estelle Doudet, la plus récente étude de fond sur le poète bourguignon, 'l'identification entre "Prince" et Louis XI semble être sciemment camouflée par Chastelain';[17] elle suppose ainsi un système subtil où le modèle se précise au fur et à mesure qu'on le nie. En fait, il n'est pas question ici de dire si l'abrégé de tous les vices du pouvoir renvoie à une personne précise ou à une construction mentale, et il n'est peut-être pas tant question de camouflage que de 'miroir' à proprement parler, en ce que le poète se contente de donner à voir. Elle ajoute: 'l'hésitation des critiques reproduit celle des contemporains, de Jean Meschinot qui lit une attaque assez précise contre le roi, à Olivier de La Marche et ses compagnons qui s'amusent de cette liste possible de portraits.'[18] Je ne suis pas sûr qu'il faille supposer une hésitation des contemporains pour prendre en compte la réception du texte de Chastelain. Les liens qui peuvent se tisser entre Chastelain et Meschinot ne peuvent relever que de l'*encomium* et du discours commun de deux grands poètes au service de leur seigneur; c'est en toute logique sur une même aversion à l'égard de l'adversaire commun qu'ils vont se fonder. Pour Olivier de La Marche et Bouton, nous sommes évidemment dans une dynamique autre qui relève du divertissement de société, comme il s'en pratique à la cour de Bourgogne, où la chose politique peut voisiner avec de grands rires.

On l'a vu dans les textes précédents, il ne s'agissait pas tant de dresser une taxinomie que d'épingler des travers qu'une même personne peut cumuler. Pour Chastelain, une chose est de dresser le portrait *du* mauvais prince, une autre de décrire les agissements *d'un* mauvais prince; même si bien des traits se retrouvent. La généralité du propos répond au projet de Meschinot qui ne parlait pas, dans ses *Lunettes,* du prince, mais de tout être humain, 'pour ce que tout homme peult estre dict prince, en tant qu'il a receu de Dieu gouvernement d'ame'.[19]

Au-delà de la simple question de l'intention, c'est aussi celle de la structure du texte qui pose difficulté; il n'est pas possible de trouver, dans la suite des strophes proposées, de fil directeur, de cheminement. Le propos est instable, et il est difficile de percevoir progression et organisation du discours d'un sixain l'autre. Comme le dit E. Doudet: 'à chaque nouvelle lecture, une cohérence nouvelle détruit la précédente, sans qu'un plan stable

---

[17] E. Doudet, *Poétique de George Chastelain (1415–1475): 'Un cristal mucié en un coffre'* (Paris, 2005), p. 460. E. Doudet s'inscrit au terme actuel de cette lignée de chercheurs (La Borderie, Kervyn de Lettenhove, Piaget et Ch. Martineau) qui ont tenté de trouver un ancrage historique aux textes de Chastelain et Meschinot.

[18] Doudet, *Poétique de George Chastelain*, p. 460.

[19] Éd. Martineau-Genieys, p. 35.

puisse être donné à l'ensemble'.[20] Il faudrait sans doute prendre en compte la symbolique des nombres dans le choix de cette série de vingt-cinq strophes; la matière est en effet d'une haute tenue morale, et se distingue radicalement des séries indéterminées qui l'entourent dans les autres séries de sixains. Vingt-cinq c'est en effet le nombre humain par excellence, en ce qu'il est le carré de cinq, qui lui-même renvoie à l'homme: on peut ajouter Science et Doctrine au trois de la Trinité, nous apprend Barthélemy l'Anglais. Ce sont là les qualités de l'homme; mais le même chiffre peut renvoyer 'aux cinq vierges folles, ou à eux qui achetèrent cinq paires de bœuf. C'est pourquoi dans 5 sont contenus les plaisirs des cinq sens de la chair.'[21] À cette charge symbolique du nombre 5, on ajoute souvent que $25 = (3^2+4^2)$, et que la tension entre les valeurs divines et les valeurs humaines (quatre est le chiffre de la matière, entre les éléments, les humeurs et les points cardinaux) y est manifestée dans son éclat. Ces approches arithmologiques ne sont pas incohérentes à la matière propre du texte de Chastelain, et on peut considérer que la diversité qui s'y manifeste restitue le foisonnement des vices humains, en accord même avec le nombre des sixains. Le mal est multiple, virtuellement infini, et s'oppose à l'unité du bien. Le prince que présente le poète bourguignon est donc autant une sorte d'archétype du mauvais souverain qu'il est figure universelle de l'être humain soumis à ses passions. Il répond exactement en cela au projet de Meschinot dans ses *Lunettes des Princes*.

Cette cohérence dans l'envoi de Chastelain à Meschinot peut également être lue en contrepoint des *Douze Dames de Rhétorique*, correspondance littéraire bien connue depuis les travaux de David Cowling. Il ne s'agit pas pour le Chroniqueur de répondre à l'*encomium*, mais d'offrir un texte en retour d'un autre, sans s'engager dans une correspondance régulière.[22] L'expérience récente de Chastelain l'amenait à une certaine prudence, et il semblait difficile de faire quelque chose de la suite des *Princes*.

La réception que fait Meschinot de cette œuvre sera au contraire dynamique; il ne s'agit pas pour lui simplement d'entériner l'échange, mais aussi de montrer sa capacité à l'*amplificatio*. J'ai montré ailleurs combien la démarche de paraphrase et de développement fait partie de la poétique de

---

[20] p. 461.
[21] 'ex additione autem unitatis ad quaternarium surgit secundus numerus impar, scilicet quinarius, qui inter impares in binario distans a ternario est secundus, et illos ideo saepe designat, qui ad Trinitatis fidem, doctrinam et scientiam superaddunt, & tamen quamvis instructi sint per fidem et per legem, nihilominus tamen quinque fatuis virginibus et quinque juga boum ementibus comparantur, quia in quique carnalium sensuum voluptatibus adhex detinentur' (Barthélemy l'Anglais, *De Proprietatibus Rerum*, lib. XIX, cap CXVIII; Francfort, W. Richter, 1601, p. 1123–4). Les cinq paires de bœufs renvoient à Luc 14:19.
[22] 'Moy non vueillant plus entendre à loenges ne à vanité de vuides parolles de main sur main renforceez, pretenz à en rompre la maniere' lettre 30, lignes 10–13. Voir *Les Douze Dames de Rhétorique*, éd. David Cowling (Genève, 2002), p. 181.

Meschinot;[23] reprenant des versets bibliques, développant une prière mariale en acrostiche de l'*Ave Maria*, il est aussi capable de composer des cycles de ballades anaphoriques aux arborescences complexes. Il y a chez lui une conscience aiguë de la nécessité de dire et de redire, de donner aux choses importantes à ses yeux la place, l'espace qu'elles méritent, et que seule une répétition, une itération sous de multiples formes peut permettre d'occuper. Les *Lunettes des princes* constituent une sorte de guide de ce qu'il faut faire pour s'approcher du salut; par symétrie, les *Ballades des Princes* pourront montrer ce qui arrive à celui qui suit la voie du mal. Si Chastelain a tracé la voie, il importe maintenant de creuser le sillon.

L'habileté de Meschinot est de reconsidérer la suite des sixains et de les percevoir non plus comme une œuvre cohérente et aboutie, mais comme un ensemble d'envois potentiels: un peu à la façon d'un Cuvier qui d'un ossement reconstituait un dinosaure, Meschinot en lisant ces *Princes* au dernier vers si bien frappé, a l'intuition des ballades comme *impliquées* par ces textes; et à vrai dire, un peu à la façon de Cuvier, on a l'impression qu'il fait surgir un texte sous-jacent, nécessaire et presque *antérieur* aux *Princes* de Chastelain. Ce travail demande une grande habileté: sur le plan formel tout d'abord, puisque la structure de la ballade est comme imposée. Un envoi fait habituellement une demi-strophe, il faudra donc que la ballade soit constituée de douzains. Le système de rimes du sixain original est bien sûr imposé sur chaque fin de strophe; pour son début, Meschinot prend le parti d'adopter le système de deux vers suivis d'un vers orphelin, sans pour autant s'autoriser la même liberté que Chastelain: c'est une forme *aab-aab+ccd-eed* qu'il adopte. La part originale de son travail se propose une contrainte plus restrictive que celle de son modèle, en composant trois fois six vers sur deux rimes seulement. Les rimes imposées par le sixain original ne sont pas forcément aisées: des rimes en -*ole* (bal. I) ou en -*ure* (bal. IV) ne tombent pas facilement sous la plume. À cela, il faut évidemment ajouter l'exigence du refrain, récurrent dans chaque strophe: Chastelain a choisi avec talent des formules souvent percutantes, qui peuvent conclure un douzain avec la même force qu'un sixain, mais il n'est pas si aisé de les incruster dans un propos autre, avec la nécessité de tenir un discours aussi cohérent sur le plan du sens que sur celui de la métrique. Par ailleurs que l'anaphore 'Prince' ne correspond pas forcément à l'adresse qui ouvre habituellement un envoi de ballade: Meschinot doit donc modifier son esthétique et sa pratique du refrain.[24]

---

[23] Voir 'Psaumes, prières, paraphrases et récritures'.

[24] Ces remarques ont déjà été formulées par Leonard W. Johnson dans 'Prince or Princes? Fifteenth-Century Politics and Poetry', *The French Review*, 68 (1995), 421–30; sa démarche, si elle recoupe la mienne, a d'autres visées et tend à montrer comment c'est une sorte de prince abstrait que montrent Chastelain et Meschinot. Il me semble au contraire que si c'est bien le but poursuivi par Chastelain, l'ambition de Meschinot est autre.

On notera, de plus, qu'il est relativement aisé de tracer en quelques vers le portrait du mauvais prince; il est plus difficile de procéder à un tel travail d'*amplificatio* sans tomber dans la redite. Les textes de Meschinot ont une tenue et une cohérence – à leur refrain, à leur envoi – telles que l'on oublie à chaque instant qu'ils sont générés par le texte qu'ils englobent. C'est là encore un portrait, moins allusif et enlevé mais plus complet, un peu pesant comme savent l'être les textes moraux du poète, mais d'une grande efficacité. La capacité d'indignation du poète fait merveille, et il a un réel talent pour dénoncer les excès de la classe dirigeante, dans une envolée dont on oublie les extrêmes contraintes formelles:

> C'est cruaulté des plus piteuses l'une
> Qui jamais fust, si par voye importune
> Le commun est par le prince destruit
> 16 Duquel il a bled, vin, rente, pecune,
> Service, honneur … Et sans luy fault qu'il june
> Car il n'est pas au labourage duit.
> En le perdant il pert sa nourriture
> 20 Et si se mect en damnable adventure,
> Car bien souvent a la fin derreniere
> Trompé se voit quant a tromper essaye.
> Et justement raison ainsi le paye
> 24 Affin qu'il sente aultruy playe premiere. (Ballade IV, fol. 57r)

> [C'est une des choses les plus pitoyables qui soit jamais, si par un détour malheureux le petit peuple est détruit par le prince, alors qu'il en reçoit grains, vin, rentes, fortune, service, honneurs: sans lui il faut qu'il jeûne, car il ne sait cultiver la terre. En le perdant, il perd qui le nourrit, et prend le risque de se damner, car bien souvent, au bout du compte, il est trompé quand il essaie de tromper, et c'est justement que la raison le paye, afin qu'il sente le mal qu'il a fait à autrui.]

Pour Meschinot, écrire, *amplifier* un texte envoyé par Chastelain, cela ne pouvait se percevoir que dans une dialectique d'hommage d'un poète à un autre, et c'est ce que prouve la ballade finale où, ayant abandonné le style sublime du douzain de décasyllabes, il s'adresse à lui en simples octosyllabes:

> O Georges, des aultres le maistre
> En la rethorique science,
> Je vous supply cruel ne me estre,
> Et vueillez prendre en patience
> Ce qu'ay faict ainsi, com si en ce
> Eusse bien sain entendement:
> Ce que non, par ma conscience,
> Mais donnez y amendement. (Ballade finale, fol. 70, vv. 1–8)

> [O Georges, le maître de tous en la science de rhétorique je vous en supplie, ne me soyez pas cruel, et supportez ce que j'ai fait, comme si en la matière j'avais eu tout mon bon sens – ce qui n'est pas le cas, j'en suis conscient – mais corrigez-le.]

Il est ici question d'hommage, de métier d'écrivain, et certainement pas d'une collaboration à une œuvre polémique! Les poètes ont la même élévation morale et ne sont pas dans la situation de plumitifs stipendiés pour une propagande immédiate, encore moins pour rédiger un tract poétique à l'occasion d'un épisode précis. Nos poètes ne sont pas des fatistes, font une œuvre originale dans la forme comme dans le fond, et sont généralement moins tributaires, par leur statut à la cour de leurs seigneurs respectifs, d'attentes ciblées dans le temps. S'il y a une responsabilité ou un commanditaire à ce cycle de ballades, ce serait peut-être Chastelain, comme le rappellent trois vers du poète breton:

> Touteffoist j'ay faict diligence
> Et par vostre commandement
> De cy monstrer mon inscience.
> (Ballade finale, fol. 70, vv. 13–14)
>
> [Toutefois, je me suis hâté, et cela sur votre ordre, de montrer ici mon ignorance.]

À ce compte, il est nécessaire de s'interroger sur le sens que pourrait porter un tel cycle de ballades, s'il n'est pas polémique:

> Quel est, dans ce long pensum, le thème que développe Meschinot? Il considère le temps qui court, où les loups sont les bergers des brebis, et il gémit sur le sort du 'commun', qui tremble de faim, de froid, de peur et de misère. Il écrit une sorte de Miroir des princes, à l'usage de tous ceux qui sont en 'dignité d'office', dans lequel ils pourront voir, pour s'en corriger, leurs vices et leurs crimes.[25]

On reconnaît ici la condescendance de Piaget à l'égard de la littérature qu'il étudiait: Meschinot est pour lui l'auteur d'un 'long pensum', et son œuvre n'apportera rien de plus que des lieux communs. Mais une telle qualification rend difficile son interprétation comme une simple polémique ancrée dans l'actualité. Je pense en effet que c'est la notion de *Miroir des princes*, évoquée par le critique, qui constitue une des clefs de l'œuvre. Depuis Gilles de Rome ou Dhuoda, il est acquis que le genre est destiné à l'éducation d'un jeune aristocrate, à qui il convient de donner justement une formation princière. C'est oublier que dans les temps médiévaux, c'est surtout une forma-

---

[25] Piaget, *'Les Princes'*, p. 199.

tion morale qu'il convient de donner aux enfants, et que le futur souverain n'a pas encore besoin de suivre les leçons de Machiavel. Le titre même de Gilles de Rome, *De Regimine principum*, nous rappelle s'il était besoin que ce n'est pas *un* prince qu'il est question d'éduquer, mais *des* princes: il en est des destinataires de cette œuvre exactement ce qu'il en était des lecteurs des *Lunettes des princes*: nous sommes tous concernés, 'pour ce que tout homme peult estre dict prince'.

Le texte de Gilles de Rome, qui se présente comme le modèle du genre, présente pourtant une table des chapitres particulièrement révélatrice, et dont il convient de reproduire la dimension itérative:

> Cap VI: Quod non deceat regiam majestatem suam felicitatem ponere in voluptatibus
> Cap VII: Quod non deceat regiam majestatem suam felicitatem ponere in divitiis
> Cap VIII: Quod non deceat regiam majestatem suam felicitatem ponere in honoribus …[26]

> [chap 6: Qu'il ne convient pas à la majesté royale de placer son bonheur dans les plaisirs; chap 7: Qu'il ne convient pas à la majesté royale de placer son bonheur dans les richesses; chap 8: Qu'il ne convient pas à la majesté royale de placer son bonheur dans les honneurs …]

On le voit, c'est la dimension répétitive qui a ici fonction pédagogique, et cette répétition a pour fonction première de nous guider vers Dieu, et non de former précisément un prince. On pourrait aisément montrer combien la plupart des facettes développées par Gilles de Rome trouvent leur équivalent dans les vers du poète, ainsi par exemple de la volupté qu'a abordée le chapitre VI de Gilles de Rome:

> Sobrieté tient la personne saine:
> De faire exces force est que mal en vienne.
> (Ballade XIII, fol. 62v, vv. 7–8)

> [La sobriété tient en bonne santé: il est fatal que les excès entraînent des maux]

Le discours reste foncièrement moral, même s'il peut s'appliquer aux activités d'un prince, et les préceptes de Meschinot pourraient avoir une portée politique.

---

[26] On a consulté l'édition Stephanum Planck de Patavia (Rome, 1482). On pourra renvoyer pour une meilleure édition à Aegidius Romanus, *De regimine principum* (Frankfurt, 1968).

> Si tu veulx donc en biens fructifier
> Et ta valeur tousjours fortifier
> En sens, honneur, paix et vertu converse:
> Ainsi pourras si bien ediffier
> Que te feras par tout magnifier
> Comme celuy qui rayson ne traverse. …
>
> (Ballade XIV, fol. 63v, vv. 25–30)
>
> [Si tu veux prospérer en vertus et renforcer ta valeur, tourne toi vers la raison, l'honneur, la paix et la vertu: tu pourras ainsi si bien construire que tu te feras partout honorer comme celui qui ne contrecarre pas la raison.]

Un peu plus loin dans son volume, Gilles de Rome développera l'importance des vertus pour un bon gouvernement: on ne sera pas étonné d'y trouver les quatre vertus cardinales, celles-là même que le poète breton avait fait parler dans ses *Lunettes des princes*. Tout se passe donc comme si le gouvernement des princes, dont le poète se fait l'écho, constituait le rappel des vertus essentielles non seulement au bon gouvernement, mais à l'homme. La dimension des *Ballades des Princes* est peut-être aussi simplement humaine, quelque vigueur qu'elle ait dans la dénonciation des tares des grands.

En fait, ce que Meschinot attaque avec le plus d'insistance, c'est l'arrogance et le manque de scrupules des puissants ou de ceux qui veulent le devenir, et qu'aucune traîtrise ne rebute. En cela, son approche ne vise pas seulement les princes, qui n'ont pas à courir après le pouvoir, mais ceux qui gravitent autour, ces membres de la cour où Meschinot lui-même est obligé de vivre, et qu'Alain Chartier avait décrits avec tant de force:

> Tourne tes yeulx de toutes pars et euvre tes oreilles pour escouter, et tu verras et orras choses espoventables a veoir et tres horribles a ouir, car publicquement et en privé nous abusons et entremeslons le droit par my le tort et le tort avecques le droit a voullenté ; contre raison ambicion preside es choses publicques, affin d'acquerir privez prouffiz.[27]
>
> [Tourne tes yeux de toutes parts, ouvre tes oreilles pour écouter, et tu verras et entendras des choses épouvantables à voir et très horribles à entendre, car publiquement comme en privé, nous commettons nos abus et mêlons l'injustice au droit et le droit à l'injustice, selon notre volonté. L'ambition prime la raison en matière de choses publiques, afin d'en obtenir des avantages personnels.]

La thématique, mais même les effets rhétoriques, sont communs:

---

[27] Alain Chartier, *Le Curial*, in *Œuvres latines d'Alain Chartier*, éd. Pascale Bourgain-Hemeryck (Paris, 1977), § 25, p. 263.

> O vous qui yeulx avez sains et oreilles,
> Voyez, ouez, entendez lez merveilles,
> Considerez le temps qui present court:
> Les loups sont mis gouverneurs des oueilles:
> Fut il jamais – Nenny! – choses pareilles?
> Plus ne voyt on que traïson au court. (Ballade XVIII, fol. 65v)
>
> [O vous qui avez des yeux et des oreilles, voyez, écoutez, comprenez les merveilles! Considérez le temps présent:les loups sont mis gouverneurs des brebis: a-t-on déjà vu – jamais! – une telle chose? Pour faire simple, on ne voit plus que trahison.]

On voit ainsi que c'est dans une tradition morale autant que politique, pas forcément ancrée dans l'actualité, que s'inscrit Meschinot. Cependant, s'il parcourt les lieux attendus de la rhétorique parénétique, il sait renouveler ces lieux communs pour éviter les poncifs.

Le 'long pensum' que dénonce Piaget est nourri de la double expérience personnelle du courtisan gravitant dans les allées du pouvoir et du petit seigneur au bord de la pauvreté qui doit tenir son rang. Cette dernière dimension est largement attestée dans son œuvre, et explique sans doute son indiscutable et attachante sensibilité aux petites gens. Meschinot a en tête l'image, héritée de l'Antiquité et réactivée par la Bible, du corps politique, et le prince reste pour lui le garant de la paix et de la bonne entente, au point qu'il invite inlassablement à la concorde et vit douloureusement toute guerre civile, on le voit dans d'autres textes.[28] Pour lui, réfléchir au pouvoir c'est fondamentalement réfléchir à l'homme et à ses tourments. Il s'inscrit ainsi dans une dynamique de réflexion qui associe non seulement la cour et l'état, mais aussi le corps politique et celui du pauvre commun. La véhémence que l'on voit dans le *Quadriloge invectif* de Chartier se retrouve chez Meschinot; mais celui-ci est peut-être plus humaniste, en ce sens que c'est à l'homme qu'elle s'attache de façon prépondérante. Son message est donc adressé à tous et pas seulement aux puissants, et invite l'homme à se conformer au dessein de Dieu:

> Pour faire fin il nous fault reformer
> Et noz vouloirs tous a Dieu conformer
> Si nous voulons a sa gloire venir.
> Assez sçavons, sans plus en informer
> Qu'il n'entendit oncques tel nous fourmer
> Pour ne vouloir l'avoir en souvenir.
>
> (Ballade XXV, fol. 70, vv. 1–6)

---

[28] 'La cause de la maladie/Du royaume et sa lesion, / Celluy qui France ama la dye: / Ce fut guerre et division. / N'en as tu pas, dy, vision, /Qui veulx rechoir en ce danger?' *Frere qui parlez...*, Tours, B.M., MS 905, f. 79v, vv. 43–8.

[Pour finir, il faut nous réformer et tous conformer nos volontés à Dieu, si nous voulons accéder à sa gloire. Sans chercher davantage, nous savons bien qu'il n'a pas eu l'intention en nous formant ainsi que nous refusions de nous souvenir de lui.]

Poésie, savoir, communauté: Meschinot certes a une maîtrise et une force poétique exceptionnelles. Il est, comme beaucoup de ceux que l'on a appelés des rhétoriqueurs, un des maîtres de la langue et le prouve ici; mais son savoir est aussi un savoir humain, et surtout un savoir qui s'attache à penser le corps politique à l'image du corps de l'Église, à rêver d'une nation unie et d'un homme en accord avec son créateur. Son approche est loin d'avoir la naïveté que l'on pourrait lui imaginer, tant elle est ancrée dans le réel et consciente d'un désir qui est une ligne d'horizon, indispensable et inaccessible. Elle a contribué cependant, l'extrême abondance des éditions du poète le montre, à mettre des mots sur une aspiration qui au début du XVIe siècle prendra d'autres formes et d'autres noms: Renaissance, Humanisme, Réforme … Et par cela même, cette poésie a contribué à la modeler.

13

Ways of Knowing in the *Songe veritable* and Christine de Pizan's *Livre de l'Advision Cristine*

THELMA FENSTER

Much human knowledge results not from scholarship but from social exchange, from the talk through which people reach the decisions and make the judgments that structure and regulate groups and communities. In the Middle Ages such talk was known as *fama*, a polyvalent term denoting both a perceived result or entity, 'common knowledge' or 'public opinion', that is, 'what everybody knows', and a process, 'what everyone is saying', and 'what everyone is saying about what everyone is saying'. In Latin *fama* was talk, report, or rumour; to be *famosus*, or famous, was to be much spoken of. *Fama* denoted *both* 'talk' and 'knowledge': talk was knowledge, knowledge was talk, and both were *fama*.[1] As socially constructed knowledge, something people agreed upon informally or in an organized way, *fama* could not belong to just one person, although it certainly could have been idiosyncratically inflected. As a force circulating socially, *fama* about a person existed outside the individual's grasp, and thus managing one's *fama* would most often have involved the kinds of dispositions and practices that Pierre Bourdieu has called a *habitus*.[2] This was not merely socially important; as a routine instrument in law courts, one's *fama* – or 'commune renommée' (sometimes simply 'renommee') – could determine the outcome of a case, as could the *fama* about a relevant event.

The legal force of *fama* is suggested in a reading of the *Songe veritable* (1406), an anonymous allegorical dream vision in octosyllabic rhyming couplets, a 'songe politique' subtitled a political pamphlet by its modern

---

[1] The term *fama*, perhaps better known to modern readers as a supplementary fame or glory, is used in this essay in its fundamental medieval meaning of something attaching to everyone – that is, knowledge about a person formed through the report of others. See the introduction and various articles in Thelma S. Fenster and Daniel Lord Smail, ed., *Fama: The Politics of Talk and Reputation in Medieval Europe* (Ithaca, NY, 2003).

[2] Pierre Bourdieu, *Outline of a Theory of Practice* (Cambridge, 1977), pp. 72–87.

editor.[3] In the poem, a large number of named and historically identifiable officers and servants of King Charles VI stand accused of having impoverished the French people. Their guilt is argued before Everyman [Chascun], who has come to the royal court to learn why he has been deprived of his goods and his livelihood. He is addressed by personifications such as Reason [Raison] and Fortune [Fortune], but also by a pair of less usual figures: Experience [Experience], in whose mirror Everyman can see the truth for himself, and Common Knowledge [Commune Renommee] who, by invoking 'what everyone knows', explains to Everyman those things that Experience's mirror cannot show. The existence in the poem of Common Knowledge and other personifications whose names evoke legal procedure (such as Excusasion, the king's magistrat) establish the *Songe*'s juridical, prosecutorial flavour.

Among medieval authors who thought about the relationship between seeing and telling, Christine de Pizan stands out for her awareness of the ways in which one's personal identity and honour could be constructed by others. But her repeated expressions of concern for reputation, and especially for women's reputations, have not always been contextualized or well understood by modern readers. Given Christine's deep suspicion of 'talk', it is not surprising that in her partly autobiographical dream allegory, *Le Livre de l'Advision Cristine* (1405), written in prose, she recurs to the proof of 'one's own eyes' – to 'experience' – in an explanation of how one may know the difference between what is true and what is false.[4] The richness of the *Advision* lies in its polysemy; what the editors have called a pilgrimage whose signifier may sometimes be autobiographical but whose signifieds may be multiple.[5] Thus, like the *Songe veritable*, the *Advision* may also be read as partly a 'songe politique' dealing with France's woes.

The *Songe veritable* was written during a tense period of conflict between the Burgundians and the Orleanists that began in 1404 with the death of Philip, duke of Burgundy, and reached a climax in 1407 with the murder of Louis, duke of Orleans and younger brother of King Charles VI. By the first decade of the fifteenth century, Charles was too ill to rule for more than a few months at a time, and in his stead Queen Isabeau and Louis held the reins of government. They were accused of lavish personal spending supported in part by Louis's excessive taxation of the people. The queen was a foreigner and a daughter of the powerful Austrian family of the Wittelsbach, and her loyalties to France had been suspect from the beginning. John the Fearless, the young duke of Burgundy and Louis's cousin, found himself distanced from the centre of power and unable to command the sums of money from

---

[3] H. Moranvillé, ed., *Le Songe véritable: Pamphlet politique d'un Parisien du XVe siècle* (Paris, 1891).

[4] Christine de Pizan, *Le Livre de l'Advision Cristine*, ed. Christine Reno and Liliane Dulac (Paris, 2001).

[5] Christine, *Advision*, pp. xvii–xviii.

the French crown that his father had enjoyed. Positions hardened and factions formed. The *Songe veritable* records the core of the dispute, taking a pro-Burgundian stance: it attacks in particular Louis d'Orléans, Jean de Montaigu, the king's 'maître d'hôtel', Queen Isabeau of Bavaria, and two of the king's uncles, Jean, duc de Berry, and Louis II, duc de Bourbon, who had helped Charles VI to govern during his minority. Notably absent is any mention of the duke of Burgundy. Many others, individually named in one of the poem's lengthy lists (showing the popularity, in this period, of listing as a literary device) are alleged to have enriched themselves at the expense of 'the people'.[6] The dreamer/author begins his narration with the conventional 'Avis me fut (line 13) [It seemed to me]', and he sees Everyman arriving at a great and richly furnished palace where the king is not arrayed as befits him, for his garments feature only 'menuettes [very tiny]' fleurs de lys. The narrative moves forward only when rubrics announce Everyman's peripetations (for example, 'How Suffering led Everyman and Poverty to Common Knowledge'), and it passes from first to third person, consisting almost entirely of speeches by the allegories. The poem concludes upon a condemnation of Jean de Berry and Jean de Montaigu in particular, prophesying atrocious punishments for them that are never carried out, for the dreamer, frightened by a storm caused by Damnation, awakens. To be persuasive, the author of the *Songe* had only to appeal to the existing *fama* about the king's unpopular wife, brother, and steward, as he himself constructed yet a further, elaborate piece of *fama*.[7]

In a brief prologue to the poem's 3,174 verses, the author calls upon the authority of the *Roman de la Rose*.[8] In the years around 1406 the *Rose* was no doubt the most famous among the group of dream allegories that constituted a popular medieval genre.[9] Re-deploying the *Rose*'s first two lines by

---

[6] See Madeleine Jeay, *Le Commerce des mots: L'Usage des listes dans la littérature médiévale (XIIe–XVe siècles)* (Geneva, 2006).

[7] Moranvillé takes pains to argue that the author was a Parisian who personally served King Charles VI (*Songe*, p. 7), and not in the duke of Burgundy's camp. With Pierre-Yves Badel, I see in him a partisan of the duke of Burgundy (*Le* Roman de la Rose *au XIVe siècle: Étude de la réception de l'œuvre* (Geneva, 1980), p. 404).

[8] The editor omits 245 verses (between lines 1860 and 2105), which he instead summarizes. Lines 2159–243 are omitted and summarized. Lines 2556–60 are also omitted. For a discussion of the *Songe* author's indebtedness to the *Roman de la Rose*, see Badel, *Le* Roman de la Rose *au XIVe siècle*, pp. 404–8.

[9] But this singular mention may also suggest that the author knew the heated debate in writing (1401–4) over Jean de Meun's portion of the *Rose*, in which Christine de Pizan and Jean Gerson, chancellor of the University of Paris, critics of the *Rose*, argued against its defenders, Jean de Montreuil and Gontier and Pierre Col, Charles's chancellery clerks. See Eric Hicks, ed., *Le Débat sur le* Roman de la Rose (Paris, 1977). See also Christine McWebb, ed., *Debating the* Roman de la Rose*: A Critical Anthology* (New York, 2007). For a study of later, related literature, see Karin Becker, 'La mentalité juridique dans la littérature française (XIIIe–XVe siècles)', *Le Moyen Age*, 103 (1997), 309–27.

recalling the claim of some that dreams contain nought but 'fables [stories/ lies]' and 'mençonges [lies]', he adds that such people have not 'tout bien essayé (line 5) [experienced everything]', a comment the full import of which will emerge later in the poem with the appearance of the character called Experience.[10]

Of the two parts of the *Roman de la Rose*, the social satire of Jean de Meun's portion of the poem would have more directly interested the author of the *Songe veritable*. Other dream allegories, often of religious inspiration and purporting to teach the way to a Christian heaven, would also have been germane, given their tendency to offer social and political criticism. I mention here a few of the better-known titles. Raoul de Houdenc's *Songe d'Enfer* (1215–16) is an allegorical journey which, much like the *Songe veritable*, intends not to edify its public but rather to criticize certain groups. Huon de Méry's *Tournoiement de l'Antéchrist* of the mid-thirteenth century, an occasionally humorous psychomachia between the armies of God and those of the 'Antecriz', is also social criticism. Rutebeuf's *Voie de Paradis*, c. 1265, formally its author's dream of a journey toward confession and paradise along a road peopled with personifications he admires, nonetheless reveals Rutebeuf's polemical and argumentative proclivities as he rails against traits that offend a Christian sensibility. The group also includes Guillaume de Deguileville's three *Pèlerinages* or pilgrimages: *de la vie humaine* (1330), *de l'âme* (1355–58), and *de Jésus Christ* (1358), as well as the *Songe de la voie d'enfer et de paradis* (1340), by Jean de le Mote. Closer in date to the *Songe veritable* were three 'songes politiques [political songs]', which supplied political lessons: the *Songe du vergier* (1376), Evrard de Trémaugon's dialogue on the relative importance of ecclesiastical and secular powers, composed in Latin then immediately translated into French; the *Songe de pestilence* (1374–76 or early 1377), which seeks to elucidate the meaning of France's misfortunes in the fourteenth century and may have been known to the author of the *Songe*;[11] and Philippe de Mézière's *Songe du vieil pèlerin* (1386–89), in which a new crusade is proposed to reinvigorate the Christian West.

Although the *Songe veritable* finds a comfortable niche in French continental literary tradition, it also joins with the broader category of late medi-

---

[10] Guillaume de Lorris et Jean de Meun, *Le Roman de la Rose*, ed. Félix Lecoy, 3 vols (Paris, 1965/1966/1970).

[11] A passage in the *Songe de pestilence* in which Sapience [Wisdom] seeks Verité, Charité and Humilité [Truth, Charity, and Humility] 'chiex les religious [among the religious]', and Prudence [Prudence] does so 'sus les nobles [among the nobles]' and 'chiex les nobles de mendre estat [among the nobles of lesser estate]', may have directly inspired a similar passage in the *Songe veritable*: see lines 182–289.

eval 'political songs'.[12] In J. R. Maddicott's description, political songs composed in English, French and Latin from the thirteenth to the fifteenth centuries in England often made propaganda for a cause, ridiculing one side while glorifying another. As social protest, they claimed to speak for the downtrodden, and they attacked those in authority; they were sympathetic to the poor, hostile to the rich, their tone 'querulous, vituperative and sometimes minatory'.[13] Maddicott's description could apply equally to the *Songe veritable*. An important difference between the 'songs' and the *Songe veritable*, however, is that whereas the former criticize the king of England, the *Songe* criticises not the king but those around him; the ailing and ineffectual Charles, the 'tres doulce creature (line 418) [very kind creature]', is as much a victim of his rapacious circle as are 'the people'.

The principal instrument of proof against those who are accused of stealing from the king is the mirror of Experience, a device which naturally recalls Narcissus's fountain in the *Roman de la Rose* as well as en entire literary genre – mirrors of the vices and virtues, mirrors for princes, and such 'mirrors of knowledge' as Vincent de Beauvais' *Speculum maius*. Experience explains that whatever is not clear in her mirror will be supplied by her partner, Common Knowledge:

> En mon mirour vous monstreray
> Ce qui en est et que j'en sçay,
> Combien que ne voyés ouvertes
> Les choses n'a plain descouvertes
> Au mains de la greigneur partie;
> Maiz ne vous en mentiray mie:
> Commune Renommee sy est,
> Qui scet bien dire où tout est.
> Et pour ce, premier vous diray
> Ceulx qu'elle scet et que j'en sçay,
> Et qu'au mirour veu les ay. (lines 981–91)
>
> [In my mirror I will show you how it is and what I know about it, although you may not see things openly or plainly exposed, at least for the most part. But I shall not lie to you: Common Knowl-

---

[12] Moranvillé claims that political pamphlets were rare in France to the end of the Middle Ages, and that only one song against the king is known from the early fifteenth century (*Songe*, p. 8).

[13] J. R. Maddicott, 'Poems of Social Protest in Early Fourteenth-Century England', in *England in the Fourteenth Century: Proceedings of the Harlaxton Symposium*, ed. W. M. Ormrod (Woodbridge, 1986), pp. 130–44 (esp. 130, 133). For the poems, see Peter Coss, ed., *Thomas Wright's Political Songs of England, from the Reign of John to that of Edward II* (Cambridge, 1996). Poems in the French of England are collected in Isabel S. T. Aspin, ed., *Anglo-Norman Political Songs* (Oxford, 1953).

edge is here, who knows how to say where everything is. And for that reason I'll first tell you about the ones she knows and that I know, and that I have seen them in the mirror.]

Experience criticises Louis d'Orléans first of all, stating that he has stolen land, even land belonging to the king, and he has had a large building erected at Coucy and another at Pierrefond (lines 1013–16). The duc de Berry has also spent money on stone constructions and other 'sotes fumées (lines 1020–1) [stupid follies]', and he has taken land belonging to the king, especially in Languedoc (lines 1023–6). As for the queen, Experience says that

> Tout son penser […]
> Est d'en prendre ce qu'elle en peut
> Maiz non pas tant comme elle vault. (lines 1035–7)

> [All her thought […] is to take as much as she can, but not as much as she wants.]

No one knows what has become of everything she has taken, except for what Common Knowledge has often said: that the queen has sent the money to her father and brother, or that she has spent it frivolously, or that she has stored it in coffers or hidden it in some way which doesn't appear in Experience's mirror (lines 1039–50). Nonetheless, she has often helped herself to money, and she has given it to her friends Semihiere and Hemonnet and to others (lines 1051–8).[14] Experience concludes, saying that she has now explained the matter:

> Com Commune Renommee m'a dist,
> Qui le m'a baillé par escript.
> En mon mirour ne l'ay pas veu
> Tres clerement ne apercu. (lines 1063–6)

> [As Common Knowledge told it to me, who gave it to me in writing. I didn't see or perceive it very clearly in my mirror.]

By far the lengthiest criticism in the *Songe* is that levelled against Jean de Montaigu, whose activities, unlike those of the queen, are plain to see in Experience's mirror. He has spent so much that he ought to be hanged; he is

---

[14] Etienne de Semihier was a knight of Charles VI's court and his wife Anne, charged with the care and purchase of the gems Isabeau wished to give to others, was a favourite of the queen (*Songe*, pp. 212–13). Hémon Raguier was the queen's treasurer until 1400, and he continued to serve both the king and queen afterward. Between 1408 and 1409 he was the queen's counsellor, responsible for paying the allowances of the queen's officers. All the sums of money said to have been spent by the queen would have passed through his hands (*Songe*, pp. 199–203).

the cause of the people's misery (lines 1072–4); witness his beautiful chateau at Marcoussis, depicted in a list of its luxurious buildings and architectural features. This *amplificatio* or 'style énumératif',[15] which parallels the later medieval taste for encyclopaedic vastness, includes the doors, steps, towers, kitchen, chambers, galleries, caves, rugs, linens, tableware, bridges, stables, ponds and park at Marcoussis, as well as its surrounding houses and buildings, and its church of the Celestines.[16] According to Experience, Everyman and Suffering can see 'clerement et appercevoir (line 1168) [clearly, and perceive]' how Montaigu has been extending his influence by going to Pierregort, Lorraine, and Aquitaine to distribute largesse. He has fêted the marriages of his friends' daughters, and his own wife and children enjoy wealth twice that of the constable's wife (lines 1211–14). He has sent one hundred thousand francs out of France to Venice, to be kept there for him (lines 1215–18). Sardonic about Montaigu's background, Experience asks:

> Est ce donc de son heritage
> Qu'il a fait faire tel ouvrage?
> 'Certes nennil! c'est chose clere'. (lines 1163–5)

[Did he have such work done out of his inheritance? 'Certainly not! That's clear'.]

Experience ends the section on Montaigu by saying:

> Or povés veoir clerement
> Que n'est pas du sien proprement:
> Car de son propre, que ne mente,
> Quatre cens frans n'a il de rente . (lines 1219–22)

[Now, you can see clearly that this does not come from what is properly his own, for – may I not lie – he hasn't got four hundred francs in income of his own.]

and:

> Bien povés veoir, ce me semble,
> Ou qui les toulst ou qui les emble,
> A vostre Roy que il gouverne,
> Il prent du vin de sa taverne:

---

[15] Jeay, *Commerce des mots*, p. 9.

[16] A list of names of the regions from which Poverty has brought 'laboureurs' to court (e.g., Normandy, the Vermandois, Picardy, and others; lines 44–51) anchors the poem in time and space, as against the transcendent abstractness of Truth, Poverty, and the like. Another (short) list supplies names of people praised for their loyalty to the king, as against a (much longer) list naming those deserving punishment for having taken advantage of Charles.

> Il ne se peut fair autrement,
> Vous le veez evidamment. (lines 1231–6)
>
> [It seems to me you can see that, whether he has taken or stolen them, he is taking wine from the tavern, from your king, whom he governs. It cannot be otherwise; you see it, plainly.]

But Experience's mirror turns out not to show what the human eye itself cannot see. Thus Everyman may not see all things as clearly as he might want, but Common Knowledge 'scet bien dire ou tout est (line 988) [can say where everything is]', for she 'voit plus cler qu'a la lune (line 1300) [sees more clearly than in moonlight]'. In addition, in spite of Experience's claims that some things are clearly visible, even in the best of circumstances they are only partly so. The spending of which Montaigu and Charles d'Orléans stand accused is deduced from the *Songe* author's description of their rich holdings, which can be seen in Experience's mirror. No such building projects or any other visual evidence are mentioned in Isabeau's case, yet 'everybody knows' that she has stolen from the French coffers.

As might be expected, the allegories of the *Songe veritable* do not function as a means of reaching a higher, metaphysical truth. The poem's packaging as allegory hardly conceals its goal as propaganda, and the absence of any reference to the duke of Burgundy can leave little doubt as to the origin of the sentiments expressed. In the end, however, the comments and opinions of such a large number of allegorical characters reinforce precisely what Common Knowledge stands for, that is, a plurality of voices that have arrived at a common point of view: this is what everybody knows. What, then, does the dream format contribute?[17] As a genre the *songe* enjoyed wide literary authority and satisfied contemporary taste. Its fundamental nature as the report of lived experience, which is in turn linked to the character of Experience, is especially pertinent in the *Songe veritable*. The narrator's initial defensive gesture, a correction aimed at those who say that dreams contain nought but fables and lies, points to the dream itself as ample authorization for its own content. Even though uttered in the third person, the assertions made in the *Songe*, because they figure as the dreamer's personal experience (what he *saw*) are irrefutable. The mirror of Experience provides a frame for the dream itself.

Christine de Pizan's *Advision Cristine* implicitly challenges the priori-

---

[17] For dreams and visions as a response to the Great Schism, see Renate Blumenfeld-Kosinski, *Poets, Saints, and Visionaries of the Great Schism, 1378–1417* (Pennsylvania, 2006). For medieval dream theory, see Steven F. Kruger, *Dreaming in the Middle Ages* (Cambridge; New York, 1992), and Kathryn L. Lynch, *The High Medieval Dream Vision: Poetry, Philosophy, and Literary Form* (Stanford, 1988). A useful collection of essays is Tullio Gregory, ed., *I sogni nel medioevo: seminario internazionale, Roma 2–4 ottobre, 1983* (Rome, 1985).

ties that the *Songe*, in its search for social and political truth, establishes as between 'experience' and 'commune renommee'. In it, the Crowned Lady [Dame Couronnee] explains to Christine all the harm that has been done to the country of France. She links experience explicitly with sight, saying: 'Helas! chiere amie, ce suis je qui a toy parle, mais, que mieulx me croies, vueil que le sens de ta veue ait *experience* du vray de ma parole [Alas, dear friend. It is I who speak to you, but so that you may believe me better, I would like for your sense of sight to *experience/prove* to itself the truth of my words].' Then she opens 'une petite fenestrelle [a little window]' to a prison where several ladies are held who represent important qualities that the kingdom of France has lost (*Advision*, pp. 27.13–28.15).[18] In yet another, autobiographic, instance, Christine explains how she and her family came to the court of Charles V at the king's invitation. Soon after they arrived, her father, Thomas, was asked to be the king's counsellor, considering 'l'*experience veue* de son savoir et science (*Advision*, p. 96.41–2) [the *manifest proof* of his knowledge and learning]'. Praising her father a few pages further on, she says: 'de ceste verité sont encore au jour d'ui maint de ses congnoiscens, princes et autres, certains comme de *experience* (*Advision*, p. 99.46–7) [of this truth today many of his acquaintances, princes and the like, are as sure as of personal *experience/proof*].'

In those examples 'experience' is adequately translated by the English 'proof' (as the editors of the *Advision* have rendered it in the glossary to their edition). But 'experience' is proof because it denotes something lived, felt, or seen, and it is the involvement of the senses that leads to proof.

At a point near the end of the *Advision* Christine unites 'experience' with 'entendement [understanding]' 'savoir [learning]', and 'estude [study]'. She says:

> Il n'est ou monde plus grant bien – et toy meismes pas ne le me nyeras – que cellui qui vient de l'entendement et qui le perfait en savoir, laquel chose fait estude qui aprent science et experience de moult de choses. Ces deux causes font la personne estre saige, se faulte d'entendement ne lui toult. (*Advision*, p. 123.17–21)

> [There is no greater good in the world – and you yourself will not deny it to me – than the one that comes from judgment completed by learning, which is what study does, which teaches knowledge and understanding of many things. These two are what make a person wise, unless lack of understanding takes it away from her.]

---

[18] Like *fama* itself, however, seeing does not always reveal what is true. Libera remarks that even though 'a veue d'ueil [according to what the eye sees]' she herself may appear young and fresh, in fact she is more than a thousand years old (*Advision*, p. 18).

Christine implies a synthesis between book-learning and first-hand experience, that is, the evidence acquired through the *moment vécu*, which leads to understanding and judgment. As in other instances in the *Advision* where the word 'experience' is used, some form of individual participation is required. This synthesis also responds to the lengthy comments of the personification named Lady Opinion, who addresses Christine in part one of the poem. Opinion, the daughter of Ignorance and Desire to Know, claims to be more powerful than capricious Fortune, the eponymous protagonist of the *Mutacion de Fortune* to whom Christine often attributed hegemony over human decisions. Opinion says that Fortune may have done all the things attributed to her, but that in doing so Fortune was merely carrying out what Opinion commanded. Opinion has inspired ideas and undertakings, but she has also encouraged false theories and fostered error, including war. She asks Christine: 'Ne vois tu pas l'*experience* de moy manifeste meismes chascun jour ? (*Advision*, p. 80.19–20) [Do you not see the *proof* of my existence made manifest every day?].' When Christine worries that Opinion may have led Christine herself to make mistakes in her writings, Opinion assures her that as long as her thinking is founded upon 'loy, raison et vray sentement (*Advision*, p. 89.40) [religion, reason and true feeling]' she will not go wrong. Religion is a system existing outside the individual, reason is an inborn human faculty, but 'vray sentement' is 'personal experience and a sense of feeling for what is right or true'.[19]

Opinion, as a form of cogitation and often the result of intercourse with books, is not *fama*, although there are significant points of overlap. When Lady Opinion is first introduced in the *Advision*, she is called L'Ombre [The Shadow]: 'une grant ombre femmenine sans corps (*Advision*, p. 51.9) [a great feminine shadow without a body]'. Christine makes a point of saying that she first perceives L'Ombre by sight, 'en haulçant mes yeulx (*Advision*, p. 51.8) [raising my eyes]', and she is assured that L'Ombre is a wonder because '*l'experience* prouvoit (*Advision*, p. 51.11) [*experience* proved [it]]':

> Celle chose veoie estre une seulle ombre mais [de] innombrables parties […] s'assembloient les parties d'ombre comme par grans tourbes si que font nuees ou ciel ou oyselles volans par tas ensemble.
> (*Advision*, pp. 51.11–52.15)
>
> [I saw that this thing was a single shadow but with numberless parts which came together in great swirls, like clouds in the sky or birds flying en masse.]

This rich description of one-and-many could equally well describe *fama* as

---

[19] This is Douglas Kelly's gloss on 'vray sentement'. See *Christine de Pizan's Changing Opinion: A Quest for Certainty in the Midst of Chaos* (Woodbridge, 2007), p. 48.

the Middle Ages inherited it from classical literature: an overwhelming mass. For Virgil *fama* is 'swift of foot and fleet of wing, a monster awful and huge, who for the many feathers in her body has as many watchful eyes beneath [...] as many tongues, as many sounding mouths, as many pricked-up ears' who 'sang alike of fact and falsehood'.[20] Ovid's *fama*, goddess of all stories both true and false, dwells where there are 'countless entrances, a thousand apertures'; 'everywhere wander thousands of rumours, falsehoods mingled with the truth, and confused reports flit about.'[21] For Geoffrey Chaucer, 'Fames Hous' is also situated so that whatever is spoken in 'hevene, erthe, and see [...] moste thider nede' (line 715). Chaucer adds later that: 'evry spech that ys yspoken [...] In his substaunce ys but aire' (lines 766–8).[22] Thus the description that Christine now applies to Lady Opinion has a long history in other, related contexts, and Opinion and *fama* share the qualities of shapelessness, porousness and multiplicity, lack of containment and uncontrollability, characterized in part by the metaphor of flight.

Not all medieval writers saw *fama* as inherently bad. In *Erec et Enide* Chrétien de Troyes showed how *fama* could be used to police behaviour and build a more cohesive aristocratic society. When 'the barons' talk about Erec as 'recreant [cowardly/lazy]', they articulate a new *fama* for him.[23] When Enide repeats it to Erec, she participates in the *fama*-making. Erec requires her to accompany him on the journey he undertakes to restore his good name (so that she may *see* the evidence of his prowess). At the end of the 'Joie de la Cour' episode, an unnamed lady steals away and returns to Erec's barons with a report of Erec's accomplishments (lines 6275–6), to make the Joy 'croistre et monter (line 6278) [grow and rise]'. All those who hear the news rejoice (lines 6279–80), showing that talk is also necessary for the creation of good *fama*. *Erec et Enide* is precisely a narrative of *fama*-management.

But as the examples from Virgil, Ovid and Chaucer suggest, other authors were not as sanguine about *fama* as Chrétien. Christine saw the results of *fama*-making as gender-bound: bad *fama* about a woman, because it was almost always created around a woman's sexual behaviour, was intractable and irremediable, and a woman's good *fama* was at best fragile.

This point requires a brief detour through Christine's *Livre du Duc des vrais amans* (1403–5).[24] It has been argued that in this work, which tells the

---

[20] H. Rushton Fairclough, ed., *Virgil, Eclogues, Georgics, Aeneid I-VI* (Cambridge, MA; London, 1999), lines 180–3, 190.

[21] Ovid, *Metamorphoses*, ed. and trans. Frank Justus Miller, 2 vols (Cambridge, Mass.; London, 1984), II, pp. 182–5.

[22] The 'House of Fame' in *Chaucer's Dream Poetry*, ed. Nicholas R. Havely and Helen Phillips (London; New York, 1997). This edition takes MS Fairfax 16 as a base.

[23] Mario Roques, ed., *Les Romans de Chrétien de Troyes I: Erec et Enide* (Paris, 1968), lines 2455–64.

[24] Christine de Pizan, *Le Livre du Duc des vrais amans*, ed. Thelma S. Fenster (Bing-

story of a love affair between a young duke and a married princess, there is no sexual consummation.[25] Instead, the lovers meet clandestinely for over a decade, perhaps practising 'ennobling' rather than sexual love. Nonetheless, those around them, who do not know the intimate details of their liaison, conclude that it must be sexual. The advice the princess receives from her former governess, Sebille de Mont Hault, who is necessarily discreet, assumes the best, presuming that there has been no carnal involvement: 'Car poson qu'il n'y ait de meffait de corps; si ne le croyent mie ceulx qui seulement orront dire: tele dame est amoureuse (*Duc des vrais amans*, p. 174) [For let us suppose that the body commits no misdeed: there are those who simply hear it said that such and such a lady is in love and they will not believe at all that there has been no wrongful act] (*Duke of True Lovers*, p. 114).'[26] In the end, the duke who, like Erec, has been thought 'recreant', can remedy the bad *fama* he has earned, but the princess's case is more complex. For her, *fama*'s destructive potential is fully realized. For Christine, bad *fama* is the Virgilian 'enormous monster' lurking outside the duke and princess's private chamber, just as it lurks outside Dido and Aeneas's cave.

Unlike the author of the *Songe veritable*, then, who gives Common Knowledge the last word, Christine is wary of 'commune renommee'. In the *Advision*, where the value of Opinion is questionable, it is 'experience', or 'vray entendement', supported by religion and human reason, that emphatically has the last word.

Like the *Roman de la Rose*, the *Songe veritable* may have been prepared as a *narration dramatisée*.[27] Putting allegory in the service of partisanship, the author innovates by creating a *mise en scène* in which metre, rhyme, and direct discourse heighten the poem's theatrical impact. Some of the characters are even said to pass from 'mansion' (or 'maison') to 'mansion', the

---

hamton, NY, 1995); English translation in *The Book of the Duke of True Lovers*, trans. Thelma S. Fenster and Nadia Margolis (New York, 1991).

[25] In *Ennobling Love: In Search of a Lost Sensibility* (Philadelphia, 1999), C. Stephen Jaeger states that the love between the princess and the duke is 'the very model of a love beyond the body, confined to the mind, the soul and spirit, confined to desire' (p. 203). Douglas Kelly agrees that 'there is no suggestion that their love is ever consummated' but that Christine de Pizan, who initially admired platonic 'chivalric love' (because it led 'to moral excellence, valor and fame'), changed her mind by the time she wrote the *Duc des vrais amans* (*Christine de Pizan's Changing Opinion*, pp. 109–10).

[26] *Duc des vrais amans*, pp. 171–80; *Duke of True Lovers*, pp. 111–20. The letter is repeated in Christine de Pizan, *Livre des Trois Vertus*, ed. Charity Cannon Willard and Eric Hicks (Paris, 1989), pp. 109–20; English translations in *A Medieval Woman's Mirror of Honor: The Treasury of the City of Ladies*, ed. Madeleine Pelner Cosman, trans. Charity Cannon Willard, (New York; Tenafly, NJ, 1989), pp. 139–47, and *The Treasure of the City of Ladies, or, The Book of the Three Virtues*, trans. Sarah Lawson (Harmondsworth, 1985).

[27] Badel, *Rose*, p. 408.

term for stations or positions in the simultaneous decor of medieval drama.[28] The octosyllable heightens the impression of 'performance' toward which the author strives through the poem's nearly ubiquitous direct discourse: the *Songe* comes as close as it can to helping its public of readers and listeners to experience for themselves the calamitous account it contains. Metre and rhyme also support the extensive listing that the poem foregrounds, rhythmically documenting and embracing a totality of names, places, misdeeds, and crimes.

The *Advision*, a far more contemplative, multilevel work than the *Songe*, requires from its readers a greater effort of interpretation. Christine de Pizan began her career with lyric and narrative poetry and often drew attention to her poetic skill, but she moved, over the first decade of the fifteenth century, toward prose composition, which she associated with the learned subjects she chose to write about. More ruminative, even theoretical, than many of her other works, the ensemble of the *Advision*'s three seemingly disparate sections asks readers to follow her thought slowly and with care, for in addition to its autobiographical and political elements, it is an epistemology, a theory of knowledge, in which what can be known by the senses is but the first step. Like so much of Christine's work, the *Advision* offers a rich series of visual images; Opinion as L'Ombre is but one of those. But the *Advision* is not a performance, nor does its prose allow it to be. Its challenge, not related to formal ornament, is in its substance.

---

[28] In Badel's view, each character seems to come to the front of the stage to speak (*Rose*, p. 407).

Conclusion
Knowing Poetry, Knowing Communities

REBECCA DIXON

As the Preface has shown, over and above the contributions that the individual chapters in this volume make to our understanding of their respective subjects, they feed into a more synthetic view of the culture of knowledge surrounding late medieval French poetry. The role of this conclusion is to draw out the main features of this culture.[1] It might usefully be characterised as a set of answers to the question: between the late thirteenth and the early sixteenth centuries in France, what makes poetry propitious to conveying knowledge and to establishing communities? These answers cluster around five issues which, while being not always specific to poetry, are more highly concentrated, more urgent, in verse than in prose. Some of these issues are to do with poetry's ability to convey knowledge as a consequence of its shape and form: knowledge is yoked to the text's physical form in quoted or recontextualized material, and in the interpretation of that material. Others concern the public character and therapeutic value of verse, which signal its propensity to carry an experiential knowledge that links the individual to the communal or the universal.

The first of these issues is the quotability of the verse text, which inheres in the formal and structural aspects of a poem that allow its ready citation. This propensity to quotation mirrors a cognitive or experiential process which Antoine Compagnon has called 'solicitation'. Why might some parts of a text be more apt to be quoted than others? Why do some passages more than others 'solicit' their severance from their context? Though Compagnon is not discussing verse texts specifically, his account of solicitation hints at a crucial way in which a poem infiltrates the consciousness of the reader and lodges itself there for later citation:

---

[1] For more on some of the ideas discussed in this conclusion, see the Introduction to Adrian Armstrong and Sarah Kay, with contributions from Sylvia Huot, Rebecca Dixon, Miranda Griffin, Francesca Nicholson, and Finn Sinclair, *Poetry and Knowledge in Late Medieval France from the Roman de la rose to the grands rhétoriqueurs*, forthcoming.

> La sonorité d'une gutturale, l'écho d'une voyelle, un rhythme adapté à ma respiration ou à mes réflexes – je ne manque jamais de souligner les alexandrins perdus dans un ouvrage de philosophie [...]: tous accidents où le texte lui-même n'est pas pour grand-chose, mais qui me sollicitent autant.[2]

The 'alexandrins' Compagnon alludes to here are the classic twelve-syllable lines of French poetry whose patterning is so ingrained in the national consciousness that they can appear unbidden – or as Compagnon puts it, become 'lost' – in non-poetic writing. Their ability to disrupt his (literally) prosaic reading-process exemplifies the way in which the structures of rhyme and metre serve a mnemonic function, permitting both the effective storage of verse in the memory and its ready retrieval and redeployment as quotation. As any schoolchild asked to learn passages of text by heart knows only too well, phonetic and prosodic patterning mean that verse can quite simply be more easily lodged in the memory than its prose counterpart. Occasional 'alexandrins perdus' may stand out against a background of amorphous prose, and impress themselves upon the reader as a result; but a Racinian tragedy consists entirely of these salient lines. Poetry, further, is memorable, and hence quotable, because it is apt to fall into clearly delimited elements – lines, couplets, stanzas – which have a formal unity that a similar volume of prose does not necessarily possess. These constituent parts of a poem, while relatively brief, possess a coherence which makes them appealing as citations and insertions in other works (on which more below). Indeed, in the fixed-form lyric genres so popular in late medieval France – the *rondeau*, *ballade*, or *chant royal* – citation is embedded within the poem itself, insofar as lines are repeated in the form of refrains which, occupying privileged formal positions, often encapsulate a poem's thematic import. Denis Hüe's essay, which describes entire *ballades* being constructed on the basis of *envois* offers a pertinent example of this.

The 'thematizing' quality of refrains underlines the obvious, but vital, fact that the process of quoting verse involves not simply grafting and transposition, but also selection on the basis of semantic import. Compagnon begins his account of citation with the seductive vignette of himself as a small boy in gleeful possession of a pair of scissors and an album of apparently disparate images – trains, planes, automobiles, animals, people – which in fact offer the young snipper 'tout ce qu'il faut pour réproduire le monde'.[3] The process, for Compagnon, is one of seemingly random excision, but ultimately of deliberate and ordered combination, of placing the cut-out fragments exactly where they fit best. This seems to mirror the act of citation in

---

[2] Antoine Compagnon, *La Seconde main ou le travail de la citation* (Paris, 1979), p. 24. Compagnon's discussion of 'sollicitation' is on pp. 23–5.

[3] *La Seconde main*, p. 15.

the later medieval francophone context which concerns us here. While we cannot know the precise cognitive processes behind an author's harvesting of quotable elements in a particular case, what is clear is that there was a definite reason, above and beyond the formal and the mnemonic, informing a quotation's deployment. To return to Racine: if every line is salient, why should some be more salient than others? It is not enough for a passage to appeal in the abstract: to be deemed quotable, it needs to have an appropriate meaning, and not necessarily that which it bore in the source text.

The knowledge conveyed by a transplanted citation differs from the knowledge inherent in the 'donor' text; for to quote or indeed to repeat anything is always to change it in some way.[4] How this change might work in practice, though, is another matter. The chapters in this book explore different modalities of transformation in fruitful and interconnected ways. As David Wrisley and Jennifer Saltzstein remind us, in the context of verse citation in prose romance and theatre respectively, the genre of the quoting text may give a new valency to the quoted fragment. Both the quotability of fragments and their function in the 'host' context are also influenced by the intention of the citing author; we see evidence for this within both Saltzstein's essay and Nancy Freeman Regalado's piece. Deborah McGrady's study similarly underlines how generic transpositions signal intention, and govern the reception of the knowledge contained in the text that is quoted (and indeed, in this instance, glossed). All these pieces, as well as Michel Zink's study of the *razo* in Chapter 5, illustrate the ways in which geographical and temporal space between quoted and quoting text can alter the meaning of the citation for the communities that produce it, and which are produced by it.

Verse, then, lends itself to excision from its source and to grafting onto a new host, where it comes to fulfil a new and distinct function.[5] Yet such transformations need not apply solely to the citation of extracts. They are also applicable to the ways in which complete verse texts can be reproduced in new settings, for example when transcribed in manuscripts alongside accompanying material that foregrounds a particular theme or technique (whether this be a systematic gloss on the transcribed text, or simply other material in an anthology). In other words, alongside its quotability, verse exhibits a further and more general property to a greater extent than does prose: recontextualizability, the second issue mentioned at the outset. Not surprisingly, perhaps, some of the reasons why this should be the case echo those

---

[4] Indeed Compagnon would take this further and suggest that even to write anything is an act of rewriting: 'écrire, car c'est toujours récrire, ne diffère pas de citer' (*La Seconde main*, p. 34).

[5] On the usefulness of the image of grafting to a discussion of citation, see Sarah Kay, 'Grafting the Knowledge Community: The Purposes of Verse in the *Breviari d'amor* of Matfre Ermengaud', *Neophilologus*, 91 (2007), 361–73. See also its companion piece, Francesca M. Nicholson, 'Branches of Knowledge: The Purposes of Citation in the *Breviari d'amor* of Matfre Ermengaud', *Neophilologus*, 91 (2007), 375–85.

discussed in connection with citation. As Regalado and Salzstein show with reference to the transposition of tags (often of just a few words' length) in refrains, just as the shortness of the verse graft and its concomitant memorability can signal its quotability, it can also enhance its propensity to be recontextualized. But this is not the whole, or perhaps the only, story. Verse's recontextualizability, like its quotability, also depends on its semantic density, its ability to establish formulations whose richness of meaning exceeds that of their more transparent and less heavily patterned prose equivalents.

Both quotation and recontextualization raise the issue of where knowledge lies: does it inhere in the 'graft', the material redeployed, or rather in the 'host', the material that frames and thereby reinterprets it, whether this be a single text citing a fragment or a manuscript collection incorporating a discrete poem? The question might usefully be posed in terms of the legitimation which Jean-François Lyotard identifies as a crucial, and problematic, feature of the construction of knowledge.[6] Which text, graft or host, is positioned as bearing knowledge, and which is positioned as able to legitimate that knowledge? For Lyotard, the quoted text bears knowledge only when it is validated through quotation elsewhere, and when it is made to 'speak' by its recontextualisation. A less radical view, however, would be that knowledge is located both in the cited passage and in the text that cites it, but the balance between the two sorts of knowledge, and the relative value accorded them, differs according to local and textual circumstances. This, in its turn, raises further complications. Is knowledge, in these circumstances, conveyed by the redeployed text alone? Or is it transmitted by a larger body of work of which it is a synecdoche – whether the whole text, in the case of a quoted portion, or, in the case of an entire recontextualised text, the tradition, genre, or authorial output of which it is part?[7]

Varying answers to these questions appear within this volume. Nancy Freeman Regalado considers the 'reciprocal reading' invited by the texts anthologised in BnF MS fr. 146; this process permits knowledge to be extended from one place to another – and vice versa – through (re)contextualization. Hence, in this manuscript, knowledge circulates around the co-present texts to generate a discourse on kingship. Lescurel's *Ditz entez*, for instance, encourage a re-reading of what Regalado calls 'moral knowledge' in the *Fauvel*, counterbalancing the hypocritical Fauvel in their condemnation of carnality. Yet the flow of knowledge in the reverse direction is less strongly in evidence:

---

[6] On legitimation, see Jean-François Lyotard, *La Condition postmoderne* (Paris, 1979), especially Chapter 8, 'La Fonction narrative et la légitimation du savoir', pp. 49–53.

[7] Compagnon makes a similar point about the synecdochic function fulfilled by the citation of a particular author within tradition: '[l]e citer, c'est alors invoquer la tradition, dans laquelle il a perdu son indentité et où son texte s'est universalisé'(*La Seconde main*, p. 219). See also the remarks on the role accorded to Ovid in the vernacular tradition in Deborah McGrady's essay.

the formal virtuosity of the Lescurel lyrics cannot be encompassed within the *Fauvel*'s didactic horizons. In this instance, then, knowledge is conveyed more by the redeployed text than by the *Fauvel*, which appears primarily to legitimate that knowledge. The case described by Deborah McGrady in Chapter 6 is altogether different, for here the recontexualization is doubled. In the first place, by the time of its recontextualisation in the thirteenth-century *Art d'amours en prose*, Ovid's material was already acknowledged as conveying certain sorts of knowledge; but the glossed translations of the *Ars amatoria* call into question the authority of this knowledge. Because Ovid's words lack contemporary relevance, as the translator-glosser makes plain, the knowledge they transmit is altered through the glossing – the Ovidian material continues to bear knowledge, but a different sort of knowledge from that on which Ovid's reputation had hitherto been founded. In the second place, the recontextualization of Ovid in the *Art d'amours en prose* and in a specific manuscript anthology (BnF, MS fr. 881) lays bare the process of legitimation: it is on contemporary vernacular verse that the poetry of classical antiquity must base any claim to authority. This not only locates a particular knowledge in the redeployed material; it also accords a synecdochic function to the Ovidian text, which represents an entire classical tradition as the bearer of knowledge that the vernacular can at last turn to appropriate account.

The glossing that McGrady discusses is only the most obvious instance of the third quality which makes of poetry a unique and fitting vehicle for knowledge: that is, the way in which it seems, precisely because it is poetry, to invite interpretation. Poetry seems to produce what Jacques Lacan has called the effect of the veil.[8] The very presence of a veil encourages us to assume that it conceals something, and that what it conceals is valuable – the veil, in short, seems to ask a question by appearing to withhold an answer. A long cultural tradition treats poetry as a veil in this way: both the Christian moralisation of pagan literature and the exegesis of biblical verse (as Mishtooni Bose and Lori Walters note) attest to poetry's propensity to invite decoding.[9] Whether this takes the form of a systematic figurative reading, as required by the *Eschés amoureux* which Amandine Mussou outlines, or simply of explaining local images or allusions, as Suzanne Akbari describes

---

[8] On the veil, see Jacques Lacan, *Le Séminaire IV: La Relation d'objet* (Paris, 1994), pp. 151–64, and Slavoj Žižek, *The Sublime Object of Ideology* (London, 1989), pp. 193–9. For a non-psychoanalytical treatment of veiledness in this context, see Suzanne Akbari's discussion of *integumenta* in the present volume.

[9] Citation and recontextualizability, too, entail a process of decoding: as the above discussion indicated, to cite anything is inevitably to raise questions in the audience's mind, to invite them to look behind the veil. Quoting implies that the passage contains knowledge, but also that the person quoting it knows something (the quotation itself; the text it is excerpted from; the author the text is by; and so on) which might be recognised by (at least some of) the addressees. The community-forming aspect of decoding is dealt with below.

in Christine de Pizan's *Epistre Othea*, poetry invites interpretation more than prose. Whatever its semantic richness, prose tends to *present* itself as transparent, in the various ways so astutely traced by David Hult in Chapter 1.[10]

Poetry's call for interpretation in our period is indicated, too, in the distinctions drawn between different kinds of verse. Jacqueline Cerquiglini-Toulet, Mishtooni Bose and Lori Walters address the distinction between *carmen* and *poema*: if the knowledge they seek to convey is to be perceived, *poemata* must be decoded philosphically, theologically or allegorically, in ways that *carmina* do not invite. In this respect the *poema* echoes the notion of *poetrie* that is so important in late medieval French literature: the use of allegorical figures, often derived from classical mythology, which yield rich insights to the reader prepared to interpret them. Marc-René Jung observes in his seminal discussion of the subject that *poetrie* is not synonymous with 'poetry' in its modern sense;[11] rather, it involves sustained figurative discourse. As Jacques Legrand puts it in his *Archiloge Sophie* (c. 1400), *poetrie* is a 'science qui aprent à faindre et à faire fictions fondees en raison et en la semblance des choses desquelles on veult parler [a science which teaches how to contrive and create fictions based on reason and on the appearance of the things of which one wishes to speak]'. Nevertheless, it is difficult if not impossible to extricate *poetrie* from verse: theoreticians had varying opinions on the matter, and Legrand himself produces the parallel claim that 'poetrie est science qui aprent à versifier et à ordonner ses moz et ses paroles par certaine mesure [poetry is a science which teaches how to versify and arrange one's words and utterances according to a fixed metre].'[12] There is, then, a privileged connection between verse and the communication of profound knowledge through figurative language; a connection that Cerquiglini-Toulet and Walters explore in the work of Gerson and Christine de Pizan.

It is significant that these two poets loom large in this respect, as their reciprocal correspondence draws attention to a further important characteristic of poetry's interpretation. The process of interpreting poetry can, and does, establish communities of interpreters. These communities might be unified, like Christine and Gerson, able to agree on what the object of their interpretation means: the Marian metaphors in devotional poetry, for example, are readily interpretable by a community united in piety.[13] Conversely, they

---

[10] Prose's apparent transparency in the period is indicated, too, by the fifteenth-century practice of the *mise en prose*, as outlined by David Wrisley. The authors of these reworked texts make explicit claims in their prefaces for the clarity of prose over verse. For more on these prologues see, for example, Richard E. F. Straub, *David Aubert, escripvain et clerc* (Amsterdam; Atlanta, GA, 1995).

[11] Marc-René Jung, 'Poetria: Zur Dichtungstheorie des ausgehenden Mittelalters in Frankreich', *Vox Romanica*, 30 (1971), 44–64.

[12] Quoted in Jung, pp. 58–9; the citation is from Paris, BnF, MS fr. 24232, fol. 61v.

[13] On the poetic expression of Marian devotion see Denis Hüe, *La Poésie palinodique à Rouen (1486–1550)* (Paris, 2002).

might cohere through antagonism, as in the two striking literary debates of the early fifteenth century: the *Querelle de la Rose*, pitting Christine and Gerson against humanist academics, and the *Querelle de la Belle Dame sans Mercy*, a series of responses to Alain Chartier's poem in which competing interpretations are themselves staged in verse.[14]

To speak of communities, of course, is to speak of an act that is in some sense public. This is in fact symptomatic of the reception of verse, which, in general if not necessarily in all cases, appears more geared than prose to public modes of presentation and reception. A number of reasons suggest themselves as to why this should be so. Performance or declamation is habitually inscribed in verse, to a much greater extent than in prose; the instances in which poems are actually texts to be sung (as are some of the works evoked by Saltzstein in Chapter 11) is only the most obvious case. We should also remember that late medieval theatre, at least to judge by the texts that have come down to us, was overwhelmingly in verse (again, Chapter 11 offers a case in point). Even leaving aside these actual contexts of public performance – contexts to which we might add the verse often declaimed or displayed during ceremonial entries, and the public nature of competitions such as the *puys* (the municipal poetry competitions of Northern France) –[15] verse contains what theoreticians of oral cultures would call an important 'oral residue'.[16] This 'oral residue' takes the form of patterning features such as rhyme and metre, whose mnemonic function we have already encountered, and which inevitably bear traces of the act of recitation and the interpersonal situation that this presupposes. In other words, even when someone sits alone reading verse, the form of this verse is impregnated with a situation involving at least two people, reciter and listener(s). Jacqueline Cerquiglini has under-

---

[14] For more on the *Rose* debate see *Le débat sur le Roman de la Rose*, ed. Eric Hicks (Paris, 1977), and *Debating the* Roman de la rose, *A Critical Anthology*, ed. Christine McWebb (New York, 2007); on the *Querelle de la Belle Dame sans mercy*, see *Le Cycle de la Belle Dame sans Mercy. Une anthologie poétique du XVe siècle (BnF MS fr 1131)*, ed. David F. Hult and Joan E. McRae (Paris, 2003). For discussion of the poetic interplay that establishes this last antagonistic community, see Emma Cayley, *Debate and Dialogue. Alain Chartier in his Cultural Context* (Oxford, 2006), especially Chapter 4, and Adrian Armstrong, *The Virtuoso Circle: Competition, Collaboration and Complexity in Late Medieval French Poetry*, forthcoming.

[15] On the use of verse in ceremonial entries see for example Cynthia J. Brown, 'From Stage to Page: Royal Entry Performances in Honour of Mary Tudor (1514)', in Adrian Armstrong and Malcolm Quainton, ed., *Book and Text in France, 1400–1600 Poetry on the Page* (Aldershot, 2007), pp. 49–72; on the *puy*, see Gérard Gros, *Le Poète, la Vierge et le Prince du puy. Etude sur les Puys marials de la France du Nord du XIVe siècle à la Renaissance* (Paris, 1994), and Hüe, *La Poésie palinodique*.

[16] See Walter J. Ong, *Orality and Literacy: the technologising of the word* (London, 1982), p. 36.

lined that earlier medieval courtly lyric is performative;[17] this performative dimension might be attenuated as the gap widens between poetry and song, and as written transmission gains precedence over oral delivery, but it is never entirely lost, for it is formally inscribed as a potential that can always be reactualized.

By contrast, prose in medieval France developed in genres that were suited much less well to performance than to a more private mode of reception, genres such as historiography or, increasingly from the thirteenth century, romance, as Hult reminds us in Chapter 1.[18] These contrasting qualities are particularly clear in the *prosimetrum* texts that formed a significant part of late medieval literary production in French. When juxtaposed with prose in these texts, verse is usually the more public form: less bound to narrative and argument, it often adopts a collective rather than individual perspective. Indeed, it sometimes reaches towards higher truths that lie beyond discursive reasoning, and is often explicitly framed as the speech not of an individual but of a group, or of a voice that stands outside the narrative world of the fiction.[19] Even the work of those poets whose output is widely regarded as distinctively personal, or perhaps pseudo-personal, displays a highly public quality in important ways. Jane Taylor has recently demonstrated that the lyrics of Charles d'Orléans must be considered as having emerged from a process of social production and exchange, as is attested by patterns of manuscript compilation.[20] The contrasting work of François Villon, however much it may present itself as poetry for knowing initiates, displays a recurrent anxiety about how it will be transmitted, received, and remembered in its particular socio-cultural context.[21] Many of the pieces in this volume indicate the irreducible public dimension of poetry. On the one hand, knowledge has a distinctively human scale, for example in the work of Christine de Pizan, while many of the texts discussed introduce personal (or ostensibly personal)

---

[17] See 'Quand la voix s'est tue: la mise en recueil de la poésie lyrique aux XIVe et XVe siècles', in Emmanuèle Baumgartner et Nicole Boulestreau, ed., *La présentation du livre. Actes du colloque Paris-X Nanterre, du 4 au 6 décembre 1985* (Paris, 1987), pp. 313–27, p. 313.

[18] On historiography, see Gabrielle Spiegel, *Romancing the Past: The Rise of Vernacular Prose Historiography in Thirteenth-Century France* (Berkeley; Los Angeles, 1993).

[19] For more on this see, for example, Jacqueline Cerquiglini, *'Un engin si soutil': Guillaume de Machaut et l'écriture au XIVe siècle* (Paris, 2001), pp. 39–49, Sylvia Huot, 'Refashioning Boethius: Prose and Poetry in Chartier's *Livre de l'Espérance*', *Medium Ævum*, 76 (2007), 268–84, and Claude Thiry, 'Au carrefour des deux rhétoriques: les prosimètres de Jean Molinet', in Peter Wunderli, ed., *Du mot au texte* (Tübingen, 1982), pp. 213–27.

[20] See Jane H. M. Taylor, *The Making of Poetry. Late-Medieval French Poetic Anthologies* (Turnhout, 2007), in particular Chapter 2.

[21] See Adrian Armstrong, 'The *Testament* of François Villon', in Simon Gaunt and Sarah Kay, ed., *Cambridge Companion to Medieval French Literature* (Cambridge, 2008), pp. 63–76.

elements into some form of abstraction and reflection. On the other hand, the level of the experiential or personal is always related to a broader, collective, indeed universal, plane. The role of allegory or *poetrie* is often to mediate between these levels, as illustrated in different ways by Suzanne Akbari, Jacqueline Cerquiglini-Toulet, Thelma Fenster, and Amandine Mussou.

The four features of poetry analysed so far, to repeat a point made earlier, are not unique to poetry but are particularly prominent there. However, the final crucial trait for consideration is integral to verse: this is its association with what we might call therapeutic order, a phenomenon that has been observed by various scholars of later medieval poetry.[22] Order in the form of quantification is of course inherent in verse; indeed, it is on the basis of verse's quantifiability that Eustache Deschamps formulates his influential definition of poetry as 'musique naturele', thereby affiliating poetry with the mathematically-based disciplines of the medieval *quadrivium*. But Deschamps' conception of poetry is not solely based on the organisation of phonemes; for that organisation produces pleasure, even consolation, for an audience. It is in these terms, for instance, that Deschamps, in the *Art de Dictier*, grounds the affinity between 'musique naturele' and 'musique artificiele' (what we would call music):

> Et aussi ces deux musiques sont si consonans l'une aveques l'autre, que chascune puet bien estre appellee musique, pour la douceur tant du chant comme des paroles qui toutes sont prononcees et pointoyees par doucour de voix et ouverture de bouche. […] La musique naturele se puet dire et recorder par un homme seul, de bouche, ou lire aucune livre de ces choses paisans devant un malade.[23]

> [And these two kinds of music are so consonant with each other, that each one can be well called music, as much for the sweetness of the melody as for that of the words that are all pronounced and made distinct by the sweetness of the voice and the opening of the mouth. […] Natural music can also be uttered and recited by one man alone aloud; or any book of these pleasing things can be read before a sick person.]

Adequate form, in other words, brings with it an aesthetic satisfaction, indeed in many circumstances an ethical one. Patterned language satisfies

---

[22] Remarks in this section reflect the analysis of Glending Olson, *Literature as Recreation in the Later Middle Ages* (Ithaca, NY; London, 1982), esp. pp. 105, 128–63. The implications of formal order are discussed in Roger Dragonetti, '"La poesie … ceste musique naturele": Essai d'exégèse d'un passage de l'*Art de Dictier* d'Eustache Deschamps', in *Fin du Moyen Age et Renaissance: Mélanges de philologie française offerts à Robert Guiette* (Antwerp, 1961), pp. 49–64, pp. 58–62.

[23] See Eustache Deschamps, *L'Art de Dictier*, ed. and trans., with introduction, by Deborah M. Sinnreich-Levi (East Lansing, 1994), lines 157–61 and 173–6. The translation is on p. 65 and p. 67.

not only the listener or reader but also the poet who produces it, both on the practical level of technical accomplishment, and on a more abstract level, by bringing the composer's thoughts and emotions into at least a temporary order.[24] Moreover, albeit in ways less particular to poetry, composition requires an engagement with literary tradition and, in many instances, with familiar exemplary narratives that can bring the pleasures of enlightenment or consolation to poets as well as to their publics. Hence the *process* of composing or receiving poetry generates a kind of knowedge: a knowledge of patterns and the satisfaction they bring, even access to a heightened order of things, where the accidents and asymmetries of ordinary life are, if not banished, then at least much less evident. The work of many of our contributors (for example, Denis Hüe, Stephanie Kamath, Deborah McGrady and Nancy Freeman Regalado) indicates the ways in which formal achievement can be manifested, and the nature of the intellectual universe that each such achievement brings into being. Poetry may often be rooted in the everyday and circumstantial, but it constantly points beyond it to a more transcendent order, whether intellectual, theological or aesthetic. It is not so much that a poem as product documents our access to this order; rather, it is the activity of composition or interpretation that perform this access. In this sense, the late medieval attitude to poetry obliquely attested in Deschamps, in later *Arts de seconde rhétorique*, and in the practices documented in this volume, rejoin Robert Lowell's classic definition of poetry as 'an event, not the record of an event'.[25] What is more, both composition and interpretation require certain types of knowledge to be deployed; and both, for the reasons we have outlined, link individual poets, readers, and listeners with the wider poetic community in a creative process where the sum of knowledge is infinitely greater than its constituent parts.

These findings lay no claim to representing the final word on the subject; in a field of this size and complexity there is inevitably scope for refinement and nuancing through further research. Nevertheless, it is hoped that future scholars will be able to ground their work in the *état présent* that this volume constitutes. The enterprise of conceiving and producing the collection has made it abundantly clear that in twenty-first-century scholarship, as in late medieval French poetry, knowledge is fundamentally a product of communities.

---

[24] On the value of technical accomplishment see Taylor, *The Making of Poetry*, Chapter 1.

[25] The phrase was delivered in one of Lowell's lectures, and is quoted in Helen Vendler, *Part of Nature, Part of Us: Modern American Poets* (Cambridge, MA; London, 1980), p. 167.

BIBLIOGRAPHY

Manuscripts

Arras, Bibliothèque municipale, MS 845
Bamberg, Staatsbibliothek, MS Lit. 115
Brussels, Bibliothèque royale Albert 1er, MS 10988
Brussels, Bibliothèque royale Albert 1er, MS 11020–33
Dresden, Sächsische Landesbibliothek, Oc. 66
Geneva, Bibliothèque publique et universitaire, MS fr. 181
Geneva, Bibliothèque publique et universitaire, MS fr. 182
Ivrea, Biblioteca Capitolare, MS115
London, British Library, MS Harley 4431
London, Lambeth Palace Archives, MS Arc.L40.2/E.44
Melbourne, State Library of Victoria, MS 096 G.94
Modena, Biblioteca Estense, MS y.G.3.20
Montpellier, Bibliothèque interuniversitaire, Section médicine, MS H196
Nantes, Bibliothèque municipale, MS 651
Oxford, Bodleian Library, MS Douce 308
Paris, Bibliothèque de l'Arsenal, MS 2319
Paris, Bibliothèque de l'Arsenal, MS 2741
Paris, Bibliothèque de l'Arsenal, MS 5198
Paris, Bibliothèque de Sainte Geneviève, MS 294
Paris, Bibliothèque nationale de France, MS fr. 226
Paris, Bibliothèque nationale de France, MS fr. 825
Paris, Bibliothèque nationale de France, MS fr. 829
Paris, Bibliothèque nationale de France, MS fr. 844–7
Paris, Bibliothèque nationale de France, MS fr. 848
Paris, Bibliothèque nationale de France, MS fr. 881
Paris, Bibliothèque nationale de France, MS fr. 1137
Paris, Bibliothèque nationale de France, MS fr. 1377
Paris, Bibliothèque nationale de France, MS fr. 1646
Paris, Bibliothèque nationale de France, MS fr. 2202
Paris, Bibliothèque nationale de France, MS fr. 12461
Paris, Bibliothèque nationale de France, MS fr. 12786
Paris, Bibliothèque nationale de France, MS fr. 24406
Paris, Bibliothèque nationale de France, MS fr. 25566
Paris, Bibliothèque nationale de France, MS nouv. acq. fr.1050
Rome, Biblioteca Vaticana, Reg. Christ. 1543
Soissons, Bibliothèque municipale, MS 208

Tours, Bibliothèque municipale, MS 905
Venice, Biblioteca Marciana, MS fr. app. 23

Primary Texts (Pre-1800)

Barthélemy l'Anglais, *De Proprietatibus Rerum* (Frankfurt: W. Richter, 1601)
Gilles de Rome, *De Regimine principum* (Rome: Stephanum Planck de Patavia, 1482)
Le Pelerinage de l'homme (Paris: Anthoine Vérard, 1511); Cambridge, MA, Houghton Library, *FC.G9455D.511v
Le pelerinaige de vie humaine (Lyons: Matias Huss, 1485); Cambridge, Cambridge University Library, Inc. 4.D.2.7 [4313]
Le premier pelerinaige in *Le Romant des trois Pelerinaiges*, (Paris: Barthole Rembolt and Jean Petit, n.d. [c. 1510–11 or 1514–18?]); Cambridge, MA, Houghton Library, *FC.G9455D.525v
Meschinot, Jean, *Les Lunettes des princes* (Nantes: Larcher, 1493)

Primary Texts (Post-1800)

Adam de la Halle, *Le Jeu de Robin et Marion*, ed. Jean Dufournet (Paris, 1989)
——, *Œuvres complètes*, ed. Pierre-Yves Badel (Paris, 1995)
Anglo-Norman Political Songs, ed. Isabel S. T. Aspin (Oxford, 1953)
Li Ars d'Amour, de Vertu et de Boneurté, ed. Jules Petit, 2 vols, (Brussels, 1867–69)
L'Art d'amours (The Art of Love), trans. Lawrence B. Blonquist (New York and London, 1987)
Boccaccio, Giovanni, *Genealogie deorum gentilium libri*, 2 vols, ed. V. Romano (Bari, 1951)
Boogaard, Nico H. J. van den, *Rondeaux et refrains du XIIe siècle au début du XIVe* (Paris, 1969)
Boutière, Jean, and A.-H. Schutz, ed., *Biographies des troubadours. Textes provençaux des XIIIe et XIVe siècles* (Paris, 1964)
Le Breviari d'amor de Matfre Ermengaud, ed. Peter T. Ricketts, 3 vols (Leiden, 1976–)
Brunetto Latini, *Li Livres dou Tresor*, ed. Francis J. Carmody (Berkeley, 1948)
Chartier, Alain, *Le Curial*, in *Œuvres latines d'Alain Chartier,* ed. Pascale Bourgain-Hemeryck (Paris, 1977)
Chaucer's Dream Poetry, ed. Nicholas R. Havely and Helen Phillips (London; New York, 1997)
Chrétien de Troyes, *Cligès*, ed. Charles Méla and Olivier Collet (Paris, 1994)
——, *Les Romans de Chrétien de Troyes I: Erec et Enide*, ed. Mario Roques (Paris, 1968)
Christine de Pizan, *The Book of the Duke of True Lovers*, trans. Thelma S. Fenster and Nadia Margolis (New York, 1991)
——, *Le Chemin de Longue Etude*, ed. and trans. Andrea Tarnowski (Paris, 2000)

——, *La Città delle Dame/Le Livre de la Cité des Dames*, ed. Earl Jeffrey Richards, trans. Patrizia Caraffi, 2nd ed (Milan, 1998)
——, *Epistre Othea*, ed. Gabriella Parussa (Geneva, 1999)
——, *Le Livre de l'Advision Cristine*, ed. Christine Reno and Liliane Dulac (Paris, 2001)
——, 'The *Livre de la cité des dames of Christine de Pisan*: A Critical Edition', 2 vols, Maureen Cheney Curnow, ed. Ph.D. diss. (Vanderbilt University, 1975)
——, *Le Livre du Duc des Vrais Amans*, ed. Thelma S. Fenster (Binghamton, NY, 1995)
——, *Le Livre des fais et bonnes meurs du sage roy Charles V*, ed. Suzanne Solente, 2 vols (Paris, 1936/1940)
——, *Le livre de la Mutacion de Fortune*, 4 vols, ed. Suzanne Solente (Paris, 1959/1964/1966)
——, *Le Livre des Trois Vertus*, ed. Charity Cannon Willard and Eric Hicks (Paris, 1989)
——, *A Medieval Woman's Mirror of Honor: The Treasury of the City of Ladies*, trans. Charity Cannon Willard, ed. Madeleine Pelner Cosman (New York; Tenafly, NJ, 1989)
——, *Œuvres poétiques*, 3 vols, ed. Maurice Roy (Paris, 1886)
——, *The Treasure of the City of Ladies*, or, *The Book of the Three Virtues*, trans. Sarah Lawson (Harmondsworth, 1985)
——, *The Vision of Christine de Pizan*, trans. Glenda McLeod and Charity Cannon Willard (Cambridge, 2005)
La Chronique métrique attribuée à Geffroy de Paris, ed. A. Diverrès (Paris, 1956)
Clasby, Eugene, trans. and intro., *The Pilgrimage of Human Life* (New York, 1992)
La Clef d'Amors, ed. Auguste Doutrepont (Halle, 1890)
'Li Commens d'Amours de Richard de Fournival (?)', ed. Antoinette Saly, *Travaux de Linguistique et de Littérature*, 10, 2 (1972), 21–55
The Continuations of the Old French Perceval of Chrétien de Troyes, Vol. IV: *The Second Continuation*, ed. William Roach (Philadelphia, 1971)
Cowling, David, ed., *George Chastelain, Jean Robertet, Jean de Montferrant, Les Douze Dames de Rhétorique* (Geneva, 2002)
Le Cycle de la Belle Dame sans Mercy. *Une anthologie poétique du XVe siècle (BnF MS fr 1131)*, ed. David F. Hult and Joan E. McRae (Paris, 2003)
Dahlberg, Charles, *The* Romance of the Rose *by Guillaume de Lorris and Jean de Meun* (Princeton, 1971)
Dahnk, E., *L'Hérésie de Fauvel* (Leipzig, 1935)
Davy, Marie-Madeleine, *Un traité de l'amour du XIIe siècle. Pierre de Blois* (Paris, 1932)
Le Débat sur le Roman de la Rose, ed. Eric Hicks (Paris, 1977)
Debating the Roman de la Rose, *A Critical Anthology*, ed. Christine McWebb (New York, 2007)
Dedeck-Héry, V. L., ed., 'Boethius' *De Consolatione* by Jean de Meun', *Mediæval Studies*, 14 (1952), 165–275
La doctrine du chant du cœur de Jean Gerson. Edition critique, traduction et

commentaire du 'Tractatus de canticis' et du 'Canticordum au pélérin', ed. Isabelle Fabre (Geneva, 2005)

Deschamps, Eustache, *L'Art de Dictier*, ed. and trans., with introduction, by Deborah M. Sinnreich-Levi (East Lansing, 1994)

——, *Œuvres complètes d'Eustache Deschamps*. ed. Le Marquis de Queux de Saint-Hilaire, 11 vols (Paris, 1878)

The 'Didascalicon' of Hugh of St. Victor: A Medieval Guide to the Arts, trans. Jerome Taylor (New York, 1961)

Doss-Quinby, Eglal, Joan Tasker Grimbert, Wendy Pfeffer, and Elizabeth Aubrey, ed., *Songs of the Women Trouvères* (New Haven, 2001)

Les Douze Patriarches ou Beniamin Minor, text and trans. by Jean Châtillon and Monique Duchet-Sucheaux, intro., notes and index by Jean Longère (Paris, 1997)

Dyson, R.W., ed. and trans., *The City of God* (Cambridge, 1998)

Évrart de Conty, *Le Livre des eschez amoureux moralisés*, ed. Françoise Guichard-Tesson and Bruno Roy (Montreal, 1993)

Ferron, Jean, and Jacques de Cessoles, *Le Jeu des eschaz moralisé*, ed. Alain Collet (Paris, 1999)

Flaubert, Gustave, *Dictionnaire des idées reçues*, texte établi et annoté par Albert Thibaudet et René Dumesnil (Paris, 1952)

Froissart, Jean, *Le Joli Buisson de Jonece*, ed. Anthime Fourrier (Geneva, 1975)

'Gérard de Nevers': Prose Version of the 'Roman de la Violette', ed. Lawrence F. H. Lowe (Princeton/Paris, 1928)

Gerbert de Montreuil, *Le Roman de la Violette ou de Gerart de Nevers*, ed. Douglas Labaree Buffum (Paris, 1928)

Jean Gerson, *The Consolation of Theology. De consolatione theologiæ*, trans. and intro. by Clyde Lee Miller (New York, 1998)

——, *Josephina*, ed. G. Matteo Roccati (Paris, 2001)

——, *Œuvres Complètes*, ed. Palémon Glorieux, 10 vols (Paris, 1960–73)

Guillaume de Deguileville, *Le Pèlerinage de la vie humaine*, ed. J. Stürzinger (London, 1893)

Guillaume de Deguileville / Anonymous, *The pilgrimage of the lyfe of the manhode*, ed. and intro. Avril Henry, 2 vols (London, 1985–88)

Guillaume de Lorris and Jean de Meun, *Le Roman de la Rose*, ed. Félix Lecoy, 3 vols (Paris, 1965/1966/1970)

Guillaume de Lorris and Jean de Meun, *Le Roman de la Rose*, ed. and trans. Armand Strubel (Paris, 1992)

Guillaume de Machaut, *Livre de la Fontaine amoureuse*, ed. Jacqueline Cerquiglini-Toulet (Paris, 1993)

——, *Le Livre du Voir Dit*, ed. Paul Imbs, révision: Jacqueline Cerquiglini-Toulet (Paris, 1999)

——, *La Louange de dames* (Edinburgh, 1972)

——, *Œuvres de Guillaume de Machaut*, 3 vols, ed. Ernest Hoepffner (Paris, 1908/1911/1921)

Hugh of Saint Victor, *Didascalicon: De Studio Legendi*, ed. Brother Charles Henry Buttimer (Washington, DC, 1939)

Jeanroy, Alfred *Anthologie des Troubadours XIIe–XIIIe siècles* (Paris, 1974)

Kervyn de Lettenhove, ed., *Œuvres de Georges Chastellain*, 8 vols (Brussels, 1863–66)
Kolsen, Adolf, *Sämtliche Lieder des Troubadours Giraut de Bornelh*, 2 vols (Halle, 1910/1935)
Langland, William, *The Vision of Piers Plowman*, ed. A. V. C. Schmidt, 2nd edn. (London, 1995)
Le Franc, Martin *Le Champion des Dames*, ed. Robert Deschaux, 5 vols (Paris, 1999)
Legrand, Jacques, *Archiloge Sophie*, ed. Evencio Beltran (Geneva, 1986)
Lieberman, Max, *Cahiers de Joséphologie*, 13 (1965), 227–72; 14 (1966), 271–314; 15 (1967), 6–113; 16 (1968), 293–316
Die Liebesgarten-Allegorie der 'Echecs amoureux': Kritische Ausgabe und Kommentar, ed. Christine Kraft (Frankfurt-am-Main, 1977)
Le Livre de Boece de Consolacion, ed. Glynnis M. Cropp (Geneva, 2006)
Li Livres d'Amours de Drouart La Vache, ed. Robert Bossuat (Paris, 1926)
'Les Lunettes des princes' de Jean Meschinot, ed. Christine Martineau-Genieys (Geneva, 1972)
Les lunettes des princes, ed. Bernard Toscani (Paris, 1971)
Lydgate, John, *The Pilgrimage of the Life of Man*, eds F. Furnivall and Katharine Locock (London, 1899, 1901, 1904)
Mehl, Jean-Michel, and Jacques de Cessoles, *Le Livre du jeu d'échecs* (Paris, 1995)
La Mort Aymeri de Narbonne, Chanson de geste, ed. J. Couraye du Parc (Paris, 1884)
Nicole de Margival, *Le Dit de la Panthère*, ed. Bernard Ribémont (Paris, 2000)
The Old French Johannes Translation of the Pseudo-Turpin Chronicle: A Critical Edition, ed. Ronald N. Walpole (Berkeley, 1976)
Ovid, *Metamorphoses*, ed. and trans. Frank Justus Miller, 2 vols (Cambridge, MA; London, 1984)
Paden, William D., trans. and ed., *The Medieval Pastourelle* (New York, 1987)
Paffenroth, K., trans., *Soliloquies: Augustine's Inner Dialogue* (New York, 2000)
Le Pelerinaige de vie humaine: Reproduced in Facsimile from the Printed Book in the Library of the Earl of Ellesmere. Intro. Alfred Pollard (Paris: Anthoine Vérard, 1499) (Manchester, 1912)
Philippe de Mézières, *Le Livre de la Vertu du Sacrement de Mariage*, ed. Joan B. Williamson (Washington, DC, 1993)
Placides et Timéo ou *Li secrés as philosophes*, ed. Claude Alexandre Thomasset (Geneva, 1980)
Le premier et le secont livre de Fauvel in the version preserved in B.N. f. fr. 146, ed. P. Helmer (Ottawa, 1997)
Raimondi, Gianmario, '*Les Eschés amoureux*. Studio preparatorio ed edizione (I. vv. 1–3662)', *Pluteus*, 8–9 (1990–98)
——, '*Les Eschés amoureux*. Studio preparatorio ed edizione (II. vv. 3663–5538)', *Pluteus*, 10 (1999), forthcoming
Rains, Ruth R., ed., *Les sept psaumes allégorisés* (Washington, DC, 1965)
Reno, Christine, 'The Preface to the *Advision Cristine* in ex-Phillipps 128', in

Reinterpreting Christine de Pizan, ed. Earl Jeffrey Richards (Athens and London, 1992), 207–27

Rhetorica ad Herennium, ed. and trans. Harry Caplan (Cambridge MA, 1981)

Richard de Saint-Victor, *The Twelve Patriarchs; The Mystical Ark; Book Three of The Trinity*, trans. and intro. by Grover A. Zinn (London, 1979)

Le Roman de Fauvel *in the Edition of Mesire Chaillou de Pesstain (facsimile of BnF MS fr. 146)*, ed. Edward Roesner. Introduction by François Avril, Nancy Freeman Regalado and Edward Roesner (New York, 1990)

Le Roman de Fauvel *par Gervais du Bus*, ed. Alfred Långfors (Paris, 1914–19)

Le Roman de Troie, ed. Léopold Constans, Vol. 6 (Paris, 1912)

Rosenberg, Samuel N., and Hans Tischler, ed. and trans., *The Monophonic Songs in the 'Roman de Fauvel'* (Lincoln, 1991)

Roy, Bruno, ed., *L'Art d'amours. Traduction et commentaire de l'*Ars amatoria *d'Ovide* (Leiden, 1974)

Scheler, Auguste, ed., *Dits de Watriquet de Couvin* (Brussels, 1868)

Sharman, Ruth Verity, *The 'Cansos' and 'Sirventes' of the Trouvadour Giraut de Bornelh: A Critical Edition* (Cambridge, 1989)

Le Songe véritable: Pamphlet politique d'un Parisien du XVe siècle, ed. H. Moranvillé (Paris, 1891)

Storer, W., and C. Rochedieu, ed. and trans., *Six Historical Poems of Geffroi de Paris, Written in 1314–1318* (Chapel Hill, 1950)

Thomas Wright's Political Songs of England, from the Reign of John to that of Edward II, ed. Peter Coss (Cambridge, 1996)

Thomas, Wyndham, ed., *Robin and Marion Motets* 3 (Newton Abbot, 1985)

Vetter, Ferdinand, *Das Schachzabelbuch Kunrats von Ammenhausen nebst den Schachbüchern des Jakob von Cessole und des Jakob Mennel*, in *Bibliotehek älterer Schriftwerke der deutschen Schweiz* (Frauenfeld, 1892)

Virgil, Eclogues, Georgics, Æneid I-VI, ed. and trans. H. Rushton Fairclough, rev. by G. P. Goold (Cambridge, MA; London, 1999)

The Works of Jehan de Lescurel, ed. N. Wilkins. (Rome, 1966)

Zink, Michel, *Le Tiers d'amour. Un roman des troubadours* (Paris, 1998)

Secondary Texts

Akbari, Suzanne Conklin, 'Death as Metamorphosis in the Devotional Allegory of Christine de Pizan', forthcoming

——, 'Nature's Forge Recast in the *Roman de Silence*', in *Literary Aspects of Courtly Culture*, ed. Donald Maddox and Sara Sturm-Maddox (Cambridge, 1994), pp. 39–46

——, *Seeing through the Veil: Optical Theory and Medieval Allegory* (Toronto, 2004)

Allen, Peter, *The Art of Love: Amatory Fiction from Ovid to the* Romance of the Rose (Philadelphia, 1992)

Arlt, Wulf, 'Jehannot de L'Escurel', in *Grove Music Online,* ed. L. Macy [15 Oct 2006], <http://www.grovemusic.com>

——, 'Jehannot de Lescurel and the Function of Musical Language in the *Roman de Fauve*l', in *Fauvel Studies*, ed. Bent and Wathey, pp. 25–34

Armstrong, Adrian, *Technique and Technology. Script, Print, and Poetics in France, 1470–1550* (Oxford, 2000)

——, 'The *Testament* of François Villon', in Simon Gaunt and Sarah Kay, ed., *Cambridge Companion to Medieval French Literature* (Cambridge, 2008), pp. 63–76

——, *The Virtuoso Circle: Competition, Collaboration and Complexity in Late Medieval French Poetry*, forthcoming

Armstrong, Adrian, and Sarah Kay, with contributions from Sylvia Huot, Rebecca Dixon, Miranda Griffin, Francesca Nicholson, and Finn Sinclair, *Poetry and Knowledge in Late Medieval France from the* Roman de la Rose *to the grands rhétoriqueurs*, forthcoming

——, and Malcolm Quainton, ed., *Book and Text in France, 1400–1600: Poetry on the Page* (Aldershot, 2007)

Atkinson, J. Keith, 'A Fourteenth-Century Picard Translation-Commentary of the *Consolatio Philosophiæ*', in *The Medieval Boethius: Studies in the Vernacular Translations of 'De Consolatione Philosophiæ'*, ed. A. J. Minnis (Cambridge, 1987), pp. 32–62

Badel, Pierre-Yves, *Le* Roman de la Rose *au XIVe siècle. Etude de la réception de l'œuvre* (Geneva, 1980)

Barolini, Teodolinda, 'The Making of a Lyric Sequence: Time and Narrative in Petrarch's *Rerum Vulgarium Fragmenta*', *Modern Language Notes*, 104 (1989), 1–38

Baumgartner, Emmanuèle, 'Les citations lyriques dans le *Roman de la Rose* de Jean Renart', *Romance Philology*, 35 (1981–82), 260–6

——, 'Sur les pièces lyriques du *Tristan en prose*', in *Études de langue et de littérature offerts à Félix Lecoy* (Paris, 1973), pp. 19–25

Beaune, Colette, *The Birth of an Ideology: Myths and Symbols of Nation in Late-Medieval France*, ed. F. L. Cheyette, trans. S. R. Huston, (Berkeley, 1991)

Bec, Pierre, *La Lyrique française au moyen âge: contribution à une typologie des genres poétiques médiévaux* (Paris, 1977)

Becker, Karin, 'La mentalité juridique dans la littérature française (XIIIe–XVe siècles)', *Le Moyen Age*, 103 (1997), 309–27

Bent, Margaret, and Andrew Wathey, ed., *Fauvel Studies: Allegory, Chronicle, Music, and Image in Paris, BnF MS fr. 146* (Oxford, 1998)

Berchtold, Jacques, ed., *Échiquiers d'encre. Le jeu d'échecs et les lettres (XIXème–XXème siècles)* (Geneva, 1998)

Bertolucci Pizzorusso, Valeria, 'Il grado zero della retorica nella "vida" di Jaufre Rudel', in *Studi Mediolatini e Volgari*, 18 (1970), 7–26

Black, Nancy B., *Medieval Narratives of Accused Queens* (Gainesville, 2003)

Blumenfeld-Kosinski, Renate, 'Jean Gerson and the Debate on the *Romance of the Rose*', in *A Companion to Jean Gerson*, ed. Brian Patrick McGuire (Leiden, 2006), pp. 317–56

——, *Poets, Saints, and Visionaries of the Great Schism, 1378–1417* (Philadelphia, 2006)

——, *Reading Myth: Classical Mythology and its Interpretations in Medieval French Literature* (Stanford, 1997)

Bolduc, Michelle, *The Medieval Poetics of Contraries* (Gainsville, 2006)

Boogaard, Nico H. J. van den, 'Jacquemart Giélée et la lyrique de son temps', in

Alain de Lille, Gautier de Châtillon, Jakemart Giélée et leur temps, ed. Henri Roussel and François Suard (Lille, 1980), pp. 333–53

Bose, Mishtooni, '*Advena, peregrinus*: Jean Gerson's charisma', in *Charisma and Authority. Jewish, Christian and Muslim Preaching, 1200–1600*, ed. Katherine Ludwig Jansen and Miri Rubin, forthcoming

Boucher, Caroline, 'Les *Eschés amoureux* d'Évrart de Conty', Appendix to 'Des problèmes pour exercer l'entendement du lecteur: Évrart de Conty, Nicole Oresme et la recherche de la nouveauté', in *Aristotle's* Problemata *in Different Times and Tongues*, ed. Michèle Goyens and Pieter de Leemans (Leuven, 2006), pp. 175–97

Boulton, Maureen Barry McCann, *The Song in the Story: Lyric Insertions in French Narrative Fiction, 1200–1400* (Philadelphia, 1993)

Bourdieu, Pierre, *Choses dites* (Paris, 1987)

——, *La distinction: critique sociale du jugement* (Paris, 1979)

——, *Outline of a Theory of Practice* (Cambridge, 1977)

Bourquin, Guy '*Piers Plowman*': *Études sur la genèse littéraire des trois versions*, 2 vols (Paris, 1978)

Brown, Cynthia J., 'From Stage to Page: Royal Entry Performances in Honour of Mary Tudor (1514)', in Adrian Armstrong and Malcolm Quainton, ed., *Book and Text in France, 1400–1600: Poetry on the Page* (Aldershot, 2007), pp. 49–72

——, 'The Reconstruction of an Author in Print: Christine de Pizan in the Fifteenth and Sixteenth Centuries', in *Christine de Pizan and the Categories of Difference*, ed. Marilynn Desmond (Minneapolis and London, 1998), pp. 215–35

Brown, Elizabeth A. R., '*Rex ioians, ionnes, iolis*: Louis X, Philip V, and the *Livres de Fauvel*', in *Fauvel Studies,* ed. Bent and Wathey, pp. 53–72

Brown-Grant, Rosalind, 'Illumination as Reception: Jean Miélot's Reworking of the *Epistre Othea*', in *The City of Scholars: New Approaches to Christine de Pizan*, ed.. Margarete Zimmermann and Dina De Rentiis (Berlin, 1994), pp. 260–72

Brownlee, Kevin, 'Jean de Meun and the Limits of Romance', in *Romance: Generic Transformations from Chrétien de Troyes to Cervantes*, ed. Kevin Brownlee and Maria Scordilis Brownlee (London, 1985), pp. 114–34

——, 'Le moi *lyrique* et la généalogie littéraire: Christine de Pizan et Dante dans le *Chemin de long estude*', in *'Musique naturele': Interpretationen zur französichen Lyrik des Spätmittelalters*, ed. Wolf-Dieter Stempel (Munich, 1995), pp. 105–39

——, 'Transformations of the Couple: Genre and Language in the *Jeu de Robin et Marion*', *French Forum*, 14 (1989), 419–33

Brusegan, Rosanna, 'Culte de la Vierge et origine des puys et confréries en France au Moyen Age', *Revue des langues romanes*, 95 (1991), 31–58

Burrows, Mark S., *Jean Gerson and 'De Consolatione Theologiæ' (1418). The Consolation of a Biblical and Reforming Theology for a Disordered Age* (Tübingen, 1991)

Butterfield, Ardis, *Poetry and Music in Medieval France: From Jean Renart to Guillaume de Machaut* (Cambridge, 2002)

——, 'The Refrain and the Transformation of Genre in the *Roman de Fauvel*', in *Fauvel Studies*, ed. Bent and Wathey, pp. 105–59
Caillois, Roger, *Les Jeux et les hommes. Le masque et le vertige* (Paris, 1967)
Callahan, Christopher, 'À l'ombre du jongleur disparu. La grammaire de la performance dans deux romans lyrico-narratifs dérimés', *Revue des Langues Romanes,* 101 (1997), 211–33
Carruthers, Mary, *The Book of Memory: A Study of Memory in Medieval Culture* (Cambridge, 1990); trans. Diane Meur as *Le Livre de la Mémoire. La Mémoire dans la culture médiévale* (Paris, 2002)
Cayley, Emma, *Debate and Dialogue. Alain Chartier in his Cultural Context* (Oxford, 2006)
Cerquiglini, Jacqueline, *'Un engin si soutil': Guillaume de Machaut et l'écriture au XIVe siècle* (Paris, 2001)
——, 'Pour une typologie de l'insertion', *Perspectives médiévales*, 3 (1977), 9–14
——, 'Quand la voix s'est tue: la mise en recueil de la poésie lyrique aux XIVe et XVe siècles', in Emmanuèle Baumgartner and Nicole Boulestreau, ed., *La présentation du livre. Actes du colloque Paris-X Nanterre, du 4 au 6 décembre 1985* (Paris, 1987), pp. 313–27
Cerquiglini-Toulet, Jacqueline, 'A la recherche des pères: La liste des auteurs illustres à la fin du Moyen Âge', *Modern Language Notes*, 116 (2001), 630–43
——, 'Leçon. Sentier de rime et voie de prose au Moyen Âge', *Po&sie*, 119 (2007), 123–31
Chavy, Paul, 'Les Premiers Translateurs français', *French Review*, 47 (1974), 557–65
Clark, A.V., 'The Flowering of Charnalité and the Marriage of Fauvel', in *Fauvel Studies*, ed. Bent and Wathey, pp. 175–86
Clark, S., and E. E. Leach, ed., *Citation and Authority in Medieval and Renaissance Music Culture: Learning from the Learned* (Woodbridge, 2005)
Cline, James M., 'Chaucer and Jean de Meun: *De Consolatione Philosophiae*', *English Literary History*, 3 (1936), 170–81
Combes, André, *La Théologie Mystique de Gerson*. II (Paris, Rome and Tournai, 1964)
Compagnon, Antoine, *La Seconde main ou le travail de la citation* (Paris, 1979)
Copeland, Rita, *Rhetoric, Hermeneutics and Translation in the Middle Ages: Academic Traditions and Vernacular Texts* (Cambridge, 1991)
Courcelle, Pierre, and Sylvie Lefèvre, 'Boèce', in *Dictionnaire des Lettres françaises: Le Moyen Age*, updated by Geneviève Hasenohr and Michel Zink (Paris, 1992 [1964]), pp. 204–8
Cropp, Glynnis M., 'The Medieval French Tradition', in *Boethius in the Middle Ages*, ed. Hoenen and Nauta, pp. 243–65
Damian-Grint, Peter, 'Translation as *Enarratio* and Hermeneutic Theory in Twelfth-Century Vernacular Learned Literature', *Neophilologus*, 83 (1999), 349–67
Dane, Joseph, *Res/verba: A Study in Medieval French Drama* (Leiden, 1985)
Delisle, Léopold, *Mélanges de Paléographie et de Bibliographie* (Paris, 1880)

——, *Recherches sur la librairie de Charles V*, Part I (Paris, 1907)
Dembowski, Peter, 'Learned Latin Treatises in French: Inspiration, Plagiarism, and Translation', *Viator*, 17 (1986), 255–69
Desmond, Marilynn, *Ovid's Art and the Wife of Bath: The Ethics of Erotic Violence* (New York, 2006)
Dillon, Emma, *Medieval Music-Making and the 'Roman de Fauvel'* (Cambridge, 2002)
Di Lorenzo, Raymond D. 'Imagination as the First Way to Contemplation in Richard of St. Victor's *Benjamin Minor*', *Medievalia et Humanistica*, 11 (1982), 77–98
——, 'The Collection Form and the Art of Memory in the *Libellus super ludo scacchorum* of Jacobus de Cessolis', *Mediæval Studies*, 35 (1973), 205–21
Doss-Quinby, Eglal, *Les Refrains chez les trouvères du XIIe siècle au début du XIVe* (New York, 1984)
——, 'The Douce 308 *chansonnier* within the Corpus of Trouvère Songbooks', in *Lettres et musique en Lorraine du XIIIe au XVe siecle,* ed. M. Chazan and N. F. Regalado, in preparation
Doudet, Estelle, *Poétique de George Chastelain (1415–1475): 'Un cristal mucié en un coffre'* (Paris, 2005)
Dufournet, Jean, *Sur 'Le Jeu de la feuillée': études complémentaires* (Paris, 1977)
Doutrepont, Georges, *La littérature française à la cour des ducs de Bourgogne* (Paris, 1909)
Dragonetti, Roger '"La poesie ... ceste musique naturele": Essai d'exégèse d'un passage de l'*Art de Dictier* d'Eustache Deschamps', in *Fin du Moyen Age et Renaissance: Mélanges de philologie française offerts à Robert Guiette* (Antwerp, 1961), pp. 49–64
Dulac, Liliane, and Christine Reno, 'L'humanisme vers 1400: essai d'exploration à partir d'un cas marginal: Christine de Pizan, traductrice de Thomas d'Aquin', in *Pratiques de la culture écrite en France au XVe siècle*, ed. Monique Ornato and Nicole Pons (Louvain-la-Neuve, 1995), pp. 161–78
Evdokimova, Ludmilla, 'Des *Douze Dames de Rhétorique* à la *Complainte*: le prolongement du débat littéraire dans la réponse de Jean Robertet', in *Poétiques en transition entre Moyen Age et Renaissance*, ed. Jean-Claude Mühlethaler and Jacqueline Cerquiglini-Toulet (Lausanne, 2002), pp. 111–28
Fabre, Isabelle, ed., *La doctrine du chant du cœur de Jean Gerson. Edition critique, traduction et commentaire du 'Tractatus de canticis' et du 'Canticordum au pélérin'* (Geneva, 2005)
Fauquet, Wilfrid, 'Le *giu parti* d'Évrart de Conty. Une version échiquéenne du *Roman de la Rose*', *Romania*, 123 (2005), 486–522
Fenster, Thelma S. and Daniel Lord Smail, ed., *Fama: The Politics of Talk and Reputation in Medieval Europe* (Ithaca, NY, 2003)
Ferrand, Françoise, 'Le *Jeu de Robin et Marion*: Robin danse devant Marion, sens du passage et sens de l'œuvre', *Revue des Langues Romanes*, 90 (1986), 87–97
Fitzgerald, A. D., ed., *Augustine Through the Ages: An Encyclopedia* (Grand Rapids, MI, 1999)

Flint, Valerie, 'Columbus, "El Romero" and the so-called Columbus Map', *Terræ Incognitæ*, 24 (1992), 19–30
Frye, Northrup, *The Great Code: The Bible and Literature* (New York, 1982)
Galderisi, Claudio, 'Vers et prose au Moyen Âge', in *Histoire de la France Littéraire: Naissances, Renaissances*, ed. Frank Lestringant and Michel Zink (Paris, 2006), pp. 745–66
Gally, Michèle, *L'intelligence de l'amour d'Ovide à Dante: Arts d'aimer et poésie au Moyen Âge* (Paris, 2005)
——, 'Le miroir mis en abyme: *Les Échecs Amoureux* et la réécriture du *Roman de la Rose*', in *Miroirs et jeux de miroirs dans la littérature médiévale*, ed. Fabienne Pomel (Rennes, 2003), pp. 253–63
Genette, Gérard, *Figures II* (Paris, 1969)
Gennrich, Friedrich, *Bibliographie der ältesten französischen und lateinischen Motetten* (Darmstadt, 1957–58)
Gibson, Margaret T., *Boethius, His Life, Thought and Influence* (Oxford, 1981)
Girard, René, *Des choses cachées depuis la fondation du monde* (Paris, 1978)
——, *Critique dans un souterrain* (Lausanne, 1976)
——, *Dostoïevski, du double à l'unité* (Paris, 1963)
——, *La Violence et le Sacré* (Paris, 1972)
Glorieux, Palémon, 'Saint Joseph dans L'Œuvre de Gerson', *Cahiers de Joséphologie*, 19 (1971), 414–28
Godzich, Wlad, and Jeffrey Kittay, *The Emergence of Prose: An Essay in Prosaics* (Minneapolis, 1987)
Gravdal, Kathryn, 'Camouflaging Rape: The Rhetoric of Sexual Violence in the Medieval Pastourelle', *Romanic Review*, 76 (1985), 361–73
——, *Ravishing Maidens: Writing Rape in Medieval French Literature* (Philadelphia, 1991)
Gregory, Tullio, ed., *I Sogni nel Medioevo: seminario internazionale, Roma 2–4 ottobre, 1983* (Rome, 1985)
Gros, Gérard, *Le Poète, la Vierge et le Prince du puy. Etude sur les Puys marials de la France du Nord du XIVe siècle à la Renaissance* (Paris, 1994)
Guichard-Tesson, Françoise, 'Évrart de Conty, poète, traducteur et commentateur', in *Aristotle's* Problemata *in Different Times and Tongues*, ed. Michèle Goyens and Pieter de Leemans (Leuven, 2006), 145–74
——, 'Le pion Souvenir et les miroirs déformants dans l'allégorie d'amour', in *Jeux de mémoire. Aspects de la mnémotechnie médiévale*, ed. Bruno Roy and Paul Zumthor (Montreal-Paris, 1985), pp. 99–108
Guynn, Noah, *Allegory and Sexual Ethics in the High Middle Ages* (New York, 2007)
Hallyn, Fernand, 'Poésie et savoir au Quattrocento et au XVIe siècle' in *Poétiques de la Renaissance. Le modèle italien, le monde franco-bourguignon et leur héritage en France au XVIe siècle*, ed. Perrine Galand-Hallyn and Fernand Hallyn (Geneva, 2001), pp. 167–217
Hanning, Robert, 'Arthurian Evangelists: The Language of Truth in Thirteenth-Century French Prose Romances', *Philological Quarterly*, 64 (1985), 347–65
Hasenohr, Geneviève, 'Aperçu sur la diffusion et la reception de la littérature de spiritualité en langue française au dernier siècle du Moyen Age', in *Wissens-*

organisierende und wissensvermittelnde Literatur im Mittelalter, Perspektiven ihrer Erforschung, Kolloquium, 5–7, Dezember 1985, ed. Norbert Richard Wolf (Wiesbaden, 1987), pp. 57–90

Hindman, Sandra, *Christine de Pizan's 'Epistre Othéa': Painting and Politics at the Court of Charles VI* (Toronto, 1986)

Heller-Roazen, Daniel, *Fortune's Faces: The* Roman de la Rose *and the Poetics of Contingency* (Baltimore, 2003)

Hexter, Ralph J., *Ovid and Medieval Schooling. Studies in Medieval School Commentaries on Ovid's* Ars amatoria*,* Epistulæ ex Ponto*, and* Epistulæ Heroidum (Munich, 1986)

Hobbins, Daniel, 'The schoolman as public intellectual: Jean Gerson and the Late Medieval Tract', *American Historical Review*, 108 (2003), 1308–37

Hoenen, Maarten J. F. M., and Lodi Nauta, *Boethius in the Middle Ages: Latin and Vernacular Traditions of the* Consolatio Philosophiæ (Leiden, 1997)

Hoffman, E. J., *Alain Chartier: His Work and Reputation* (New York, 1942)

Holford-Strevens, Leofranc, 'Fauvel Goes to School', in Clark and Leach, ed., *Citation and Authority in Medieval and Renaissance Musical Culture*, pp. 59–66

——, 'The Latin *Dits* of Geffroy de Paris', in *Fauvel Studies*, ed. Bent and Wathey, pp. 247–75

Hüe, Denis, 'Du Je courtois à la Prosopopée, Jean Meschinot', *Figures de l'Écrivain au Moyen Âge*, ed. Danielle Buschinger (Göppingen, 1991), pp. 151–65

——, *La Poésie palinodique à Rouen (1486–1550)* (Paris, 2002)

——, 'Psaumes, prières, paraphrases et récritures', *Le Moyen Français*, 51–52–53 (2003), 349–73

Hult, David, 'Language and Dismemberment: Abelard, Origen, and the *Romance of the Rose*', in *Rethinking the* Romance of the Rose*: Text, Image, Reception*, ed. Kevin Brownlee and Sylvia Huot (Philadelphia, 1992), pp. 101–30

Huot, Sylvia, *Allegorical Play in the Old French Motet: The Sacred and the Profane in Thirteenth-Century Polyphony* (Stanford, 1997)

——, '"Ci parle l'aucteur": The Rubrication of Voice and Authorship in the Roman de la Rose Manuscripts', *SubStance*, 56 (1988), 42–8

——, *From Song to Book: The Poetics of Writing in Old French Lyric and Lyrical Narrative Poetry* (New York, 1987)

——, 'Intergeneric Play: The Pastourelle in Thirteenth-Century French Motets', in *Medieval Lyric: Genres in Historical Context*, ed. William D. Paden (Urbana, 2000), pp. 297–316

——, 'Refashioning Boethius: Prose and Poetry in Chartier's *Livre de l'Espérance*', *Medium Ævum*, 76 (2007), 268–84

——, 'Seduction and sublimation: Christine de Pizan, Jean de Meun, and Dante', *Romance Notes*, 25 (1985), 361–73

——, *The 'Romance of the Rose' and its Medieval Readers: Interpretation, Reception, Manuscript Transmission* (Cambridge, 1993)

Ignatius, Mary Ann, 'Christine de Pizan's *Epistre Othea*: An Experiment in Literary Form', *Mediævalia et Humanistica*, n.s. 9 (1979), 127–42

Jaeger, C. Stephen, *Ennobling Love: In Search of a Lost Sensibility* (Philadelphia, 1999)

Jeauneau, Édouard, 'L'Usage de la notion d'*integumentum* à travers les gloses de Guillaume de Conches', *Archives d'histoire doctrinale et littéraire du moyen âge*, 24 (1957), 35–100

Jeay, Madeleine, *Le Commerce des Mots: L'usage des listes dans la littérature médiévale (XIIe–XVe siècles)* (Geneva, 2006)

Jodogne, Omer, 'La Naissance de la prose française', in *Académie royale des sciences, des lettres et des beaux-arts, Bulletin de la classe des lettres et des sciences morales et politiques* (Brussels, 1963), pp. 296–308

Johnson, Leonard W., 'Prince or Princes? Fifteenth-Century Politics and Poetry', *The French Review*, 68 (1995), 421–30

Jung, Marc-René, 'Poetria: Zur Dichtungstheorie des ausgehenden Mittelalters in Frankreich', *Vox Romanica*, 30 (1971), 44–64

Kamath, Stephanie A. V. G., 'Unveiling the "I": Allegory and Authorship in the Franco-English Tradition, 1270–1450', Ph.D. diss. (University of Pennsylvania, 2006)

Kay, Sarah, 'Grafting the Knowledge Community: The Purposes of Verse in the *Breviari d'amor* of Matfre Ermengaud', *Neophilologus*, 91 (2007), 361–73

——, *The Place of Thought: The Complexity of One in Late Medieval French Didactic Poetry* (Philadelphia, 2007)

——, *Subjectivity in Troubadour Poetry* (Cambridge, 1990)

Kelly, Douglas, *Christine de Pizan's Changing Opinion: A Quest for Certainty in the Midst of Chaos* (Woodbridge, 2007)

——, '*Translatio Studii*: Translation, Adaptation, and Allegory in Medieval French Literature', *Philological Quarterly*, 57 (1978), 287–310

Kerby-Fulton, Kathryn, *Books Under Suspicion. Censorship and Tolerance of Revelatory Writing in Late Medieval England* (Notre Dame, IN, 2006)

Kibler, William, 'The Development of the Pastourelle in the Fourteenth Century: An Edition of Fifteen Poems with an Analysis', *Mediæval Studies*, 45 (1983), 22–78

Koch, John, 'Anglonormannische Texte im Ms. Arundel 220 des Britischen Museums', *Zeitschrift für romanische Philologie*, 54 (1934), 20–56

Köhler, Erich, *Trobadorlyrik und Höfischer Roman* (Berlin, 1962)

Kruger, Steven F., *Dreaming in the Middle Ages* (Cambridge; New York, 1992)

Lacan, Jacques, *Le Séminaire IV: La Relation d'objet* (Paris, 1994)

Laistner, M. L. W., 'Notes on Greek from the Lectures of a Ninth-Century Monastery Teacher', *Bulletin of the John Rylands Library*, 7 (1923), 421–56

Langlois, Ch.-V., 'Jean de Lescurel, poète français', in *Histoire Littéraire de la France,* 36 (Paris, 1927), 109–15

Langlois, Ernest, 'La Traduction de Boèce par Jean de Meun', *Romania*, 42 (1913), 331–69

Lefèvre, Sylvie, 'Christine de Pizan et l'Aristote Oresmien', in *Au champ des escriptures: IIIe Colloque international sur Christine de Pizan*, ed. Eric Hicks (Paris, 2000), pp. 231–43

Legaré, Anne-Marie, 'La réception du *Pèlerinage de Vie humaine* de Guillaume de Digulleville dans le milieu angevin', in *Religion et mentalités au Moyen Âge: Mélanges en l'honneur d'Hervé Martin*, ed.. Sophie Cassagnes-Brouquet et al. (Rennes, 2003), pp. 543–52

Lieberman, Max, 'Chronologie Gersonienne IV: Gerson poète', *Romania*, 76 (1955), 289–333

Lynch, Kathryn L., *The High Medieval Dream Vision: Poetry, Philosophy, and Literary Form* (Stanford, 1988)

Lyotard, Jean-François, *La Condition postmoderne* (Paris, 1979)

Maddicott, J. R., 'Poems of Social Protest in Early Fourteenth-Century England', in *England in the Fourteenth Century: Proceedings of the Harlaxton Symposium*, ed. W. M. Ormrod (Woodbridge, 1986), pp. 130–44

McGrady, Deborah, *Controlling Readers: Guillaume de Machaut and His Late Medieval Audience* (Toronto, 2006)

——, 'Maîtriser Ovide: Exemple d'une traduction de l'*Ars amatoria* à la fin du moyen âge', in *Ovide métamorphosé: les lecteurs médiévaux d'Ovide*, ed. Laurence Harf-Lancner, forthcoming

McGuire, Brian Patrick, ed., *A Companion to Jean Gerson* (Leiden, 2006)

——, *Jean Gerson and the Last Medieval Reformation* (Leiden, 2005)

Mehl, Jean-Michel, *Jeu d'échecs et éducation au XIIIe siècle: recherches sur le 'Liber de moribus' de Jacques de Cessoles*, Thèse de 3ème cycle (Strasbourg, 1975)

——, *Les Jeux au royaume de France, du XIIIe au début du XVIe siècle* (Paris, 1990)

Meneghetti, Maria Luisa, 'La forma-canzoniere fra tradizione mediolatina e tradizioni volgari', in *L'Antologia poetica, Critica del Testo II/1*, 1999, 119–40

——, *Il Pubblico dei trovatori. Ricezione e riuso dei testi lirici cortesi fino al XIV secolo* (Modena, 1984)

Minnis, Alastair, *Magister Amoris: The 'Roman de la Rose' and Vernacular Hermeneutics* (Oxford, 2001)

——, *Medieval Theory of Authorship: Scholastic Literary Attitudes in the Later Middle Ages* (Philadelphia, 1984)

Monfrin, Jacques, 'Humanisme et Traductions au Moyen âge', *Journal des Savants*, 148 (1963), 161–90

Morin, J. C., ed. and trans., 'The Genesis of Manuscript Paris, Bibliothèque Nationale, Fonds Français 146, with Particular Emphasis on the *Roman de Fauvel*', diss. (New York University, 1992)

Mullally, Robert, 'Balerie and Ballade', *Romanica*, 104 (1983), 533–8

Murray, Harold J., *A History of Chess* (New York; Oxford, 1913)

Newman, Barbara, *God and the Goddesses: Vision, Poetry, and Belief in the Middle Ages* (Philadelphia, 2003)

Nicholson, Francesca M., 'Branches of Knowledge: The Purposes of Citation in the *Breviari d'amor* of Matfre Ermengaud', *Neophilologus*, 91 (2007), 375–85

Olson, Glending, *Literature as Recreation in the Later Middle Ages* (Ithaca, NY; London, 1982)

Ong, Walter J., *Orality and Literacy: the technologising of the word* (London, 1982)

Ott, Muriel, ed., *L'Épopée médiévale et la Bourgogne* (Dijon, 2006)

Ouy, Gilbert, 'Discovering Gerson the humanist: fifty years of serendipity', in McGuire, ed., *A Companion to Jean Gerson*, pp. 79–132

——, 'Gerson, émule de Pétrarque: le *Pastorium Carmen*, poème de jeunesse de Gerson, et la renaissance de l'églogue en France à la fin du XIVe siècle', *Romania*, 88 (1967), 175–231

Paden, William D., 'Flight from Authority in the Pastourelle', in *The Medieval Opus: Imitation, Rewriting, and Transmission in the French Tradition*, ed. Douglas Kelly (Amsterdam, 1996), pp. 299–325

——, 'Old Occitan as a Lyric Language: The Insertions from Occitan in Three Thirteenth-Century French Romances', *Speculum*, 68.1 (1993), 36–53

——, 'Rape in the Pastourelle', *Romanic Review*, 80 (1989), 331–49

Paris, Gaston, 'Chrétien Legouais et autres traducteurs et imitateurs d'Ovide au moyen âge,' *Histoire littéraire de la France*, 29 (1885), 489–97

——, 'Par ci le me taille', *Romania*, 18 (1889), 288–9

Piaget, Arthur, '*Les Princes* de Georges Chastelain', *Romania*, 47 (1921), 161–206

Pomel, Fabienne, 'Enjeux d'un travail de réécriture', *Le Moyen Âge*, 109 (2003), 457–72

Regalado, Nancy Freeman, 'Allegories of Power: The Tournament of Vices and Virtues in the *Roman de Fauvel* (BN MS fr. 146)', *Gesta*, 32 (1993), 135–46

——, 'Des contraires choses: la fonction poétique de la citation et des exempla dans le *Roman de la Rose* de Jean de Meun', Littérature, 41 (1981), 62–81

——, 'The *Chronique métrique* and the Moral Design of BN fr. 146: Feasts of Good and Evil', in *Fauvel Studies*, ed. Bent and Wathey, pp. 467–94

——, 'Masques réels dans le monde de l'imaginaire: le rite et l'écrit dans le charivari du *Roman de Fauvel*, MS. B.N. Fr. 146', in M. L. Ollier, ed., *Masques et déguisements dans la littérature médiévale* (Montreal, 1998), pp. 112–26

Ribémont, Bernard, 'Vers et prose dans l'écriture à caractère scientifique médiévale: L'exemple de l'encyclopédisme', in *Actes du XXe Congrès International de Linguistique et Philologie Romanes*, ed. G. Hilty (Tübingen, 1993) vol. 5, section 8 ('L'art narratif aux XIIe et XIIIe siècles'), pp. 341–52

Richards, Earl Jeffrey, 'Christine de Pizan and Jean Gerson: An Intellectual Friendship', in *Christine de Pizan 2000: Studies on Christine de Pizan in honour of Angus J. Kennedy,* ed. John Campbell and Nadia Margolis (Amsterdam, 2000), pp. 197–208

——, 'Water without Salt and Ballades without Feeling, or Reintroducing History into the Text: Prose and Verse in the Works of Christine de Pizan', in *Christine de Pizan and Medieval French Lyric*, ed. Earl Jeffrey Richards (Gainesville, 1998), pp. 206–29

de Riquer, Martin 'La *avventura*, el *lai* y el *conte* en María de Francia', *Filologia Romanza*, 2 (1955), 1–19

Robertson, Anne Walters, *Guillaume de Machaut and Reims: Context and Meaning in his Musical Works* (Cambridge, 2002)

Roccati, G. Matteo, 'A Gersonian text in defense of poetry: *De Laudibus Elegie Spiritualis* (ca. 1422–1425)', *Traditio*, 60 (2005), 369–85

——, 'À propos de la tradition manuscrite de l'œuvre poétique latine de Gerson: les manuscripts Paris, Bibl. Nat., Lat. 3624 et 3628', *Revue de l'Histoire des Textes*, 10 (1980), 277–308

——, 'Gerson e il problema dell'espressione poetica: note su alcuni temi e immagini ricorrenti nelle poesie latine', *Studi Francesi*, 77 (1982), 278–85

——, 'Humanisme et préoccupations réligieuses au début du XVe siècle: Le

Prologue de la *Josephina* de Jean Gerson', in *Preludes à la Renaissance. Aspects de la vie intellectuelle en France au XVe siècle*, ed. Carla Bozzolo and Ezio Ornato (Paris, 1992), pp. 107–22

——, 'La "Josephina" di Jean Gerson (1418): un poema virgiliano di contenuto biblico', *Studi Francesi*, 121 (1997), 4–15

——, 'Note a proposito delle poesie latine di Jean Gerson', *Studi Francesi*, 65–66 (1978), 341–9

Roesner, Edward, 'Labouring in the Midst of Wolves: Reading a Group of *Fauvel* Motets', *Early Music History*, 22 (2003), 169–245

Rouse, Mary, and Richard Rouse, *Manuscripts and their Makers: Commercial Book Producers in Medieval Paris, 1200–1500*, 2 vols (Turnhout, 2000)

Saltzstein, Jennifer, *Wandering Voices: Refrain Citation in Thirteenth-Century French Music and Poetry*, Ph.D. diss. (University of Pennsylvania, 2007)

Semple, Benjamin, 'The Critique of Knowledge as Power: The Limits of Philosophy and Theology in Christine de Pizan', in *Christine de Pizan and the Categories of Difference*, ed. Marilynn Desmond (Minneapolis and London, 1998), pp. 108–27

Seznec, Jean, *La Survivance des dieux antiques: essai sur le rôle de la tradition mythologique dans l'humanisme et dans l'art de la Renaissance* (Paris, 1993)

Sheingorn, Pamela, '"Illustris patriarcha Joseph": Jean Gerson, Representations of Saint Joseph, and Imagining Community among Churchmen in the Fifteenth Century', in *Visions of Community in the Pre-Modern World*, ed. Nicholas Howe (Notre Dame, IN, 2002), pp. 75–108

Sherman, Claire Richter, *Imaging Aristotle: Verbal and Visual Representation in Fourteenth-Century France* (Berkeley, 1995)

Spanke, Hans G., *Raynaud's Bibliographie des altfranzösischen Liedes* (Leiden, 1955)

Speer, Mary B., and Alfred Foulet, 'Is *Marques de Rome* a derhymed romance?', *Romania*, 101 (1980), 336–65

Spiegel, Gabrielle, *Romancing the Past: The Rise of Vernacular Prose Historiography in Thirteenth-Century France* (Berkeley and Los Angeles, 1993)

Straub, Richard E. F., *David Aubert, escripvain et clerc* (Amsterdam; Atlanta, GA, 1995)

Symes, Carol Lynne, *The Makings of a Medieval Stage: Theatre and the Culture of Performance in Thirteenth-Century Arras*, Ph.D. diss. (Harvard University, 1999)

Tanay, Dorit, *Noting Music, Marking Culture: The Intellectual Context of Rhythmic Notation, 1250–1400* (Holzgerlingen, 1999)

Taylor, Jane H. M., *The Making of Poetry. Late-Medieval French Poetic Anthologies* (Turnhout, 2007)

——, 'The Significance of the Insignificant: Reading Reception in the Burgundian *Erec* and *Cligés*', *Fifteenth-Century Studies*, 24 (1998), 183–97

Tesnière, Marie-Hélène, 'Les manuscrits copiés par Raoul Tainguy: un aspect de la culture des grands officiers royaux au début du XVe siècle', *Romania*, 107 (1986), 282–368

Thiry, Claude, 'Au carrefour des deux rhétoriques: les prosimètres de Jean

Molinet', in Peter Wunderli, ed., *Du mot au texte* (Tübingen, 1982), pp. 213–27
Thompson, John, 'Chaucer's *An ABC* in and out of Context', *Poetica*, 37 (1993), 38–48
Thompson, John L., *Writing the Wrongs. Women of the Old Testament among Biblical Commentators from Philo Through the Reformation* (New York, 2001)
Tischler, Hans, *Trouvère Lyrics with Melodies: Complete Comparative Edition* (Neuhausen, 1997)
Turcan-Verkerk, Anne, 'Le *prosimetrum* des *Artes dictaminis* médiévales', *Archivum Latinitatis Medii Aevi* (2003), 111–74
Tuve, Rosamund, *Allegorical Imagery. Some Mediæval Books and their Posterity* (Princeton, 1966)
Vendler, Helen, *Part of Nature, Part of Us: Modern American Poets* (Cambridge, MA; London, 1980)
Venuti, Lawrence, ed., *The Translation Studies Reader* (New York, 2004)
Vielliard, Françoise, 'La traduction du *De excidio Troiæ* de *Darès le Phrygien* par Jean de Flixecourt', in *Medieval Codicology, Iconography, Literature, and Translation: Studies for Keith Val Sinclair*, ed. P. R. Monks and D. D. R. Owen (Leiden, 1994), pp. 284–95
Vitz, Evelyn Birge, *The Crossroad of Intentions; A Study of Symbolic Expression in the Poetry of François Villon* (The Hague, 1974)
Walters, Lori J., 'Christine de Pizan, Primat, and the *noble nation françoise*', *Cahiers de Recherches médiévales,* 9 (2002), 237–46
Weinberg, Bernard, 'Guillaume Michel, dit de Tours. The Editor of the 1526 *Roman de la Rose*', *Bibliothèque d'Humanisme et Renaissance*, 11 (1949), 72–85
Woledge, Brian, 'La légende de Troie et les débuts de la prose française', in *Mélanges de linguistique et de littérature romanes offerts à Mario Roques*, 2 vols (Baden-Baden, 1953), II, pp. 313–24
Woledge, Brian, and H. P. Clive, *Répertoire des plus anciens textes en prose française depuis 842 jusqu'aux premières années du XIIIe siècle* (Geneva, 1964)
Wrisley, David J., 'Burgundian Ideologies and Jean Wauquelin's Prose Translations', in *The Ideology of Burgundy: The Promotion of National Consciousness, 1364–1565*, ed. D'Arcy Jonathan Dacre Boulton and Jan R. Veenstra (Leiden, 2006), pp. 131–50
Yates, Frances A., *L'Art de la mémoire*, trans. Daniel Arasse (Paris, 1975)
Zink, Michel, *La Pastourelle: poésie et folklore au Moyen Age* (Paris, 1972)
——, *Poésie et Conversion au Moyen Age* (Paris, 2003)
——, *La subjectivité littéraire autour du siècle de saint Louis* (Paris, 1985)
——, 'Suspension and Fall: The Fragmentation and Linkage of Lyric Insertions in *Le Roman de la rose (Guillaume de Dole)* and *Le Roman de la Violette*', in *Jean Renart and the Art of Romance: Essays on* Guillaume de Dole', ed. Nancy Vine Durling (Gainesville, 1997), pp. 105–21
Žižek, Slavoj, *The Sublime Object of Ideology* (London, 1989)

INDEX

Abelard, Peter 19, 122
Adam de Givenci 182
Adam de la Halle 4, 155, 183
   Congé 171
   Jeu de la Feuillée 183, 184
   Jeu de Robin et de Marion 174–76,
      178–80, 182, 184, 186
      Gautier 176, 178
      Marion 173–74, 176–81, 186
      Robin 173–74, 176–80
Adultery (personification) 153
Aelred de Rievaulx
   De amicitia spirituali 19
Alain de Lille 140
   De planctu Naturae 36, 136
Aliénor d'Aquitaine 88, 89
allegory 13, 43, 49, 50, 51, 53, 59, 64, 65,
   74, 77, 113–17, 119, 121–23, 136–39,
   141, 143, 146–47, 209, 213, *see also*
   Guillaume de Deguileville
   allegorical authority 118
   allegorical characters 113, 115, 204
   allegorical dreams/ dream allegory
      114, 202–5
   allegorical exposition 136, 138, 139
   allegorical fiction 73
   allegorical journey 137, 205
   allegorical meaning 120
   allegorical narrative 119, 139
   allegorical techniques 113
   allegorical voice 113, 114, 115, 117,
      122, 123
   allegorized moralisation 76
   of architecture 139, 146
   of marriage 63
   of pilgrimage 111, 112, 114
Allen, Peter 98
Altercatio Phillidis et Florae 9
Amour (personification) 4, 5
amour de loin 6

André Le Chapelain 8, 10
   Ars honneste amandi 7
Anne de Bretagne 188
antifeminism 10, *see also* misogyny
Aquinas, Thomas 89, 143
Aristotle 11, 73, 145, 146
   Metaphysics, 1, 143, 144, 147
   Problèmes 43
Arlt, Wulf 157
Arnauld de Corbie 107
Arras 181, 182, 183, 184
Ars d'amour, de vertu et de boneurté 15
Art (personification) 5
Art d'amours en prose 8, 99–102, 104,
   106–10, *see also* Ovid
Arthur (King)
   Arthurian court 129
Audiarde de Malemort 95
Augustine 72, 73, 81
   City of God 13, 71, 72
   Civitas 77
   Confessions 72
   Ennarationes in Psalmos 77
   Soliloquies/ Seul parlers 72
Azalaïs de Boissezon 91, 93
Azalaïs de Mercœur 95

Barolini, Teodolinda 152
Barthélemy l'Anglais 194
Bâtard de Bourgogne 191
Benoît, *see also* Dares
   Roman de Troie 29, 30
bergerie 176, 180, 181, 185, 186
Bernard d'Anduze 95
Bernard of Clairvaux 119
Bernard de Ventadour 88, 89, 97
Blonquist, Lawrence 100
Boccaccio 5
   Genealogie deorum 12
Boethius 11, 12, 21, 22, 31, 40, 57,

60, 61, 67, 74, 140, 143, *see also* Philosophie
De consolatione Philosophiae/ Consolation of Philosophy 10, 19, 20, 21, 22, 24, 59, 137, *see also Livre de Boece de consolacion*
Boniface de Montferrat 89
Boogaard, Nico H. J. 181, 182, 184
Borderie, Arthur de la 188
Bose, Mishtooni 69, 74, 79, 81
Boulton, Maureen 130
Bourdieu, Pierre 202
Boutière, Jean 87, 94, 95
Bouton, Claude 191, 192, 193
Brown, Elizabeth A. R. 154, 166, 169
Brownlee, Kevin 174
Brunetto Latini 27
Tresor 26, 31
Burgundian court *see* Court of Burgundy
Butterfield, Ardis 100, 106, 178, 179, 182

Caillois, Roger 53
Callahan, Christopher 125, 126
canticordum (song of the heart) 62, 78
carmen/ carmina 15, 60, 61, 65, 66, 68, 69, 70, 71, 72, 79
Carnality (personification) 153
Carruthers, Mary
Book of Memory 51
Cato 100, 104, 107
Chaillou de Pesstain 153, 165
Chanson de Guillaume 127, 133, 134, 135
Chanson de Roland 30
chanson de toile 132
Marote 132
Charlemagne 134
Berthe (mother) 134
Charles I de Nevers 125
Charles V 6, 24, 40, 76, 80, 140, 210, *see also* translation
Charles VI 203, 204
Charles VII 75
Charles d'Orléans 209
Charles Martel 134
Chartier, Alain 5, 190, 199
Bréviaire des Nobles 187
Quadriloge invectif 200
Chastelain, George 195–97
Les Princes 190–94
Chaucer, Geoffrey
House of Fame 58, 212

Chrétien de Troyes
Cligès 7, 129
Erec et Enide 7, 129, 212, 213
Christ 64, 67, 74, 76, 77, 78, 79, 80, *see also* New Testament
Christine de Pizan 2–7, 9–15, 32, 69, 136–48
L'Art de Chevalerie selon Végèce 7
Autres Balades 15
Cent Balades d'Amant et de Dame 1, 11, 12, 70, 77, 78
Chemin de longue estude 1, 2, 4, 6, 11, 137, 138, 146
Epistre au Dieu d'amour 10
Epistre Othéa 6, 12, 76, 77, 136–39, 141, 145
Livre de l'Advision Cristine 2, 3, 5, 12, 14, 15, 74, 79, 137, 139, 140–41, 143–47, 203, 209–11, 214, for Philosphy (personification), *see* Philosophie/ Philosophy
Chaos (personification) 144, 145
Opinion (personification) 141, 144, 145, 147, 211, 212, 213, 214
Silva (personification) 144
Livre de la Cité des dames 9, 77, 79, 99, 137, 139, 146, 147
Livre du Duc des vrais amans 77, 212
Sebille de Mont Hault 213
Livre des Fais d'armes et de chevalerie 7
Livre des Fais et bonnes meurs du sage roy Charles V 1, 73, 76, 78, 139, 141, 142
Livre de la Mutacion de Fortune 2, 12, 137, 139, 145, 211, *see also* Fortune
Livre de Prudence 76
Livre des Trois Vertus 75, 77
love and knowledge 2, 4
Sept Psaumes allegorisés 76, 78
Thomas (father) 6, 11, 12, 210
Chronique métrique 153, 154, 157, 166, 168, 169, 171
Cicero 7, 61
citation 100, 104, 106, 132, 133, 151, 152, 157, 158, 172, 184, *see also* refrain citation
Clef d'amours 7, 101, *see also* Ovid
Clement V 171
Cline, James 23
Col, Pierre 32
Colart le Boutelier 182

INDEX

Combes, André 57
Comfort (personification) 78
Commens d'Amour 8
Copeland, Rita 19, 21, 22
Council of Constance 57, 66, 67, 68
Cour d'Amour 182
Court of Burgundy 125, 128, 129, 133, 134, 135
    library 134
    prosators 128, 129
    prose 126, 127, 130
Cowling, David 194
Cropp, Glynnis 25
Cycle de la gageure 127

Daedalus 73
Dante 5, 13, 152
    Commedia 14, 140
    Convivio 1, 152
    Inferno 11
    Vita nova 14
Daphne, myth of 77
Dares 29, *see also* Benoît
Dauphin d'Auvergne 97
Dean, Jeffrey 169
Death (personification) 122
Dembowski, Peter 25, 26
dérimage 111–13, 116–17, 119–23, 126, *see also* mise en prose
Deschamps, Eustache 99, 107, 109
Dhuoda 197
Diane (goddess) 6, 43
didacticism 43, 48, 50, 53, 110
Dido and Aeneas 213
Dostoïevski
    L'éternel Mari 91
Doudet, Estelle 193
Dous Penser (personification) 5
Doutrepont, Georges 135
Douze Dames de Rhétorique 194
Drouart La Vache
    Li Livres d'Amours 7
Duke of Burgundy 102, 209, *see also* John the Fearless, Duke of Burgundy

Eloquence Theologienne (personification) 32
Enguerran de Marigny 171
epithalamium 62, 64
Erasmus 61
Eschés amoureux 2, 4, 10, 42–4, 48, 49–50, 52
    Beauté 52

Déduit 42, 43, 44, 46, 53
    Regard 52
Espérance (personification) 2, 5, 6, 51
euphemism 33
Evrard de Trémaugon
    Songe du vergier 205
Evrart de Conty 42, 49, 53, 55
    Livre des Eschez amoureux moralises 43, 48, 51

fable 13, 73, 87, 142, 205
Fabre, Isabelle 58
fama 202, 204, 211, 212, 213
Fauquet, Wilfred 52
fin'amors 98, 100, 110
Flaubert, Gustave
    Dictionnaire des idées reçues 44, 48
Foi (personification) 2
Folquet de Marseille 95
forme-fixe 152, 155, 157
Fortune (personification) 203, 211, *see also* Christine de Pizan, *Livre de la Mutacion de Fortune*
François Ier, Duke of Brittany 188
François II, Duke of Brittany 188
Froissart, Jean 107
    Joli buisson de Jonece 10

Gally, Michèle 49, 100
Gaucelm Faidit 93, 94, 95
Gautier, Pierre 120
Geffroi de Paris 153, 154, 157, 166, 168, 169, 171
Geoffrey of Monmouth 31
Gérard de Nevers 125–35, *see also* Gerbert de Montreuil
Gerbert de Montreuil
    Roman de la Violette 125, 127–28, 130–5, *see also Gérard de Nevers*
        Aiglente 131, 133
        Euriaut 127, 132
        Florentine 131, 132
        Gerard, count of Nevers 127, 129, 131, 132, 134
        King Louis 127, 131
        Lisiart 127, 134
Gerson, Jean 32, 35, 40, 56, 69
    'Ad Deum vadit' sermon 78, 80
    'Ave Maria' sermon 71
    Carmen dicendum tempore tentationis 59
    De canticis 60, 62–5, 68, 72

De consolatione theologiae 57, 60–3, 68, 74
Descriptio peregrine 67
ego 58, 59, 68
Epithalamium mysticum theologi et theologiae 59, 62, 64–5, 67
Josephina 57, 58, 59, 60, 66, 68
Montaigne de contemplation 70
Obsecro vos 67
Œuvres 58
Pastorium carmen 58, 68
Pratique du psalterium mystique 78
Schola mystica 59
super-ego 58, 59, 65, 67
Tractatus de canticis 58, 71, 77
Traictié d'une vision faite contre Le Ronmant de la Rose 26
Ut festum Joseph celebratur 67
Gervès de Bus 153, 169
Gillebert de Berneville 182, 183
Gilles de Rome 197, 199
De Regimine principum 198
Girard, René 91
Girart de Roussillon 133
Giraud de Barri
Topographica hibernica 19
Glorieux, P. 58
gloss/ *glose* 23, 34, 37, 49, 50, 52, 65, 71, 76, 77, 79, 98, 99, 100, 101, 102, 105–8, 125, 130, 131, 137, 138, 141, 142
god of love/ dieu d'amours 2, 7, 9, 43, 45, 48, 49, 114, 115
Godefroy de Bouillon 133
Grace of God (personification) 116, 117, 118, 120, 122, 123
Grandes Chroniques de France 80, 81, see also St Louis
grands rhétoriqueurs 123
Guiart 101
Guichard-Tesson, Françoise 42, 51
Guilhem de Balaun 94, 95, 96
Guilhem de la Tor 85
Guillaume au court nez 134, 135
Guillaume de Deguileville 111–15, 117, 123, 124, 205
Deguileville, Thomas de (father) 115, 117, 120
Pèlerinage de la vie humaine 111, 117–19, 123–4, see also allegory manuscripts 115
Guillaume de Lorris 2, 35, 40, 113, 114, see also Jean de Meun; *Roman de la Rose*
Guiraut de Bornelh 97

Hanning, Robert 27
Heller-Roazen, Daniel 20
Heloise 19, 122
Hercules 62, 135
Hesiod 13
Holford-Strevens, Leofranc 159, 169
Homer 11, 74
Horace 11
Hugh of Saint Victor 34
Didascalicon 33, 36
Hugues le Brun 93
Hugues de Lusignan 93
Huitace de Fontaines 176, 183
Huon de Méry
Tournoiement de l'Antéchrist 205

integument 140, 141–3
Isabeau de Bavière 5, 75, 203, 204, 209

Jacquemart Giélée 182
Jacques d'Amiens 101
Jacques de Cessoles
Liber de moribus hominum vel officiis nobilium sive super ludo scacchorum 51
Jean V, Duke of Brittany 188
Jean, duc de Berry 102, 204, 207
Jean the Celestine 61
Jean de Flixecourt 29
Jean de Meun 2, 5, 19, 32, 35, 75, 113, 114, 122, 185, 190, 205, see also Guillaume de Lorris; *Roman de la Rose*
De confort 25
preface 25
translations 20, 21, 23, 25, 26, 35
Jean de Montaigu 204, 207, 208, 209
Jean de le Mote
Songe de la voie d'enfer et de paradis 205
Jean Renart
Roman de la Rose, ou de Guillaume de Dole 128
Jeanne de Bourgogne 154, 166, 168
Jeanne de Lanval 111
Jehan de Prunai 31
Jeunesse (personification) 51
Jodogne, O. 30

Johannes
    Chronique de Turpin 27
John the Fearless, Duke of Burgundy 203,
    see also Duke of Burgundy
John, St 77, 79
Joseph, St 57, 66, 67, 68, *see also* Old
    Testament
jouissance 93, 95
    de l'autre 90, 95, 96
Jung, Marc-René 73
Juno (goddess) 14, 46, 50

Kay, Sarah 129, 146
Kelly, Douglas 26
Köhler, Erich 96

Lefèvre, Jean 108, 109
Legrand, Jacques
    Archiloge Sophie 10
Lescurel, Jehannot de 152–5, 157–9, 161,
    164, 166–7, 169, 171–2
Lettenhove, Kervyn de 190, 192
Lieberman, Max 56
Livre de Boece de consolacion 25
Livre de la Rose 13, *see also Roman de
    la Rose*
Louis II, Duke of Bourbon 204
Louis X 154, 171
Louis XI 188, 190, 192, 193
Louis d'Orléans 75, 203, 204, 207
Louis, St 80, *see also Grandes Chroniques
    de France*
Lucan, 74
Lulle, Raymond
    Arbre de Philosophie d'amour 8
lyric insertions 128–33
lyric refrains *see* refrain

Machaut, Guillaume de 3, 4, 5, 10, 14, 15,
    99, 107, 108, 109, 110, 152, 155
    Louange des dames 109
    Voir dit 4
Machiavelli 198
Maddicott, J. R. 206
Maistre Elie 101
Marguerite d'Aubusson 93
Marguerite of Burgundy 171
Marie de France 87
Marie de Ventadour 95
Marot, Jean
    Doctrinal des Princesses 187
Martianus Capella 74, 140

Martin le Franc
    Champion des Dames 10
Martin of Laon 37
Martineau, Christine 188, 189
Mary (Virgin) 63, 64, 66, 71, 75, 76, 77,
    78, 80
Matfre Ermengaud
    Breviari d'amor 8, 87
melancholie/ melancholy 47
Meliacin 182
Meneghetti, Marie Louisa 86, 87, 96
Merlin 31
Meschinot, Jean 187–90, 192–193, 195–7,
    199–201
    Ballades des princes 187, 190, 192,
        195, 199
    Lunettes des princes 187, 189, 190,
        192–5, 198, 199
metaphor 33
Minnis, Alastair 35, 50
Miroir des princes 197
mise en prose 125–7, 129–30, 135, *see
    also dérimage*
misogyny 101, 108, *see also* antifeminism
Molinet, Jean
    Roman de la Rose moralisé 13
Molinier, Guilhem
    Leys d'amor 1, 8
Montreuil, Jean de 32, 76
Morin, Joseph 158
La Mort Aymeri de Narbonne 28, 31
Murray, Harold James 52
musical refrains *see* refrain
Musique (personification) 5
myth 141, 143

Nantes 189, 192
Narcissus 43, 206
natural philosophy 143
Nature (personification) 4, 5, 9, 12, 43,
    see also Nourreture
New Testament 74, *see also* Christ
Nicolas de Senlis
    Pseudo-Turpin (trans.) 30, *see also
    Pseudo-Turpin*
Nicole de Margival
    Dit de la Panthère 9
Nicole Oresme 143
Nourreture 9, *see also* Nature

Odilon de Mercœur 95
Oiseuse (personification) 44

Old Testament 63, 64, 71, 74, *see also* St Joseph
  Abraham 63
  Adam 63
  allegorical exegesis 63
  Bala 63, 64
  Benjamin 64
  Daniel 74
  David 71, 76, 77
  Delilah 120
  Eve 75
  Genesis 63
  Hagar 63, 64
  Herod 66
  Jacob 63, 64
  Jeremiah 71
  Job 65, 71
  Joseph 63, 64
  Laban 63
  Levi 67
  Lia 63, 64
  Moses 67, 71
  Rachel 63, 64
  Samson 120
  Sarah 63
  Solomon 71, 74, 100, 104
  Zelpha 63, 64
Olivier de La Marche 193
  Dames 191
Orpheus 11, 13, 36, 62, 74, 77
Ouy, Gilbert 58, 59, 70
Ovid 10, 11, 13, 74, 77, 98–110, 113, 114, 117–19, 123, 212, *see also Art d'amours en prose; Clef d'amours; Ovide moralisé*
  Ars amatoria/ Art d'amour 7, 8, 10, 26, 98–101, 104, 106, 109
  Bible des poètes 98
  Ibis 117
  Metamorphoses 98, 112
  Remedia 98, 99, 109
Ovide moralisé 13, 98 see also Ovid

Paden, William 178, 185
Pallas (goddess) 6, 10, 11, 43, 46, 48, 49, 50
Paris
  and Helen 8
  Judgement of 6, 14, 49
Paris, Gaston 99
pastourelle 173–81, 183, 185–6
Paul, St 63, 71, 78, 122
Peirol 97

Perlesvaus 30
Perrin d'Angecourt 179, 182, 183
Petit, Jean 57
Petrarch 58, 59, 81
  Rime sparse 152
Philip V 153, 154, 166
Philip VI 171
Philip Augustus 31
Philip, Duke of Burgundy 203
Philip the Fair 19, 25, 153, 154, 167
Philip the Good 135
Philippe de Mézières
  Livre de la Vertu et du sacrament de marriage 13
  Songe du vieil pélerin 205
Philippe de Vitry 159
Philosophie/ Philosophy (personification) 10, 12, 14, 41, 67, 74, 145, 146, 147
Piaget, Arthur 188, 190, 192, 197, 200
Pierre II, Duke of Brittany 188
Pierre de Beauvais
  Bestiaire 31
Pierre de Blois
  De amicitia christiana 7
Pierre de Corbie 182
Pizzorusso, Valeria Bertolucci 86
Placides et Timéo, 1
Plaisance (personification) 5
Plato 74, 143
  Timaeus 142
poema/ poemata 15, 60, 69
poesie/ poetria 73, 74, 136, 139–44, 148
Pons de Chapteuil 94, 95
Premierfait, Laurent de
  De casibus virorum illustrium (trans.) 5, 13
prophecy 147
Prophetia Merlini 28
prosimetrum 24, 74, 77, 136, 189
proverbs 101, 104, 109, 120–3
Pseudo-Turpin 30, *see also* Nicolas de Senlis
Pygmalion 40

Querelle de la Rose 5, 32, 68, 70, 72, 76, *see also Roman de la Rose*, criticism of

Raimbaut de Vaqueiras 89, 90
Raimon de Miraval 91, 92, 93
Raimondi, Gianmario 42
Raison/ Reason (personification) 9, 115, 117, 120–2, 203

Raoul de Houdenc
    Songe d'enfer 205
Raoul de Presles 13
refrain 174, 176, 178–9, 181, 195–6
    lyric refrains 104, 109, 161
    musical refrain 164
    refrain citation 175, 176, 180, 182–4, 186, *see also* citation
    refrain song 173–4
Remedia amoris 10
Renart le Nouvel 181, 182
Renaut de Louhan 25
Rhétorique (personification) 5
Richard de Fournival
    Bestiaire d'amours 1
    De vetulla 108
Richard of St Victor 63, 64, 65
    De duodecim patriarchis 63
Richards, Earl Jeffrey 138
Richtmyer, Alan 161
Rigaut de Barbezieux 95
Riquer, Martin de 87
Robertson, Anne Walters 152
Roccati, Matteo 58
Roesner, Edward 155, 158, 159
Roman du Chastelain de Couci 125
Roman de Fauvel 153–5, 158, 161, 164–6, 169, 171–2
    Dame Constance 168
    Fortune (personification) 153, 164, 165
    Vainglory (personification) 153
Roman de la Rose 2, 3, 5, 10, 11, 12, 13, 19, 24, 27, 43, 52, 113, 115, 123, 124, 185, 204–5, 206, 213, *see also* Guillaume de Lorris; Jean de Meun; *Livre de la Rose*; *Querelle de la Rose*; Narcissus
    l'Amant/ the Lover 20, 32, 34
    Ami 37, 38
    Art 40
    art d'amour 9
    as allegory 13, 52
    Bel Accueil 9, 19
    criticism of 56, 68, 70, 75
    Death 38, 39
    Faus Semblant 38
    Genius 36, 38, 40, 114, 123
    Jalousie 19
    Male Bouche 37
    manuscripts 114
    Nature 36, 38, 39, 40
    Raison/ Reason 20–1, 25, 32–4, 36, 122, *see also* Raison
    la Vieille 9, 37
Roman de Troie see Benoît
Roman de la Violette, *see* Gerbert de Montreuil
Rouse, Mary, and Richard Rouse 157, 169
Roy, Bruno 51, 100, 108
Rutebeuf
    Voie de Paradis 205

Sail de Claustra 97
Sannazaro 59
Sapientia/ Sapience 71, 79
School of Chartres 33
Scylla and Charybdis 64
Sens (personification) 5
Sheingorn, Pamela 66, 68
Sherman, Claire 143
Sibyl 4, 11, 77, 138, 147
    sibylline verse 138
Sickness (personification) 122
Simon de Hesdin, 23
Simun de Freine
    Roman de Philosophie 25
Song of Songs 59, 63, 64, 65, 74
Songe de pestilence 205
Songe veritable 202–7, 209–10, 213–14, *see also* Fortune; Raison/ Reason
    Chascun/ Everyman 203, 204, 208
    Commune Renommee/ Common Knowledge (personification) 203, 204, 206, 207, 209, 213
    Damnation (personification) 204
    Experience (personification) 203, 205, 206, 207, 208, 209
    Poverty (personification) 204
    Suffering (personification) 204, 208
Strubel, Armand 33
Suso, Henri
    Horologium sapientiae 10

Tainguy, Raoul 107–10
Taylor, Jane 129
Testament 40
Théologie/ Theology (personification) 14, 62, 74, *see also* Wisdom
Thomas, *Tristan* 96
Thomas III de Saluces
    Le Chevalier errant 2
three ages of man 14
Titus Livius 107
Tournoi de Chauvency 182
translatio 21

translation 19, 21, 25, 80, 99, 101, 105–7, 125, 136, *see also* Charles V
    theory of 23, 76
Trevet, Nicholas 143
Tristan and Yseut 8

Uc de Saint-Circ 86

Valerius Maximus 100, 107
    Memorabilia 23
Venus (goddess) 6, 12, 43, 50
vernacular literature 1
Villehardouin 30
Vincent of Beauvais
    Speculum maius 206
Virgil 11, 74, 212, 213

Virginity (personification) 153
Vitz, E. B. 165

Wace 31
Wauchier de Denain
    Second Continuation of the *Conte du Graal* 29
    Vie des pères (trans.) 29
Wilkins, N. 169
William of Conches 142, 143
Wisdom (personification) 62, 64, *see also* Théologie/ Theology

Yates, Frances 51

Zink, Michel 179

Already Published

1. *Postcolonial Fictions in the 'Roman de Perceforest': Cultural Identities and Hybridities*, Sylvia Huot
2. *A Discourse for the Holy Grail in Old French Romance*, Ben Ramm
3. *Fashion in Medieval France*, Sarah-Grace Heller
4. *Christine de Pizan's Changing Opinion: A Quest for Certainty in the Midst of Chaos*, Douglas Kelly
5. *Cultural Performances in Medieval France: Essays in Honor of Nancy Freeman Regalado*, eds Eglal Doss-Quinby, Roberta L. Krueger, E. Jane Burns
6. *The Medieval Warrior Aristocracy: Gifts, Violence, Performance, and the Sacred*, Andrew Cowell
7. *Logic and Humour in the Fabliaux: An Essay in Applied Narratology*, Roy J. Pearcy
8. *Miraculous Rhymes: The Writing of Gautier de Coinci*, Tony Hunt
9. *Philippe de Vigneulles and the Art of Prose Translation*, Catherine M. Jones
10. *Desire by Gender and Genre in Trouvère Song*, Helen Dell
11. *Chartier in Europe*, eds Emma Cayley, Ashby Kinch
12. *Medieval Saints' Lives: The Gift, Kinship and Community in Old French Hagiography*, Emma Campbell